# The Dawn of Chinese Pure Land Buddhist Doctrine

SUNY Series in Buddhist Studies
Kenneth Inada, Editor

# The Dawn of Chinese Pure Land Buddhist Doctrine

## Ching-ying Hui-yüan's Commentary on the *Visualization Sutra*

Kenneth K. Tanaka

STATE UNIVERSITY OF NEW YORK PRESS

Published by
State University of New York Press, Albany



Printed in the United States of America



For information, address the State University of New York Press,
State University Plaza, Albany, NY 12246

**Library of Congress Cataloguing-in-Publication Data**

Tanaka, Kenneth K., 1947-
The dawn of Chinese pure land Buddhist doctrine : Ching-ying Hui-yüan's Commentary on the Visualization sutra / Kenneth K. Tanaka.
p. cm. — (SUNY series in Buddhist studies)
Includes bibliographical references.
ISBN 0-7914-0297-5. — ISBN 0-7914-0298-3 (pbk.)
1. Hui-yüan, 523-592. Kuan wu liang shou ching i shu. 2. Kuan wu liang shou ching—Commentaries. 3. Pure Land Buddhism—China—Doctrines—History. I. Title. II. Series.
BQ2025.H853T36 1990
294.3'85—dc20 89-21685
CIP

10 9 8 7 6 5 4 3 2 1

To Kimie's parents,
Mr. and Mrs. Kenzo Nishikawa, and to my parents.

# Contents

## Part I

## Part II    Translation of the *Commentary*

# Preface

This book sheds new light on four areas. First, this study of Hui-yüan's highly scholarly commentary contradicts the conventional perception that Pure Land Buddhism comprises a popular teaching for only the religiously inferior. Secondly, the findings extend to Hui-yüan a long overdue recognition of his contribution to Chinese Buddhism and, more specifically, to Pure Land doctrine. Third, the study further broadens the traditional boundaries of Pure Land teaching. This challenges the adequacy of previous definitions. Fourth, and perhaps most crucially, this study considers the question of the sectarian formation of the Pure Land school in China.

Numerous factors contribute to the formation of a school. Modern writers generally cite the historical events confirming the eschatological message on the arrival of the Last Period of Dharma (*mo-fa*) as one of the primary factors contributing to the emergence of the Pure Land school. The actual process, however, was immensely more complex. A fuller accounting and understanding must consider other factors such as doctrine, institution, and religious environment.

Among these factors, this book deals with the doctrinal element and, specifically, examines the critical role played by a commentary written by Ching-ying Hui-yüan (523–592 C.E.). Ironically, this Hui-yüan differs from the earlier Lu-shan Hui-yüan (334–416), known for his traditional association as founder of the Pure Land school. Ching-ying Hui-yüan's *Kuan wu-liang-shou ching i-shu* (Commentary on the Sutra of Visualization on the Buddha of Immeasurable Life; henceforth, *Commentary*) figures as the oldest extant commentary on the *Kuan wu-liang-shou ching* (*Kuan-ching*). This treatise played a vital role in the commentarial tradition of this sutra. Yet, its "heretical" status within the later orthodox Pure Land tradition has discouraged its subsequent study.

The introduction discusses the status of the commentary in modern scholarship on Chinese Pure Land Buddhism with special attention to the reasons for its heretical treatment. Chapter 1 examines the problems and origins associated with Pure Land as a distinct teaching or school, and surveys the doctrinal development of Pure Land thought in India and China prior to Ching-ying Hui-yüan.

Chapter 2 considers the life and thought of Hui-yüan. As a prominent ecclesiastic leader and eminent scholar of the Sui Dynasty, Hui-yüan was better known for his non-Pure Land doctrinal innovations, the *ālaya-vijñāna* (storehouse consciousness) and *tathāgatagarbha* (Buddha womb or embryo) theories, than for those in Pure Land thought. Contrary to his image as a strict scholastic, Hui-yüan in reality not only effectively propagated but also staunchly defended the Dharma, as demonstrated by the account of his gallant debate with Emperor Wu of Northern Chou.

Chapter 3 takes up the textual background of the *Commentary.* This includes the consideration of the controversial origins of the *Kuan-ching* as well as of the dating and authenticity of the *Commentary.* Moreover, given that tradition does not regard Hui-yüan as a Pure Land proponent, this chapter explores the possible reasons that prompted him to write a commentary on a Pure Land sutra.

Chapter 4 locates Hui-yüan's treatment of the text in the context of other Buddhist works through the examination of the "five-essentials," his *p'an-chiao* classification and exegetical style. Hui-yüan consciously treated a disparate group of Pure Land scriptures as a consistent set, thus suggesting his recognition of Pure Land as a distinct teaching. As it turns out, the *Commentary* is the earliest surviving text to refer to two of the major Pure Land scriptures by their abbreviated titles, a practice that even the orthodox Pure Land tradition adopted.

Chapter 5 focuses on Hui-yüan's analysis of the two aspects of rebirth, the causal practices and the spiritual ranking. Contrary to previous assessment, Hui-yüan acknowledged not only oral recitation as a legitimate cause for rebirth but also the ability of Pṛthagjanas (ordinary seekers who have yet to reach the higher levels of the sages) to engage in visualization practices. The ranking of the nine grades of rebirth generated fervent interest among all the commentators of this sutra. But apparently the *Commentary* appears to be the earliest to initiate this schema of rankings that exerted considerable impact on subsequent commentaries.

Chapter 6 ascertains the effect of the *Commentary* on the main writing of the preeminent orthodox Pure Land figure, Shan-tao. By selecting doctrinal topics from Shan-tao's commentary on the *Kuan-ching,* Hui-yüan's influence on Shan-tao's doctrinal framework can be uncovered. Chapter 7 offers some conclusions to close out Part I.

Part II contains a full translation of the *Commentary.*

I am extremely indebted to the myriad of causes and conditions that have made the completion of this book possible. Without the generous grant from the Mabelle McLeod Lewis Memorial Fund, progress would have been severely hampered. Supplementary support from the Reverend G. Kono Memorial Fund and the Sunao Kikunaga scholarship supported travel and the acquisition of research materials. I am grateful to the Institute of Buddhist Studies for allowing my research time to be devoted to the completion of this project.

To Professor Lewis Lancaster, I extend my deepest appreciation for his encouragement and invaluable suggestions for the early drafts. I am grateful for the supportive and critical guidance accorded me by Professors Haruo Aoki, Robert Bellah, Carl Bielefeldt, Cyril Birch, P. S. Jaini, Whalen Lai, and Michel Strickmann. The initial support and encouragement given to me by Professor Hisao Inagaki of Ryukoku University, Professor Yoshihide Yoshizu of Komazawa University and Professor Kyoko Fujii of Yokohama City University served as sources of inspiration throughout the research. I am especially indebted to Professor Robin Matthews for her critique of the manuscript and many stylistic suggestions. Ms. Kimi Hisatsune has kindly edited the text and assisted with the tedious task of compiling the index.

The completion of this book was greatly facilitated by the personal support for my work by the trustees and many people affiliated with the Institute of Buddhist Studies, notably Bishop Seigen Yamaoka, Professor Kakue Miyaji, Dr. Jack Fujimoto, Dr. Walter Hashimoto, Reverend Russell Hamada, Reverend LaVerne Sasaki, Reverend Hiroshi Abiko, Reverend Shojo Oi, Reverend Haruyoshi Kusada, Reverend Eijun Kujo, Reverend Kanya Okamoto, and the late Mr. Roy Iwamoto. My colleagues, fellow staff, and students at the Institute have created for me a "Pure Land," an environment conducive for my enhanced productivity. For this, I am also grateful, especially to Dean Alfred Bloom, Rika Wagner, Yuki Matsumoto, Venerable Bhante Seelawimala, Dr. Ronald Nakasone, Dr. Richard Payne, Dr. Ronald Davidson, Azel Jones, Sonoe Jitodai, Reverend Carol Himaka, Sumi Hirabayashi, Gregory Gibbs, Kathy Velasco, Charles Niimi, Masami Hayashi and Joseph King. Finally, I thank Kimie, Aaron, and Nathan, for their sacrifices in allowing me to forego many of my family obligations.

# Abbreviations and Conventions

| | |
|---|---|
| *Bussho* | *Bussho kaisetsu daijiten* |
| *Chih-i Commentary* | *Fo-shuo kuan wu-liang-shou fo ching shu* attributed to Chih-i, *Taishō* 1750. |
| *Commentary* | *Kuan wu-liang-shou ching i-shu* by Ching-ying Hui-yüan, *Taishō* 1749. |
| *Further Biographies* | *Hsü kao-seng chuan* by Tao-hsüan, *Taishō* 2060. |
| *Kaidai* | *Butten kaidai jiten* ed. by Mizuno Kōgen, et. al. |
| *Kuan-ching* | *Kuan wu-liang-shou ching, Taishō* 365. |
| *Mahayana Encyclopedia* | *Ta-ch'eng i-chang* by Hui-yüan, *Taisho* 1851. |
| *Nakamura* | *Bukkyōgo dai jiten,* Nakamura. |
| *Pure Land Treatise* | *Ching-t'u lun* by Chia-ts'ai, *Taishō* 1963. |
| *Ryūkoku* | *The Sutra of Contemplation on the Buddha of Immeasurable Life as Expounded by Śākyamuni Buddha.* Ryūkoku University Translation Center, trans. and annot. |
| *Shan-tao Commentary* | *Kuan wu-liang-shou fo ching shu* by Shan-tao, *Taishō* 1753. |
| *T* | *Taishō shinshū daizōkyō* 85 vols. Tokyo, 1914–22. |
| *Tsukamoto Festschrift* | *Tsukamoto hakushi shōju kinen: bukkyō shigaku ronshū.* Kyoto: Tsukamoto hakushi shōju kinen kai, 1961. |
| *Rebirth Treatise* | *Wu-liang-shou ching yu-po-t'i-she yüan-sheng chieh,* attributed to Vasubandhu. *Taishō* 1524. |

| | |
|---|---|
| *T'an-luan Commentary* | *Wu-liang-shou ching yu-po-t'i-she yüan sheng chieh-chu* by T'an-luan. *Taishō* 1819. |
| *ZZ* | *Dai nihon zokuzōkyō.* Kyoto, 1905–22. |

The following are treated as English terms (hence, no diacritical marks), except when they appear in untranslated titles of Sanskrit works or as technical terms: Hinayana, karma, Mahayana, nirvana, and sangha.

No macrons are affixed on names of modern Japanese writers, except in the Bibliography section at the end.

# Introduction: Challenge to the Orthodoxy

## Limitations of previous scholarship

Modern discussion of Chinese Pure Land Buddhism has been severely limited with regard to the issues and the personalities treated. Kenneth Ch'en's *Buddhism in China,* the standard modern historical work on Chinese Buddhism in English, provides a good case in point. The section on the Pure Land School through the T'ang period (618–907 C.E.) only encompasses Lu-shan Hui-yüan (334–416), T'an-Luan (476–542 or 488–554), Tao-ch'o (562–645), Shan-tao (613–681), Tz'u-min (680–748) and Fa-chao (eighth century).[1] Ch'en's selection of these figures undoubtedly reflects the concerns and findings of modern Japanese scholarship, which served as a basis for much of his treatment. In addition, dissertation topics on Chinese Pure Land Buddhism through the T'ang period submitted to North American universities are similarly confined either to these traditional figures or to their works: for example, T'an-luan by Ching-fen Hsiao and Roger Corless; Tao-ch'o by David Chappell; Shan-tao by Julian Pas, Ingram Seah, and Nobuo Haneda.[2]

The scope of modern Japanese scholarship, in turn, has been delimited sharply by the interests of the Pure Land schools. In his *Senchaku-shū* (Treatise on the *Nembutsu,* Selected by the Original Vow), Hōnen (1133–1212), the founder of the Jōdo School, sets forth Lu-shan Hui-yüan (not the Ching-ying Hui-yüan of this study), Tz'u-min and Tao-ch'o/Shan-tao as the founders of the three Chinese Pure Land lineages. Shinran (1173–1262), the founder of the Jōdo-Shinshū School, considered T'an-luan, Tao-ch'o, and Shan-tao the Chinese patriarchs of his Dharma-transmission lineage.[3]

Since scholars affiliated with these Pure Land schools carry out the bulk of the studies, modern Japanese scholarship on Chinese Pure Land Buddhism has produced volumes on what this study shall call the "orthodox" Pure Land figures, namely, T'an-luan, Tao-ch'o, Shan-tao, and, to a lesser extent, Lu-shan Hui-yüan, Tz'u-min, and so forth. But as the bibliographical catalogues of modern works on Pure Land Buddhism readily demonstrate, these studies, with very few exceptions, have concentrated on doctrinal and historical issues pertaining to the orthodox Pure Land figures. They have preemptorily excluded as significant objects of research those figures who fall outside this restricted group.[4]

In China the orthodox figures received similar recognition as important contributors to Pure Land Buddhism, as indicated by their inclusion in the Dharma-transmission lineages of the Sung and Yüan periods.[5] However, because these lineages were concocted hundreds of years later—eight hundred in the case of Lu-shan Hui-yüan—they sometimes lack historical warrant. As a prime example, Lu-shan Hui-yüan was foisted off as the founder of the two lineages created by the Lotus Society (*lien-she*). But no corroborating evidence has been uncovered of any influence either by way of his thought or by historical connection through his disciples to the later figures in the lineages to validate his eminent status as founder.

It therefore appears that Hui-yüan's actual contribution to Chinese Pure Land Buddhism was substantially less than purported by the lineages of the Sung Lotus Society or Hōnen.[6] In fact, modern scholars now question the authenticity of the name "White Lotus Association," (*pai-lien she*) that coterie of one hundred and thirty-eight devotees who made a collective vow on Mt. Lu to be reborn together in Sukhāvatī under Hui-yüan's leadership, which thereby effected Hui-yüan's fame as a Pure Land devotee.[7]

This emphasis on the limited scope of previous scholarship does not minimize the contributions of any of these orthodox figures. Unquestionably, Shan-tao did significantly advance doctrinal systematization and propagation. He was so highly regarded by later Chinese and Japanese Pure Land followers that subsequent Pure Land luminaries were called "the second Shan-tao," (*hou Shan-tao*) as in the case of Fa-chao and Shou-k'ang (d.805).[8] Rather the crucial claim here contends that modern studies have concentrated unduly on these orthodox Pure Land Buddhists, particularly on T'an-luan, Tao-ch'o, and Shan-tao at the expense of others who have also decisively affected Pure Land Buddhism.

A more adequate appraisal of early Pure Land Buddhist development awaits research into areas that have been regrettably overlooked to date. The body of literature known as "apocryphal sutras" (*wei-ching*) comprises one such neglected area of research.[9] A revered text in Chinese and later in Japanese Pure Land Buddhism, Tao-ch'o's *An-le chi* (Collection of Passages on the Land of Peace and Bliss), quotes extensively from a number of sutras considered apocryphal by such modern scholars as Makita Tairyo.[10] In one instance, Tao-ch'o cites several sutras that he then interprets as advocating rebirth in the Pure Land. Two of the texts, the *Sui-yüan shih-fang wang-sheng ching* (Sutra on the Rebirth in the Ten Directions in Accord with Aspiration) and the *Shih wang-sheng ching* (Sutra on the Rebirth in the Ten Directions), are considered apocryphal.[11] Among other apocryphal sutras, the latter is also quoted in two of Shan-tao's five extant works.[12] Yet a detailed study of the role of the apocryphal sutras in the *An-le chi* as well as in Shan-tao's two works has apparently been discouraged in a scholarly field dominated by strong orthodox Pure Land interests. Such a study would undoubtedly provide a more complete picture of the emergence of Pure Land Buddhism in the sixth and seventh centuries.[13]

Another neglected category of literature includes the "apologetic" writings of the late seventh, eighth, and early ninth centuries. The representative works of this literature include the *Shih ching-t'u ch'ün-i lun* (Treatise Clarifying the Many Doubts Concerning the Pure Land Teaching), the *Ching-t'u shih-i lun* (Treatise Clarifying the Ten Doubts Concerning the Pure Land Teaching), the *Nien-fo ching* (Mirror of Buddha-contemplation) and the *Nien-fo san-mei pao-wang lun* (Treatise on the Jeweled King of Buddha-contemplation *Samādhi*).[14] This set of writings emerged after the Pure Land teaching had reached a stage of development in which its basic doctrine had solidified and its proponents had turned to defending its position against rival groups. For example, sections of the *Nien-fo ching* directly respond to criticisms or questions posed by specific groups, such as the Ch'an (Zen) and Maitreya. The *Ching-t'u shih-i lun* dwells on two of ten questions that presumably Ch'an and Maitreya proponents raised.[15] These writings are especially valuable not only for reflecting what the Pure Land proponents took as their doctrinal uniqueness but also for revealing how they articulated this uniqueness in light of their opponents' critique of the Pure Land position.

The last neglected category of literature comprises commentaries on the *Kuan wu-liang-shou ching* (Sutra of Visualization on the Buddha of Immeasurable Life; hereafter, *Kuan-ching*). The exception to this is, of course, Shan-tao's commentary, the *Kuan wu-liang-shou fo ching shu,* (hereafter, the *Shan-tao Commentary*). Due to the interests of Japanese Pure Land schools, it has been one of the central foci of Chinese Pure Land studies in modern Japanese scholarship.[16] From the Sui to Sung period, at least forty commentaries of the *Kuan-ching* are known, most of which were compiled prior to the year C.E. 800.[17] Nine have survived, and two more have been partially restored.[18] The *Kuan-ching,* more than any other Pure Land sutras including the *Larger Sukhāvatīvyūha Sutra* (Larger Sutra on the Adornments of the Realm of Bliss) or the *Smaller Sukhāvatīvyūha Sutra,* attracted considerable commentarial attention. Thus it and its attendant literature acquire crucial importance in penetrating the early history of Pure Land Buddhism.[19] That Shan-tao's 'magnum opus' was a commentary on the *Kuan-ching* rather than on the aforementioned two Pure Land sutras underscores its centrality. Similarly, despite the title of the work, Ta-ch'o's *An-le chi* was essentially a commentary on the same sutra.

While "apologetic" literature inform us about the mature phase, these commentaries on the *Kuan-ching* will reveal more about the formative stage of Chinese Pure Land Buddhism. While "apocryphal" literature will reveal more about those practices that attracted interest in China, these commentaries will increase our understanding of the formal doctrinal developments. As formal Buddhist writing, most of these commentaries were authored by highly placed ecclesiastical scholar-monks such as Ling-yü (518–605), Chi-tsang (549–623), and Ching-ying Hui-yüan himself.

The subject of this study concerns one of these commentaries, the *Kuan wu-liang-shou ching i-shu* (hereafter, *Commentary*) by Ching-ying Hui-yüan (523–592). The *Commentary* is especially critical for interpreting early Pure Land Buddhism because, according to modern writers on the subject, it constitutes the earliest commentary on the *Kuan-ching.*[20] While the adequacy of this view will be assessed later, the *Commentary* certainly appears to be the earliest *extant* commentary.

Also, Etani Ryukai and Fujiwara Ryosetsu maintain that the *Commentary* became paradigmatic for many subsequent commentaries on the *Kuan-ching.*[21] Further, Etani suggests Hui-yüan exerted a major influence on Korean Pure Land Buddhism. According to his view, the commentators of Pure Land sutras during the Silla Dynasty can be grouped into one of two lines of transmission. One originates in Hui-yüan and the other in Hsüan-tsang (596–664) and [K'uei-]chi (632–682). Hui-yüan's 'lineage' includes such commentators as Chajang (608–677), Wŏnhyo (617–686), Ŭisang (620–702), Ŭijŏk (fl. seventh—early eighth centuries), Pŏbwi (fl. seventh century) and Hyŏnil (fl. seventh—early eighth centuries).[22] Though the cogency of Etani's proposal requires further evaluation, it nevertheless conveys the potential scale of Hui-yüan's role in the development of Korean Buddhism. The extent of his activities becomes all the more impressive, because these Silla Pure Land commentaries directly and vitally participated in the development of Japanese Pure Land doctrine during the Nara and early Heian periods.[23]

There is no evidence in the *Commentary* of any influence of T'an-luan's *Wang-sheng lun chu* (Commentary to the *Rebirth Treatise;* henceforth, *T'an-luan Commentary*), the only known major antecedent Chinese Pure Land treatise.[24] Yet conversely, as will be argued in this study, the *Commentary* did have an impact on the writings of the orthodox Pure Land Buddhists, Tao-ch'o and Shan-tao. This impact forces a reappraisal of the position held by Shinran's patriarchal lineage that Chinese Pure Land Buddhism developed exclusively and linearly from T'an-luan through Tao-ch'o and then to Shan-tao. Instead Hui-yüan's *Commentary* played a greater shaping role than previously acknowledged, and it would be more accurate in one sense to place Hui-yüan between T'an-luan and Tao-ch'o in the lineage above.

## Orthodox criticism of the Commentary

Despite the importance that Etani and Fujiwara accorded to Hui-yüan's *Commentary* in the early development of Pure Land Buddhism, the *Commentary* has not been seriously studied on its own terms. What discussion has arisen on the *Commentary* invariably occurs in its comparison with the *Shan-tao Commentary.*[25] The *Commentary* has not escaped its polemic role as a "straw man" in Japanese orthodox Pure Land scholarship (*shūgaku*). Since premodern times, *shūgaku* scholarship has churned out massive studies extolling the virtue of Shan-tao's interpretation while disparaging that of Hui-yüan and others. These belittled opponents (which include Hui-yüan) were collectively referred to either as "Masters" (*shoshi*), based on the *Shan-tao Commentary*[26], or as those of the "gate of the path of the sages" (*shōdōmon*). Although the other two commentaries on the *Kuan-ching,* attributed to Chih-i (538–597) and Chi-tsang (549–623) also shared in the *Shan-tao Commentary's* disagreement with the *Commentary,* Hui-yüan, nevertheless, has continued as the "spokesman" of the "Masters" and their "heretical" position.

Perhaps the most representative *shūgaku* scholar of the *Kuan-ching* is Rei'ō (1774–1851). In his *Bussetsu kanmuryōjukyō-kōki* (Lecture Notes on the *Kuan-ching* Expounded by the Buddha) he attacked the positions held by Hui-yüan and others and delineated twenty-two points on which the Masters (though principally Hui-yüan) and Shan-tao differed.[27] The twenty-two points are:

| **Masters** | **Shan-tao** |
|---|---|

1. Two or three parts to the preface (*hsü*) of the sutra:

| | |
|---|---|
| two parts | three parts |

2. Three or five divisions to the sutra:

| | |
|---|---|
| three divisions | five divisions |

3. Place for dividing the preface from the main (*cheng*) section:

| | |
|---|---|
| shorter preface | much longer |

4. Reasons for preaching the *Kuan-ching*:

| | |
|---|---|
| two reasons | seven reasons |

5. Distribution of meditative good acts (*ting-shan*) and non-meditative good acts (*san-shan*):

| | |
|---|---|
| All sixteen visualizations are meditative | thirteen visualizations are meditative and three are non-meditative |

6. Source requesting the teachings for the two types of good acts:

| | |
|---|---|
| Vaidehī requested both | Vaidehī requested the meditative but Amitābha taught the non-meditative without being requested |

7. Choice of Buddha-visualization (*kuan-fo*) or Buddha-contemplation (*nien-fo*) as sutra import (*tsung*):

| | |
|---|---|
| Buddha-visualization | both |

8. One or two teachings in the sutra:

| | |
|---|---|
| one teaching by Śākyamuni | two teachings: one by Śākyamuni and one by Amitābha |

9. Visualizations: phenomenal (*shih*) or noumenal (*li*):

| | |
|---|---|
| noumenal | phenomenal |

10. Amitābha: Rewarded-body (*pao-shen; saṃbhogakāya*) or Transformed-body (*hua-shen; nirmāṇakāya*):

| | |
|---|---|
| Transformed-body | Rewarded-body |

11. Nine grades of rebirth (*chiu-p'in wang-sheng):* Āryapudgalas (*sheng-jen*; sages) or Pṛthagjanas (*fanfu*; ordinary seekers below the Ārya-pudgala ranks in the Path):

| | |
|---|---|
| Āryapudgala | Pṛthagjanas |

12. Lady Vaidehī: Āryapudgala or Pṛthagjana:

| | |
|---|---|
| Āryapudgala | Pṛthagjana |

13. Place in the sutra when Vaidehī attained Insight of the Non-arising of *dharmas* (*wu-sheng jen*):

| | |
|---|---|
| end of the main part | at the seventh visualization |

14. Ranking of Vaidehī's Insight of Non-arising:

| | |
|---|---|
| seventh or first Bhūmi (the Āryapudgala stages in the Path) | Ten-Faiths stage |

15. Reason for the Buddha's smile:

| | |
|---|---|
| Vaidehī's attainment of Insight | Pure Land teaching was revealed for future sentient beings |

16. Vaidehī's vision of the Buddha in the seventh visualization: a skillful means [*upāya*] leading into the visualization or an integral part of the visualization:

| | |
|---|---|
| a skillful means | an integral part |

17. Buddha-contemplation (*nien-fo*): visualization (*kuan*) or recitation (*ch'eng*):

| | |
|---|---|
| visualization | recitation |

18. Division of the nine grades of rebirth:

| | |
|---|---|
| five sections | nine sections |

19. Three minds (*san-hsin*): application to the grades of birth:

| | |
|---|---|
| applies to highest three grade | applies to all nine grades and more |

20. Conversion of Hinayanists of the three middle grades to Mahayana:

| | |
|---|---|
| converts at deathbed | converts once in the Pure Land |

21. Resolution of the problem of those of the two-vehicles not being able to be reborn in the Pure Land:

| | |
|---|---|
| resolved in *Lotus Sutra* | no problem; Pure Land sutras provide resolution |

22. Oral recitation: degree of application:

| | |
|---|---|
| applies to the three lowest grades | applies to all nine grades |

Modern writers often cite these twenty-two points to criticize Hui-yüan or to applaud the uniqueness of Shan-tao's views.[28]

A few remarks here should be made about Hui-yüan's commentary to a recension of one of the other major Pure Land sutras, the *Larger Sukhāvatīvyūha Sutra,* entitled the *Wu-liang-shou ching i-shu* (Commentary to the Sutra on the Buddha of Immeasurable Life).[29] If the *Commentary* has received scant attention from modern scholars, then this commentary has been accorded virtually none at all.[30] Just as the *Commentary* is the earliest extant commentary on the *Kuan-ching,* so is this *Wu-liang-shou ching i-shu* the earliest extant commentary on the *Wu-liang-shou ching.* A thorough study of this work is imperative for a fuller understanding of Hui-yüan's overall position on Pure Land teachings. Though this commentary is not the primary object of this study, frequent reference will be made to it. For example chapter 4 will address Hui-yüan's attempt to reconcile the discrepancies between the two Pure Land sutras.

The sharp attack leveled by Shan-tao against a doctrinal position similar to one found in Hui-yüan's *Commentary* largely accounts for the focused criticism of Hui-yüan's position by orthodox Pure Land Buddhists. Shan-tao's main contention dealt with the ranking of the nine grades of rebirth (cf. chapter 6 under section "The Ranking of the Nine Grades") discussed by the *Kuan-ching.* In keeping with his fundamental advocacy of the Pure Land teaching's availability to the Pṛthagjanas, Shan-tao ranked the nine grades much lower on the Buddhist Path (*mārga*). (See chapter 5 and appendix 1 for details.) In contrast, Hui-yüan ranked them higher so that even Bodhisattvas of the Bhūmi stages, or the Āryapudgalas (sages), were counted among those reborn in the Pure Land. Shan-tao must have considered this difference crucial for validating the uniqueness of his basic interpretation of the *Kuan-ching,* for he devotes much of the first chapter to criticizing Hui-yüan's position.[31] Another point of contention concerned Shan-tao's judgment that Hui-yüan incorrectly categorized all sixteen visualizations as "meditative good acts" (*ting-shan*). Instead he regarded only the first thirteen as meditative good acts and the last three as "non-meditative acts" (*san-shan*).[32]

Their differences derive from basic disagreements over the efficient cause of rebirth in the Pure Land. On the one hand, Hui-yüan advocated raising the "mind set for enlightenment" (*bodhicitta*) and, on the other hand, Shan-tao proposed Amitābha Buddha's vow (*fo-yüan*).[33] Precisely on account of the vow, beings of inferior capacity could be reborn without themselves raising the mind set for enlightenment. Shan-tao did not wholly reject the efficacy of mind set for enlightenment. But the centrality of the vow in his overall doctrinal system extended and elaborated a tendency initiated by T'an-luan's writings.[34]

I contend that "*orthodox* Pure Land Buddhists" should not be considered a separate breed apart from those of "Pure Land Buddhism." Rather they should be regarded as members of the latter. As will be documented below, T'an-luan, Tao-ch'o and Shan-tao did not work in isolation but were products of a greater Pure Land Buddhist milieu. In this study, the term "orthodox Pure Land Buddhists" shall encompass specifically T'an-luan, Tao-ch'o, and Shan-tao. Others in the Chinese Pure Land lineages mentioned earlier, such as Lu-shan Hui-yüan and Fa-chao, will be incorporated into the larger rubric of "Pure Land Buddhism," in keeping with the definition given at the outset of chapter 1. Those not in any of the lineages but who did write commentaries or treatises related to Pure Land scriptures, such as Ching-ying Hui-yüan, will also be categorized under "Pure Land Buddhism" because they fall within the framework of the definition.

In part, this study distinguishes these two groups because of their doctrinal differences. In larger measure, however, it conforms to the general practice of previous scholarship. Although this study takes issue with many assumptions and conclusions of prior research, its adoption of this established distinction provides continuity with past scholarship and a common framework for carrying out the objectives of this analysis. It should be noted that despite the adoption of "orthodox Pure Land Buddhists," I am aware that they neither espoused a uniform set of ideas, as we are often led to believe, nor constituted a direct line of transmission. After all, Tao-ch'o was born at least ten years after T'an-luan's death, and some basic doctrinal differences existed between Tao-ch'o and Shan-tao.[35]

A distinction will also be maintained in this study between "orthodox Pure Land Buddhists" and "Japanese orthodox Pure Land Buddhists." The latter group includes Honen, Shinran, and their followers of the Jōdoshū and Jōdo-Shinshū schools. There will be frequent references to "Japanese orthodox scholars or writers," those who were trained in the traditional studies, *shūgaku.* Due to the very nature of the training in *shūgaku,* they were in most instances predisposed to support and defend the doctrinal position of their school. This distinction needs to be underscored, since what they say about Shan-tao, for example, may not always coincide with what Shan-tao himself said.[36] For this reason, we must exercise caution with the findings of the orthodox scholars with respect to both Shan-tao and to the other figures and topics related to Chinese Pure Land Buddhism.

Most of what we know about the *Commentary* and Hui-yüan suffers from limitations in scope and is prejudiced toward the orthodox perspective. This results in three shortcomings hampering our knowledge of the *Commentary* and its contribution to Pure Land Buddhism. First, in the absence of a more balanced reading of the *Kuan-ching,* judgment cannot be rendered on the adequacy of orthodox Pure Land criticism. Very possibly Hui-yüan's interpretation was more compatible with the more objective reading of the *Kuan-ching* than was Shan-tao's. Second, orthodox criticisms do not shed light on the claims Hui-yüan himself made in the *Commentary,* since sectarian interests have filtered virtually all that we know about the *Commentary.* Third, these sectarian criticisms have inhibited the development of a more complete picture of the *Commentary*'s impact, not only on the writings of orthodox Pure Land Buddhists but also on the *Shan-tao Commentary* in particular.

Since many previous authors have concurred that the *Kuan-ching* was the single most important sutra for the emergence of Pure Land Buddhism, then Hui-yüan's *Commentary* as its oldest surviving commentary should give us some clue for the sutra's popularity among the scholar-monks of the period. This would in turn provide some basis for interpreting the sudden surge of Pure Land Buddhism in the sixth century. Also, as Hui-yüan wrote commentaries on a broad range of scriptures, his *Commentary* constitutes a source for discovering the relations of Pure Land teaching to other streams of Buddhist thought. For example, Hui-yüan's knowledge of the *Nirvāṇa-sūtra* or of Vasubandhu's commentary on the *Daśabhūmika-sūtra* (Sutra on the Ten Bhūmis) must have shaped his interpretation of the *Kuan-ching.* Given the general perception of Pure Land Buddhism as a teaching for only the lay followers (who are of inferior ability compared to the monastics), the *Commentary,* along with the other commentaries of the *Kuan-ching,* indicates that this form of Buddhism attracted the interest not only of monks but also of high caliber exegetes and practitioners.

# Part I

# Chapter One

## Pure Land Buddhist Development in India and China Prior to Hui-yüan

### The term "Pure Land Buddhism"

"Pure Land Buddhism" refers to a set of beliefs and practices that espouses for its aspirants the realization of the stage of non-retrogression (*avaivartika; pu t'ui-chuan*) either in the present life or through rebirth in a Buddha land or realm (*Buddha-kṣetra; fo-kuo*) called "Sukhāvatī" (Land of Bliss).[1] According to the Pure Land sutras, the *Larger Sukhāvatīvyūha* and the *Smaller Sukhāvatīvyūha,* Sukhāvatī lies billions of Buddha lands away in the western direction from this world, the Sahā world-realm (*loka-dhātu*).[2] The Buddha Amitāyus (*Wu-liang-shou;* Immeasurable Life) or Buddha Amitābha (*Wu-liang-kuang;* Immeasurable Light) is the 'transcendant' Buddha who presides over the Sukhāvatī world-realm. The following will refer to this Buddha as "Amitābha" unless "Amitāyus" is more appropriate.

According to the *Larger Sukhāvatīvyūha Sutra,* Amitābha established through his compassionate vows (*praṇidhāna*) Sukhāvatī in order to lead sentient beings to Buddhahood. He made the vows as a Bodhisattva, named "Dharmākara" (storehouse of Dharma), and after five Kalpas (aeons) of contemplation followed by innumerable Kalpas of cultivation his vows were consummated. For the past ten Kalpas, Buddha Amitābha has dwelled in Sukhāvatī and has continually preached the Dharma. The sutras exhort both monks and laity, who aspire for rebirth in Amitābha's Sukhāvatī, to engage in a broad range of practices that include: meditation, observances of precepts, virtuous acts, building of *stūpa* (relic monument), and contemplation. Those reborn in Sukhāvatī acquire an ideal environment unlike this world for consummating their practices. Rebirth guarantees the attainment of the stage of non-retrogression and the eventual realization of the Mahayana goal of perfect enlightenment (*samyaksaṃbodhi*). Upon attainment of enlightenment, some return to this Sahā world-realm to carry out the Bodhisattva task of leading others to rebirth and ultimately to Buddhahood.[3]

This set of beliefs and practices surrounding Amitābha and Sukhāvatī has come to be referred to as "Pure Land Buddhism" and in its Chinese sectarian development as the "Pure Land school" (*ching-t'u tsung*) or "Pure Land teaching" (*ching-t'u chiao*). It is of interest to note, however, that the term "Pure Land" in specific reference to Sukhāvatī does not occur in any of the 'Pure Land' sutras translated prior to the middle of the eighth century.[4] Sukhāvatī is, instead, normally rendered into Chinese as "An-le kuo" (Country of Peace and Bliss) or "Chi-le" (Extreme Bliss). Apparently the identification of these two ideas, Sukhāvatī and Pure Land, began among Chinese commentators. One of the earliest textual sources for this occurs in the *T'an-luan Commentary,* which speaks of "the Pure Land of Sukhāvatī" (*An-le ching-t'u*).[5]

T'an-luan is also the earliest known writer to employ the term "Pure Land" to denote a distinct form of Chinese Buddhism. The *T'an-luan Commentary,* compiled around 540, includes a phrase "the Dharma-gate for the rebirth in the Pure Land" (*wang-sheng ching-t'u fa-men*), which refers to the five kinds of practices necessary for rebirth.[6] Approximately half a century later, Tao-ch'o in his *An-le chi* advocated the "path of rebirth in the Pure Land" (*wang-sheng ching-t'u men*) as one of two primary Buddhist paths, the other being the "path of the sages" (*sheng-tao men*).[7] Elsewhere in the same work appear such terms as "the singular gate of Pure Land" (*ching-t'u i-men*) and "the Dharma-gate of Pure Land" (*ching-t'u fa-men*).[8] The works of the preeminent Pure Land Buddhist, Shan-tao, also include the term "Pure Land teaching" (*ching-t'u chiao*).[9] Thus, the use of "Pure Land" to designate a distinct form of Buddhism had apparently begun around the first half of the sixth century and had become standard by the mid-seventh century.[10]

In the larger Mahayana context, Amitābha, along with Akṣobhya and Bhaiṣajyaguru, is the best known of the countless Buddhas in the cosmology who preside over the equally numerous Buddha-lands. While the traditions of the latter two Buddhas require greater research, unquestionably the Amitābha tradition has been the most pervasive and enduring of the three, if not on the Indian subcontinent, then clearly in China, Korea, and Japan. This is especially true of its scholastic tradition, which gave rise to Dharma-transmission lineages, not only in China, as we shall see, but also in the sectarian institutions of Japan. Its impact on East Asian popular religious devotion has been equally extensive and abiding, ranking with the traditions of such well-known Bodhisattvas as Maitreya, Avalokiteśvara, and Kṣitigarbha.

**Background and development of the doctrine and practice**

India offers no evidence of an independent Pure Land school or lineage. The diaries of early Chinese pilgrims to India do not refer to Pure Land at all. Instead, the second century stone foundations for an Amitābha image dated 104 C.E. from Mathurā comprise the only nonliterary trace of exclusive Amitābha devotion.[11] The next oldest epigraphical evidence is found in Sañcī and dates from the late seventh century. But it forms only a fragment of a verse of praise dedicated to Avalokiteśvara. Devotion to Amitābha, thus, appears to have been a limited movement during the Kuṣāṇa period (ca. 50–200 C.E.) with no impact on the continuing development of Buddhism during the Gupta period (ca. 320–570) either at Mathurā or any other location in Northern India.[12]

Mention of Pure Land practice occurs only in the early eighth century. During his India pilgrimage begun in 702, Hui-jih (later called "Tz'u-min," d. 748) reported that when he inquired about the swiftest means for seeing the Buddha, all the scholars encouraged him to pursue the Pure Land teaching. In Gandhāra Hui-jih received a revelation related to rebirth in the Western Realm. But his account must be treated with caution in the absence of corroborating evidence about the prevalence of Pure Land devotion in India. His reports could very well be a pious accounting of a Pure Land devotee who, on his return to China, became one of the major Pure Land proponents of the mid-T'ang period.[13]

The process of generalization and disassociation incurred by Pure Land teaching may explain the absence of any significant Pure Land school. Gregory Schopen's study of early Sanskrit literature proposes that Sukhāvatī may have become disassociated from the specific cult of Buddha Amitābha as early as second century C.E. Devotion not only to Amitābha but also to Śākyamuni, Bhaiṣajyaguru or other Buddhas could also affect rebirth in Sukhāvatī. Aspirants to Sukhāvatī could now broaden their devotion beyond Amitābha to a host of other Buddhas. Also, Sukhāvatī became generalized as a realm epitomizing an ultimate religious goal. Just as Mt. Meru symbolized unshakability and imperturbability, so did Sukhāvatī become the standard literary simile for magnificance, loveliness, charm, and splendor. The appropriation by non-Pure Land Buddhists of Sukhāvatī not only rendered it accessible to them but also weakened the coherence of Pure Land's soteriological foundations as formed by Amitābha, Sukhāvatī, and the aspirant's practice.[14]

The earliest Indian textual sources for Pure Land Buddhism are the *Larger Sukhāvatīvyūha Sutra* and the *Smaller Sukhāvatīvyūha Sutra.* Their subsequent translations and linguistic and internal evidence suggest they were compiled in Northwest India around 100 C.E. during Kuṣāṇa Dynasty. Examination of the Chinese transliteration determines the original language of the sutras to be Gandhārī (or a related dialect), a Northwestern Prākrit language of Northwest India and Central Asia extant from the third century B.C.E. to third century C.E.[15] In these sutras are found the essential components of Pure Land doctrine: (1) the career of Bodhisattva Dharmākara before becoming Buddha Amitābha, (2) his vows to establish Sukhāvatī as a Buddha land, (3) a description of the features of Sukhāvatī, (4) the practices required of the aspirants for rebirth, and (5) the character of rebirth in Sukhāvatī and the attainment of enlightenment.

With these two sutras as reference points, the development of Pure Land teaching and practice seems to proceed in the following five stages: (1) the initial dominance of the concept of multiple Buddhas of the past and future (from fifth century B.C.E.), (2) the subsequent shift to the idea of transcendent contemporary Buddhas (from second century B.C.E.), (3) then the emergence of Buddha Amitābha, (from first century C.E.), (4) the adoption of visualization and recitative techniques (from ca. third century), and (5) the establishment of a critical commentarial tradition (from ca. fifth century). While the dates cannot be exact given the absence of solid evidence, this scheme nevertheless offers a general chronology for the major developments. As we have defined it, Pure Land Buddhism begins in stage three with the prior two stages comprising its major conceptual background.

*Stage one: multiple Buddhas of the past and future*

The idea that Buddhas other than Śākyamuni existed in the distant past seems to have emerged soon after Śākyamuni Buddha's death in ca. 486 B.C.E. The theory of the "seven past Buddhas" best represents this notion of previous Buddhas. It maintained that six earlier Buddhas, Vipaśyin, Śikhin, Viśvabhū, Krakucchanda, Kanakamuni and Kāśyapa preceded Śākyamuni. Śākyamuni was, in a sense, the spiritual heir to a lineage of Buddhas. The early literary sources along with Aśokan inscriptions establish the idea of seven past Buddhas no later than mid-third century B.C.E.[16] Subsequent theories posited fifteen, twenty-four and even a much larger number of past Buddhas. Regarded by many early schools as the first Buddha, Dīpaṃkara acquires special prominence among these Buddhas as the foreseer of Śākyamuni's enlightenment.[17]

One impulse for this idea derived from efforts to account for Śākyamuni's achievement of Buddhahood in this life, a feat unattained by any of his contemporaries. This also prompted the compilation of the *Jātaka* Tales that detailed the great accomplishments of the Buddha in his previous lives as a Bodhisattva.

If Buddhas existed in the past, it followed that there would be future Buddhas. Towards the end of the second century B.C.E., such inferences led to the belief in the best known of the future Buddhas, Maitreya. This belief held that like Śākyamuni Maitreya awaits in Tuṣita Heaven to be reborn in this world 5,000 to billions of years after Śākyamuni's death. The Maitreya faithful hoped for rebirth either in Tuṣita Heaven or in the world at the time of Maitreya Buddha's messianic appearance.[18]

These past and future Buddhas universalized the enlightenment of the historical Buddha. Śākyamuni no longer retained a monopoly on Buddhahood, because those in the past as well as the future could obtain it. This reinforced the pronouncement attributed to Śākyamuni Buddha: "Whosoever sees me sees the Dharma and whosoever sees the Dharma sees me."[19]

### *Stage two: Transcendent contemporary Buddhas of other world-realms*

Although previously confined to this Sahā world-realm, Buddhist cosmology gradually expanded so that the immediate universe came to be described as "the three thousand great-thousand world-realm" consisting of one billion smaller worlds. By the second century B.C.E., its cosmology underwent a still greater expansion by addition of innumerable numbers of world-realms in all ten directions. Since Buddhas presided over many of these world-realms, they were referred to as "Buddha realms." Thus, the cosmos in the ten directions became populated with countless transcendent Buddhas. Unlike the past and future Buddhas, these Buddhas existed contemporaneously, albeit in distant realms beyond the Sahā world-realm.[19]

Although criticized by the Theravādins and Sarvāstivādins, this new idea apparently found currency within the Mahāsaṃghika and Lokottaravāda schools. The *Kathāvatthu* of the Theravādins credited the Mahāsaṃghikas with a doctrine that the Buddhas pervade all the directions of the universe.[20] Further, the Lokottaravādin's *Mahāvastu* expressed this same doctrine, which later commentators of other schools also corroborated as the idea of the Lokottaravādins.[21] The doctrine of multiple contemporary Buddhas must have existed by the seconds century B.C.E. since the *Kathāvatthu* was completed by the end of the same century.[22]

In the absence of this conception by these pre-Mahayana proponents or their critics, modern scholars have turned to Mahayana sources as the possible doctrinal origins for the emergence of multiple contemporary Buddhas. Some have suggested that the thesis of contemporary Buddhas directly derived from the realization that large numbers of Bodhisattvas upon becoming Buddhas had nowhere to go. From very early on, Buddhists had tacitly ruled that only one Buddha could inhabit at one time the Sahā world. Thus, the "one Buddha to one world-realm" premise forced the issue about the dwelling place of the contemporary Buddhas.[23] Although Asaṇga (ca 390–470) offered this explanation (of the Bodhisattvas having nowhere to go upon becoming Buddhas) in the fifth century C.E., it is unlikely that it had anything to do with an idea that arose at least five centuries earlier.[24] While the concept of a distinct Bodhisattva path existed in the second century B.C.E., it instead referred specifically to Śākyamuni prior to his becoming the Buddha rather than to multiple Mahayana Bodhisattvas. Thus, the earlier conception lacked the doctrinal necessity to find "homes" for them in the transcendent realms.

Instead, the concept of Buddha-realm may provide a more likely doctrinal explanation for the emergence of these contemporary Buddhas. Under this view, the Buddhist cosmos is not an objective and material but a subjective and spiritual reality. The transcendent Buddhas and their realms that fill the universe are concretized expressions of the eternal Buddha-principle (*dharma*), which as the basic reality of the universe is ever active to lead all beings to enlightenment. In other words, the universe is the domain of the Buddhas and is, thus, fashioned and sustained by their work to lead beings to enlightenment.[25] The idea that the Buddhist universe is spiritually determined finds expression in other genres of Buddhist literature, for example, in the *Jātaka* with respect to Śākyamuni Buddha:

> Now at the moment when the future Buddha made himself incarnate in his mother's womb, the constituent elements of the ten-thousand world systems (i.e. entire universe) quaked, trembled and shook violently.[26]

While further research might determine with greater certainty the doctrinal factors for the idea of transcendent contemporary Buddhas, the religious demands of the believer cannot be neglected. Social and political ferment in North India followed the relative stability of the golden age of Mauryan and, in particular, of King Aśoka's dynastic rule (r. 269–232 B.C.E.). Competing with the non-Buddhist Śaivaites and Bhāvagatas, the Buddhists sought innovative responses to the cultural and religious demand for a theistic, saviour-centered devotionalism.[27] Accordingly, the contemporary Buddhas assured devotees that in the absence of a Buddha in this world, Buddhas yet resided elsewhere who could answer their calls and in whose land they could be reborn.[28]

This new religious milieu required a new soteriological scheme, which in turn changed the earlier assumption about personal karma as the sole responsibility of the individual. Now, the devotees could expect the "intervention" or "grace" of these saviour Buddhas that drastically altered the karmic makeup of these devotees. The concept of "merit transference" (*pariṇāma/pariṇāmanā*) expresses this soteriological process wherein an accomplished practitioner can transfer to others his accumulated good merit for their benefit. Those with higher spiritual attainments were able to transfer greater amount of merit. Hence, the transcendent Bodhisattvas and Buddhas could dispense benefits on a greater scale due to their immense stock of accumulated merit. The transference also took place among ordinary devotees of this Sahā realm. These benefits took either the worldly form of good health and wealth or the religious form of attainments closer to enlightenment. In performing virtuous acts of devotion, one can transfer the merit accrued from the action to his family members, either alive or deceased.[29] A similar idea finds expression in the *Questions of King Milinda* (*Milindapañha*), a non-Mahayana text compiled in Northern India around the beginning of the common era. According to this well-known work revered also by the Theravādins, offerings made to the relics of Śākyamuni Buddha create goodness that can assuage and allay the fever and the torment of the threefold fire of desire, hatred, and delusion. Though the Buddha has passed away, such offerings to him have value and bear fruit.[30]

*Stage three:*
*Emergence of the Amitābha Pure Land movement*

The compilation of the sutras around 100 C.E. implies that Pure Land thought and practice became established by the latter half of the first century C.E. In this process, Buddha Amitābha appeared as one of the transcendent contemporary Buddhas. He presides over Sukhāvatī, one of the innumerable transcendent world-realms located billions of Buddha-lands away in the western quarter. Thus, the concepts in stage two of multiple contemporary Buddhas and of transcendent world-realms now converge to form a specific cult of Amitābha Buddha to which the *Larger* and *Smaller Sukhāvatīvyūha Sutras* give expression. The Pure Land sutras assert that Amitābha constitutes one of the contemporary Buddhas. Nāgārjuna (ca. 150–250 C.E.) also confirms this by regarding Dīpaṃkara, Amitābha, and Maitreya as representatives of, respectively, the past, contemporary and future Buddhas.[31]

As initially mentioned, the original Sanskrit name for this Buddha was either "Amitābha" (immeasurable light) or "Amitāyus" (immeasurable life).[32] But by the time of their compilation, the two Pure Land sutras used both names but with different frequencies. While the *Larger Sukhāvatīvyūha Sutra* favored "Amitābha," the *Smaller Sutra* preferred "Amitāyus."[33] In the East Asian context, the names of this Buddha originate not only from translations of Amitābha as "Wu-liang-kuang" or of Amitāyus "Wu-liang-shou," but also from its transliteration as "A-mi-t'o" (Chinese), "Amit'a" (Korean) or "Amida" (Japanese).[34]

Modern scholars have diversely advocated either non-Buddhist or Buddhist origins for Amitābha Buddha. In general, Western scholars comprise the former group, often citing Zoroastrian sun gods such as Mithra whose theme of light is cognate with "immeasurable light" of Amitābha.[35] Also, the Zoroastrian primordial principle of *zrvan akarana,* "infinite time," may have influenced Amitāyus, "immeasurable life."[36] Others have postulated non-Buddhist Indian sources such as the Viṣṇu mythology, Amitaujas ("immeasurable power") of Brahmaloka Heaven and the deity Varuṇa of western quarter.[37]

Represented largely by Japanese scholars, those unconvinced by this contend, instead, that the Buddhist tradition offers a sufficient doctrinal basis.[38] For instance, Fujita cites numerous passages from early sutras and pre-Mahayana school literature on the Buddha's exceedingly long or immeasurable life and immense or immeasurable light.[39] A doctrine attributed to the Mahāsaṃghikas and its related schools states: "The power of the Tathāgatas is unlimited, and the life of the Buddhas is unlimited."[40] Since "power" (Chinese *wei-li*; Tibetan *mthu*) in this context is intimately connected with "light," this passage could refer to the two qualities (light and life) that later became ascribed to Amitābha Buddha.[41]

Theories about the derivation of Sukhāvatī have similarly generated scholarly debate. Advocates of a non-Buddhist provenance point to various prototypes: an island off the coast of Africa called "Scotra," Brahma's realm, Varuṇa's realm of Sukhā and Yāma's realm, and even the Garden of Eden.[42] A more recent hypothesis centers around a Taq-i-Bustan Cave in eastern Iran.[43] In contrast, theories of a Buddhist source cite the city of Kusāvatī of King Mahāsudassana, the northern continent of Uttarakuru in the Buddhist cosmology, the heavens within the Desire (Kāma) and Form Realms (Rūpa-dhātu) and the *stūpas* dedicated to Śākyamuni.[44]

The ensuing debates of the last fifty years about both Amitābha and Sukhāvatī have not established any decisive conclusions. With regard to the genesis of Amitābha, Fujita maintains that, while external influences cannot be totally excluded, the origin of Amitābha Buddha can be adequately explained as a development within mainstream Buddhist thought.[45]

In my view, a theoretical framework for the interreligious transmission of ideas would enhance the clarity of Fujita's conclusion. I shall suggest that transmission may occur in one of three modes which I term "direct," "eclectic," and "stimulative." In direct transmission, Amitābha, for example, would be identified with the Zoroastrian sun-god Mithra. In the absence of a precedence, Buddhists would find sufficient rationale to subsume it under a new Buddhist name. Eclectic transmission would entail a Buddhist assimilation of certain elements from an external tradition. For example, a prominent characteristic of external deities, such as light, would be incorporated into the Buddhist framework as a trait of a Buddha. The stimulative mode, however, does not involve any borrowing as in the direct and eclectic transmissions. Rather, Buddhists would be stimulated to meet the challenges of external traditions by turning to resources of its own heritage.

In my estimation, Fujita's position exemplifies primarily a stimulative and, only secondarily, an eclectic mode. The strong presence of Persian, Hellenistic, and other occidental elements in the cultural milieu of first century C.E. in Northwestern India under Kuṣāṇa rule suggests a non-Buddhist provenance for Amitābha. If the non-Buddhist gods with salvific powers associated with light and life enjoyed popularity and influence in that region, then they might have served as an impetus for a Buddhist Amitābha. They amplified the valued qualities of light and life which, as shown above, already existed within the Buddhist tradition. If elements were borrowed and assimilated in an eclectic transmission, they would most likely be physical features belonging to Yāma and Varuṇa. But no compelling evidence of direct transmission occurs in the development of Amitābha Buddha or Sukhāvatī in Pure Land Buddhism.

We have discussed Pure Land's two key doctrinal components, Amitābha Buddha and Sukhāvatī. But Pure Land Buddhism would not have achieved its complete soteriological form without these other doctrinal components: the career story of Bodhisattva Dharmākara, the Bodhisattva vow, and the practices of the aspirants for rebirth. These components do not suggest extraneous influences, and it is safely assumed that they evolved internally within the Buddhist fold. The career story of Dharmākara becoming Amitābha follows the basic model of the earlier Buddhist *Jātaka* literature. The Bodhisattva vow accords with the general practice of Bodhisattvas within pre-Mahayana and early Mahayana models. The maintenance of monastic precepts, the performance of such virtuous acts as *stūpa* building and sutra copying, and mindfulness on the Buddha all conform to the Buddhist devotional practice.

### *Stage four: Adoption of visualization and recitation*

The range of practices for Pure Land devotees expanded significantly with the adoption of visualization (*anusmṛti*; *kuan*) and oral recitation of the name (*ch'eng-ming*) of Amitābha, which neither the *Larger* nor *Smaller Sukhāvatīvyūha Sutras* discussed. In the development of Pure Land Buddhism in India and beyond, both practices attracted many devotees to the

Pure Land path. A commentary to the *Daśabhūmika-sūtra* attributed to Nāgārjuna advocates recitation as a means for rebirth in any one of the multiple transcendent world-realms.[46] This work, however, is not technically a Pure Land text and its authorship is questionable.[47] Hence, the earliest Pure Land resource for visualization and recitation practices would be the *Kuan-ching.*[48] Believed to have been compiled in the late fourth century, this sutra undoubtedly describes practices of the early fourth, if not third, century.[49]

The sutra refers to visualization practice as the "*samādhi* (concentration) of contemplation on the Buddha" (*nien-fo san-mei*).[50] Thus, Pure Land visualization may be regarded as one among many of the early Mahayana *samādhis* such as the Śūraṃgama-samādhi (concentration of the heroic Buddha in which the defilements are destroyed) and Pratyutpanna-samādhi (concentration in which the Buddhas stand before one).[51] The textual background and content of the *Kuan-ching* suggest that it belongs to a group of so-called visualization sutras (*kuan-ching*) devoted to Mahayana Bodhisattvas and Buddhas. These meditational techniques gained popularity in India and more notably, Central Asia, particularly from about the fourth century. The Central Asian popularity of visualization may be partially seen in the inordinately large number of Central Asians involved in translating "visualization sutras" into Chinese in the early fifth century.[52]

In the *Kuan-ching* aspirants for rebirth visualize (*hsiang*) the features of Sukhāvatī, Amitābha and his attendant Bodhisattvas. Once accomplished each feature is individually inspected (*kuan-ch'a*). This leads to the next step in the attainment of a vision (*chien*). Properly done, the vision of the object appears clearly before the practitioner, whether the eyes are open or shut. *Samādhi* and its attendant psychological and spiritual tranquility or resolve are thereupon realized.[53] For example, the sutra remarks, "Therefore, when you perceive a Buddha in your mind, . . . your mind becomes a Buddha and your mind is a Buddha; and the wisdom of the Buddhas, true, universal and ocean-like, arises from this mind."[54] The Pure Land soteriological scheme generally conceived such *samādhi* states as assurances to practitioners of their rebirth in the Pure Land and their ultimate Buddhahood.

Compared to the more difficult visualization discipline, oral recitation is more accessible to the faithful. The *Kuan-ching* offers recitation to spiritually inferior beings on their deathbed. For instance, beings in the lowest of the nine grades of birth, who had committed the five grave offenses and the ten transgressions, cannot be mindful of the Buddha as instructed by even a virtuous teacher. But if they follow their teacher's exhortation to recite with sincere mind the name of Buddha Amitābha, they thereby eradicate their karmic retribution (*tsui*) of eight billion Kalpas and are assured of rebirth.[55]

Recitation brought with it the eradication of karmic retribution. The prototype of recitation occurs in earlier Buddhist scriptures but invariably exemplifies a magical nature that often wards away imminent dangers. In the *Mahāvastu,* for example, 500 merchants in a boat were devoured by a giant fish but were saved when collectively they recited aloud: "We take refuge in the Buddha."[56] The type of recitation, however, found in the *Kuan-ching* differs in its nature and application from this early self-serving form. A related genre of sutras that dealt primarily with visualization or contemplation (*anusmṛti*) and with Buddha names (*Buddha-nāma*) also represented this type of recitation. Almost invariably these sutras closely associated recitation with practices of repentance (*ch'an-hui*). Recitation and repentance together led to the elimination of karmic retribution. This, in turn, promoted the realization of *samādhi* as the ultimate soteriological goal.[57] However, recitation in the *Kuan-ching* differed in that recitation led, not to *samādhi,* but to rebirth in Sukhāvatī.

A fifth century Chinese translation (ca. 529) by Bodhiruci of a work attributed to Vasubandhu (ca. 400–480), the *Rebirth Treatise* (*Sukhāvatī-vyūhopadeśa*), discussed both visualization and recitation.[58] While its primary concern lies with visualization, it also advocates oral recitation. The recitation assists in explaining "praise," which along with worship, aspiration for rebirth, visualization and transference of one's merit comprise the "Five Contemplative Gates" (*wu-nien men*). To praise the Tathāgata means to orally recite the name of Buddha Amitābha as a form of verbal action (*vāk-karman*).[59] The treatise then elaborates extensively the issue of visualization, which has as its object the seventeen features of the physical aspects of the Pure Land, the eight features of Amitābha, and the four features of the two attendant Bodhisattvas. These visualizations are, for the author of the treatise, none other than "insight" (*vipaśyanā*), a traditional Buddhist expression of meditative realization.[60]

### *Stage five: Critical commentarial tradition*

Very few treatises on Pure Land have been found in India. In fact the only extant work devoted exclusively to Amitābha Pure Land Buddhism is the previously mentioned fifth century work attributed to Vasubandhu that survives only in its Chinese translation, the *Rebirth Treatise.* There are, however, a few older writings that comment on aspects of Pure Land doctrine. Among these the earliest documents are attributed to Nāgārjuna (hence, dated around 200 C.E.), the *Ta chih tu lun* (Great Perfection of Wisdom Treatise) and the aforementioned commentary on the

*Daśabhūmika-sūtra.*[61] In the latter text's chapter on "Easy Practice," the author discusses the attainment of the non-retrogressive state and then distinguishes two paths. The first follows the "easy practice" (*i-hsing*) of devotion, which is likened to riding on a vessel over water. The "difficult" (*nan*) path resembles a Bodhisattva walking on land to his destination.[62] Amitābha is one among numerous transcendent Buddhas to whom devotion of easy practice may be directed. In East Asia, the distinction between the difficult and the easy path served as one of the primary doctrinal bases for the establishment of Pure Land as an independent school.

In the *Mahāyānasaṃgraha* (Compendium of the Mahayana), Asaṅga criticizes Pure Land doctrine as an expedient teaching solely to lure spiritually inferior and morally indolent people. In a doctrine called "intended for another time" (*kālāntarābhiprāya*; *pieh-shih-i*), he argues that Pure Land teaching encourages rebirth in the Pure Land and enlightenment as benefits to be attained in the immediate future. But in actuality, he adds, enlightenment is only realized in the distant future after one consummates long and arduous practice.[63] This doctrine had a lasting impact on Pure Land Buddhism. It became a standard criticism by Yogacāra advocates in India and China.[64]

In the previously alluded to *Rebirth Treatise,* the author sets forth the five kinds of practices for rebirth, the Five Contemplative Gates: worship, praise, aspiration for rebirth, visualization, and the transfer of merit. Significantly, the author places the five practices within traditional Mahayana categories. He identifies the aspiration for rebirth with concentration (*śamatha*) and visualization with insight (*vipaśyanā*). He further correlates the first four gates with the concept of benefit for oneself (*svārtha*; *tzu-li*) and the fifth gate with the benefit for others (*parārtha*; *li-t'a*).[65] The treatise also disqualifies Hinayanists, women, and the disabled for rebirth in the Pure Land. This exclusion provoked harsh criticism in China and preoccupied Pure Land apologists.[66]

Thirty-one Sanskrit texts and over one hundred Chinese and Tibetan translations refer to Amitābha and/or Sukhāvatī.[67] For example, the author of the *Ratnagotravibhāga-śāstra* (Treatise on the Buddha-womb Theory) concludes his highly technical work on the *tathāgatagarbha* (Buddha-womb or embryo) doctrine by stating: "By the merit I have acquired through [writing] this [treatise], may all living beings come to perceive the Lord Amitāyus endowed with infinite light."[68] Such references attest to the influence wielded by Pure Land thought in the devotional lives of the commentators. Some reference, however, did not presuppose the Amitābha devotion of the *Sukhāvatīvyūha Sutras.* For example, the Bodhisattva names in Amitābha's previous life do not include Dharmākara but range over fifteen other apellations.[69] This suggests a more diffused Pure Land thought.

The processes of disassociation had disengaged Amitābha not only from Sukhāvatī, as discussed earlier, but also from the Dharmākara story.

These surviving literary sources imply that despite numerous passing references, a Pure Land commentarial tradition in India was virtually nonexistent. Further, as seen above, the questions surrounding the authenticity of the major Pure Land treatises attributed to Nāgārjuna and Vasubandhu leave little solid evidence of active scholarship on Pure Land doctrine in India. In fact, many doctrinal categories associated with Pure Land doctrine awaited the creative contributions of the Chinese commentators. Their innovation bears particularly on the following discussion of the Three-body (*trikāya*) doctrine and Amitābha as either Transformed-body or Rewarded-body.

## Chinese development

### *First scriptural transmission*

Of the Chinese translations of the *Larger Sukhāvatīvyūha Sutra,* two of the five extant recensions belong to what we are calling the "first transmission" that occurred around 200 C.E. The earliest was translated either in the second half of the third century or possibly even in the second century. Chih-ch'ien may have translated the *A-mi-t'o san-yeh-san-fo-sa-lou-fo-t'an kuo-tu-jen-tao ching* (hereafter, by its common title the *Ta a-mi-t'o ching* (Great Sutra on Amitābha) between 222 and 253. Yet, Lokakṣema (Chih Lou-chia-ch'en) may have translated it around 167. The translation of the second, *Wu-liang ch'ing-ching p'ing-teng-chüeh ching* (hereafter, *P'ing-teng-chüeh ching,* Sutra on the Enlightenment of Equanimity) ascribed to Lokakṣema, has recently been attributed to Po-yen and dated almost a century later around 258.[70] Strictly speaking, the *Pan-chou san-mei ching* (Sutra on the *Samādhi* in which the Buddhas Stand Before One) is not considered a Pure Land sutra because its primary concern centers on meditative practice, the Pratyutpanna-samādhi.[71] But because it refers to Amitābha and his land as the object of Pratyutpanna-samādhi, this sutra played a crucial role in the early phase of Chinese Pure Land Buddhism.[72] It served as a canonical source for Lu-shan Hui-yüan in his promulgation of the Pure Land practice of the "*samādhi* of contemplation on Buddha Amitābha (*nien-fo san-mei*).[73]

### *Pure Land devotees*

Western Chin accounts identify the earliest known Pure Land devotees to be Ch'üeh Kung-tse (d. 265–274), his student Wei Shih-tu (d. ca. 323) and

Wei's mother, who reportedly aspired to and gained rebirth in the Western Realm.[74] Then there was also a certain Seng-hsien, who left the war torn North and arrived in the Eastern capital of Chien-k'ang in 321. According to *Biographies of Eminent Monks:*

> Later when he became seriously ill for a long time, he concentrated his thoughts upon the Western Realm as he endured extreme pain. He then saw the Buddha of Immeasurable Life descend in his true appearance to shine upon his body, at which time his pain completely disappeared.[75]

Chih-tun (314–366) represents one of the earliest known Pure Land practitioners among the intellectual non-ethnic Chinese. The aristocracy and the learned circles of the newly established Western Chin society respected him as a scholar of Neo-Taoist philosophy of Dark Learning (*hsüan-hsüeh*). He interpreted contemporary religio-philosophical issues and offered a metaphysical meaning for the term *li* (noumenal).[76] Besides his philosophical writings, he composed several eulogies, one of which expresses his faith in Buddha Amitābha and Sukhāvatī. E. Zürcher's translation captures the sense of the deeply introspective and intimate expression of the earliest surviving personal testimony of Amitābha Pure Land devotion:

> In this country there is no arrangement of royal regulations, ranks and titles. The Buddha is the ruler, and the three Vehicles are the [state] doctrine. . . . Whosoever in this country of Chin, in this era of sensual pleasures, serves the Buddha and correctly observes the commandments, who recites the Scripture of Amitābha, and who [furthermore] makes a vow to be [re]born in that country of [Sukhāvatī] without ever abandoning his sincere intention, will at the end of his life, when his soul passes away, be miraculously transported thither. He will behold the Buddha and be enlightened in his spirit, and then he will realize the Way. I, Tun, born at this late time, [can only] hope to follow the remaining traces [of the doctrine], and I do not dare to expect that my mind is bound for that spiritual country. Hence I had a painting made by an artisan, and erected this as a manifestation of the divine [power]; respectfully I look to the noble appearance [of this Buddha] in order to confront myself with Him whom [I adore like] Heaven.[77]

He envisioned an unstructured and egalitarian Pure Land, perhaps in keeping with his Neo-Taoist orientation. Here also are the germs of some of the common themes that appear in the "mature" writings of later Pure Land Buddhists: the acknowledgement of the degeneracy of his time, the low estimation of one's spiritual capacity to realize the goal on his own, and the reliance on Buddha's power. The painting of Amitābha constitutes one of the earliest examples in China of an icon used for devotional purposes.

The devotion expressed by Chih-tun was overshadowed approximately fifty years later by Lu-shan Hui-yüan who led perhaps the most famous event associated with Chinese Pure Land Buddhism. Hui-yüan figured as a prominant contemporary Buddhist. The courts of the Eastern Chin dynasty in the South and the Yao Ch'in dynasty in the North as well as local rulers regarded him as the paragon of Buddhist virtues. He fostered translation activities and also composed the influential treatise *Sha-men pu-ching wang-che lun* (Monks Do Not Pay Homage to the Ruler), which defended the autonomy of Buddhist clergy.[78]

Moreover, his Pure Land devotional groups exemplify his most enduring influence on Chinese Buddhism. In 402, Hui-yüan and his coterie of 123 lay and clerical disciples made a collective vow to be reborn together in Sukhāvatī. Accompanied by an offering of incense and flowers, the participants expressed before an icon of Buddha Amitābha their desire to be reborn together in Sukhāvatī. But because of individual differences in karmic maturity, they realized that some participants would gain rebirth before others. Thus, they vowed that the early arrivals in Sukhāvatī would not simply revel in their bliss but exert themselves to share their salvation with those lagging behind. If they could adhere to this pact, they would in the end all be reborn and together "miraculously behold the great appearance [of Amitābha] and open their hearts in [his] pure brightness."[79]

Upon Hui-yüan's death, his disciples transmitted their master's teaching to much of southern China, including Chiang-ling, Ch'eng-tu and Chien-k'ang. Also, Hui-ch'ih (d. 412), an active proponent of in the Ch'eng-tu area, was known for his devoted Pure Land faith. Having had two known disciples, he undoubtedly transmitted Pure Land devotion to them.[80] Hui-yüan's name heads the list of Pure Land masters of the first half of the seventh century and is resurrected as the "founder" of several Pure Land lineages later in the Sung dynasty. The transmission lines of his direct disciples, however, apparently did not continue for more than a few generations. None of his disciples are credited either with any writings or with the formation of identifiable Pure Land groups. This may have resulted from the exclusivistic, other-worldly nature of Hui-yüan's Pure Land group that did not reach out to the larger society for broader support.[81]

### *Second scriptural transmission*

In the first half of the fifth century, the translation of another group of Pure Land sutras played a more substantial role in subsequent developments of Pure Land Buddhism than did those of the first transmission two centuries earlier. The translation of the *Wu-liang-shou ching,* one of the recensions of the *Larger Sukhāvatīvyūha Sutra,* is ascribed to a Sogdian K'ang Seng-k'ai (Saṃghavarman) of the Wei dynasty (220–265). The Pure Land tradition has long accepted this ascription. But modern scholarship regards Buddhabhadra (359–429) and Pao-yün (376–449) as its actual translators, thereby moving back its date of translation nearly two centuries to about 421.[82] The commentators of the Sui and T'ang periods and the entire Pure Land tradition of China, Korea, and Japan quickly rated this text, known in the catalogues as the *New Sutra on the Buddha Amitāyus* (*Shin wu-liang-shou ching*), as of greater importance than its two earlier recensions.[83] Around 402, Kumārajīva (344–413 or 350–409) translated the *Smaller Sukhāvatīvyūha Sutra* (*A-mi-t'o ching*). Catalogues report another translation by Guṇabhadra (394–468). But it was lost, probably as early as the beginning of sixth century.[84]

Kālayaśas (383?–442?) is credited with the translation of the *Kuang-ching* between 424 and 442 during the Yüan-chia era of the Liu-Sung period. Unlike the previous two, this sutra has no Sanskrit, Tibetan, or variant Chinese recension.[85] Consequently, as discussed below, scholars contest the date and general location of its compilation. The *Kuan-ching,* nevertheless, played the most central role of the three sutras in the emergence of Pure Land Buddhism as a major Buddhist school in Sui-T'ang China.

### *Devotional and scholastic activities in the South*

Along with the translation of the *A-mi-t'o ching,* the translations in the South of the new *Wu-liang-shou ching* and the *Kuan-ching* attracted the attention of scholar-monks who lectured on them. For example, Fa-tu (d. 500) on Mt. She, a devotee of the Pure Land teaching, lectured on the *Wu-liang-shou ching.*[86] Pao-liang (d. 509), a noted scholar of the *Nirvāṇa-sūtra* in the Liang capital of Chien-yeh, lectured to large audiences of over 3,000 on a wide range of sutras. While he favored such sutras as the *Nirvāṇa* and *Śrīmālādevī* (Queen Śrīmālā), Pao-liang lectured on the *Wu-liang-shou ching* on nearly ten occasions.[87]

Despite this attention, Pure Land scriptures remained relatively minor texts, overshadowed by such better known sutras as the *Lotus,* the *Nirvāṇa,* the *Prajñāpāramitā* (Perfection of Wisdom), and the *Vimalakīrti* (Questions of Vimalakirti). No lecturer appears to have written Pure Land treatises or commentaries on these sutras. In contrast, the *Nirvāṇa-sūtra* boasted numerous commentaries by the early sixth century. Pao-liang and others compiled these commentaries into a voluminous seventy-one scroll commentary, the *Ta-nieh-p'an-ching chi-chieh,* in response to Liang Emperor Wu's edict of 509.[88] The nonexistence of Pure Land commentaries attests to weak scholarly interests in Pure Land scriptures. In such a climate, any school or lineage of scholarly Pure Land transmission would not likely arise in the South.

### *Devotional and scholastic activities in the North*

In contrast, the North exhibited both popular and scholarly activities. Popular Pure Land found expression in the stone images built primarily by lay supporters during the Northern Wei period. The two oldest surviving images of Amitābha were both erected by lay women in 518, and constitute two of twelve extant from this period. The inscription of one of these surviving images in the Lung-men Cave records the widow's desire that her deceased husband be quickly reborn in the Western Realm. Earlier images reveal syncretistic devotion in which the image is of Maitreya, Śākyamuni or other Buddhas. But their inscriptions affirm desires for rebirth in the western quarter or Sukhāvatī.[89]

The earliest known lineage of Pure Land transmission compiled by Tao-ch'o suggests an active scholarly development in the North. The Six Worthies (*liu ta-te*) of this lineage were Bodhiruci, Hui-lun, Tao-ch'ang, T'an-luan, Ta-hai, and Fa-shang.[90] Although the status of some of these Worthies as actual devotees of Pure Land teaching has not been fully documented, Bodhiruci and, especially T'an-luan did make major contributions. Bodhiruci translated the *Rebirth Treatise* in 531. This gave impetus to Pure Land studies as the treatise gained the attention of scholars associated with the so-called Ti-lun school that Bodhiruci helped to found. In addition to T'an-luan's commentary on the *Rebirth Treatise* is another commentary, now lost, attributed to Ling-yü, a scholar monk also associated with the Ti-lun school.[91]

T'an-luan was not only a believer of the Pure Land path but also the first major Pure Land writer with three works to his credit. His major work, the *T'an-luan Commentary,* is a commentary to the *Rebirth Treatise*.[92] His search for immortality with a Taoist master, his subsequent conversion to Pure Land, and his successes as a healer greatly esteemed by the emperor have been well-chronicled in the Pure Land tradition.[93] T'an-luan's memorial epitaph inspired the conversion of Tao-ch'o, to Pure Land teaching, who in turn served as teacher to Shan-tao.[94] A later Pure Land lineage of the Yüan period included T'an-luan as a member.[95] T'an-luan's doctrinal insights profoundly influenced Shinran of the Japanese Pure Land tradition, who venerated him as the first of the three Chinese patriarchs, the others being Tao-ch'o and Shan-tao.[96]

The doctrinal justification for the independence of the Pure Land Buddhist path constitutes one of T'an-luan's contributions. He took Nāgārjuna's division of the "easy and difficult paths," which originally applied to the attainment of the non-retrogressive stage on the Bodhisattva path, and ingeniously adapted the "easy path" to the Pure Land teaching.[97] As we saw above, he is credited with the earliest known term that denoted Pure Land practice as a distinct path, "the Dharma-gate for the rebirth in the Pure Land."[98]

His successes derived partly from his ability to synthesize Pure Land practice with indigenous Chinese religious elements.[99] He explains, for example, the efficacy of reciting the name of Amitābha by citing a spell from the *Pao p'u-tzu,* a Taoist text, for curing edema and an incantation for protecting soldiers on the battlefield. Also, after noting the common use of quince moxibustion to cure sprains, he remarks that everyone is aware that the sprain can also be cured simply by reciting the name "quince."[100] T'an-luan further utilized phrases from Taoist and Confucian classics including the *Lao-tzu,* the *Chuang-tzu,* and the *Lun-yü* (Analects).[101] His expertise in non-Buddhist literature was later acknowledged by Tao-hsuan, who describes him as being "well versed in both Buddhist and non-Buddhist scriptures."[102]

In terms of doctrinal contribution, T'an-luan stressed the concept of the "vow power of Buddha [Amitābha]" (*fo-yüan li*) or "other power" (*t'a-li*) in his soteriological scheme to a much greater degree than did the Pure Land sutras in their original formulation. In T'an-luan's scheme, the devotee's practice carries little weight in comparison to that of Buddha's vow power. Recitation of the name with firm faith sufficed for rebirth since the efficient cause lay not in the devotee's action but in the vow power of Amitābha. The following statement epitomizes T'an-luan's emphasis on "other power":

> "The way of easy practice" means that simply by resolving to be reborn in the Pure Land, through faith in the Buddha, and by availing oneself of the power of the Buddha's vow, one attains rebirth in that Pure Land. Sustained by the Buddha's power, one joins the assembly of those who are properly settled in the Mahayana.[103]

Thus, his stress on the centrality of the Buddha's vow power, which belonged implicitly to his inherited Pure Land tradition, contributed decisively to the development of that tradition.

But, despite the creative identification of the Pure Land path as a unique and independent path, neither the *T'an-luan Commentary* nor T'an-luan's other writings generated sub-commentaries by subsequent writers. In fact, its absence in any of the catalogues after *Nei-tien lu* (Catalogue of Buddhist Scriptures) (compiled 664) or in the Sung and Ming canons has led to a suggestion that this work was excluded from the canon sometime during the T'ang period after the compilation of the *Nei-tien lu.*[104] While Tao-ch'o and Shan-tao inherited and developed the legacy of the "other-power" doctrine, their major writings instead comprise commentaries on the *Kuan-ching,* not on the *Rebirth Treatise* or the *T'an-luan Commentary* as one might expect.[105] T'an-luan actively propagated the Pure Land teaching during his years at Hsüan-chung Monastery in Fen-chou, which was his residence in his latter years.[106] But very little is known about his direct disciples; apparently his following was confined predominately to lay persons in the proximity of Hsüan-chung Monastery.

# Chapter Two

## Hui-yüan's Place in Buddhism of North China

### Hui-yüan's Image

Hui-yüan was an exegete, a lecturer of the highest caliber, and an ecclesiastic leader of distinguished prominence within the Buddhist community from the latter part of Northern Ch'i (550–577) to his death in 592 in the early years of the Sui period (581–618). His contemporaries include such eminent figures in Chinese Buddhist history as T'an-luan, Hui-szu (515–577), Fa-lang (508–581), Hui-k'o (487–593), Hsin-hsing (540–594), Chih-i, Chi-tsang, and Tu-shun (557–640). They represented a period not only that embodied great creativity in the areas of doctrine and practice but also that laid the foundations for essentially all of the schools now associated with Chinese as well as with Korean and Japanese Buddhism. These schools are regarded by modern scholars as the "new Buddhism" of the Sui-T'ang period. They signified the emergence of truly sinified forms of Buddhism that relied less on the interpretations of the Indian commentators than on the indigenous formulations of doctrine and practice derived from direct engagement with the sutras themselves.[1]

Modern discussions of Hui-yüan invariably associate him with either the Ti-lun or the She-lun school.[2] But surviving sources do not provide any historical basis for his purported affiliation with the She-lun school.[3] His Ti-lun school affiliation must also be questioned, for evidence does not support the traditional assumption that a school called "Ti-lun" existed. None of the figures who are considered members of this school—Hui-kuang (468–537), Fa-shang (495–580), and Ching-ying Hui-yüan—ever referred to themselves in their writings as belonging to this school. It is only later in the Sui and early T'ang writings of Chih-i, Chi-tsang and others that we first encounter the term "Ti-lun shih" (Ti-lun masters).[4] But in these instances, the reference remains unclear. Furthermore, it appears that the appellation "Ti-lun masters" constituted a pejorative term like "Hinayana" when used by the Mahayanists.[5]

For these reasons, there is little reason to associate Hui-yüan with the Ti-lun school. Instead, with respect to Hui-yüan's connections, it would be more accurate to speak of a 'Hui-kuang lineage' because of specific accounts associating him with a cadre of monks who were disciples of Hui-kuang. As an erudite scholar and Ecclesiastic Head of the Sangha (*shang-t'ung*), Hui-kuang traditionally, but without historical warrant as noted above, retains the status of 'founder' for the southern branch of the Ti-lun school. It was with a number of Hui-kuang's disciples acting as witnesses that Hui-yüan was ordained. Moreover, he studied for nine years with Fa-shang, a disciple of Hui-kuang.[6]

Hui-yüan's accomplishment as an exegete proves remarkable in virtue of the vast size and range of his writings. No doctrinal study of this period (ca. 550–592) spanning Northern Ch'i, Northern Chou, and early Sui periods in north China can be complete without a thorough study of Hui-yüan's works, of which ten have come down to us, either in part or in their entirety. The *Commentary*, presently under study, is one of these. But only a few exegetical works by north Chinese commentators from this period have survived.[7] In fact, there are almost as many extant works by Hui-yüan as there are by all other writers from this group; thus, this attests to the importance of his writings for modern research.

Aside from commentaries on the two "Pure Land" sutras (the *Kuan-ching* and *Wu-liang shou-ching*), many of these writings have influenced later works, including several attributed to Chi-tsang. Modern researchers have reported their influence on the following works:

1. *Commentary on the Śrīmālādevī-sūtra*: influenced a commentary on the same sutra by Chi-tsang.[8]
2. *Commentary on the Treatise on the Awakening of Faith:* influenced commentaries on the same treatise by Wŏnhyo and Fa-tsang (643–711).[9]
3. *Commentary on the Vimalakīrtinirdeśa-sūtra*: influenced commentaries by Chih-i and Chi-tsang.[10]
4. *Commentary on the Kuan-ching*: influenced the *Shan-tao Commentary* and others.[11]

Further research is in order for a full accounting of the extent and nature of Hui-yüan's impact on these subsequent works. For the *Śrīmālādevī-sūtra,* however, Hui-yüan's commentary became paradigmatic for the sutra's commentarial tradition. Chi-tsang's commentary, the *Sheng-man pao-k'u,* has been regarded as the standard text in the commentarial tradition of this sutra in East Asia. But this work by Chi-tsang owes many of its ideas to Hui-yüan's commentary as evidenced by his adoption of passages from it.[12] Furthermore, his *Mahayana Encyclopedia* is cited by later exegetes, including Chih-i, Chi-tsang, [Kuei-]ch'i, Wŏnhyo, Chih-yen (602–668), Fa-tsang, and Ch'eng-kuan (738–839).[13]

Also, Hui-yüan brought significant innovation to the development of two major doctrinal issues of the Sui-T'ang period, the *tathāgatagarbha* (Buddha womb or embryo) and *ālayavijñāna* (storehouse consciousness) theories, as will be discussed below. This fact is of significant interest, because according to Kamata Shigeo, Hui-yüan's treatment served as one of the bases for the fully developed theories of the later Hua-yen and T'ien-t'ai traditions.[14] Moreover, the *Mahayana Encyclopedia,* his work of Buddhist concepts and terms, not only served as a reference text for writers of the Sui and T'ang period but also serves today as a valuable source for analyzing that period's doctrinal development.[15]

Despite the importance and availability of Hui-yüan's writings, they have suffered surprising neglect. Thus, his doctrinal contributions have remained relatively unknown. In large measure, this resulted from the failure of his writings to attain canonical status in later Buddhist schools, unlike the writings of the T'ien-t'ai master Chih-i. Furthermore, the sheer volume and variety of sutras and *śāstras* encompassed by his writings have complicated a ready understanding of his overall thought. There is no clear, committed doctrinal stance from which Hui-yüan carried out his exegesis, as Ocho Enichi has succinctly stated:

> . . . Hui-yüan strove to maintain his objective approach and [unlike Chi-tsang] refrained from advocating in his writings the transmitted [doctrinal position] of his masters.[16]

Present knowledge of Hui-yüan's thought remains fragmentary. Most modern writings on Hui-yüan have focused on narrowly defined doctrinal topics such as 'Buddha-nature' and 'pure land.' Moreover, these writings proceed primarily on the narrow base of those chapters in the *Mahayana Encyclopedia* dedicated specifically to these issues.[17]

The modern image of Hui-yüan persists as a mere academician rather than as a practitioner like Hsin-hsing of the Three Stage school, Hui-szu of the T'ien-t'ai, and Tu-shun of the Hua-yen traditions. According to Kamata, Hui-yüan did not actively incorporate his meditative experience into his doctrinal system but, instead, concentrated on the intellectual understanding of the scriptures.[18] For this reason, Kamata excludes Hui-yüan from the "new Buddhism" of Sui and early T'ang mentioned earlier and, instead, characterizes him as a "transitional" figure bridging the old and new Buddhism.[19]

While this portrayal of Hui-yüan retains some truth, it so obscures his other traits and accomplishments that it conveys an incomplete picture of him as an individual. As discussed below, the account of Hui-yüan's daring debate in defense of Buddhism against Emperor Wu's (Wu-ti; 543–78) persecution testifies to his fervor and commitment to Buddhism.

He also effectively communicated the teaching, as evidenced by the large number of students who flocked to study with him. He was not uninterested in practice, but rather he openly lamented that his ecclesiastic duties left him little time for pursuing meditation.[20] In the *Commentary,* he articulates his high regard for practice:

> In entering Buddha Dharma, there are generally three approaches: teaching, interpretation and practice. Teachings are shallow, interpretation is profound, but practice is supreme. [174c17]

**Biographical sketch including his debate with Emperor Wu**

The best textual source for Hui-yüan's biographical sketch is the *Further Biographies.* Other sources include the *Kuang hung-ming chi* (Expanded Record to Spread and Elucidate the Teaching), and two works on transmission lineages, *Fo-tsu t'ung-chi* and *Fo-tsu li-tai t'ung-tsai.* As these accounts are limited to Hui-yüan's debate with Emperor Wu of Northern Chou, they offer no new information beyond the accounts in the *Further Biographies.*[21] Based principally on the *Further Biographies* and supplemented by other sources when appropriate, Hui-yüan's life can be divided into five periods: (1) the period prior to his going to the Eastern Wei capital of Yeh (up to age 16), (2) his residence at Yeh (until age 32), (3) the interim at Ch'ing-hua monastery in Che Chou (–577 until age 55), (4) his seclusion during the Buddhist persecution (577–580 to age 58), and (5) his stay in Lo Chou and Ch'ang-an (–592 to age 70).

Born in 523 in Tun-huang to a family named Li, Hui-yüan went to live with his uncle upon his father's death. At the age of seven he began formal studies; according to recorded information he excelled. At the age of thirteen, Hui-yüan left his uncle and went to Ku-hsien-ku Monastery on Tung-shan in Tse-chou (Modern Chin-ch'eng District Shansi Province). There he met Dhyāna Master Seng-szu, a renowned monk, who gave him his tonsure ordination. Hui-yüan later went to Tan-ku on Pei-shan in Huai-chou, where he queried his teachers on the essential meaning of the sutras. Typical of these hagiographical accounts, it is stated that all of his questions were profound and revealed exceptional intelligence and great promise.

At the age of sixteen he followed his teacher, Vinaya Master Li-chan, to Yeh, which at the time was the capital of Eastern Wei. In that setting, Hui-yüan studied both Mahayana and Hinayana scriptures, but he soon came to regard Mahayana as more fundamental to the Buddhist path.

When Hui-yüan reached the age of ordination, monks of the highest Ecclesiastic rankings and fame within the Buddhist community of Eastern Wei attended the ceremony. Fa-shang, the Ecclesiastic Head of the Sangha, served as his master, and the National Preceptor Hui-shun presided as the ceremony head. Ten disciples of the eminent Hui-kuang witnessed the ceremony.

During the next seven years in Yeh, Hui-yüan studied the *Szu-fen lü* (Four-Part *Vinaya*) with Vinaya Master Ta-yin. Moreover, during this period Hui-yüan studied with Fa-shang, the Ecclesiastic Head of the Sangha. The latter was an expert on Vasubandhu's commentary on the *Daśa-bhūmika-sūtra* (Sutra on the Ten Stages), the *Shih-chu p'i-p'o-sha lun,* and other texts revered by the 'Hui-kuang' lineage, such as the *Avataṃsaka-sūtra* (Flower Garland Sutra).

After seven years of study under Fa-shang and others, Hui-yüan returned to Kao-tu in Tse-chou, where he had spent his early childhood. He established residence at the Ch'ing-hua Monastery, which became his home for over twenty-three years (554–577). A number of scholar-monks, who aspired to study with him, gathered at Ch'ing-hua Monastery. As his reputation grew, people from all over the empire came to hear his lectures.

In the second year of Ch'eng-kuang (577), Emperor Wu of Northern Chou invaded Northern Ch'i and instigated the severe persecution of Buddhists in the newly conquered territory.[22] According to the *Kuang hung-ming chi,* the devastating Ch'i repression effected the confiscation of forty thousand temples by the imperial and aristocratic families, the laicization of three million monks and the conscription of many others into military service. Buddhist images were burned, and government officials seized monastic property.[23]

At the outset of this persecution in Northern Ch'i, Emperor Wu ordered over five hundred of the sangha elders to gather. Emperor Wu himself then ascended the throne to proclaim his new policy toward religion. He gave three reasons for abolishing Buddhism. First, Buddhists had built monasteries and *stūpas* in flagrant violation of Buddhism's own claim that true Buddhas were formless. Second, building temples was wasteful, for it unnecessarily burdened people who, out of ignorance, contributed to the endeavor. Third, the renunciation by Buddhist monks of the ordinary householder's way of life conflicted with the practice of filial piety.[24]

The proclamation stunned the monks, including the ecclesiastic head. But they were unable to refute the Emperor's accusations and instead turned pale and wept in silence. At this point, Hui-yüan became convinced that silence would only confirm the truth of Emperor Wu's contention and decided to refute the Emperor.[25] His outspoken defense of Buddhism's legitimacy and right to exist in China was so effective that the Emperor was silenced on several occasions. Hui-yüan retained the offensive throughout most of the debate and at one point even threatened the Emperor with rebirth in hell. The debate ended abruptly when Emperor

Wu, humiliated by his own collapse before Hui-yüan's reasoning, curtailed the debate. But he ordered his officials to take the names of all the attendant monks present before dismissing them.[26]

The debate's account of Hui-yüan's bravery and tenacity reveals his deep personal commitment to Buddhism, which was hardly that of a dispassionate armchair academician. The following reiterates the discussion between Hui-yüan and Emperor Wu.

> "Emperor, you have come to rule the great city and gained sole reverence. And in accordance with the worldly sentiments, you are now regulating the three teachings.[27] As for the proclamation "true Buddhas have no images" (*chen-fo wu-hsiang*), it is certainly correct as stated in your imperial decree [from the viewpoint of ultimate truth]. But living beings, who [depend] solely on their ears and nose, must rely on the scriptures to hear the Buddha and depend on the images for the truth to be revealed. If you now destroy them, there would be nothing for them to revere.
>
> "Since the formless true Buddhas can be known completely on their own, they have yet to rely on scriptures and images [to make themselves known].
>
> "[If what you say is true,] why didn't the Chinese people know about the formless true Buddha prior to Emperor Ming of the Han Dynasty[28] when [the Buddhist] scriptures and images had not yet reached China?"
>
> The Emperor had no response.
>
> "If without relying on the scriptural teachings one can know on his own the existence of the Dharma, then people living before the time of the Three Emperors,[29] when no writings yet existed, should have known about the Five Norms.[30] Why would people at the time know only their mother but not their father, which would render them equal to fowls and beasts?"[31]
>
> The Emperor again had no response.
>
> "If you maintain that [Buddhist] images must be destroyed because there is no benefit in serving them on account of their not having feelings, then how can you foolishly honor and serve the images of the seven ancestral temples of the country, believing that they have feelings?"
>
> The Emperor did not respond to this criticism and instead merely went on to state:
>
> "Since Buddhist scriptures contain the teachings of a foreign country, this country has no use for them. By destroying them they would not be used. The seven ancestral temples of the country, how-

ever, were built by former emperors. I therefore do not regard them [as I do the Buddhist scriptures]; if I did, I would destroy them in the same way [as were the Buddhist scriptures].

"If you claim foreign scriptures should not be used, then what Confucius preached originated in his Country of Lu and not from the Country of Ch'in-chin.[32] [Being that Confucian teaching came from another country just as Buddhism came from another country,] the Confucian [teaching] should be destroyed and not be practiced. [If that is actualized and] you regard the seven mausoleums to be without value and wish to destroy them, then you would not be honoring your ancestors. Not to honor your ancestors amounts to an abrogation of proper burial order[33], which means that the five Confucian Books[34] are not being practiced. But earlier you stated how you would preserve the right conduct of the Confucian teaching and firmly establish it. If in that case [where the Confucian teaching is destroyed], then all three religions would be destroyed. Then, what will regulate the country?

"Even though the boundaries of the Country of Lu and Ch'in-chin do differ, the two are under the same rule of the emperor. So, the situation differs from the Buddhist scriptures."

The Emperor was, however, unable to comprehend the [reasoning] of the criticism concerning the seven mausoleums.

"If the countries of Lu and Ch'in-chin respect the same rule and the teachings of the scriptures are similarly practiced [in both countries], then even though China and India are separate countries they are within the four oceans of the Jambudvīpa under the same rule of the Cakravartin.[35] Why do you not honor the Buddhist scriptures in the same way [you do the Confucian scriptures] rather than to single them out for destruction?"

The Emperor again had no answer.

"Your decree calls for the returning of the monks to lay life and for the monks to revere the practice of caring for their parents. The *Book of Filial Piety* says, 'To establish oneself in life and to follow the right path to bring glory to one's parents constitutes the practice of filial piety.' Why then do you force them to return to lay life [when the Buddhist monks are indeed living up to the Confucian ideals]?

"Parental concern is extensive; they have provided quality upbringing [for the children]. And [for the monks] to abandon parents to seek separation does not constitute living up to [the practice of] filial piety.

"If that is how you feel, then what of your servants who have parents of their own. Why do you not let them leave, rather than holding them in service for five long years without allowing them to see their parents!

"I do, in fact, allow them to take turns returning home to serve their parents.

"The Buddha also permitted the monks in winter and summer to cultivate their [Buddhist] path according to their circumstances, and in the spring and autumn to return to their homes to serve [their parents]. Therefore, Maudgalyāyana begged for food to feed his mother, while the Buddha carried [his father's] casket to the funeral pyre.[36] Since this principle [of filial piety] has been widely practiced, [Buddhism] should not be singled out for destruction."

The emperor again had no response.

"Oh Emperor, presuming upon the prerogatives of imperial power, you are destroying the Three Jewels [of Buddhism]. This is the work of a person of perverted views. Avīci Hell does not discriminate the noble from the lowly. Emperor, are you not afraid?"

The Emperor's face suddenly turned red in great anger, and glaring at Hui-yüan said:

"If I can bring happiness to the peasants, then I would not even refuse the numerous kinds of suffering of Hell [for myself]!

"Oh Emperor, by resorting to a wrong teaching to rule your subjects, you are manifesting various karmic actions that will lead to suffering. Your subjects will, then, be headed for Avīci Hell with you. Where will they, then, be able to find happiness."

With his reasoning defeated, the Emperor was unable to respond as [Hui-yüan's] calculated aim in his earlier statements [to confound the Emperor] was fully effective. He instead merely ordered:

"Monks, return immediately. Officers, take down and report to me the monks' last names."[37]

According to the account in the *Further Biographies,* Hui-yüan's defense of Buddhism against Emperor Wu so infuriated the Northern Chou soldiers in the hall that they threatened to crush and boil Hui-yüan's bones. In contrast, his fellow Buddhist monks, who had remained silent through the debate, came over to Hui-yüan to express their gratitude for standing up to Emperor Wu. Among them was T'an-yen, the Ecclesiastic Head of the Sangha, who in tears grasped Hui-yüan's hands, praising him as the "Bodhisasttva, the protector of the Dharma" (*hu-fa p'u-sa*) espoused by the *Nirvāṇa-sūtra.* Hui-yüan responded that truth needed to be defended even at the sacrifice of his own life. Hui-yüan then offered that the persecution was a sign of the times but that the Dharma would not perish; and he admonished them not to mourn the state of affairs.[38]

Hui-yüan went into hiding during the persecution at Hsi-shan in Chi-chun (modern Chi District, Honan Province). During those three years in hiding, he devoted himself to various forms of practice. He chanted the *Lotus Sutra, Vimalakīrti-sūtra* and other sutras more than one thousand times, while maintaining the precepts and engaging in meditation practices.[39]

These activities disclose another side of Hui-yüan. He was attracted not only to intellectual comprehension but also to the active cultivation of meditation and the observance of precepts. As seen above, he had earlier engaged in intensive study of the Vinaya text, *Szu-fen lü,* during his stay in Yeh. While this probably constituted more of a scholastic endeavor, such studies must have contributed to his strict adherence to the precepts during this period. He is reported to have later severely punished, in accordance with the Vinaya precepts, those monks who fell asleep or arrived late to his lectures. Hui-yüan also referred to his meditational practices while at Yeh that cultivated the breath-counting meditation. His teacher informed him that he had experienced a state attained only by adepts and that he was close to realizing the goals of this meditation.[40]

Hence, Hui-yüan's limited involvement with actual practice did not stem from a lack of interest. Rather, it resulted largely from the lack of opportunity for practice because of the demands of his ecclesiastical positions. In fact, Hui-yüan admitted: "I regret the fact that duties of the office do not leave me enough time to cultivate the mind, which is simply a shame!"[41] Probably this kind of underlying sentiment prompted Hui-yüan's reluctance to accept the imperial appointment as Sangha Head of Lo-chou. When freed of such duties during the previous three years of exile, he had immersed himself in vigorous practices.

The proscription against Buddhism was lifted in 580 with the death of Emperor Wu and the ascension of his son, Emperor Hsüan (Hsüan-ti) to the throne. In each of the two capitals, a Chih-hu monastery was built, which housed the newly established long-haired "Bodhisattva monks" (*p'u-sa seng*).[42] Amidst the atmosphere of renewed Buddhist support, Hui-yüan was appointed senior lecturer at Shao-lin Monastery. On hearing of Hui-yüan's reputation, Emperor Wen (Wen-ti; r.581–604) appointed him the Sangha Head of Lo-chou (modern Loyang County in Honan) in the year following the establishment of the Sui dynasty. Although hesitant for probably the reasons noted above, he nevertheless accepted the position because of its imperial status. After four years in that position, Hui-yüan returned to Tse-chou at the request of the imperial emissary of that region and was highly successful in reviving Buddhism there. Then in the spring of 587, Hui-yüan went to Ting-chou (modern Ting County, Honan) where he held a series of lectures for two consecutive summers.[43]

In the same year the Emperor Wen invited Hui-yüan to Ch'ang-an as one of the Six Worthies who, in the eyes of the Emperor, comprised the most eminent monks in the empire. These six along with over one hundred and twenty learned monks gathered in the Emperor's hall, where Hui-yüan lectured on Buddhist teachings, the family, and the nation. Impressed and elated by what Hui-yüan had to say, Emperor Wen appointed him to the Ta-hsing-shan Monastery. Being the hub of the capital's Buddhist activities, however, the new residence proved too hectic for Hui-yüan. Recognizing the problem, the Emperor built a temple for him, naming it "Ching-ying Monastery," the name with which Hui-yüan has ever since been associated.[44]

Hui-yüan's reputation as a scholar and lecturer attracted over seven hundred of the empire's most learned monks to Ching-ying Monastery. Many who came to the capital of Ch'ang-an in search of the Dharma congregated at Ching-ying Monastery and regarded it as the "arena for the way of the Dharma" (*fa-tao ch'ang*). The final months of his life were engaged, by imperial order, in the study of translated texts and the editing of speeches. He passed away on the twenty-fourth day of the sixth month of the twelfth year of the K'ai-huang Era (592). He was seventy years old with fifty years of sacerdotal life behind him. "The country has lost two treasures," lamented the Emperor as he mourned the loss of Hui-yüan and Li Te-lin, who died in the same month.[45]

## Writings

The earliest surviving record of the writings, mostly commentaries, attributed to Hui-yüan is the *Further Biographies,* which lists the following:[46]

1. *Ti-ch'ih [lun i-]shu,* 5 fascicles (on *Bodhisattvabhūmi-śāstra*)
2. *Shih-ti [ching-lun i-]shu,* 7 fascicles (on *Daśabhūmika-vyākhyāna*)
3. *Hua-yen [ching] shu,* 7 fascicles (on *Avataṃsaka-sūtra*)
4. *[Ta-pan] nieh-p'an [ching i-]shu,* 10 fascicles (on *Nirvāṇa-sūtra*)
5. *Wei-mo [ching i-chi]* (on *Vimalakīrti-sūtra*)
6. *Sheng-man [ching i-chi]* (on *Śrīmālādevī-sūtra*)
7. *[Wu-liang-]shou kuan [ching i-shu]* (on *Kuan-ching*)[47]
8. *Wen-shih [ching i-shu]* (on *Warm Room Sutra*)
9. *Ta-ch'eng i-chang,* 14 fascicles (*Mahayana Encyclopedia*)

The next oldest source on the subject, the *Tō'iki dentō mokuroku* (Catalogue of Scriptures Transmitted to the Eastern Region) compiled by Eichō in 1014, lists Hui-yüan as the author of six additional works:[48]

10. *Chin-kang pan-jo ching shu,* 1 fascicle (on *Diamond Sutra*)
11. *Fa-hua ching shu,* 7 fascicles (on *Lotus Sutra*)

12. *Wu-liang-shou ching i-shu,* 1 fascicle (on *Sutra on the Buddha of Immeasurable Life*)
13. *Chin kuang-ming ching shu,* 1 fascicle (on *Golden Light Sutra*)
14. *Chin-kang pan-jo lun shu,* 3 fascicles (on *Treatise on the Diamond Sutra*)
15. *Ta-ch'eng ch'i-hsin lun i-shu,* 4 fascicles (on *Treatise on the Awakening of Faith in the Mahayana*)

Of the above fifteen works, five have not survived: the *Hua-yen shu* from the first list and all from *Tō'iki dentō mokuroku* except the *Wu-liang-shou ching i-shu* and the *Ta-ch'eng ch'i-hsin lun i-shu* (henceforth, *Awakening of Faith Commentary*). In all the ten that have survived, of which four are incomplete, as indicated by the following list of surviving works, the titles of extant works are listed in their entirety, for some discrepancies appear in the title and the number of fascicle of the same work recorded in the *Further Biographies.*

1. *Ti-ch'ih ching lun i-chi,* 10 fascicles[49] (incomplete) (*ZZ* 1.61.3)
2. *Shih-ti ching-lun i-chi,* 4 fascicles[50] (incomplete) (*ZZ* 1.71.2 and 3)
3. *Ta-pan nieh-p'an ching i-chi,* 10 fascicles (*T* 1764.37)
4. *Wei-mo i-chi,* 8 fascicles (*T* 1776.38)
5. *Sheng-man ching i-chi,* 1 fascicle (incomplete) (*ZZ* 1.30.4)[51]
6. *Wu-liang-shou ching i-shu,* 2 fascicles (*T* 1745.37)
7. *Kuan wu-liang-shou ching i-shu,* 2 fascicles (*T* 1749.37)
8. *Wen-shih ching i-chi,* 1 fascicle (*T* 1793.39)
9. *Ta-ch'eng i-chang,* 26 fascicles[52] (incomplete) (*T* 1851.44)
10. *Ta-ch'eng ch'i-hsin lun i-shu,* 4 fascicles (*T* 1843.44)

The extent of his writings is certainly remarkable, as is the fact that much of it has survived. It should, however, be kept in mind that such an accomplishment was not unusual among some of his contemporaries. According to *Further Biographies,* Ling-yü is accredited with even a larger number of works, which numbered over one hundred fascicles.[53] Though not as prolific as Ling-yü, T'an-yen is another contemporary of Hui-yüan with a large corpus of work attributed to him.[54] More well-known, though slightly younger, is Chi-tsang, who is credited with twenty-six works, amounting to one hundred and twelve fascicles—these are only the ones that have survived.[55]

Of the surviving works listed above, only the authorship of the *Awakening of Faith Commentary* and the *Mahayana Encyclopedia* has been seriously questioned in modern times. The main arguments against Hui-yüan's authorship of the *Awakening of Faith Commentary* rest on largely textual grounds.[56] Neither is the writing style in the usual four-character phrase pattern of his other works nor does this work make any reference, as do his other writings, to the *Mahayana Encyclopedia.* One finds in this work a phrase, "Dharma Master Hui-yüan (*Yüan-fa shih chieh*) understands . . . ," which has not been found in any of his other writings. Lastly, as seen above, the *Further Biographies* does not list this among the nine works attributed to Hui-yüan.[57]

Yoshizu Yoshihide defends Hui-yüan's authorship of this work primarily on the compatibility of its formulations with those of his other works. In responding to each of the four points above, Yoshizu first finds unproblematic the absence in the work of the four-character phrase pattern that is present in Hui-yüan's other writings. This problem would be removed, Yoshizu asserts, if this work were based on a rough draft of Hui-yüan's later finished draft. Also lack of any reference to the *Mahayana Encyclopedia* in this work might simply indicate its earlier date of completion. Further the occurrence of the phrase "Dharma Master Hui-yüan" suggests for Yoshizu the high likelihood of its later insertion. Lastly for Yoshizu, the *Further Biographies*'s silence on this text is not decisive, since quite possibly it could have simply omitted it.[58]

Tsujimori Yoshu has proposed that the *Mahayana Encyclopedia,* the best known of Hui-yüan's works, was not written solely by Hui-yüan. Instead, he argues that the text's tightly organized structure and flawlessly rendered cross references, which are unusual in such a voluminous work (twenty-six of the original thirty-two fascicles), mitigate against a single authorship. He suggests, instead, that Hui-hsiu (548–?) first organized and edited the draft that subsequently Hui-yüan used as his reference and which he continuously revised throughout his career. This would explain Hui-yüan's citation in the *Mahayana Encyclopedia* of a treatise, the *Mahāyānasaṃgraha* translated by Paramārtha, which only became available to him late in his career. Tsujimori supports his thesis on the existence of a work, though not extant, which was attributed to Hui-hsiu and also entitled "*Ta-ch'eng i-chang*" (*Mahayana Encyclopedia*) in forty-eight fascicles. He believes this work actually referred to Hui-yüan's *Mahayana Encyclopedia.*[59]

Tsujimori further conjectures that when Hui-yüan worked on this text, he relied on his teacher Fa-shang's *Tseng-shu fa-men* and revised it according to his own understanding. This work by Fa-shang, which has not survived, is believed to have been a similar encyclopedic text with entries arranged in numerically increasing order.[60] This conjecture would, thereby, not only explain how Hui-yüan might have written a text of such magnitude prior to his other works, including the *Commentary,* but also account for why many of his subsequent works defer to the *Mahayana Encyclopedia* in their explanation of key Buddhist concepts.[61]

Accurately dating Hui-yüan's works is difficult, if not impossible. The primary difficulty arises from the absence of independent sources that could throw light on this matter. The *Further Biographies*'s description of his works simply lists the writings without alluding to any dates or order of compilation. Scholars have suggested dates of individual works, but none has systematically attempted to determine either the approximate dates of compilation or even the order of Hui-yüan's entire body of works. If Tsujimori's above suggestion is correct, the *Mahayana Encyclopedia* existed as a text early in Hui-yüan's career, though probably not necessarily in the same form as the present version.

Comment on some of the other works should be made. Hui-yüan lectured on the *Daśabhūmika-sūtra* during his seven summers in the capital of Yeh.[62] Quite possibly his commentary to the sutra, *Shih-ti ching-lun i-chi,* was compiled sometime during this period (ca. 540–548) and was derived from his lectures.[63] Given the *Further Biographies,* the *Ti-ch'ih ching lun i-chi,* his commentary on the *Yogacārabhūmi,* was apparently written prior to the commentary on the *Nirvāṇa-sūtra,* and both were compiled during his residence at Ch'ing-hua Monastery (553 or 554 and 578).[64] In his study both of Tun-huang manuscripts of the *Śrīmālādevī-sūtra* and of its commentaries that circulated in the northern dynasties during the Nan-pei Chao period, Fujieda Akira proposes 572 as the approximate year in which Hui-yüan wrote the commentary to the *Śrīmālādevī-sūtra.*[65]

**Thought beyond Pure Land Doctrine**

A survey not only of Hui-yüan's position on major non-Pure Land doctrinal issues but also of his importance in contemporary doctrinal development would be a daunting task given his dealing with a broad range of doctrinal topics. Kamata Shigeo's study was the first serious attempt to inspect a range of Hui-yüan's doctrinal positions and to analyze them in the context of Mahayana developments of sixth-century China. As mentioned earlier, he concludes:

> . . . [Hui-yüan's] thought did not develop into a thorough going Mahayana as [found] in the T'ien-t'ai concept of "the true characteristics of *dharmas*" (*chu-fa shih-hsiang*) and the Hua-yen concept of "non-obstruction of phenomena" (*shih-shih wu-ai*). . . . His Mahayana thought can be understood as being transitional in nature and as leading up to the new Buddhism of the Sui and T'ang periods.[66]

With Kamata's observation as point of reference, I shall focus on Hui-yüan's innovations on the following three issues: (1) the doctrinal classification (*p'an-chiao*), (2) the concept of the mind, and (3) the concept of "Tathāgatagarbha-dependent origination."[67] In the *Mahayana Encyclopedia,* Hui-yüan sets forth his views on doctrinal classification:[68]

| | | |
|---|---|---|
| 1. Doctrine that establishes nature | Causation doctrine | Shallow Hinayana (*Abhidharma*) |
| 2. Doctrine that destroys nature | Provisional-name doctrine | Profound Hinayana (*Ch'eng-shih lun*) |
| 3. Doctrine that destroys form | False doctrine | Shallow Mahayana |
| 4. Doctrine that manifests the real | True doctrine | Profound Mahayana |

Hui-yüan has here adopted the format of a doctrinal classification scheme that is attributed to Hui-kuang.[69] Hui-yüan's major innovation is that he did not cite specific sutras or treatises for the two Mahayana doctrines. Thus, he departed from Hui-kuang's scheme that had cited, respectively, the *Larger Prajñāpāramitā Sutra* and the three treatises,[70] and *Nirvāṇa-sūtra, Avataṃsaka-sutra,* and so forth.[71]

His reluctance to identify specific Mahayana texts contrasts with the common practice of most other doctrinal classification schema, including, for example, Chih-i's famous "Five Periods, Eight Teachings" (*wu-shih pa-chiao*).[72] In defense of this unique practice, he argues that a given Mahayana sutra can simultaneously expound two separate doctrines, and thus it would be incorrect to identify a sutra with only one doctrine. As an example, Hui-yüan notes that the *Nirvāṇa-sūtra* teaches the doctrines of emptiness as well as of non-emptiness, which, in Hui-yüan's scheme, correspond, respectively, to the false and true doctrines.[73] For this reason, Hui-yüan advocated listing doctrines rather than texts as a basis for his doctrinal classification schema.

For Hui-yüan, the third doctrine (false doctrine) reveals the provisional nature of forms or the nonexistence of *dharmas.* It is "analogous to a person who, in seeing a mirage in the distance, takes it as water, but in approaching it realizes that there is actually no water." In contrast, the fourth doctrine (true doctrine), "advocates that *dharmas* exist on the basis of deluded thoughts, which are without substance and necessarily rely on truth.

This truth is none other than the 'nature of *tathāgatagarbha'* (*ju-lai-tsang hsing*)."[74]

Although Hui-yüan refuses to identify the two Mahayana doctrines with either specific texts or a corpus of texts, clearly the "false doctrine" refers to the doctrine of emptiness as contrasted with the "true doctrine" of non-emptiness expressed in the *Nirvāṇa-sūtra.* Kamata correlates the former with the doctrine of emptiness espoused by the *Prajñāpāramitā-sūtras* and Nāgārjuna.[75] For Yoshizu also, the third doctrine refers to the Mādhyamika teaching of emptiness in the texts translated and propounded by Kumārajīva and his disciples.[76] The fourth and true doctrine for Hui-yüan, as noted above, is the doctrine of the "nature of *tathāgatagarbha,*" which is elsewhere rendered "the Dharma-gate of Co-dependent Origination of Dharma-dhātu" (*fa-chieh yüan-ch'i fa-men*).[77]

His reluctance to associate doctrines with specific scriptures, Yoshizu suggests, lies in Hui-yüan's understanding of the "main import" (*tsung*) of a particular text, of which there are two kinds: (1) "that which is taught" (*so-shuo*) (or "practicing virtue;" *hsing-te*), and (2) "that which is manifested" *so-piao* (or "manifested Dharma"; *piao-fa*). As the latter is too difficult to reveal, the former is employed to reveal the Dharma. Some examples of the 'main import that is taught' include the *samādhi* of the *Avataṃsaka-sūtra* and *Lotus Sutra,* the one-vehicle (*ekayāna*) of the *Śrīmālādevī-sūtra* and the *prajñā* found in the corpus of the *Prajñāpāramitā-sūtras.* These are a few of the countless varieties of main import that is taught that express the fundamental 'main import to be manifested.' Hui-yüan's central emphasis in his doctrinal classification concerned the first kind of main import, that is, main imports that are taught. Since he maintained that any given scripture could have more than one "import," he relied on the import for his doctrinal classification rather than on its scriptural source.[78]

Yoshizu suggests that Hui-yüan's stress on the "main import" bore deep implications for his exegetical style. This freed him from the obligation to advocate the perspective of a particular scripture or set of scriptures. All Mahayana scriptures had the potential of possessing what he called the "false" as well as the "true" doctrines, the third and fourth terms in his classification. This approach to the scriptures allowed him to regard scripture with a greater balance and openness, as evinced by the wide range of sutras and treatises on which he commented. It also promoted in his scriptural commentaries the employment of a broad range of concepts and ideas from the entire corpus of Buddhist literature. As a result, these very characteristics of objectivity and inclusiveness excluded him from the 'new Buddhism,' whose members displayed a more subjective and exclusivistic approach.[79]

As evident in his doctrinal classification theory, Hui-yüan highly valued the doctrine of *tathāgatagarbha* (*ju-lai-tsang*). His valuation reflects in part a growing interest by sixth-century Chinese Buddhists in the *tathāgatagarbha* doctrine, that syncretic doctrine of the *ālaya-vijñāna* (storehouse consciousness) and *tathāgatagarbha* concepts espoused in such texts as the *Laṅkāvatāra-sūtra* and *Awakening of Faith.* This syncretic doctrine, manifest in Hui-yüan's view on the 'concept of the mind,' proved to be a pivotal doctrinal issue for Buddhist thinkers during the one hundred years between the mid-sixth and mid-seventh centuries. The ensuing controversies surrounding it focused on the nature of *ālaya-vijñāna*: is it pure or impure, seventh or eighth consciousness, conditioned or unconditioned, and so forth?

Hui-yüan's teacher Fa-shang is credited with one of the earliest extant works on this subject, the *Shih-ti-lun i-shu* (*Commentary on the Daśabhūmika-śāstra*). Based on this, Fa-shang's fundamental position on *ālaya-vijñāna* can be described as follows:[80]

1. The *ālaya-vijñāna* constitutes the seventh consciousness.
2. The *ālaya-vijñāna* is essentially impure and functions as the foundation of birth and death [*saṃsāra*], which produces through the process of dependent-origination the other six consciousnesses, the world of false conceptualization.
3. The eighth consciousness is the true consciousness.
4. It is upon this pure and true eighth consciousness that the *ālaya-vijñāna* and the other six consciousnesses depend, since neither the false nor deluded can sustain itself.
5. The relationship between the *ālaya-vijñāna* and the true consciousness involves both "function" (*yung*) and "essence" (*t'i*). The *ālaya-vijñāna* embodies the function of the true consciousness that is the essential or fundamental reality. The relation is not dualistic, however, for the function is none other than essence as there is no essence apart from function.

Hui-yüan adopted much of Fa-shang's basic position, but with clarifications and modifications. The most prominent contribution established the eighth consciousness scheme in which *ālaya-vijñāna* constituted the eighth, not the seventh consciousness. While essentially pure, the *ālaya-vijñāna* served nonetheless as the basis for illusion, that is, the first seven consciousnesses. But for Hui-yüan the *ālaya-vijñāna* itself was not fundamentally false as it was in Fa-shang's scheme. Instead the basis for the illusion that arises from it was ascribed to the seventh consciousness, *ādāna-vijñāna.*[81] The *ālaya-vijñāna* was further identified with *tathāgatagarbha,* an identification which Fa-shang had left vague but which Hui-yüan clarified in his explanation of the various Chinese rendering of the term *ālaya-vijñāna*:

> First, it is rendered "storehouse consciousness" (*tsang-shih*), since *tathāgatagarbha* is this [storehouse] consciousness. The sutra (*Laṅkāvatāra-sūtra*) states, "*Tathāgatagarbha* is called the 'storehouse consciousness.'"[82]

Hui-yüan's third major doctrinal contribution is the concept of "*tathāgatagarbha* dependent-origination" (*ju-lai-tsang yüan-ch'i*), a term believed to have been coined by Hui-yüan and later popularized by Fa-tsang, the third patriarch of the Hua-yen school. Hui-yüan offers this concept as a partial response to the controversy over the nature of the two-truths (*erh-ti*), another of the main doctrinal preoccupations of the period.

The two main aspects of this concept are that of essence, *tathāgatagarbha,* and that of function, *saṃsāra* and nirvana. Hui-yüan explains:

> Relying on the previously [-discussed] essence, i.e. the *tathāgatagarbha* of ultimate reality, [both] *saṃsāra* and nirvana are produced through dependent-origination. These [*saṃsāra* and nirvana] constitute its function. As the sutras state, "the twelve[-membered scheme of] dependent-origination is all a creation of the mind," and "the three realms [of existences] are the creation of the mind," and also "the *dharmakāya* transmigrating in the five paths [of existences] is called 'sentient beings.'" This is the *saṃsāra* that is produced by [the *tathāgatagarbha* of] ultimate reality. Also, just as the sutra [states], "the nature of *tathāgatagarbha* reveals and establishes *dharmakāya,*" a principle such as this (nature of *tathāgatagarbha*) produces nirvana.[83]

For Hui-yüan, the *tathāgatagarbha* establishes the basis of both true reality and of *saṃsāra* and nirvana, since *tathāgatagarbha* produces both delusion (*saṃsāra*) and enlightenment (nirvana).

When compared to the later Hua-yen concept of "the non-obstruction of phenomena" (*shih-shih wu-ai*), Hui-yüan's "*tathāgatagarbha* dependent-origination" is not as thoroughgoing. The question of this concept's functional reality suggests that if Hua-yen's concept could be characterized as "non-dualistic," then Hui-yüan's would be "dualistic" and is closer in meaning to another Hua-yen concept, "the non-obstruction of principle and phenomena" (*li-shih wu-ai*). Hui-yüan clearly distinguishes the functional aspect, *saṃsāra* and nirvana, which belongs to the level of mundane truth (*shih-ti*), from the aspect of essence, of *tathāgatagarbha,* belonging to ultimate truth (*chen-ti*). Function, moreover, cannot independently exist, for it dependently arises on essence. A function is real only because its support, the *tathāgatagarbha,* is real. Hence, "function" in Hui-yüan's scheme differs from the concept "phenomena" (*shih-shih*), in the Hua-yen concept of "the non-obstruction of phenomena," because the latter describes realities as existing independently.

# Chapter Three

## Textual Background of the *Commentary*

### The Kuan-ching

Controversy surrounding the origins of its compilation

Tradition claims that Kālayaśas (Chiang-liang-yeh-she, 383?–442) translated the *Kuan-ching* sometime in the Yüan-chia Era (424–453) of the Liu-Sung period.[1] Since this sutra has neither been found in a Sanskrit version nor cited by extant Sanskrit texts, the original was probably not compiled in India. The absence of a Tibetan translation further undermines the theory of an earlier Sanskrit text. A Uigur manuscript fragment appears to be only a translation from the Chinese. Had Kālayaśas translated a Sanskrit text, the original would have existed in India by the early fifth century, but evidence fails to corroborate this possibility.[2] Thus, most modern scholars reject the hypothesis that locates the compilation of the extant *Kuan-ching* in India proper. But their views divide into two camps concerning its actual place of compilation, one favoring Central Asia and the other China.[3] As outlined below, Fujita Kotatsu has made a detailed study of this issue.[4]

Three basic premises undergird the Central Asian compilation theory. The first concerns the place of origin for Kālayaśas and the "translators" of the other so-called visualization sutras, with which the *Kuan-ching* is closely related.[5] On the one hand, information on Kālayaśas' activities in the Western region only reveals the fact of his birth there. On the other hand, we know more about the translators of the other visualization sutras. For example, Chü-ch'ü Ching-sheng, the translator of the *Kuan mi-le p'u-sa shang-sheng tou-shuai-t'ien ching* (Sutra of Visualization on Bodhisattva Maitreya) was trained in meditation techniques in Khotan and other areas in Central Asia. In the Turfan area he reportedly obtained two visualization sutras, one on Avalokiteśvara and the other on Maitreya.[6] References found in Chü-ch'ü Ching-sheng's biography to meditation-visualization should not be surprising because the Turfan area exhibited considerable interest in the powers of meditational-visualization and the paranormal.[7]

The iconographic descriptions of Buddhas and Bodhisattvas in the

*Kuan-ching* reveal characteristics suggestive of actual images existing in central Asia. This is most pronounced in the focused attention given to descriptions of Bodhisattvas' auspicious primary and secondary marks. For example, the ninth visualization describes the bodily marks of Amitābha Buddha as follows: "The height of the Buddha's body is as many *yojanas* as six hundred thousand *koṭis* of *nayutas* of the sands of the Ganges River." Some suggest that this refers to the colossal Buddha image of Bāmiyan. An art historian has proposed that the Śākyamuni Buddha of the tenth visualization actually depicts the thirty-five meter Buddha image located in the eastern part of Bāmiyan.[8]

In addition to the colossal size, other iconographic descriptions may refer to images found in central Asia. The seventh and eighth visualizations of the *Kuan-ching* detail a large number of transformed Buddhas standing at an angle, and lined up in a radiating pattern within the halo. This resembles a common central Asian art motif associated with Buddha Amitābha and his two attendant Bodhisattvas. In the thirteenth visualization, the *Kuan-ching* states, "All beings can recognize Avalokiteśvara and Mahāsthāmaprāpta just by looking at the head features." A passage such as this in all likelihood could only have been written by someone very familiar with the actual images.[9]

Given the above iconographical features, the descriptions in the *Kuan-ching* were probably not based on images existing in China prior to ca. 400 C.E., because most of the period's surviving gilt bronze images were small, measuring thirty to forty centimeters in height. Images of human size or larger occur only in the carvings of the Yün-kang caves of the second half of the fifty century. Yet in central Asia colossal Buddha images, transmitted in nearly original form from Gandhāra, were already being made around 400 C.E.[10]

In contrast, arguments in support of the Chinese compilation theory derive primarily from textual evidence. The most convincing arguments rest on the similarity of some passages in the *Kuan-ching* with those in earlier Chinese translations of other sutras. This suggests that the Chinese compilers of the *Kuan-ching* adopted these passages during its compilation. One such strata is the *Wu-liang-shou ching* from which the passage "the forty-eight vows of Bhikṣu Dharmākara" may have been taken. Other sutras that may have been used include translations of the *Vimalakīrti-sūtra* (*Wei-mo ching*) and the *Pratyutpanna-sūtra* (*Pan-chou san-mei ching*). In this regard, the *Kuan-ching* may have relied on the other visualization sutras mentioned above, because undeniable parallels in doctrine, terminology, and style of translation exist among them. Lastly, a passage from the sixteenth visualization section in the *Kuan-ching,* "We praise the names and the opening titles of the twelve divisions of the Mahayana sutras," suggests the Chinese base of the translated text. This follows from the fact that sutra titles of Sanskrit texts do not generally appear at the beginning, as in the Chinese texts, but are placed at the very last line.[11]

Fujita believes that while both compilation theories have substantial merit neither has summoned decisive evidence in its favor. He believes that the core of the *Kuan-ching* transmitted a form of meditation that was practiced at that time somewhere in central Asia, possibly in the Turfan area. In the process of translation, concepts and expressions assumed a Chinese coloring from the numerous Chinese scriptural translations that were consulted and utilized, including the *Wu-liang-shou ching* and other visualization sutras.[12]

In recent years, Yamada Meiji has contributed evidence to strengthen the Chinese-compilation theory. His theory argues that the *Kuan-ching* resulted from an amalgamation effected in China of four previously unrelated parts: (1) the preface based on Ajātaśatru story, (2) the first thirteen visualizations, (3) the last three visualizations on the nine grades of rebirth, and (4) the conclusion. His theory's major argument asserts that the Chinese terms referring to "Amitābha/Amitāyus Buddha" clearly reflect each of the above four parts of the *Kuan-ching*: the first part employs almost exclusively the term "A-mi-t'o fo," the second "Wu-liang-shou fo," the third "A-mi-t'o fo," and the fourth "Wu-liang-shou fo." The preface shows only three occurrences of "A-mi-t'o fo"; the second part on the thirteen visualization reveals fifteen occurrences of "Wu-liang-shou fo" and one "A-mi-t'o fo"; the third part on the last three visualizations contains nine instances of "A-mi-t'o fo" and one occurrence of "Wu-liang-shou fo"; the last part includes only three occurrences of "Wu-liang-shou fo." Thus, each part displays a clear preference for one name over another. Yamada resolves the problematic anomolous occurrences, "A'mi-t'o fo" in part two and "Wu-liang-shou fo" in part three by theorizing that the compiler of the *Kuan-ching* attempted to combine independent sections by 'connectors' for transitions from one part to the next. Thus, the one occurrence of "A-mi-t'o fo" in part two smoothed the transition to the third part that contained nine occurrences of "A-mi-t'o fo" as opposed to one "Wu-liang-shou fo," which in turn served as a connector to the next part.[13]

### *Kuan-ching's status prior to the compilation of the commentary*

During the approximately hundred years between the translation (424–442) and the compilation of Hui-yüan's *Commentary,* attempts to determine the status of the *Kuan-ching* in the Buddhist community uncover very little information. Other than the *T'an-luan Commentary* discussed below, commentarial literature from this period does not mention the *Kuan-ching.* The *Kuan-ching* is also not listed in Hui-yüan's *Mahayana Encyclopedia,* which, as seen earlier, reflected not only Hui-yüan's views but also those inherited from his predecessors of the Northern dynasties.[14] There are, however, indications that the *Kuan-ching* was utilized for devotional purposes, as the *Biographies of Eminent Monks* comments:

> As a technique for turning back obstacles and a great cause [for leading to rebirth in] the Pure Land, the two sutras were widely chanted and circulated throughout the (Liu-)Sung Empire.[15]

The other sutra referred to here is the *Yao-wang Yao-shang kuan ching* (Sutra of Visualization on Yao-wang and Yao-shang), whose translation is also attributed to Kālayaśas but which has now been lost.

The *Biographies of Eminent Monks* also refers to the devotional chanting of the *Kuan-ching.* T'an-hung (d. 455) who traveled through southern China and died in Chiao-chih (near modern Vietnam), reportedly "recited the *Wu-liang-shou [ching]* and the *Kuan ching* in pledging to make the mind at peace."[16] Another monk associated with the *Kuan-ching* is a certain Fa-lin (d.495) of the Szu-ch'uan area, where it is said there were no monks or nuns who did not respect him. He constantly recited the "*Wu-liang-shou* [*ching*]" and the "*Kuan ching*" in order to seek a peaceful mind. When he fell ill, he contemplated on the Western Realm and died holding the palms of his hands reverently together.[17] While it should be cautiously proposed, nonetheless were the "*Kuan ching*" in these two reports indeed to refer to the *Kuan-ching,* it would then follow that the *Kuan-ching* would have been used for devotional purposes soon after its translation and circulated in areas as remote as extreme southern China and the Szu-ch'uan region.[18]

The earliest identifiable exegetical work, which either mentions or quotes passages from the *Kuan-ching,* is the *T'an-luan Commentary.*[19] On seven occasions it quotes the *Kuan-ching* by name. The first three instances discuss the physical features of the Pure Land, while the remaining four relate to the question of rebirth in the Pure Land for those who have committed the Five Grave Offenses or the Vilification of the True Dharma.[20] Fujiwara cites one passage from the *Kuan-ching* as supportive of T'an-luan's advocacy of rebirth through the oral recitation of Amitābha's name.[21] Consequently, T'an'luan is usually credited as the first proponent for the efficacy of oral recitation and for the doctrinal basis adopted by Tao-ch'o and Shan-tao, who advocated the enhanced importance of recitation in the Pure Land soteriological scheme.[22]

But outside these references by those two orthodox Pure Land figures and by Chia-ts'ai's (620–680) *Pure Land Treatise* (compiled ca. 650), it does not appear that the *T'an-luan Commentary* circulated widely in the Sui and T'ang periods.[23] This work neither appears in any of the catalogues after Tao-hsüan's (596–667) *Nei-tien lu* (664) nor is included in any of the extant versions of the Sung and Ming canons.[24] Kōgatsuin Jinrei (b. 1749) has concluded from this that T'an-luan's work was excluded from the canon sometime during the T'ang after the compilation of the *Nei-tien lu.*[25] Instead it gained much more attention in Japan, where it was transmitted possibly as early as 639. Its first known sub-commentary was written in the mid-eighth century.[26] Although the *T'an-luan Commentary* is the earliest known Chinese exegetical work to treat the *Kuan-ching,* it apparently did not significantly rescue the *Kuan-ching* from its earlier obscurity.[27]

## The commentary

### *Authenticity of Hui-yüan's authorship*

Unlike his *Mahayana Encyclopedia* and the *Awakening of Faith Commentary,* no serious doubt has been cast on the authenticity of Hui-yüan's authorship of the *Commentary.* Although the *Commentary* and his other surviving works were not included in any of the printings of the Buddhist canon of the Sung, Yüan, and Ming periods, as seen below, accounts as early as the beginning of the T'ang period credit the *Commentary* to Hui-yüan.

The earliest extant text to corroborate Hui-yüan's authorship of the *Commentary* is Chia-ts'ai's *Pure Land Treatise,* which was compiled sometime around 650. In this work, Chia-ts'ai refers to Hui-yüan as "Yüan fa-shih" (Dharma Master Yüan), and quotes extensively from the *Commentary,* especially with respect to the nine grades of people to be reborn in the Pure Land. Though Chia-ts'ai does not mention the *Commentary* by title, the passages clearly cite it rather than any other of Hui-yüan's works.[28] Other treatises from the mid-seventh to the mid-eighth centuries cite passages from the *Commentary.*[29]

The earliest surviving catalogues to list the *Commentary* were compiled in Japan. It was certainly transmitted to Japan by 914, for in that year this work, Hui-yüan's *Mahayana Encyclopedia,* the *Awakening of Faith Commentary* and others, were listed in the *Sanron-shū shō sho* (Collection of Works Belonging to the Sanron School), the oldest surviving catalogue to list the *Commentary.* This catalogue was compiled by the Sanron School in compliance with an imperial decree mandating the disclosure by Buddhist schools of their scriptural holdings.[30] Since the Tendai, Kegon, Ritsu, or Hossō School catalogues presented in response to the imperial decree do not list the *Commentary,* it is safe to assume that it was transmitted to Japan and circulated among those affiliated with the Sanron School.[31] The title appears again in the *Tō'iki dentō mokuroku* compiled by Eichō in 1014.[32]

Outside of Japan the oldest extant catalogue to list the *Commentary* was compiled in 1090 by Koryŏ monk Ŭich'ŏn (ca. 1055–1101), *Sinp'yŏn chejong kyojang ch'ongnok* (Catalogue of the New Collection of Works of the Various Schools). This catalogue contains works by East Asian Buddhists that Ŭich'ŏn either collected in China or obtained by his buyers and collectors from other parts of China and Japan.[33] Since the catalogue does not specify the country from which the texts were obtained, possibly the *Commentary* was acquired in Japan rather than in China. Yet the Chinese origin of the *Commentary* in Ŭich'ŏn's catalogue acquires greater likelihood from his reported contact with Yüan-chao (1048–1116), who was familiar with and quoted the *Commentary* in his extant sub-commentary on Chih-i's commentary on the *Kuan-ching.*[34]

*Dating: the first commentary on the Kuan-ching*

Without more substantial evidence, dating the compilation of the *Commentary* with any certainly is virtually impossible. Nogami Shunjo suggests Hui-yüan wrote the *Commentary* after the Northern Chou persecution (577–580), which had confirmed for Hui-yüan the arrival of the Last Period of Dharma *(mo-fa).*[35] Yet none of Hui-yüan's writings expresses alarm over the "End of Dharma," so that concerns about the state of the Dharma cannot necessarily base the dating of the compilation. He could very well have written the *Commentary* before the Chou persecution.

The *Commentary* quotes extensively from the *Nirvāṇa-sūtra* and the *Ti-ch'ih ching-lun.*[36] Yoshizu suggests that Hui-yüan[36] studied and lectured on the *Ti-ch'ih ching-lun* and *Nirvāṇa-sūtra* during and after his residence at Ch'ing-hua Monastery (554–577).[37] If Yoshizu is correct, Hui-yüan must have written the *Commentary* after 577, when at the age of fifty-five, he left Ch'ing-hua Monastery.

Another clue may be found in contrasting the introductions of Hui-yüan's works. The result of the contrast increases the possibility that the *Commentary*'s authorship was later than the others. Hui-yüan employed a similar format in the introductions of all his commentaries. Yet the extreme conciseness of his introduction to the *Commentary* seems to presume prior exposure to his earlier and more extended introductions. The introduction in the *Commentary* is not only more polished and organized than the others, but also the only one with a nomenclature, the "five essentials" (*wu-yao*) ascribed to it.[38] Moreover, with the exception of the *Wu-liang-*

*shou ching i-shu,* the *Kuan-ching* is not mentioned in his other writings.[39] In light of these factors, the lower limit for the *Commentary*'s compilation date falls sometime around 570. This would have given him sufficient time to study and lecture on the *Nirvāṇa-sūtra,* which, as suggested above, was the focus of his concern prior to his taking an interest in the *Kuan-ching.* The upper limit for the compilation date would be the spring of 592. Since he remained an active lecturer and writer almost until the end, he conceivably could have finished it immediately prior to his death in 592.

Modern scholars generally assume that Hui-yüan composed the first commentary on the *Kuan-ching.*[40] While no available evidence decisively refutes this, one other candidate exists for the honor of being the compiler of the first commentary on the *Kuan-ching.* According to *Further Biographies,* Ling-yü (518–605) is also credited with a commentary on the *Kuan-ching,* which has neither survived nor been cited by later works.[41] Unfortunately, the account does not indicate when he wrote the commentary. One clue, however, has surfaced in an epigraphic text entitled *Ta-fa-shih hsing-chi* (Record of the Eminent Dharma Master). Makita Tairyo reports that sometime between the age of forty-three and forty-seven Ling-yü wrote a commentary to the *Wu-liang-shou ching* (though not on *Kuan-ching*), *Wu-liang-shou ching-shu.*[42] At the latest, that would correspond to 565, Hui-yüan's twelfth or thirteenth year at Ch'ing-hua Temple, thereby antedating the suggested lower limit of 570 for Hui-yüan's compilation of the *Kuan-ching.*

Problematically, the *Further Biographies* does not list this work among Ling-yü's writings. Since the *Further Biographies* listings are not always exhaustive, this, of course, does not preclude his authorship. Alternatively, the epigraphic text referred to by Makita may have erred and should have stated that it was the commentary on the *Kuan-ching,* which the *Further Biographies* corroborates.[43] If, however, Ling-yü's commentary had been compiled during the period between 561 and 565, then this would antedate the lower limit for Hui-yüan's compilation, namely, 570. Thus, Hui-yüan would not have produced the first commentary on the *Kuan-ching.*[44]

A commentary by an anonymous author on the *Kuan-ching,* which does not correspond to any of the extant commentaries on this sutra, has been found among the Tun-huang manuscripts.[45] Mochizuki suggests this is the "lost" commentary by Ling-yü, on the grounds that the text was compiled prior to Hsüan-tsang (ca. 650) and includes citations from the same scriptures on which Ling-yü wrote commentaries.[46] But any one of the several known lost commentaries on the *Kuan-ching* could just as easily be so identified with the Tun-huang find. The text mentions the *Mahāyāna-saṃgraha* in connection with the theory of "intended for a later time" (*pieh-shih i*),[47] which the proponents of the *Mahāyānasaṃgraha* employed in their criticism of the Pure Land position. They argued that the Pure Land practice, in particular the ten contemplations (*shih-nien*), was merely a preliminary form that by itself could not lead to rebirth in the Pure Land. Rebirth, therefore, was not attained immediately but "intended for a later time" after one had accomplished more difficult practices.

Pure Land proponents Tao-ch'o, Chia-ts'ai, Shan-tao, and Huai-kan responded vigorously to this attack. But since these Pure Land texts were written slightly before either in the middle or the second half of the seventh century, the issue appears to have been taken seriously by contemporary rather than earlier Pure Land proponents. Both Hui-yüan and Chi-tsang did not mention this topic in their commentaries to the *Kuan-ching*. It thus makes it somewhat unlikely that Ling-yü, who died in 605, would have regarded it as an issue important enough to discuss in a commentary to the *Kuan-ching*.

In addition, this commentary cites an opinion that seems to appear first in Chi-tsang's commentary on the same sutra.[48] If it does cite Chi-tsang's view, this argues against Mochizuki's attribution of this commentary to Ling-yü. It is unlikely that he would have cited an opinion from a writing by Chi-tsang, who was quite a bit younger than he.

These considerations suggest that the Tun-huang manuscript is later than the *Commentary*, which then appears to be the earliest *extant* commentary on the *Kuan-ching*. It was followed by numerous other commentaries on the *Kuan-ching*, particularly during the Sui and T'ang periods. Of the approximately one hundred known commentaries through the Ch'ing period, the following are the extant commentaries written through the Sung period.[49]

1. *Kuan wu-liang-shou ching i-shu*, by Hui-yüan (523–592) (*T* 1750.37)
2. *Fo-shuo wu-liang-shou ching shu*, by T'ien-tai Chih-i (538–597) (*T* 1750.37) (an 'apocryphal' compiled as late as mid-eighth century)[50]
3. *Kuan wu-liang-shou ching i-shu*, by Chi-tsang (549–623) (*T* 1752.37)
4. *Kuan wu-liang-shou fo ching shu*, by Shan-tao (613–681) (*T* 1753.37)
5. *Wu-liang-shou kuan ching tsan-shu*, author unknown[51]
6. *Kuan wu-liang-shou-fo ching chi*, Tun-huang manuscript; author unknown (*T* 2760.85)[52]
7. *Kuan wu-liang-shou-fo ching chi*, Fa-ts'ung (*ZZ* 1.32.4) (compiled by 817)[53]
8. *Kuan wu-liang-shou-fo ching shu miao-tsung ch'ao*, Chih-li (960–1028) (*T* 1751.37)
9. *Kuan wu-liang-shou-fo ching i-shu*, Yüan-chao (1048–1116) (*T* 1754.37)

Besides the above, Etani Ryukai has partially reconstructed two commentaries based on quotations found in Japanese texts from the late Heian and early Kamakura periods.[54]

10. *Kuan-wu-liang-shou ching shu,* Etani ascribes this to Tao-yin (contemporary of Shan-tao in Ch'ang-an)[55]
11. *Kuan wu-liang-shou ching chi,* Etani ascribes this to Lung-hsing (655–711?)[56]
12. *An-le chi,* Tao-ch'o (*T* 1958.47)

This last work by Tao-ch'o is not the same sort of commentary on the *Kuan-ching* as those listed above. The title does not reflect the name of the *Kuan-ching,* and the text does not engage in the line by line exegesis characteristic of most of the above commentaries. Nevertheless, Tao-ch'o regarded his work to be a commentary on the *Kuan-ching,* for in the introductory section he states: "Here, this *Visualization Sutra* (the *Kuan-ching*) [which is being commented upon] received its title on the basis of the person (*jen*) and of the Dharma (*fa*); 'Buddha' is the person and the 'Discourse on the [Sutra] on Visualizing the [Buddha] Amitāyus' is the Dharma."[57]

While subsequent chapters will discuss the influence of Hui-yüan's *Commentary* in detail, it is possible here to obtain a bird's-eye view of its impact. We have noted that (1) the *Commentary* is quoted or mentioned by name in two works (nos. 9, and 10 from the above list); (2) that its concepts or issues were adopted or criticized in three (nos. 3, 4, and 12); and (3) that its passages are adopted wholesale in the compilation of one (no. 2).

Of the commentaries listed above, the one attributed to Chih-i has been most greatly influenced by the *Commentary.* According to Sato Tetsuei and others, this commentary is not an actual work by Chih-i but one compiled about a century later. But ever since the mid-T'ang this remains one of the best, if not the most studied, commentary on the *Kuan-ching.*[58] This is attested to by the proliferation of sub-commentaries on it by Fa-ts'ung, Chih-li and Yüan-chao (nos. 7, 8, and 9 in the above list). Sato has documented the extensive indebtedness of Chih-i's commentary to Hui-yüan's *Commentary* in virtue of the former's wholesale borrowing of entire sections from the latter.[59] In contrast, the reported lost commentary by Ling-yü has neither been quoted nor even mentioned in any surviving works.

### *Possible reasons for writing the Commentary*

Several reasons may have motivated Hui-yüan to write his commentary on the *Kuan-ching.* On this matter Ocho Enichi states:

> Though I have yet to examine the *Commentary* and *Wu-liang-shou ching i-shu* thoroughly, it would be safe to assume that Hui-

> yüan took a deep interest in Amitābha's Pure Land because of the influence of his teacher Fa-shang's devotion to Maitreya cult.
>
> His interest may not have been as thoroughgoing as the [teaching based on] *nien-fo* of the other power, but was related to [his interest in Pure Land Buddhist concepts] such as the Buddha land espoused in the *Vimalakīrti-sūtra.*
>
> As was the case with Fa-shang, Hui-yüan's interest [in Pure Land teaching] was rooted in his disillusionment with the state of affairs brought on by the destruction of Dharma, but not in an introspective realization of his nature as an inferior and incapable being.[59]

Similarly Mochizuki Shinko points out Fa-shang's Maitreya devotion as a major factor in contributing to Hui-yüan's interest in Pure Land thought.[60] Initially, Ocho's and Mochizuki's suggestions seem curious, since a pure land such as Amitābha's Sukhāvatī and a heavenly realm such as Maitreya's Tuṣita clearly belong to different cosmological categories. The former lies beyond the Three Realms (*tridhātuka*), while the latter belongs to one of the realms, the Realm of Desire (*kāmadhatu*).

But this may not be as unreasonable as it appears from the traditional Buddhist standpoint. In the chapter on the pure lands in his *Mahayana Encyclopedia,* Hui-yüan treats the heavenly realms (*t'ien*) and pure lands (*ching-t'u*) as virtually identical.[61] Because Hui-yüan treated Maitreya's Tuṣita as one of these heavenly realms, Tuṣita heaven, for him, belonged to the same category as Sukhāvatī Pure Land. Such a treatment was not totally foreign to popular understanding during the Nan-pei Chao period, as syncretistic fusion both of Maitreya and Amitābha and of their respective lands appears in numerous epigraphic inscriptions from this period. One such inscription reads: "I request that my deceased son rid himself of this defiled [physical form], meet Maitreya and be reborn in the Western Realm [of Amitābha]."[62]

Despite the apparent affinity of the two traditions, it still does not adequately answer why he wrote commentaries on the sutras pertaining to Amitābha rather than to Maitreya, as one would expect. Several sutras on Maitreya were already translated into Chinese before Hui-yüan's time:[63]

1. *Mi-le hsia-sheng ching*—translated by Dharmarakṣa (239–316)
2. *Mi-le hsia-sheng ch'eng-fo ching*—translated by Kumārajīva (350–409)
3. *Mi-le ta-ch'eng-fo ching*—translated by Kumārajīva
4. *Kuan mi-le p'u-sa shang-sheng tou-shuai-t'ien ching*—translated by Chü-ch'ü Ching-sheng (ca. 400)

The striking absence of a single commentary by Hui-yüan on any of the Maitreya sutras weakens all arguments that account for his interest in Pure Land sutras in terms of his personal devotion to Maitreya.

Ocho also cites the 'destruction of Dharma' as a motivating factor. Normally expressed as the arrival of the Last Period of Dharma, this concept has been the orthodox scholars' standard reason for the emergence of Pure Land Buddhism in sixth century China.[64] This suggestion assumes that the events destructive to Buddhism, such as the Northern Chou persecution, led Hui-yüan to take an interest in the *Kuan-ching,* a teaching that was appropriate for the decadent times. The mere recitation of the name of Amitābha was sufficient for rebirth. Though he did not reject oral recitation as a legitimate cause for rebirth, Hui-yüan regarded the '*samādhi* of Buddha-visualization' as the main import of the *Kuan-ching.* His remarks to his fellow monks after his gallant defense of Buddhism in his debate with Emperor Wu do not betray despair over the future of the Dharma:

> Truth must be expressed. How can I be concerned about my own life! . . . Such is the fate of the time! But even the Sage cannot banish the [the Dharma]. The fact that we cannot presently serve the [Dharma] is a great regret. The Dharma, however, is truly indestructible. Oh Venerables, please understand this, and I ask that you not be so sad and distressed.[65]

Such an affirmation undermines the traditional explanation of Hui-yüan's motives for writing the *Commentary.*

Another factor that requires mentioning regards the apparently active presence of Amitābha devotion among Hui-yüan's predecessors and contemporaries in the 'Hui-kuang lineage.'[66] The earliest known description of the lineage for the transmission of Pure Land teaching in China is Tao-ch'o's Six Worthies (*liu ta-te*) mentioned in his *An-le chi.* The six are: (1) Bodhiruci, (2) Dharma Master Hui-ch'ung, (3) Dharma Master Tao-ch'ang, (4) Dharma Master T'an-luan, (5) Meditation Master Ta-hai, and (6) the Ecclesiastical Head of the Ch'i Dynasty (*Ch'i-ch'ao shang-t'ung*).[67] Putting aside their alleged status as actual devotees of the Pure Land teaching or as famous names employed for authenticating Pure Land Buddhism, one cannot ignore their collective association with the 'Hui-kuang' lineage.

Bodhiruci was a teacher of Hui-kuang and is intimately associated with Pure Land Buddhism, especially in his role of converting T'an-luan to Pure Land teaching. Reportedly he gave T'an-luan a text called the "*Kuan ching,*" which has sparked controversy among modern scholars as to the identity of this "Kuan ching."[68] Also, included among the numerous texts that he translated was Vasubandhu's *Rebirth Treatise,* which has perhaps been the most influential Indian *śāstra* of Pure Land Buddhism in China as well as in Japan. According to Mochizuki, the second in the lineage, Hui-ch'ung, refers to Tao-ch'ung. Like Hui-kuang he was a disciple of Bodhiruci and regarded as a rival to Hui-kuang as head of the Northern branch of the Ti-lun school. Next in the lineage was Tao-ch'ang, a disciple of Hui-kuang. T'an-luan, the fourth Worthy, was converted to Pure Land teaching by Bodhiruci, Hui-kuang's teacher. Lastly, the Ecclesiastic Head, none other than Fa-shang, was a disciple of Hui-kuang and Hui-yüan's direct master.[69]

According to *Further Biographies,* Hui-kuang himself also appears to have been a devotee. He constantly aspired to be reborn in a Buddha-land, and at the end of his life he specifically prayed for rebirth in the "Land of Peace and Sustenance" (*An-yang shih-chieh*). Another disciple of Hui-kuang, Tao-p'ing, reportedly desired rebirth in the Western Quarter and had a vision of light at his deathbed. Tao'p'ing's disciple, Ling-yü (whom we have discussed earlier), died facing the western direction and is credited with commentaries on the *Kuan-ching* and the *Rebirth Treatise* as will be discussed below.[70]

The treatment the *Rebirth Treatise* evidences greater Amitābha Pure Land devotion among members of the 'Hui-kuang' lineage than previously thought. It suggests the possibility that Amitābha devotion was far more extensive than has been previously believed. To my knowledge, the following consideration has not been addressed before.

As will be discussed in the next chapter, Hui-yüan regarded the *Rebirth Treatise* as scriptural authority and virtually equal to the *Kuan-ching* and the *Wu-liang-shou ching.* But more important for our immediate discussion is the finding that the *Commentary* appears to be the oldest extant text that refers to Vasubandhu's treatise by the short title, *Rebirth Treatise,* the title by which later commentators in China as well as in Japan have known it. The practice of referring to this short title may very well have begun among the members of this 'Hui-kuang' lineage. Their deployment of the short title emphasizes the devotional aspect of this treatise.

In the *Taisho* edition, the full title of the *Rebirth Treatise* is *Wu-liang-shou ching yu-po-t'i-she yüan-sheng chieh* (The Treatise on the Sutra of the [Buddha] of Immeasurable Life and the Verses on the Aspiration for Rebirth).[71] This treatise is also known by another title, *Ching-t'u lun* (Treatise on the Pure Land ).[72] It is by these two shorter titles that this treatise has been commonly known, especially within Pure Land Buddhism. For example, orthodox Japanese Pure Land tradition knows this work as *Ōjō ron* (*Rebirth Treatise*) or *Jōdo ron* (*Pure Land Treatise*). In fact, today, these shorter titles are oftentimes used as if they were the original. Not unexpectedly, the present examination does not uncover any study on the origins for referring to the treatise by these shorter titles.[73]

The *T'an-luan Commentary* might be expected to be the earliest to employ the shorter titles. Aside from its title (*Wang-sheng lun-chu*), it is not only the oldest extant but also the earliest known commentary on Vasubandhu's treatise. No reference, however, to the shorter titles occurs either in his commentary or in his other shorter works.[74] Thus, the *Commentary* by Hui-yüan is the first to refer to this treatise by one of the two shorter titles.[75] In fact, the *Commentary* never refers to this treatise by its full title, but only by the *Rebirth Treatise.*

Despite the scriptural status that it has enjoyed in China and especially in Japanese Pure Land schools, no one has recognized that the *Commentary* by Hui-yüan is the earliest extant writing that uses the title *Rebirth Treatise.* For example, one of the best-known studies on the *T'an-luan Commentary* suggests early T'ang as the first usage of the short title on the basis of Chia-ts'ai's (ca.620–680) reference to the treatise as a "*Wang-sheng lun*" (Treatise on Rebirth.)[76] But this short title had already been used in the *Commentary* more than half a century earlier.

In the earliest catalogues, none of the entries refers to either of the abbreviated titles of the *Rebirth Treatise, Wang-sheng lun* or *Ching-t'u lun*; instead, they use "*Wu-liang-shou ching lun*" (Treatise on the Sutra of [the Buddha of] Immeasurable Life) or "*Wu-liang-shou yu-po-t'i-she ching lun*" (Treatise on the Sutra of Instructions on [the Buddha of] Immeasurable Life).[77] Among exegetical works written after Hui-yüan, Tao-ch'o's *An-le chi* is the oldest work to employ the short title, the "*Ching-t'u lun.*" "*Wang-sheng lun*" is found, for example, in the *Ching-t'u lun* by Chia-ts'ai and in the *Ching-t'u shih-i lun* previously alluded.[78]

In summary, the *Commentary* is the oldest extant text to designate the title as the *Rebirth Treatise.*[79] Moreover, some evidence suggests that this short title was coined by members of the 'Hui-kuang' lineage. The *Further Biographies* credits Ling-yü, a member of the 'Hui-kuang' lineage and a contemporary of Hui-yüan, with a commentary to the *Rebirth Treatise,*[80] unfortunately, now lost. No other references occur to a text from the sixth century as "*Wang-sheng lun.*"

Not unexpectedly, Ling-yü is credited with a commentary on this treatise, for this treatise would be held in high esteem by a member of the 'Hui-kuang' lineage. The author of the treatise was the eminent Vasubandhu, whose writings, particularly the *Daśabhūmika-śāstra,* constituted the focus of study and lectures by those of this lineage. Even though the interest of this lineage focused on the Yogacara or consciousness-only doctrine, derived primarily from the latter treatise, it should not be surprising that members of this lineage, such as Ling-yü and Hui-yüan, also valued the *Rebirth Treatise* as one of Vasubandhu's works.

Unlike the original full title, the title of the *Rebirth Treatise* centers on the highly devotional theme of "rebirth" (*wang-sheng*) in the Pure Land.

This poses the question as to its name. That is, the full title could instead have been easily shortened to "*Wu-liang-shou ching lun*," as it was in the Fa-ching catalogue *Chung-ching mu-lu,* alluded to above.[81] The "*Wang-sheng lun*" is probably related to the "*Yüan-sheng*" (Vow to be Reborn) of the full title (*Wu-liang-shou ching yu-po-t'i-she yüan-sheng chieh*), since their ideas are very similar. Yet the two are not exact, and the question still remains as to why *Wang-sheng lun,* and not simply *Yüan-sheng lun,* was selected.

Hui-yüan does not address this issue directly. But a passage in his *Wu-liang-shou ching i-shu* might serve as a clue for its abridgement:

> Question: When Vasubandhu compiled the Verses on Rebirth (*wang-sheng chieh*), he stated that women, the disabled and those of the class of the Two Vehicles are all unable to be reborn in the Pure Land.[82]

Of particular interest is the phrase "the *Verses* on Rebirth," which refers to the verse, as opposed to the commentarial prose section of this treatise. If "Verses on Rebirth" refers only to the verse section, then perhaps the commentarial prose section came to be called the "*Treatise* on Rebirth," that is, *Wang-sheng lun.* This suggestion finds support in Vasubandhu, who at the end of the verse section states: "I have compiled the treatise in order to explain the verses."[83]

Evidence tends to identify the 'Hui-kuang' lineage as the milieu in which the short title, *Rebirth Treatise,* was coined. This would add credence to Mochizuki's proposal that Pure Land Buddhism was quite active among those who are traditionally not counted among orthodox Pure Land Buddhists. In short those who belonged to a lineage that is conventionally regarded as exclusively scholastic in fact may have had an interest in the devotional dimension of Pure Land Buddhism. Thus, the Hui-kuang lineage's unexpectedly active interest in scriptures centering on Buddha Amitābha must be included as one of the factors motivating Hui-yüan's writing of the *Commentary* and *Wu-liang-shou ching i-shu.*

# Chapter Four

## Treatment of the *Kuan-ching*

### Background

Significantly, Hui-yüan became the first known exegete not only to treat the *Kuan-ching* on an equal footing with the other Mahayana sutras of the period but also to assemble it into a set with two other Pure Land texts. This set acquired scriptural authority for later Chinese Pure Land proponents and became canonical for Japanese Pure Land Buddhists.[1] As will be discussed below, by placing the *Kuan-ching* among the major sutras of his time, Hui-yüan legitimatized the *Kuan-ching* as a crucial text for Buddhist exegesis.

Hui-yüan's inclusion of the *Kuan-ching* among the major Mahayana sutras is especially noteworthy, since from the time of its translation until Hui-yüan's compilation of the *Commentary,* the *Kuan-ching* only ranked as a minor text. While utilized for liturgical purposes, it lacked the scholarly stature of such major sutras as the *Avataṃsaka, Lotus, Nirvana* or the *Vimalakīrti.* In fact, outside of the *T'an-luan Commentary,* the *Kuan-ching* is not discussed at any length in the extant exegetical works compiled prior to Hui-yüan's *Commentary.* Even in the work by T'an-luan, the coverage given to the *Kuan-ching* was limited.[2] Moreover, the fact that Seng-yü (445–518) in his *Ch'u san-tsang chi chi* (A Collection of Notices Concerning the Issuance of the Canon) included the *Kuan-ching* in a section called the "Records of miscellaneous sutras by anonymous translators" (*shih-i tsa-ching lu*) reflects its tenuous status among the sutras.[3]

This chapter focuses on four issues: (1) the 'five-essentials' (*wu-yao*), (2) the exegetical style, (3) the 'reconciliation of inconsistencies, and (4) the title "Ta-ching." The five-essentials are a set of categories appearing at the beginning of the introductory section of the *Commentary* in which Hui-yüan analyzes the *Kuan-ching.* First of all, his employment of virtually the same categories in all of his commentaries provides a common standard for relating his interpretation of the *Kuan-ching* to other Mahayana literature. Second, his exegetical style in the *Commentary* was in keeping with the orthodox style of his time. The section on the 'reconciliation of sutras and treatises' discloses his understanding of the relationship between the *Kuan-ching* and the *Wu-liang-shou ching* and the *Rebirth Treatise*. He consciously reconciles the differences among these Pure Land scriptures that were later elevated to canonical status.

**Five-essentials**

The discussion of the five-essentials that initiates the *Commentary*'s introductory section includes questions concerning (1) the identification of the teaching as Hinayana or Mahayana (*chiao-chih-ta-hsiao*), (2) the nature of the teaching as limited, gradual, or sudden (*chiao-chü-chien-tun*), (3) the main import of a sutra (*ching-chih-tsung-ch'ü*), (4) the differences in the sutra titles (*ching-ming pu-t'ung*), and (5) the distinctions in [the five kinds of] speakers of the sutras (*shuo-jen ch'a-pieh*).

Six other commentaries by Hui-yüan utilize the same categories.[4] Two of these categories are found in the scriptures, the first category in the *Ti-ch'ih ching* and the fifth in the *Ta chih tu lun*.[5] Therefore, apparently Hui-yüan took these scattered categories and adopted them as exegetical terms in his commentaries. Among Hui-yüan's writings in which they are found, only the *Commentary* refers to the entire set of categories as the "five-essentials," a term that he most likely coined.

The first essential is a form of *p'an-chiao* classification that distinguishes Hinayana from Mahayana, or in Hui-yüan's terms "Śrāvaka Piṭaka" (*sheng-men tsang*) from the "Bodhisattva Piṭaka" (*p'u-sa tsang*). Hui-yüan places the *Kuan-ching* in the Bodhisattva Piṭaka, which includes texts that espouse the Bodhisattva teaching. While the *Commentary* offers no further explanation, Hui-yüan's *Wu-liang-shou ching i-shu* explains that Śrāvaka Piṭaka represents a teaching belonging to both the Śrāvakas and the Pratyekabuddhas. Then in elaborating on the Bodhisattva Piṭaka, he remarks:

> The *Ti-ch'ih ching* states, "The Buddha preached the sutras in order for the Śrāvakas and the Bodhisattvas to practice leaving the realm of suffering. . . . To explain what the Śrāvakas practice [the Buddha taught] the Śrāvaka Piṭaka, and to explain the Bodhisattva practice [he taught] the Bodhisattva Piṭaka."[6]

Elsewhere in his commentary to the *Nirvāṇa-sūtra* Hui-yüan adds:

> The treatise (*Ta chih tu lun*) says, "Among the twelve canonical divisions, only the Vaipulya (Mahayana) division is the Bodhisattva Piṭaka, while the remaining eleven divisions constitute the Śrāvaka Piṭaka.[7]

The presence of this first essential in the Hui-yüan's extant commentaries demonstrates his conviction that the sutras and treatises on which he commented belonged to the Bodhisattva Piṭaka. He included none of these scriptures among the Śrāvaka Piṭaka, and the *Kuan-ching* was no exception.[8]

The second essential is another *p'an-chiao* category that divides the teachings into "limited" (*chü*), "gradual" (*chien*), and "sudden" (*tun*). Limited teaching is the Hinayana teaching, while the gradual teaching is the Mahayana form that is entered from the Hinayana teaching (*ta-ts'ung-hsiao-ju*). The "sudden" is the Mahayana teaching that is not entered through the Hinayana teaching (*ta-pu-yu-hsiao*). As to which of the three teachings the *Kuan-ching* belonged, Hui-yüan explains:

> It is known because this sutra was taught specifically for Vaidehī, who, as will be explained below, was a Pṛthagjana. Since it is taught for the sake of Pṛthagjanas and not entered by way of Hinayana, this teaching is known as the "sudden teaching."[9]

Gradual and sudden teachings were not new categories for *p'an-chiao* classification. In fact they formed the main criteria for the two earliest known *p'an-chiao* schemes of Liu-ch'iu (438–495) and Hui-kuan (d. ca. 424–453).[10] In both of these cases, however, "gradual" and "sudden" carried different meanings. "Sudden" referred specifically to the *Avataṃsaka-sūtra* and "gradual" to the rest of the Hinayana and Mahayana teachings that were divided into five periods. T'ien-t'ai monk Chih-i's famous "five-period eight-teachings" classification also regarded "sudden" as the teaching of the *Avataṃsaka-sūtra* and "gradual" as including both Hinayana and some Mahayana teachings.[11] Hui-yüan's deployment of the two categories, therefore, differs significantly from other well-known classifications. He was not unaware of the other classifications, for in his *Mahayana Encyclopedia* he mentions Liu-ch'iu's and proceeds to criticize it for applying the two categories to both Hinayana and Mahayana. In his view the two apply only to Mahayana.[12]

The *Commentary* neither elaborates nor offers any clue as to the nature and source of this rather unique interpretation of the sudden and gradual teaching. Fortunately, however, Hui-yüan's other commentaries include a passage that enhances our understanding of the subject. Hui-yüan states:

> Within the Bodhisattva Piṭaka there are two kinds of teachings taught: (1) the gradual entrance and (2) the sudden awakening. The term "gradual entrance" refers to those who had in the past cultivated the Mahayana doctrine, but had then left to dwell in the Hinayana

> [doctrine], only to return later to enter Mahayana. To enter Mahayana from Hinayana is referred to as "gradual." Hence, the sutra stated, "I shall now lead those who have rejected their previous cultivation and studies of Hinayana to enter the [Mahayana] doctrine." They are the Bodhisattvas of gradual entrance.[13]

Thus, for Hui-yüan the "gradual teaching" applies to those who reenter the Mahayana fold after having spent some time following the Hinayana doctrine.

Further explanations for leaving and returning to Mahayana appear in the *Mahayana Encyclopedia.* According to it, the Bodhisattva in a past life generated the mind committed to Mahayana, but as he transmigrated in *saṃsāra,* he lost his original thought of enlightenment and temporarily turned to Hinayana teaching. Even though the "Bodhisattva" attained the Hinayana fruit, he again turned to Mahayana in the present life, as he realized there was still more to be attained.[14]

With regard to the "sudden teaching," Hui-yüan explains:

> The term "sudden awakening" refers to those sentient beings who after a long period of cultivating wholesome faculties in keeping with Mahayana [teaching] see the Buddha for the first time, enabling them to enter Mahayana. Mahayana [teaching] that is not [entered] by way of Hinayana is categorized as "sudden." Hence, the sutra explained, "There are some beings who for generations had always accepted the teaching regarding the [false notion of the] self, but in seeing myself for the first time and on hearing what I had to explain about [the self], they all entrusted themselves [in the teaching] and entered the Tathāgata's wisdom." This is sudden awakening. While Bodhisattvas of the gradual entrance must traverse extensively the [numerous] superficial steps, the Bodhisattvas of sudden awakening gain understanding of Mahayana in one leap (*i-yueh*).[14]

While Hui-yüan found scriptural authority in this sutra for his understanding of the "sudden" teaching, his interpretation went beyond the sutra. He distinguished two paths that sound very much like both the distinction in the later Ch'an controversy between "sudden" and "gradual"[15] and the Pure Land Buddhist distinction between the "path of difficult practice" and the "path of easy practice."[16] For Hui-yüan, the gradual entrance comprises a long tortuous path, but sudden awakening is attained in "one leap" without undergoing Hinayana practices. Despite the differences between two paths, their end results are the same, as Hui-yüan explains, "Even though the sudden and the gradual are distinct, when the time comes to receive the Mahayana [teaching, those of the two groups] will dwell together."[17]

As a sutra of sudden teaching, the *Kuan-ching* assumes the company of three others sutras on which he also commented: the *Wu-liang-shou ching,* the *Śrīmālādevī, Vimalakīrti* and, indirectly, the *Daśabhūmika.*[18] In contrast, he deems the *Wen-shih ching* and the *Nirvāṇa-sutra* to belong to the gradual teaching. Regarding the latter sutra, he comments, "The gradual teaching for sentient beings is a Dharma-gate of protracted nurturing."[19]

Only the *Kuan-ching* and the *Wu-liang-shou ching* among the "sudden" teaching are stipulated to be for Pṛthagjanas, whom Vaidehi represents in the *Kuan-ching.* With regard to the *Wu-liang-shou ching,* Hui-yüan explains in his *Wu-liang-shou ching i-shu*:

> How do we know [this sutra is of the] sudden [teaching]? It is because this sutra is precisely for those Pṛthagjanas who are weary of birth and death and seek to be properly settled. They are taught to raise the mind of [bodhi] in order to be reborn in the Pure Land. They [enter] Mahayana not by way of Hinayana. Thus, [this sutra] is to be known as a sudden [teaching].[20]

Those "who are weary of birth and death . . ." in the *Wu-liang-shou ching* and Vaidehī in the *Kuan-ching* have much in common. Further it is striking that among the sutras of the sudden teaching, only the Pure Land sutras were designated as teachings for the Pṛthagjanas.

The third essential concerns the main import of a sutra, which Hui-yüan explains:

> The main import advocated by each sutra differs. For example, the *Nirvāṇa-sūtra* advocates nirvana as its main import; the *Vimalakīrti-sūtra* advocates incomprehensible liberation as its main import; the *Larger [Prajñāpāramitā]-sūtra* advocates *prajñā* as its main import; the *Avataṃsaka-sutra, Lotus Sutra* and *Wu-liang-i [ching]* advocate *samādhi* as their main import; the *Ta chi ching* advocates esoteric formula (*dhāraṇī*) as its main import. Hence there is not just one main import. This sutra (the *Kuan-ching*) advocates the *samādhi* of Buddha-visualization its main import.[21]

The fourth essential concerns differences among sutra titles. Hui-yüan enumerates the following criteria for sutras titles, for example, "doctrine" (*fa*), "person" (*jen*), "analogy" (*yü*), "objects" (*shih*), "location" (*ch'u*), "time" (*shih*), "person and doctrine" (*jen fa*), "objects and doctrine" (*shih fa*), "doctrine and analogy" (*fa yü*). As he explains, the *Kuan-ching* title is determined by person and doctrine, "'the Buddha' is the person and the

'Discourse on Visualizing the [Buddha of] Immeasurable Life' is the doctrine." Hui-yüan goes on to list the four kinds of sutra titles based on persons: (1) the speaker, (2) the interlocutor, (3) the person being discussed, and (4) the person for whom the sutra is preached. The *Kuan-ching* is included in the first group, that is to say, in that based on the speaker, who (as the fifth essential will show) is the Buddha himself.[22]

The fifth essential concerns the distinction based on the kind of person who discourses on the sutra:

> As for the fifth [essential], one ought to know there are distinctions based on the person doing the discourses; in carrying out the discourse there are roughly five kinds of sutras as explained, for example, by Nāgārjuna: those discoursed on (1) by the Buddha himself, (2) by [Buddha's] holy disciples, (3) by the hermits, (4) by the gods and (5) by transformed beings. Of the five, this sutra belongs to those [sutras] discoursed on by the Buddha.[23]

A comparison of this to the original passage from Nāgārjuna's *Ta chih-tu lun* (Perfection of Wisdom Treatise) discloses that Hui-yüan has employed somewhat different characters for the five classes of beings.[24] In contrast, Chi-tsang's commentary on the *Kuan-ching* carried over directly the character rendering for the five speakers from the *Ta chih-tu lun.*[25]

Based on the five-essentials, several observations can be made about Hui-yüan's perception of the *Kuan-ching.* For Hui-yüan, the *Kuan-ching* is a Mahayana sutra par excellence, as evidenced by its inclusion among the sudden teaching of the Bodhisattva Piṭaka and its company of such prominent sutras as the *Śrīmālādevī-sūtra, Daśabhūmika-sūtra* and *Vimalakīrti-sūtra.* Further, its main import (Buddha-visualization *samādhi*) was counted among those of other major Mahayana sutras, such as the *Lotus, Avataṃsaka, Nirvana* and *Prajñāpāramitā.* As indicated by the fifth essential, he accorded further credibility to the *Kuan-ching* because he included it among sutras preached by the Buddha himself. In sum these observations acquire greater significance because aside from a few citations in the *T'an-luan Commentary,* the *Kuan-ching* did not receive any scholarly treatment by extant literature prior to the *Commentary.*

Some of the five-essentials occur in subsequent commentaries on the *Kuan-ching,* including those by Chi-tsang, Tao-ch'o, Shan-tao, Chih-i, and its sub-commentaries.[26] In explaining the title of the sutra, the *Chih-i Commentary* states:

> The two Piṭakas clarify the principle [of a sutra,] which [for the *Kuan-ching*] is included in the Bodhisattva Piṭaka. Between the gradual and the sudden entrances, this [sutra] is of the sudden teaching. It was

> appropriately [taught] for Vaidehī and her female attendants, who are all Pṛthagjanas and have not yet realized the Hinayana fruits. Therefore, one should know this [sutra] as of the sudden and not of the gradual entrance. The sutra title says "Buddha's Discourse," since it differs from the other four [kinds of] people [who discourse], [Buddha's] disciples, hermits, heavenly beings and transformed beings, etc.[27]

These correspond to the first, second and fifth essentials of Hui-yüan's five-essentials.

## Exegetical style

According to Ocho Enichi's analysis of the history of Buddhist commentaries in China, what he calls the "*shu*" commentarial style dominated exegetical form during the Nan-pei Chao period (420–589) after it supplanted the so-called *chu* commentaries. For Ocho, this distinction does not denote a clear-cut transition, for he is aware that the *chu* commentaries by no means disappeared during this period as attested to by Liu-chiu's (438–495) *Chu fa-hua ching* (Commentary on the *Lotus Sutra*) and Liang Wu-ti's *Chu ta-p'in ching* (Commentary on the *Larger Prajñāpāramitā Sutra*).[28] Fujieda Akira also recognizes similar changes in exegetical style, though he does not explicitly identify the two styles by name. He believes the transition occurred around the end of the fifth century but not earlier than 420.[29]

According to Ocho, the three representative *chu* commentaries are the *Yin-ch'ih-ju ching-chu* (Commentary on the *Sutra on the Fundamental Elements*) by Ch'en-hui (n.d., Wu period), *Jen-pen-yü-sheng ching-chu* (Commentary on the *Mahānidāna-sūtra*) by Tao-an (312–385) and *Chu wei-mo ching* (Commentary on the *Vimalakīrti-sūtra*) by Seng-chao (384–414).[30] The salient characteristics common to the *chu* commentaries are: (1) the introductory section is separate from the main body of the commentary; (2) there is no 'dividing into sections' as a means of understanding the sutra passages; (3) the titles include the character "*chu*."[31]

In Ocho's opinion, the *Miao-fa lien-hua ching shu* (Commentary on the *Lotus Sutra*) by Tao-sheng (355–434) represents the earliest work of the *shu* commentaries. Some of its characteristics are: (1) the introductory section is no longer separate from the main body and is much more developed in its content with an introductory discussion that Ocho calls "*hsüan-ta'n*"; (2) the introductory discussion includes the issues of *p'an-chiao* and the text's main import; (3) the practice of 'dividing into sections' is adopted as a method of comprehending the text.[32]

Like *chu* commentaries, the introductory section of the *shu* style generally explains the title of the sutra and the background of the text's translation. But it adds a *p'an-chiao* of one sort or another and a discussion of the 'main import' of the text. The practice of dividing into sections, however, features prominently in the *shu* commentaries. In its developed form, it divides the sutras into sections with the following standard nomenclature: "preface," "main body," and "conclusion."[33] In its more elaborate form, such as in Fa-yün's (467–527) commentary to the *Lotus Sutra,* each of the three sections becomes further subdivided. For example, the preface branches into (1) "general preface," also referred to as "preface for verification of faith," and (2) "specific preface" or "preface for initiating [the instruction]."[34] Fujieda also cites the dividing into sections as the principal characteristic of the exegetical style from the end of the fourth century.[35] Viewed in this context, Hui-yüan's *Commentary* exhibits all the characteristics of a *shu* commentary, thus rendering it the oldest extant Pure Land work to be written in the *shu* format.

In contrast, the only extant Pure Land treatise prior to the *Commentary,* the *T'an-luan Commentary,* primarily features characteristics of a *chu* commentary. Both the inclusion of "chu" in its title and the designation of T'an-luan's authorship in the phrase "*chu* commentary by Śramaṇa T'an-luan" marks as a *chu* commentary. While the introductory section is not separate from the main body of the text, it contains no discussion on the main import of Vasubandhu's treatise. Unlike the *chu* commentary, however, it does include a simple *p'an-chiao* formulation of "the path of difficult practice" and "the path of easy practice."[36]

Moreover, T'an-luan's treatise lacks what both Ocho and Fujieda consider the most prominent feature of the *shu* commentaries, the three-fold division into preface, main body, and conclusion. T'an-luan does, however, divide Vasubandhu's text into two parts as T'an-luan explains:

> This treatise from beginning to end has roughly speaking two parts, the general explanation and the elucidation of meaning.[37]

The first part refers to the verse section at the beginning of the treatise, while the second part points to the prose section that follows.[38] However, this distinction is purely mechanical, as it issues from a very obvious difference between a verse and a prose section. Thus, the two sections merely reflect two distinct literary forms rather than an analytic division of the treatise's interpretive labors.

T'an-luan's treatment may partly stem from his personal standpoint on the practice of 'scripture-dividing.' He is later quoted criticizing this practice that was prevalent in south China, particularly in Chien-k'ang:

> Such detailed division is [nothing but] a smoke screen, an alloyed ore and scattered mental obstruction.[39]

In contrast, Hui-yüan's *Commentary* exhibits all the features of a *shu* commentary. The title includes the character *shu.* Its introductory section, comprised primarily of the five-essentials, constitutes a well-developed discussion on (1) the *p'an-chiao* formulation (the first two of the five-essentials), (2) the main import (the third essential), and (3) the elucidation of the title of the sutra (the fourth and fifth essential plus the subsequent subsection).

In the *Commentary,* the practice of sutra-division fully proliferates into sections and further subsections, whose main demarcations can be enumerated as follows:[40]

| | |
|---|---|
| 1. Preface | A. Preface on Initiating the Teaching |
| | B. Preface on Proving the Credibility of the Teaching |
| 2. Main Body | A. Vaidehī's General Request |
| | B. Buddha's General Manifestation |
| | C. Vaidehī's Specific Request |
| | D. Buddha's Specific Revelation |
| 3. Conclusion | A. Conclusion at the King's Palace |
| | B. Conclusion at Gṛdhrakūṭa |

Since it exhibits all the characteristics of a *shu* commentary, the *Commentary* conforms to the dominant exegetical style of its period, as identified by Ocho Enichi. Its conformity accords with Fujieda's description of the dominant exegetical style, which he suggests came into vogue around the end of the fifth century. He cites the dividing into sections as one of the two primary features of the new style. The other is the enlarged listing of differing explications of particular passages. As one of the classic examples of this style, Fujieda specifically cites Hui-yüan's commentary on the *Śrīmālādevī-sūtra.*[41]

Even if the *Commentary* had been compiled somewhat later in the Sui period, it still would have been consistent with the dominant exegetical style of the next period in Ocho's scheme. Ocho calls Sui and the period prior to Hsüan-tsang's return (649) the "period of introductory discussion." The following features characterize the writings of this period: (1) the expansion in size of the introductory discussion, (2) the division of the introductory discussion section, (3) the development of the exegetical categories, (4) the three-section division of texts, and (5) the comprehensiveness of citation and criticism.[42] The *Commentary* largely accords with these points, with the possible exception of the last.

During this period, introductory discussions underwent extensive development, as demonstrated by Chi-tsang's and Chih-i's works. Not only did they expand in size but also proliferated into a greater number of sections. Chi-tsang's "three meanings" and "four gates" and Chih-i's "five important profound meanings" designate some of the well-known nomenclature of these sections. Hui-yüan's "five-essentials" represent this development, though not as extensively as those in the commentaries on the *Kuan-ching* by Chi-tsang or Shan-tao, or that attributed to Chih-i. The overall writings of Chi-tsang and Chih-i are once again replete with references to the third point, the adoption of exegetical categories such as Chi-tsang's "reliance on name," "causes and condition," "revealing the path," and "absence of method."[43]

Hui-yüan's *Commentary* also reveals many similar categories including "features," "benefits," and "meaning" that explained the visualization of Dharmakāya (180b12–15). Along with the *Commentary,* Hui-yüan's commentaries adhere to this three-fold division. Similarly, Chih-i and Chi-tsang adopted this method in their writings. In particular, Chi-tsang extensively discussed this method of division, thereby attesting to its prevalence during this period.[44]

This examination of Ocho's and Fujieda's analyses of this period's commentarial style and exegesis may safely conclude that the compilation of the *Commentary* accorded with the orthodox commentarial format of the second half of Nan-pei Ch'ao and the early T'ang. The exegetical style of the *Commentary* was, therefore, more 'orthodox' than was that of the *T'an-luan Commentary,* which is traditionally considered the earliest surviving Chinese commentary on a Pure Land scripture. Moreover, as will be discussed later in this study, the *Commentary* had a definite impact on subsequent commentaries on the *Kuan-ching.* Many of the *Commentary*'s exegetical features also appear in these commentaries, especially in the *Shan-tao Commentary* and the *Chih-i Commentary.*

**Reconciliation of apparent inconsistencies**

Customarily the Japanese Pure Land tradition of Hōnen regards the *Wu-liang-shou-ching* ('Large Sutra'), the *A-mi-t'o fo ching* ('Small Sutra'), the *Kuan-ching* and Vasubandhu's *Rebirth Treatise* as canonical Pure Land scriptures.[45] Kōgatsuin Jinrei (b. 1749) as well as more recent writers, such as Roger Corless, maintain that T'an-luan did consider these three sutras a related set. This would make the latter the earliest known commentator to have so treated them.[46]

However, evidence seems insufficient to support this widely held assumption. Evidence for such a claim would require either a clear statement by the author to that effect or, in the absence of such a statement, a concerted attempt by the author to reconcile apparent inconsistencies among them. The *T'an-luan Commentary* offers only minimal evidence in this regard. In contrast, Hui-yüan's *Commentary* does reveal a conscious effort to treat the Pure Land scriptures as a consistent set, especially in the section on the reconciliation of discrepancies among the sutras and treatises.

According to a survey of the sutras quoted in the *T'an-luan Commentary,* the above Pure Land sutras are quoted forty out of a total of sixty-three times, the *Wu-liang-shou ching* twenty times, the *Kuan-ching* sixteen and the *A-mi-t'o fo ching* four times. Based on the number of citations, there is little skepticism about T'an-luan's high regard for the Pure Land sutras. There were, however, also two non-Pure Land sutras that either equalled or surpassed the number of citations of the *A-mi-t'o fo ching,* namely, the *Lotus Sutra* with six and the *Vimalakīrti-sūtra* with four.[47]

In one instance, T'an-luan attempts to resolve an apparent contradiction between the *Kuan-ching* and the *Wu-liang-shou-ching* on the qualifications for rebirth in the Pure Land. The *Wu-liang-shou-ching* excludes rebirth to those who have committed the Five Grave Offenses and vilified the true Dharma. Yet the *Kuan-ching* allows even those guilty of the Five Grave Offenses and the Ten Evils to be reborn there. T'an-luan's solution fundamentally contends that only the Vilification of the Dharma rather than the Five Grave Offenses (or the Ten Evils) constitutes the grounds for preventing one's rebirth. Thus, the *Wu-liang-shou-ching* proscribed their rebirth since the group included those who vilified the True Dharma. Had the group been comprised only of those committing the Five Grave Offenses, T'an-luan would have permitted their rebirth. To the contrary, the *Kuan-ching* permitted rebirth since those guilty of the Vilification of the Dharma were not included among the people under question.[48]

As evidence for T'an-luan's treatment of the three sutras as a unit, the proponents assert that the "*Wu-liang-shou ching,*" the first part of the full title of Vasubandhu's treatise (i.e. *Wu-liang-shou ching yu-po-t'i-she yuan-sheng-chieh*), not only refers to the *Wu-liang-shou ching,* but also actually encompasses all three Pure Land sutras. They base their argument on the interpretation of a statement in the *T'an-luan Commentary*:

> Śākyamuni Buddha spoke, in the city of Rājagṛha and the [city-] state of Śrāvastī, in the midst of great congregations, on the merits of the adornments of Buddha Amitāyus. Thus that Buddha's Name embodies the sutras (*ching*).[49]

Because the *Kuan-ching* and the *Wu-liang-shou-ching* were preached in Rājagṛha and the *A-mi-t'o fo ching* at Śrāvastī, these three Pure Land sutras are 'embodied' in the name "Wu-liang-shou," found in the full title of the *Rebirth Treatise.*[50] While provocative, this view is not sufficiently compelling in the absence of adequate evidence to substantiate that T'an-luan did in fact regard the three as a compatible unit. The only instance of T'an-luan's dealing with the sutras as related texts was his attempt, seen above, to reconcile the discrepancies between the two of them.

In contrast, subsequent modern writers have not recognized Hui-yüan's attempt to reconcile the *Kuan-ching* with the other Pure Land scriptures. In fact he established a subsection in the *Commentary* called, "Reconciliation of Sutras and Treatises" (*shih-hui ching-lun*), in which he specifically answered questions about the discrepancies between the *Kuan-ching,* on the one hand, and the *Rebirth Treatise* and the *Wu-liang-shou ching* on the other. This is noteworthy because this section constitutes a far more intensive endeavor than T'an-luan's, not only in terms of its dedication of a section to the resolution of these inconsistencies but also in terms of the number of discrepancies he confronted.

Hui-yüan does not mention the *A-mi-t'o fo ching* in the *Commentary,* and instead holds Vasubandhu's *Rebirth Treatise* to be virtually on the same footing as the other sutras. In part, as was argued in the previous chapter, the high regard in which Hui-yüan held the *Rebirth Treatise* probably derived from its status among those affiliated with the 'Hui-kuang lineage.' It should be noted that this treatise maintained its high esteem among later exegetes of Pure Land scriptures well into the T'ang period.[51]

The first issue that Hui-yüan attempts to reconcile turns on the question of rebirth in the Pure Land for those of the Two Vehicles (the Śrāvakas and Pratyekabuddhas). The *Rebirth Treatise* denies, while the *Kuan-ching* accedes to their rebirth.[52] Hui-yüan agrees with the *Kuan-ching*'s position and maintains the possibility of their rebirth in the Pure Land through Mahayana practice. He cites the *Wu-liang-shou-ching*'s admonition 'to generate the bodhi mind' as the Mahayana practice par excellence for that purpose. Hence for Hui-yüan, the *Rebirth Treatise*'s exclusion of the Hinayanists refers to the end of their career, in which they have not undergone the conversion to Mahayana required for rebirth in the Pure Land. In contrast, the *Kuan-ching*'s liberal attitude refers to the beginning of their career. Thus, even if they are Hinayanists, they can still 'convert' to Mahayana in time to generate the bodhi mind for rebirth in the Pure Land.[53]

The second issue concerns reconciling the *Rebirth Treatise* statement that women and the disabled cannot be reborn in the Pure Land with that of the *Kuan-ching* in which Lady Vaidehī and all her five hundred female attendants do attain rebirth.[54] Hui-yüan resolves this by regarding the

*Rebirth Treatise* passage as a statement on the "end" of their career, which in this context is a reference to their lives in the Pure Land. He thus affirms the position that neither women nor disabled persons dwell in the Pure Land. At the same time, however, he is not rejecting their rebirth. Although they can be reborn as any other beings, in the Pure Land they undergo transformation and are no longer either women or disabled. There are no such people in the Pure Land, since rebirth constitutes a purified physical reward and a separation from passion.[55]

The third inconsistency that Hui-yüan tackles is that which T'an-luan himself had earlier attempted to reconcile, namely, the rebirth of those guilty of the Five Grave Offenses. The *Wu-liang-shou-ching* excluded them, while the *Kuan-ching* permitted their rebirth. By responding in terms of the person (*jen*) and the practice (*hsing*), Hui-yüan's solution, however, displays more sophistication than does T'an-luan's. Based on the degree of transgression and of repentance, there are superior and inferior persons among the guilty. Even among the superior, like King Ajātaśatru, can be found those of lesser crimes and of greater repentance. The *Kuan-ching* referred to this latter type, rather than to the inferior person with greater crimes and lesser repentance, who concerned the *Wu-liang-shou-ching.*

In terms of practice, Hui-yüan argues that the meditative practice of Buddha-visualization *samādhi* is strong enough to erase the evil karma of the transgressions. All other non-meditative practices are too weak to erase evil karma. The *Kuan-ching* subscribes to the former, while the *Wu-liang-shou-ching* to the latter. Hence, the *Kuan-ching* permitted rebirth for these transgressors precisely because they can overcome the negative effects by cultivating the meditative practice of visualization.[56]

Besides the three issues in this section devoted specifically to reconciling discrepancies, on six other occasions Hui-yüan attempts either to resolve differences or to compare the *Kuan-ching* and the *Wu-liang-shou-ching.* First, the *Wu-liang-shou-ching* divides the people of rebirth in the Pure Land into three grades as opposed to nine for the *Kuan-ching* (183b8ff). Second, the *Wu-liang-shou-ching* speaks of the present being beset by evil karma, while the *Kuan-ching* speaks of evil karma only in the past (183c14–17). Third, Hui-yüan compares the quality of the Buddha seen by the different grades of aspirants in the two sutras (183c25–184a2). Four, in the *Wu-liang-shou-ching* everyone of the middle category gains a vision of the Buddha, but in the *Kuan-ching* only some do. Because the *Kuan-ching*'s description of this category is more detailed than that of the *Wu-liang-shou-ching,* the former is able to indicate the lowest one-third in the category who are prevented from gaining the vision. The *Wu-liang-shou-ching,* on the other hand, speaks only in general terms so that it did not indicate the minority in this category who are unable to gain a vision (184a4–7). Five, in the *Wu-liang-shou-ching* none of the low grade beings are able to see the Buddha, but in the *Kuan-ching* some are. This is possible because those of the *Kuan-ching* are able to destroy their evil karma because they cultivate visualization (184a7–10). Six, this is related to the preceding one. In the *Wu-liang-shou-ching* the quality of the Buddha seen in the visions is of a lower grade than that of the nine grades in the *Kuan-ching.* Again the explanation lies in the superior efficacy of the visualization ( 184a10–15). These attempts further strengthen the contention that Hui-yüan was highly conscious of the affinity between the two sutras and strove to reconcile them to a greater degree than did either T'an-luan or previous extant commentaries.[57]

## The title "Ta-ching"

Throughout the *Commentary* Hui-yüan refers to the *Wu-liang-shou-ching* as "*Ta-ching*" (the Large or Great Sutra), the same title by which later Pure Land commentators called it. Japanese Pure Land Buddhists also used the same epithet "*Dai kyō,*" as in Shinran's *Ken jōdo shinjitsu kyōgyōshō monrui* (A Collection of Passages Revealing the True Teaching, Practice, and Enlightenment of Pure Land Buddhism).[58] In modern times, Max Müller, in translating the Sanskrit text of this sutra, rendered its title as "*The Larger Sukhāvatī-vyūha.*"[59] Despite the widespread practice of referring to this sutra as the "Large Sutra," the earliest reference to this sutra as "*Large Sutra*" ("*Ta-ching*") was in Hui-yüan's *Commentary.*[60] Texts compiled after *Commentary* contain numerous references to this sutra as either "Ta-ching" or as inclusive of the character "Ta" in its title. The Tao-ch'o's *An-le chi,* Chia-ts'ai's *Pure Land Treatise* and the *Shan-tao Commentary,* for example, refer to the *Wu-liang-shou-ching* as "*Ta-ching.*"[61] It should be noted that this work is known by other abbreviated titles, "*Ta-pen*" (the Large Text),[62] "*Shou-ching*" (Sutra on [the Buddha of Immeasurable] Life),[63] and "*Shuang-chuan ching*" (the Two Fascicle Sutra).[64]

Hui-yüan seems to have abbreviated the longer title also. *Ta-ching* just as he had abbreviated the titles of other texts into two characters such as, "*Kuan-ching*" for *Kuan-ching.*[65] On one occasion he refers to the sutra as "*Wu-liang-shou ta-ching,*" so that *Ta-ching* could very well have been the abbreviation of the full title by which Hui-yüan knew this sutra.[66] If this were the full title, it would be rendered as "*The Great Sutra on the [Buddha] of Immeasurable Life.*" This, however, is the only occurrence of such a title in either the *Commentary* or in his other writings, including the *Wu-liang-shou ching i-shu.* All the other occurrences of its full title are invariably the "*Wu-liang-shou ching*" *(Sutra on the [Buddha] of Immeasurable Life)* and never include the character "Ta." Among subsequent commentators, Tao-ch'o refers to the sutra as "*Wu-liang-shou ta-ching.*[67]

Yet these titles with the character "Ta" appear to have been anomalies in the overall picture. The extant catalogues compiled up to the second half of seventh century do not refer to this sutra with a character "Ta" as part of the title. For example:

1. In *Ch'u san-tsang chi-chi*: (a) "Hsin wu-liang-shou ching" and (b) "*Wu-liang-shou ching*".[68]
2. In *Chung-ching mu-lu* by Fa-ching, et al.: (a) "*Hsin wu-liang-shou ching*" and (b) "*Wu-liang-shou ching.*"[69]
3. In *Chung-ching mu-lu* by Yen-ts'ung, et al.: "*Wu-liang-shou ching.*"[70]
4. In *Li-tai fa-pao chi* by Fei Ch'ang-fang: (a) "*Wu-liang-shou ching*" and (b) "*Hsin wu-liang-shou ching.*"[71]
5. In *Chung-ching mu-lu* by Ching-t'ai: "*Wu-liang-shou ching.*"[72]

These catalogues indicate that the common full title by which the sutra was known was either "*Wu-liang-shou ching*" or "*Hsin wu-liang-shou ching*" but not "*Wu-liang-shou ta-ching.* Further, Hui-yüan himself also referred to this sutra by its full title as "*Wu-liang-shou ching,*" with the exception of that one occasion when he called it "*Wu-liang-shou ta-ching.*" Of course, Hui-yüan's reference to this latter title is not the only occurrence among Chinese Buddhist texts that includes the character "Ta" in its full title. For example, Tao-ch'o also referred to the sutra as "*Wu-liang-shou ta-ching.*"[73] The *Ching-t'u shih-i lun* (believed to have been compiled sometime between 695 and 774) also refers to a "*Ta wu-liang-shou ching.*"[74] An entry with the same title appears in Ŭich'ŏn's catalogue, the *Sinp'yŏn chejong kyojang ch'ongnok.*[75] But all of these references appear in texts that were compiled subsequent to Hui-yüan's *Commentary.*

The above findings support arguments that the titles that include "Ta" (Large or Great)—be it *Ta-ching* or *Wu-liang-shou ta-ching*—reflect the enhanced regard that this sutra came to acquire. For instance, those who regard the *Nirvāṇa-sūtra* as a main canonical scripture symbolized their high esteem by referring to it by the more elevated "*Ta-ching.*"[76] While Hui-yüan used the title *Ta-ching* in reference to this sutra, there is no reason to believe that he regarded the *Wu-liang-shou-ching* as the most important scripture for either exegetical or devotional purposes. In short, as discussed earlier, no compelling evidence demonstrates that the *Wu-liang-shou-ching* played a central role in his personal doctrinal position or devotional commitment.

Another possibility is that "Ta" implied size, not importance, as in the case of the *Nirvāṇa-sūtra* and that it functioned to set it apart from a related sutra of shorter length. Unfortunately, Hui-yüan himself nowhere refers to a title that includes the word "Hsiao" (Small). The most likely candidate for this shorter sutra could have been the "*Hsiao wu-liang-shou ching*" translated by Guṇabhadra (394–468), which is recorded in Yen-tsung's catalogue *Chung-ching mu-lu.*[77] Also known as the *A-mi-t'o ching,* the "*Smaller Sukhāvatīvyūha Sutra* constitutes one of the triple Pure Land canonical sutras of the Japanese Jōdo and Jōdo Shinshū schools.[78] Hui-yüan, however, does not mention this sutra in either the *Commentary* or the *Wu-liang-shou ching i-shu.*

Tao-ch'o's *An-le chi* is the oldest extant treatise other than the above catalogue to associate the character "Hsiao" with the title of this sutra, "*Hsiao-chüan wu-liang-shou ching.*"[79] This text is listed along with "*Ta-ching*" and "*Kuan-ching*" as three of the six sutras that Tao-ch'o recognized as advocating the abandonment of this world and the aspiration for the Pure Land.[80] Whether Tao-ch'o consciously juxtaposed the "*Hsiao-chüan wu-liang-shou ching*" with the "*Ta-ching*" is unclear, but his use of the word "small" in the same context as "*Ta-ching*" is significant. In some later works, the word "Small" in the title of this *Smaller Sukhāvatīvyūha Sutra* is contrasted instead with an early recension of the *Larger Sukhāvatīvyūha Sutra* translated by Chih-ch'ien.[81]

The rationale remains uncertain not only for Hui-yüan's reference to this sutra as "*Ta-ching*" but also for his inclusion of the word "*Ta*" in the title. It is clear, however, that the *Commentary* is the earliest surviving text to refer to this sutra by a common title that later Pure Land Buddhists in China and Japan then employed. This strongly strengthens the possibility that the practice of referring to the *Wu-liang-shou-ching* as "*Ta-ching*" emerged outside the orthodox Pure Land milieu.

# Chapter Five

## Rebirth: Causes and Ranking

### Causal practices for rebirth: devotion and visualization

*Overall position*

This section examines Hui-yüan's perspective on devotion (*kuei-hsiang*) and on visualization (*kuan*), which in Pure Land Buddhism have been the principal forms of practice for rebirth in the Pure Land. Moreover, it is generally believed that recitation (*ch'eng*), as one form of devotional practice, played a vital role in the popularity and emergence of Pure Land Buddhism. In their view, recitation made Buddhism more accessible to a larger number of lay people than did the more inhibiting and less appealing practice of visualization.[1]

In the section on causes for rebirth, Hui-yüan enumerates the views of the *Larger Prajñāpāramitā Sutra, Nirvāṇa-sūtra, Vimalakīrti-sutra* and Vasubandhu's *Rebirth Treatise.* The causes are "wisdom based on emptiness" for the *Larger Prajñāpāramitā Sutra,* precepts, giving, wisdom and protecting the Dharma in the *Nirvāṇa-sūtra,* the "eight doctrines" for the *Vimalakīrti-sūtra,* and the "five gates," of worship, praise, vow, visualization, and transference of merit in the *Rebirth Treatise.*[2]

He then follows with a list of four causes which, in his view, are explicated by the *Kuan-ching,* namely, (1) the cultivation of visualization (*hsiu-kuan*), (2) the cultivation of acts (*hsiu-yeh*), (3) the cultivation of mind (*hsiu-hsin*), and (4) devotion (*kuei-hsiang*). The first cause is the sixteen visualizations, to which the *Kuan-ching* is primarily devoted, while the second refers to the three purified acts that were taught to Lady Vaidehī at the beginning of the *Kuan-ching.* The third cause, the cultivation of the mind, involves the three minds discussed among the highest grades of rebirth, the sincere mind, the deep mind, and the mind aspiring for rebirth by transferring merit. The fourth refers to the following devotional forms, contemplation (*nien*), worship (*li*), praise (*t'an*), and recitation of his (Amitābha Buddha's) name (*ch'eng-ch'i-ming*).[3]

Even though he deemed visualization the main import of the *Kuan-ching,* his teaching about the four causes reveals Hui-yüan's recognition of a range of other practices. That he did give space to a variety of teachings weakens Yuki Reimon's statement:

> The masters (Hui-yüan, Chi-tsang, etc.) interpreted all forms of Buddha-contemplation . . . in the *Kuan-ching* as the visualization (as opposed to recitative) type of contemplation; and in determining that *this sutra did not advocate the oral recitative [type of contemplation],* they, as previously stated, deemed Buddha-visualization as the main import of this sutra. (emphasis added)[4]

*Devotional*

In light of Yuki's statement above, Hui-yüan's recognition of devotional acts as a legitimate cause for rebirth is of interest. It also points out a serious omission in a description of Hui-yüan's position on the causes for rebirth by a modern scholar:

> In Ching-ying [Hui-yüan's] explanation found in his *Commentary,* he sets forth *three* kinds of methods for rebirth in the Pure Land: (1) rebirth by cultivating, visualization, (2) rebirth by cultivating [purified] acts and (3) rebirth by cultivating the mind.[5]

The failure to mention the fourth cause, devotion, distorts the real nature of Hui-yüan's work, since the causes are explicitly delineated as a set of four in the *Commentary.* The Japanese Pure Land tradition was aware of the four, for Genshin (942–1017) specifically cited them as a set in his *Ōjōyōshū* (Essentials of Pure Land Birth).[6]

Further, Hui-yüan's understanding of devotional acts does not differ drastically from that of the orthodox Pure Land proponents. In regards to the lowest three grades of rebirth, Hui-yüan states:

> Despite the fact that those of the lowest grades have created evil karma in this life, they will gain rebirth [in the Pure Land] through the power of devotion (*kuei-hsiang chih li*) with the virtuous teacher guiding them.[7]

The power derived from carrying out devotional acts with the guidance of the teacher destroys the accumulated evil karma of past transgressions, which the aspirants themselves are unable to overcome on their own.

Moreover, among the four causes, devotion is the only one that Hui-yüan does not regard as an object of cultivation (*hsiu*). This suggests that, for Hui-yüan, actualization of devotion relied less on the efforts of the devotee than did the other three causal practices. Rather, the virtuous teacher plays a greater role than the devotee himself in initiating the devotional acts of the aspiring devotee. The virtuous teacher may either discourse on the three treasures or praise the virtuous qualities of Amitābha Buddha, Bodhisattva Avalokiteśvara, Bodhisattva Mahāsthāmaprāpta, and the exquisite features of the Pure Land. Only as a response to these initiatives can an aspirant for the Pure Land engage in single-minded devotion, in the form of contemplation, worship, praise, or the recitation of the name.

Modern writers contend that the orthodox Pure Land proponents popularized and legitimized recitation as one of the central causal practices.[8] As the first and earliest of these proponents prior to Hui-yüan, T'an-luan discussed the efficacy of recitation in the following passage from his *T'an-luan Commentary:*

> Although those of the lowest grades [of rebirth] cannot comprehend that *dharmatā* (true reality) is unproduced, simply by the power derived from reciting the Buddha's name they produce the resolve to be reborn and aspire to be reborn in that land.[9]

T'an-luan here acknowledges recitation as a practice for rebirth. The recitation, however, generated the resolve and the aspiration but was not, by itself, sufficient for rebirth in the Pure Land.

In another reference to recitation, T'an-luan explains, "'To recite the name of that Tathāgata' means to recite the name of the Tathāgata of Unhindered Light." This provides a straightforward exegesis of a passage from the *Rebirth Treatise,* but does not disclose his own understanding of recitation. Several lines later, T'an-luan responds to a question concerning recitation:

> Question: A name indicates a thing, just as a finger indicates a moon. If, by reciting the name of the Buddha, our aspiration [for rebirth] is fully actualized, then a finger indicating the moon should be able to destroy darkness. But if the finger indicating the moon cannot destroy darkness, then how can reciting the name actualize the aspiration [for rebirth]?
>
> Answer: All things are different and cannot be treated as the same. There are names that are the same as the things [which they indicate], while there are names that are different from the things [they purport to indicate]. The names of Buddhas and Bodhisattvas, of the *Prajñāpāramitā[-sūtra]* and its *dhāraṇī* section, of the incantations and such sound phrases are "names that are the same as the things [they indicate]."[10]

There is another major reference to recitation as a causal practice for rebirth.[11] But this is simply a direct quotation from the section on people of the lowest of the low grade and, thus, does not reveal T'an-luan's own position on the subject.[12]

Besides the above three major references to recitation, there is another in his treatise, the *Lüeh-lun an-le ching-t'u i*:

> Also several like-minded companions should join together in an agreement so that when the end of life [of one of the companions] approaches, they will take turns until dawn reciting the name of the Buddha Amitābha and wish for the rebirth [of the dying companion] in Sukhāvatī. Voice follows upon voice until the ten-contemplations are accomplished.[13]

Like the first example, this again reaffirms that recitation still remains the attainment of a proper state, which in this case is that of the ten-contemplations.

In sum, three of T'an-luan's own discussions on oral recitation do not indicate that oral recitation was for him either a *direct* causal practice or a *sufficient* cause in itself for rebirth. Moreover, he does not express a concerted advocacy of this practice. Thus, it would be difficult to accept the view that T'an-luan advocated oral recitation to the same degree as did the modern writers alluded to earlier. Therefore, coming as it does prior to Tao-ch'o and Shan-tao (though after T'an-luan), Hui-yüan's position on oral recitation takes on greater significance for understanding the historical development of this vital form of practice in Chinese Pure Land Buddhism.

Among those surviving Chinese commentarial texts discussed, Hui-yüan's *Commentary* is the earliest to include recitation as a formal, comprehensive category of causal practice for rebirth comparable to the acclaimed Five Contemplative Gates (*wu-nien-men*) in the *Rebirth Treatise*.[14] It is one thing to recognize a particular form of practice as T'an-luan did, but it is quite another to incorporate it as a formal category of practice as did Hui-yüan.

I contend that the *Commentary*'s formal categorical scheme internalizes to a higher degree an interpretive framework than does a mere incidental reference. A formal category such as Hui-yüan's Four Causes reflects a basic position on a given subject. Moreover, Hui-yüan espouses the Four Causes in the same context as the major Mahayana sutras, namely, the *Larger Prajñāpāramitā,* the *Vimalakīrti,* the *Nirvāṇa* and the Five Contemplative Gates of the *Rebirth Treatise.* That Hui-yüan placed the practice of recitation in the same context as the causal practices expounded in these authoritative scriptures indicates the high degree of legitimacy Hui-yüan accorded to recitation.

Orthodox Japanese Pure Land scholarship, beginning with Hōnen, has made much of Shan-tao's so-called Five Correct Practices (*wu cheng-hsing*), which are believed to represent his basic position on the means of rebirth. They entail single-minded concentration in carrying out, (1) chanting [of sutras], (2) visualization, (3) worship, (4) recitation, and (5) praise and offering.[15] Orthodox Pure Land writers often take Shan-tao's distinction between the "main action" (*cheng-ting-yeh*) of recitation and the four "supportive actions" (*chu-yeh*) as evidence for his emphasis on recitation.[16]

However, the term "five correct practices" does not appear in the *Shan-tao Commentary* but appears for the first time in Hōnen's *Senchakushū.* The five are, thus, a reformulation by Hōnen of Shan-tao's position, one which Shan-tao explained as follows:

> What are the [correct] practices? They are to chant (*tu-sung*) with singleminded concentration (*i-hsin chuan-chu*) this *Kuan-ching,* the *A-mi-t'o ching,* the *Wu-liang-shou ching,* etc.; to formulate in the mind, inspect and recollect (*szu-hsiang kuan-ch'a i-nien*) with singleminded concentration the two-fold rewarded adornments (the animate and the inanimate objects) of that land (*Sukhāvatī*); when worshipping, one should worship (*li*) with singleminded concentration Buddha Amitabha; when orally reciting, one should recite (*ch'eng*) with singleminded concentration the [name of] that Buddha; when praising and making offerings, one should praise and make offerings (*tsan-t'an kung-yang*) with singleminded concentration [to the Buddha]. These are called the "correct [practices]."
>
> Of these correct [practices,] there are again two kinds. One is to contemplate with singleminded concentration the name of Buddha Amitābha, whether walking, standing, sitting or lying, without concern for the length of time, at every moment without abandoning [the practice]. This is called the "main action," as it is in accord with the Buddha's vows. [The practices that] rely on worship, chanting, etc., are called "supportive actions."[17]

It is interesting to point out the similarity between Shan-tao's Five Correct Practices and Hui-yüan's Four Causes, since all the elements of the former can be found in the latter's earlier category. More importantly, the practices retain the same meaning in both lists.[18] Although it is possible that Shan-tao may have partly based the Five Correct Practices on Hui-yüan's category, no conclusive evidence can yet be cited. But Shan-tao's famous list reveals a suggestive comparison with Hui-yüan's little known precedent. Therefore, the allegedly anti-Pure Land Hui-yüan had already recognized recitation as a legitimate cause for rebirth approximately seventy-five years prior to Shan-tao.

### *Visualization*

According to Hui-yüan, "cultivation of visualization" (*hsiu-kuan*) refers to the sixteen visualizations enumerated in the *Kuan-ching.* Hui-yüan's estimation of the '*samādhi* of visualization of the Buddha' (*kuan-fo san-mei*) as the main import of the *Kuan-ching* testifies to the high value he placed on visualization. For Hui-yüan the visualization of the *Buddha* represents all sixteen forms of visualization, including visualizations of the features of the Pure Land and of the Bodhisattvas.[19] In the examination of Hui-yüan's understanding of visualization in general, the focus will be on the "visualization of the Buddha" (henceforth, "Buddha-visualization").

Orthodox backers of Pure Land have portrayed visualization as an extremely difficult form of meditation, hopelessly beyond the capability of the Pṛthagjanas, for whom they felt the Pure Land sutras were written. They deemed those of the "gate of the path of the Āryapudgalas" as the only practitioners capable of visualization.[20] This alleged inaccessibility of visualization to the Pṛthagjanas (the perceived rightful audience of Pure Land teaching) in part accounts for the virtual absence of serious study on visualization related to the *Kuan-ching.*[21] But as seen above, Hui-yüan clearly states that the main import of the *Kuan-ching* is Buddha-visualization and, more importantly, that the *Kuan-ching* is taught for the Pṛthagjanas.[22]

In elucidating the meaning of the title of the *Kuan-ching,* Hui-yüan defines "*kuan-fo*" (Buddha-visualization):

> There are two kinds of Buddha-visualization: the True-body visualization (*chen-shen kuan*) and the Response-body visualization (*ying-shen kuan*). To visualize the Buddha as the body of the impartial Dharma gate is the "True-body visualization." In contrast, to visualize the Buddha as the body of the Tathāgata who shares [characteristics] with a worldly body is called the "Response-body visualization."[23]

Of the two visualizations, Hui-yüan regards the Response-body visualization as the one taught by the *Kuan-ching.* The True-body visualization is expounded in the "Chapter on Visualizing Buddha Akṣobhya" of the *Vimalakīrti-sūtra.* According to the latter sutra, one visualizes the real form (*shih-hsiang*) of the body that "neither comes from the past, departs for the future, nor dwells in the present."[24]

In contrast, the Response-body visualization is said to be taught in the *Kuan-fo san-mei ching* (Sutra on the *Samadhi* of Visualization of the Buddha).[25] This form of visualization calls for the practice of "beholding the Buddha's features and restraining thoughts [in order] to examine [them]." Hui-yüan, then, enumerates two types of Response-body visualization, specific (*pieh*) and general (*t'ung*). He goes on to claim that the *Kuan-ching* expounds the first form, while the above-mentioned *Kuan-fo san-mei ching* explains the latter.[26]

Hui-yüan further divides this specific form of Response-body visualization into the "vision of unrefined pure-faith" (*ts'u ching-hsin chien*) and the "vision of true reality" (*chen-shih chien*), also referred to as the "beginning" (*shih*) and "end" (*chung*) respectively. In the former case, the practitioner listens to the teachings of the Bodhisattva Piṭaka and learns that there are an infinite number of Buddhas in the ten directions of the universe. He then restrains his thoughts and examines [the object], thereby, clearing the mind. In the vision of true reality, the practitioner either has through supernatural powers direct audience or is reborn in a Buddha-land where he is personally able to make offerings to the Buddha.[27]

Since Hui-yüan does not elaborate these points in the *Commentary,* inquiry must look to other texts for a more precise understanding of his "vision of unrefined pure-faith" as one of the two forms of "Response-body visualization." One such text is the *Kuan fo san-mei ching,* which Hui-yüan regards as a scriptural basis for his understanding of the Response-body visualization. Unfortunately, this sutra has not survived, and no extant texts quote passages from it that would be pertinent to our present discussion.[28] It is quite possible that this refers to another sutra with a similar title, the *Kuan fo san-mei hai ching.*[29] Hui-yüan could very well have omitted the character "hai" (sea) from the title. But even in this text there is no quotation from the lost *Kuan-fo san-mei ching.*

A passage in the *T'i-ch'ih ching* (*Bodhisattvabhūmi*) throws light on this visualization:

> [For a Bodhisattva] in this Stage [of Rejoicing] (first Bhūmi) there are two causes for gaining vision of the immeasurable number of Buddhas. [As the first cause,] *by hearing the discourses of the Bodhisattva Piṭaka, he comes to firmly believe and to know about the numerous Buddhas of the immeasurable number of world-realms in the ten quarters.* This is called the "*vision of unrefined pure-faith,*" [whose attainment] then enables him to attain the "*vision of true reality.*" This is the first [of two] causes.[30] (The italicized passages are the same as those in *Commentary.*)

This passage from the *Ti-ch'ih ching* bears a striking resemblance to that of the *Commentary* under discussion. Since he wrote a commentary on this work and cites it on numerous occasions throughout his writings, it is quite safe to assume that Hui-yüan adopted this passage as a basis for the *Commentary's* passages under discussion.[31]

While the meaning of this passage is not wholly clear, a somewhat better understanding of the key terms does emerge. The "vision of unrefined pure-faith" together with "vision of true reality" constitutes the first of two causes for gaining a vision of the Buddhas. The second cause consists in making a vow, as the *Ti-ch'ih ching* explains:

> One also makes the vow, saying "Because the Buddha appeared in the world, I will be reborn there [in that world]." According to such a vow, he will be reborn in the same way as in the vision of unrefined pure-faith, namely by the power of the vow."[32]

Since he uses them interchangeably in the *Commentary,* the "*vision* of unrefined pure-faith" discussed here would be, for Hui-yüan, none other than the "*visualization* of unrefined pure-faith."[33] Also since Hui-yüan would regard the "visualization of unrefined pure-faith" as the same visualization advocated in the *Kuan-ching,* the "vision of unrefined pure-faith" holds the key to unlocking Hui-yüan's understanding of visualization in the *Kuan-ching.*[34]

The above passage from the *Ti-ch'ih ching* does not clarify the vision's relationship to unrefined pure-faith. It is not certain whether the vision is the object or the result of unrefined pure-faith. A later recension of the *Yogācārabhūmi-śāstra,* the *Yü-chia-shih ti-lun* translated by Hsüan-tsang, includes a less ambiguous and more detailed explanation of the same section than did the earlier translation of the *Ti-ch'ih ching*:

> For the Bodhisattvas dwelling in this Stage [of Rejoicing] there are two causes by which they can envision the Buddhas.
>
> By listening to the discourses of the Bodhisattva Piṭaka or by generating a conviction in the mind, they come to believe that there exist numerous Buddhas, Tathāgatas of varying names in the numerous world-realms of varying names in the ten directions. *On account of the mind accompanied by unrefined pure-faith, they seek and desire to manifest the vision [of the Buddhas].* Having completed seeking in this way, true reality is actualized. This is to be known as the first cause. . . .
>
> *Accordingly, the Bodhisattvas gain vision of the Buddhas based on the unrefined trust* and the power of the correct vow. (emphasis added)[35]

A corresponding section from the Sanskrit text of *Bodhisattvabhūmi* reveals virtually the same idea as the above Chinese text.[36] The underscored passage clearly explicates that vision (*chien*; *darśana*) is the outcome of unrefined pure-faith or of the "mind of unrefined pure-faith" (*audārikā-prasāda-sahāgatena cetasā*). If this agrees with Hui-yüan's understanding of the terms, it follows that he understood the term to mean "vision *derived from* unrefined pure-faith." In other words, the realization of unrefined pure-faith leads to the vision of the Buddhas.

This is the initial level of visualization, which finally culminates in the "vision of true reality." But this "vision of true reality" is not the kind advocated in the *Kuan-ching.* Hence, for Hui-yüan, the visualization that the *Kuan-ching* advocates is only the third of the three types of visualization which he mentions: (1) visualization of the True-body, (2) visualization of true reality as one form of visualization of the Response-body, and (3) visualization of unrefined pure-faith within visualization of the Response-body. This suggests that Hui-yüan ranked these three in the order of difficulty with the first being the most difficult to perform and attain. As Hui-yüan referred to them as "end" and "beginning" for the second and third types, respectively, the precise relationship for the latter two is clearly stated.

*Chih-kuan* (*śamatha-vipaśyanā*) is the best known meditation technique of Chinese Buddhism. A comparison of visualization with that meditative form should be helpful in clarifying Hui-yüan's understanding of visualization. Chih-i defines *chih-kuan* in the *Mo-ho chih-kuan*:

> *Chih* and *kuan* each have three meanings, which [in the case of *chih*] are: 1) ceasing, 2) stopping and 3) the combating of non-*chih*. . . . *Kuan* also has three meanings: 1) the piercing, 2) the penetration of *kuan* and 3) the combating of non-*kuan.*[37]

Even a cursory glance discloses how much closer the visualization of Hui-yüan is to *chih* (*śamatha*) than to *kuan* (*vipaśyanā*). "To behold the Buddha's features and restrain one's thoughts from examining them"[38] describes Hui-yüan's visualization, which accords closely with Chih-i's definition of ceasing and stopping. According to Chih-i, "ceasing" encompasses the quieting and ceasing of deluded thoughts and concepts, while "stopping" involves the "restraining of present thoughts so that they stay stationary and not move."[39]

In contrast, *kuan* for Chih-i takes on an element of wisdom that Hui-yüan's understanding of visualization lacks. One of the meanings of *kuan,* "piercing," is described by Chih-i as "wisdom which through its incisive usage pierces through and destroys blind passion.[40] Another meaning of *kuan,* "penetration," also takes on a quality of wisdom as it characterizes, "the penetration of the wisdom of *kuan* which leads one to merge with suchness."[41] The following statement in his *Commentary* further demonstrates that Hui-yüan's emphasis on visualization finally rested on concentration and calming the mind (i.e., *śamatha*): "The *samādhi* of Buddha-visualization is called '*ting*' (concentration or meditation).[42] His *Mahayana Encyclopedia* sets forth "concentration" as, "Because the mind dwells on one object and does not scatter or move, it is called 'concentration'."[43] Again, the element of wisdom (*vipaśyanā*) found in Chih-i's definition of "kuan" is conspicuously absent.

The next question concerns the stage in the Path (*mārga*) at which this form of visualization is practiced. A definitive answer to this question would be crucial for challenging the traditional claim that denied to the Pṛthagjanas the capacity to cultivate visualization.

As seen above, Hui-yüan regarded the *Kuan-ching* to be for Pṛthagjanas and the import of the *Kuan-ching* to be the '*samādhi* of Buddha-visualization.' Thus, clearly Hui-yüan did not regard the Āryapudgalas as the prime practitioner in the context of the *Kuan-ching.* Another statement in the *Commentary* further supports this:

> Further, coarse lands are generally for the rebirth of Pṛthagjanas whose life spans are limited and subject to transmigration. The subtle lands, however, are only for Āryapudgalas who are capable of creating their bodies at will in the realm of transmigration. The country of Buddha Amitābha is among the coarse pure lands. . . . The *Kuan-ching* is concerned only with coarse pure land.[44]

Hui-yüan does not elaborate in the *Commentary* on the exact Pṛthagjana stages at which the visualization is practiced. But a clue to this appears in Hui-yüan's understanding of "unrefined pure-faith." Though not exactly "*unrefined* pure-faith," Hui-yüan's *Mahayana Encyclopedia* on "pure-faith" states:

> [The Buddhist Path] is sometimes divided into five [categories]. That of the Good Destinies (*shan-ch'ü*) is the first. Because one understands and cultivates pure-faith, this [category] is called [the stage of] Ten-Faiths in the *Ying-lo [ching].*[45]

In another statement from the same text, Hui-yüan explains:

> At the rank of Good Destinies, one cultivates pure-faith to separate oneself from the actions of the Icchantikas (one destitute of virtuous nature). The [pure-faith] is then established at the stages of Lineage (*gotrabhū) (chung-hsing*) and Practice of Resolution (*adhimukticaryā) (chieh-hsing*).
>
> One shall, thereby, be eternally separated from the three kinds of evil actions [of the Icchantikas]: the Vilification of Dharma, the Four Grave Transgressions and the Five Grave Offenses.[46]

In the *Commentary,* Hui-yüan regards the thirteenth visualization in the *Kuan-ching* to be meant for even the lowest among the Pṛthagjana ranks:

> The following gate (thirteenth visualization) repeats the description of the visualization of the Buddha and of the [two] Bodhisattvas [which was previously discussed as the eighth visualization]. "Why was

> it necessary to repeat?" It was necessary because the visualization of the Buddha and the Bodhisattvas discussed earlier could not be fathomed by the lowest among the Pṛthagjanas; hence, it is repeated to teach [all] Pṛthagjanas to visualize and inspect [the images].[47]

Based on these passages, practitioners begin the cultivation of pure-faith quite early in the Path, at the stage of the Good Destinies. They then realize their goals in the two higher Pṛthagjana stages of Lineage and of the Practice of Resolution. As seen above in the *Yogācārabhūmi-śāstra,* because pure-faith constituted the basis for the attainment of visualization, it is safely concluded that Hui-yüan believed visualization to be cultivated by practitioners in the stages of Lineage or the Practice of Resolution. Moreover, according to the last passage, he recognized one of the sixteen visualizations to be meant specifically for inferior beings as low on the Path as those of the lowest Pṛthagjana rank.

The *Yogācārabhūmi-śāstra* construes the stages of Good Destinies, Lineage and Practice of Resolution as Pṛthagjana stages, which constitute one of the traditional Buddhist Paths.[48] These correspond to ranks belonging to another well-known Path: Good Destinies correspond to Ten-Faiths (*shih-hsin*) and below, Lineage to Ten-Dwellings (*shih-chu*) and Ten-Practices (*shih-hsing*), and Practice of Resolution to Ten-Transferences (*shih hui-hsiang*). In addition the Pṛthagjanas are divided into two categories of the Inner (*nei-fan*) and the Outer (*wai-fan*). This can be illustrated as follows (see appendix 1 for further detail):

| | | |
|---|---|---|
| Bhūmis. . . . . . . . . | Bhūmis. . . . . . . . . . . . . . | .Āryapudgalas |
| Practice of. . . . . . Cultivation | .Ten-Transferences | Inner Pṛthagjanas |
| Lineage. . . . . . . . | Ten-Practices<br>Ten-Dwellings (or Ten-Understandings) | |
| Good Destinies . . . | Ten-Faiths | . . . Outer Pṛthagjanas |

The accessibility of visualization practice accorded to Pṛthagjanas by Hui-yüan differs markedly from its inavailability to them, which orthodox Pure Land writers adamantly maintained. The following statement summarizes the orthodox position on the "visualization" formulated by Hui-yüan and other masters of the 'path of the sages':

> First, both the visualization of the Buddha and visualization of the pure lands are visualizations based on the wisdom of emptiness, which is not in keeping [with the capability of] Pṛthagjanas.[49]

Differences arise in the interpretation of the term "*fan-fu*" (Pṛthagjana; Japanese *bonpu*) and "*sheng-jen*" (Āryapudgalas; Japanese *shōnin*) between Hui-yüan and the orthodox Pure Land school. First, as the following three passages from the *Mahayana Encyclopedia* indicate, Hui-yüan understood *fanfu* to mean 'those in the stages below the first Bhūmi':[50]

> 1) How do we know they are prior to the Bhūmis?
> The sutra (*Nirvāṇa-sūtra*) itself calls those below the Bhūmis, "*fan-fu*."
> 2) Those below the Bhūmis are called "*fan[-fu],*" while those in the Bhūmis are called "*sheng[-jen].*"
> 3) Because the term "*sheng*" is used in a restricted sense, those prior to the Path of Insight (*darśana-mārga*) are called "*fan-fu*" and those with the truth of [the Path of] Insight and above are called "*sheng.*"

But the orthodox Japanese Pure Land position as represented by Rei'ō has maintained "*fan-fus*" to mean those below the Ten-Faith stages.[51] Ohara Shojitsu, for example, concurs; he argues that Hui-yüan ranked *all* nine grades as Āryapudgalas (*sheng-jen*), simply because, in his eyes, Hui-yüan ranked even the lower three grades either as Outer Pṛthagjanas or as those of the Ten-Faith stages.[52] For the orthodox Pure Land position, therefore, the "Pṛthagjanas" (*fan-fu*) are those below the Ten-Faith stages, while the "Āryapudgalas" refer to those of the Ten-Faith or Outer Pṛthagjanas and above. Thus, this reveals a difference in the definition of "*fan-fu.*" But modern writers either do not make this distinction or are not precise in their usage of the term *fan-fu*. Consequently, they assume Hui-yüan agreed with their own definition of the term.[53]

Hui-yüan meant *sheng-jen* to include those in the Bhūmi stages as stated in the following *Mahayana Encyclopedia* passage:

> In dividing the [Path] into two [categories], one is *fan* (Pṛthagjanas) and the second is *sheng* (Āryapudgalas). . . . Those of the Bhūmis are called "*sheng.*"[54]

The orthodox Pure Land view lowers the limit to admit those of the Ten-Faiths stages, as discussed above in Ohara's assessment of Hui-yüan's ranking. The orthodox position assumes more ranks on the Path under the category of Āryapudgalas than does Hui-yüan's. Thus, the point of contention narrows to interpreting the forty stages below the Bhūmis, that is, the Ten-Transferences, the Ten Practices, the Ten-Dwellings (or Ten-Understandings), and the Ten-Faiths. Hui-yüan calls them "Pṛthagjanas," while the orthodox writers refer to them as "Āryapudgalas."

This practice of modern Japanese writers harkens back to the Chinese master Shan-tao. In the *Shan-tao Commentary,* Shan-tao describes the upper three rankings of the nine grades of rebirth by the so-called masters:

> The highest of the high grade refers to the Bodhisattvas from the fourth Bhūmi up to the seventh Bhūmi. The middle of the high grade refers to Bodhisattvas from the first Bhūmi up to the fourth Bhūmi. . . . The lowest of the high grade refers to Bodhisattvas from the Lineage stages up to the first Bhūmi. . . . All these people of the three grades constitute the ranks wherein the Āryapudgalas of Mahayana are reborn.[55]

The Bodhisattvas of Lineage and above (the lowest of the high grade) listed here are equal to the Inner Pṛthagjanas discussed above. But Shan-tao clearly includes them in the category that he calls the "Āryapudgalas of Mahayana." This ranking of the "masters," which will be discussed in greater detail in the next section, is clearly Hui-yüan's. While Shan-tao's description remains, by in large, faithful to Hui-yüan's, the reference to those at the levels of Lineage and above as "Āryapudgalas" departs from Hui-yüan's *Commentary.*[56] Chia-ts'ai, a contemporary of Shan-tao and a proponent of Pure Land teaching, also regarded the Inner and Outer Pṛthagjanas as Āryapudgalas in his *Pure Land Treatise.*[57] It appears that the other Chinese Buddhists of this period were divided on this subject.[58]

Hence, the apparent differences in the two rankings of the visualization practitioners are largely rooted in the diverse understanding of the term *fan-fu* (Pṛthagjanas). When the orthodox writers exclude visualization as a practice for the *fan-fu,* they are really dismissing the Pṛthagjanas below the Ten-Faiths level. On the one hand, they fall into agreement with Hui-yüan who similarly withholds cultivation of visualization from Pṛthagjanas of such *low* rankings. On the other hand, when orthodox writers extend visualization to only the Āryapudgalas, they intend only those at the stage of Ten-Faiths and above. But, for Hui-yüan, the same group is not composed of Āryapudgalas but of Pṛthagjanas. Both sides concur that the Bhūmi stages are for Āryapudgalas. But they differ on the stages from the Ten-Faiths up to the Ten-Transferences.

Aside from semantics, another possible reason surfaces for the difference of opinion surrounding the Pṛthagjanas' ability to cultivate visualization. This arises from orthodoxy's assertion that Hui-yüan regarded Lady Vaidehī, the main interlocutor and the cultivator of visualization in the *Kuan-ching,* as an Āryapudgala. Thus, the visualizations espoused in the *Kuan-ching* were evidently meant for Āryapudgalas such as Lady Vaidehī. As primary evidence for their argument, the orthodox writers have traditionally cited the following statement from Hui-yüan's *Commentary*:

> In sub-segment five, "The Buddha saying to Vaidahī, 'you are a Pṛthagjana'" refers to her capabilities. "You are unable to see far" reveals what Vaidehī is incapable of [doing]. Lady Vaidehī is in reality a great Bodhisattva (*ta p'u-sa*). At this setting in the sutra, "she obtained the Insight of Non-arising" reports how [the Buddha] knew that she was not of the small [vehicle] (Hinayana) but that she appeared as a [Mahayana] Pṛthagjana.[59]

The Pure Land orthodox position has interpreted the term "great Bodhisattva" as referring to an Āryapudgala. In this term's single occurrence in the *Commentary,* Hui-yüan regarded Vaidehī as having realized the "Insight into the Non-arising of *dharmas*," attained by Bodhisattvas of the seventh, eighth, and ninth Bhūmis.[60] These Bhūmi stages belonged to the Āryapudgalas and not to the Pṛthagjanas.

However, even if she were in reality a great Bodhisattva, this would not directly bear on the immediate issue of visualization as a practice for the Pṛthagjanas. Based on Hui-yüan's above statement, Lady Vaidehī embodies a great Bodhisattva only in the sense of ultimate reality. But in actual existence she remains a Pṛthagjana. Ultimately, she is a great Bodhisattva. But in the penultimate context of performing the visualization, she is still a Pṛthagjana who had to receive instructions from the Buddha on the sixteen visualizations.[61] By receiving instruction, she becomes not a great Bodhisattva but an enfeebled Pṛthagjana, as the Buddha expressly stated in the *Kuan-ching*:

> You are but a Pṛthagjana, and your mental faculties are feeble and inferior. Since you have yet to attain divine perception, you are unable to see far. But the Tathāgatas possess various provisional means to enable you to see [that land].[62]

Orthodox writers have failed to correctly locate the *context* in which Hui-yüan identified Vaidehī as a "great Bodhisattva." His description in no way should be construed, as they do, to argue that Hui-yüan regarded visualization as practice meant for the Āryapudgalas and not for the Pṛthagjanas.

## The ranking of the nine grades of rebirth

### *Background*

Undoubtedly, the most widely discussed and hotly debated issue of the *Kuan-ching* by its commentators of the Sui and early T'ang periods focused on the ranking of the nine grades of people (*chiu-p'in wang-sheng*) for rebirth in the Pure Land. The nine grades are: (1) the highest of the high grades, (2) the middle of the high grades, (3) the lowest of the high grades, (4) the highest of the middle grades, (5) the middle of the middle grades, (6) the lowest of the middle grades, (7) the highest of the low grades, (8) the middle of the low grades, and (9) the lowest of the low grades.[63] Every known author of extant commentaries on the *Kuan-ching* tried his hand at ranking the nine grades within the framework of the traditional Buddhist Path. Although the *Kuan-ching* was the only sutra to discuss the nine grades, this issue so captivated Pure Land exegetes that even authors in treatises and commentaries on other sutras felt compelled to express their views on the subject.[64]

Previous studies on this subject have highlighted the different rankings formulated by the various commentators, with particular attention paid to those of Hui-yüan and Shan-tao. The authors of these modern studies contrast what they regard as Hui-yüan's unduly high ranking of the nine grades with Shan-tao's comparatively low ranking.[65] They often use these discussions as foils for their criticism of Hui-yüan's overall interpretation of the *Kuan-ching.* But they have not allowed Hui-yüan to speak for himself. They have failed not only to examine the context in which Hui-yüan assigned the rankings but also to appreciate the significance of Hui-yüan's contributions to this subject.

Hui-yüan's contribution is all the more significant because it is the earliest known ranking of the nine grades. In the absence of later reference to Ling-yü's lost commentary to the *Kuan-ching,* it is unknown if this work considered this issue. But Hui-yüan's views are cited in several of the later works as seen below. His views were well-known and apparently were even regarded by some of the later commentators as the standard statement on this subject. As a prime example, it was Hui-yüan's ranking that Shan-tao attacked.

*Unjustified criticism of Hui-yüan's ranking*

Hui-yüan's ranking of the nine grades can be delineated as follows:[66]

| | | |
|---|---|---|
| 1. highest of high | Mahayana | Fourth Bhūmi and above |
| 2. middle of high | " | First three Bhūmis |
| 3. lowest of high | " | Practice of Resolution and Lineage stages |
| 4. highest of middle | Hinayana | People of the initial three [Ārya-pudgala] stages (Stream-winner, Once-returner, Non-returner) |

| | | | |
|---|---|---|---|
| 5. | middle of middle | " | Inner and Outer Pṛthagjanas prior to Path of Insight |
| 6. | lowest of middle | " | Worldly Pṛthagjanas prior to Path of Insight |
| 7. | highest of low | Mahayana | Outer Pṛthagjanas. Those who have begun to train in the Mahayana path. They are not even in the Path ranking.[67] |
| 8. | middle of low | " | " |
| 9. | lowest of low | " | " |

Shan-tao's ranking is as follows:[68]

| | | | |
|---|---|---|---|
| 1. | highest of high | Mahayana | [Pṛthagjanas] of utmost virtue |
| 2. | middle of high | " | Mahayana Pṛthagjanas |
| 3. | lowest of high | " | [Pṛthagjanas] who generate the Mahayana mind |
| 4. | highest of middle | Hinayana | Pṛthagjanas who observe Hinayana precepts |
| 5. | middle of middle | " | Pṛthagjanas without virtues |
| 6. | lowest of middle | " | [Pṛthagjanas] who have not encountered the Buddha Dharma [prior to their deathbed] |
| 7. | highest of low | Mahayana | Pṛthagjanas who require the help of a teacher |
| 8. | middle of low | " | [Pṛthagjanas] who cannot maintain [precepts] |
| 9. | lowest of low | " | [Pṛthagjanas] who commit such evil acts as the Five Grave Transgressions and the Ten Evils |

As is evident here, the ranks assigned by Hui-yüan are clearly higher. Shan-tao's ranking of the highest of the high grade is ranked equal to or even lower than Hui-yüan's lowest of the low. No one disputes this fact. But this poses the question about Hui-yüan's rationale for the higher ranking.

Orthodox writers have traditionally explained Hui-yüan's higher ranking by citing Chia-ts'ai's statement in his *Pure Land Treatise.*

> I shall now rank the nine grades of persons of rebirth based on the *Kuan-ching*. Since of old, the eminent Dharma Master Hui-yüan and others have ranked the persons by looking at the effect (*kuo*); consequently, the ranks have been quite high. I will now rank them based on the cause [*yin*), thereby, the ranks will be somewhat lower.[69]

They have understood Hui-yüan's assigned ranks as pertaining to rebirth in the Pure Land, rather than to life in the present Sahā world. The high rankings were intended to motivate the aspirants to higher birth. In contrast, the rankings of both Shan-tao and of Chia-ts'ai denote the various spiritual stages of the aspirants while they are still in this world.

Hui-yüan's *Commentary,* however, does not support this explanation, since his rankings are also attained in this world. The rank distinctions are acquired *prior* to the practitioners reaching the Pure Land, since their ranks determine the lengths of time to be spent in the lotus flower of the Pure Land before their ultimate rebirth. For example, those of the highest of the high grade spend virtually no time, the middle of the high grade spend overnight, while those of the lowest of the high one day and one night.[70] Moreover, the one rank that is attained in the Pure land is the Insight of Non-arising. No other rank is mentioned. The varying lengths of time required upon rebirth for the attainment of the Insight of Non-arising are based on the ranking acquired prior to reaching the Pure Land.[71]

Since the *Commentary* does not corroborate the traditional orthodox answer, an explanation for Hui-yüan's comparatively higher ranking must be properly sought in the context of the *Commentary* itself. For Hui-yüan, the nine grades comprised the object of the fourteenth, fifteenth, and sixteenth of the sixteen visualizations. In initiating the discussion on the section on the nine grades, Hui-yüan explains:

> The following three visualizations are to be consolidated into the same category under "visualizations on the rebirths of other [people]," in which one visualizes the features involved in the rebirths of the nine grades of people.
>
> "Why does one visualize them?" They are visualized in order to make the people of the world realize that they can ascend to higher [grades] or descend to lower [grades] based on their actions causing rebirth and that it is possible for them to cultivate and be reborn [in the higher grade]. For this reason, the *Kuan-ching* encourages this set of visualizations.[72]

Hui-yüan explicitly assigns the nine grades as *objects* of visualization that directly inspire the devotees engaged in the visualizations towards higher ranks of rebirth in the Pure Land.

Shan-tao, in contrast, treated the nine grades not as objects of visualization but as descriptive statements of the nature and capability of the devotees, with Vaidehī as an example of such a devotee. Shan-tao's fundamentally different approach appears in his criticism of Hui-yüan's assignment of the upper two grades for Bodhisattvas of the First to Sixth Bhūmis. To substantiate that such Bodhisattvas could not possibly be treated on the same level with the lowly Vaidehī, Shan-tao enumerates a litany of superior accomplishments for such Bodhisattvas, which include the absence of suffering, the span of the Bodhisattva career over two great immeasurable Kalpas, the cultivation of virtues and wisdom as well as the dual emptiness of person (*jen; pudgala*) and *dharmas* (*fa*), the freedom of their supernatural powers, their unrestricted ability to be transformed, their dwelling in the Rewarded-land, and their compassionate preaching to beings of the ten directions. For Shan-tao, therefore, such Bodhisattvas need not resort to a Pṛthagjana such as Vaidehī who would petition the Buddha on their behalf to teach them about rebirth in the Pure Land.[73] These concerns make it clear that Shan-tao regarded the aspirants of the nine grades in the same context as that of Vaidehī.

Based on Shan-tao's argument in the *Shan-tao Commentary,* modern commentators have rejected Hui-yüan's ranking because they insist that the instruction of the *Kuan-ching* was for the Pṛthagjanas, not, as Hui-yüan and other masters claim, for the Āryapudgalas.[74] Therefore, they argue that the nine grades cannot be assigned to the Āryapudgala stages as Hui-yüan did.

The basis of this rejection, however, rests on an inadequate understanding of Hui-yüan's position. Hui-yüan never contended that the *Kuan-ching* was intended for the Āryapudgalas. In fact, he expressly makes this point in the very beginning of the *Commentary*:

> It is known [to be a sutra of the sudden teaching] because this sutra was taught specifically for Vaidehī, who, as will be explained below, was a Pṛthagjana.[75]

Later Hui-yüan reaffirms this position in his explanation of the nature of Sukhāvatī, which he regards as belonging to the category of coarse rather than subtle pure lands. In the coarse pure lands, only the Pṛthagjanas whose life-spans are limited, are reborn.[76] Hence, even given the nature of Pure Land, Hui-yüan considered the *Kuan-ching* as instruction for Pṛthagjanas and not for Āryapudgalas.

These modern writers have based their criticism of Hui-yüan's position on Shan-tao's statement in the *Shan-tao Commentary.* In response to questions raised about his contention that the *Kuan-ching* was preached for the sake of Pṛthagjanas rather than for Āryapudgalas, Shan-tao cites ten passages from the *Kuan-ching* and concludes the section by explaining:

> Even though the above ten passages are not exactly the same [in content], they prove my point that the Tathāgata taught the sixteen visualization methods solely for the sake of sentient beings who are continually wallowing [in *saṃsāra*] and not for the Āryapudgalas of Mahayana or Hinayana.[77]

Yet Hui-yüan would have no qualms with this position. As he also advocated the compatibility of the Pṛthagjanas with that visualization, this quotation provides an invalid basis for refuting Hui-yüan's higher ranking.

This poses the question about Shan-tao's employing this inappropriate argument against Hui-yüan's ranking. As discussed above, Shan-tao and others assumed that practitioners of the visualizations comprised the same kind of people as those of the nine grades. The section on the nine grades, therefore, amounts to a description of the aspirants who are, if not identical, then at least in a similar predicament as Vaidehī and the other Pṛthagjanas, for whom the *Kuan-ching* was preached. This is most clearly reflected in Shan-tao's statement:

> What worries could they (Bodhisattvas of the Bhūmis) still have which would make them rely on [the lowly] Vaidehī to request the Buddha, on their behalf, [for a teaching] to aspire to be reborn in Sukhāvatī?[78]

Here Shan-tao assumes that the Āryapudgalas (in Hui-yüan's ranking) are in the same position as Vaidehī in being recipients of the teaching of the *Kuan-ching*. Shan-tao, of course, rejects the notion that Āryapudgalas would depend on Vaidehī. But crucial for this immediate discussion is Shan-tao's operating assumption that the Āryapudgalas of the nine grades can be treated in the same context as Vaidehī.

In contrast, Hui-yüan treats them as two separate groups of people. While the people comprising the nine grades of rebirth are the objects of Vaidehī's visualization, Vaidehī and the other Pṛthagjanas are themselves the practitioners of the visualization for whom the *Kuan-ching* was preached. Previous writers have noted that Hui-yüan regarded the people of the nine grades as objects of Vaidehī's visualization.[79] Yet no one has recognized Hui-yüan's implicit treatment of Vaidehī and the nine grades of people as two distinct categories of persons. It is for this reason that Hui-yüan could, on one hand, agree with Shan-tao that the *Kuan-ching* was taught for the Pṛthagjanas, while, on the other hand, rank some of the nine grades as Āryapudgalas. Hence, Shan-tao's argument is invalid, since it fails to take into account the different premise on which Hui-yüan bases his position.

*The significance of Hui-yüan's ranking*

Beside the unjustified criticism discussed above, Hui-yüan's ranking has not received proper recognition for its significant accomplishments and for its role in the subsequent commentarial tradition of the *Kuan-ching.* In short, Hui-yüan's contribution lies in having successfully integrated the nine grades into the orthodox Buddhist Path. Furthermore, it not only constituted the earliest known ranking of this sort but also served as the standard interpretation of this subject for many subsequent commentators.

It appears that the *Jen-wang ching* (The Benevolent King Sutra) provided the scriptural basis for Hui-yüan's ranking of the highest three grades. These grades correspond generally to the five kinds of Insight (*jen*; *kṣānti*), which Hui-yüan identified elsewhere in the *Commentary* as the *Jen-wang ching* position on the subject: (1) the Suppressive Insight (*fu-jen*) attained in the Lineage and Practice of Resolution stages, (2) the Faith Insight (*hsin-jen*) attained in the Second and Third Bhūmi stages, (3) the Accordance Insight (*shun-jen*) realized in the Fourth, Fifth, and Sixth Bhūmi stages, (4) the Non-arising Insight (*wu-sheng jen*) acquired in the Seventh, Eighth, and Ninth Bhūmi stages, and (5) the Extinction Insight (*chi-mieh jen*) attained in the Tenth Bhūmi and above.[80] The following illustrates the correspondence between the Five Insights and Hui-yüan's ranking with the highest grade listed first:

| *Five insights of Jen-wang ching* | Hui-yüan's ranking |
|---|---|
| 1. Extinction Insight | |
| 2. Non-arising Insight: 7th, 8th, and 9th Bhūmis | Highest of the high: 4th Bhūmi and above[81] |
| 3. Accordance Insight: 4th, 5th, and 6th Bhūmis | |
| 4. Faith Insight: [1st], 2nd, and 3rd Bhūmis | Middle of the high: 1st, 2nd, and 3rd Bhūmis[82] |
| 5. Suppressive Insight: Lineage and Practice of Resolution | Lowest of the high: Lineage and Practice of Resolution stages |

While the Insights from the *Jen-wang ching* provided the framework, it was the temporal duration required for attaining the Insight of Non-arising, the second of the five Insights, that constituted the main criterion for correlating the three grades with three of the five Insights. In other words, what prevented Hui-yüan from assigning the middle of the high grade to Accordance Insight rather than to the Faith Insight? The overriding yardstick was the Non-arising Insight. Hui-yüan explains:

> They are the Bhūmis of the Non-arising [Insight], since those [of the highest of the high grades] obtain the Insight of Non-arising *immediately* upon being reborn there. . . . Those Bodhisattvas of the first, second and third Bhūmis who have obtained Faith Insight are ranked as the middle of the high grades. Because of this the sutra (*Kuan-ching*) states that they obtain the Insight of Non-arising in one small Kalpa after being reborn there.[83]

Hui-yüan ranked the three middle grades in the context of the traditional Hinayana path. Since these ranks possess a general nature and no specific sutra is associated with the Hinayana path in the *Commentary,* it would be difficult, if not impossible, to locate the scriptural source for these rankings. Nonetheless, the time required for the attainment of the Arhat and Stream-winner ranks served as the primary criterion in Hui-yüan's ranking.

Hui-yüan assigned the highest of the middle grades to the first three Āryapudgala stages on the basis of the *Kuan-ching*'s statement that those of this grade attain the Arhat rank immediately upon rebirth in the Pure Land. He reasoned that if one attained Arhatship immediately on rebirth, then he must occupy a rank immediately prior to that of the Arhat. That the middle of the middle grades is ranked as a stage of the Inner and Outer Pṛthagjanas follows from the *Kuan-ching* passage in which those of this grade attain the Stream-winner rank seven days after rebirth in the Pure Land. The lowest of the middle is the rank of the secular Pṛthagjana. This issues from the *Kuan-ching* statement that one full Kalpa, compared to half a Kalpa for the middle of the middle grades, passes in the Pure Land before the Arhat rank is attained.[84]

Previous writers have determined that Hui-yüan ranked the three lowest grades as Outer Pṛthagjanas.[85] However, this is not quite accurate, for he assigned these grades to more ranks than that of the Outer Pṛthagjanas. His opening remark in the section on the ranking of the lowest three grades states, "Among the Mahayanists, the Outer Pṛthagjanas with karmic evil are of the [three] lowest grades."[86] Hui-yüan further explains that the three grades include those who have just initiated training in the Mahayana, and are ranked by the kind of transgressions committed. Since they have not yet entered the Path, it is difficult to determine their exact ranking.[87] Elsewhere, Hui-yüan ranks those of the three grades even lower, that is to say, at levels below Good Destinies.[88]

Thus, based on the three explanations of the *Commentary,* the assigned ranks for the lowest three grades encompassed a wide range of ranks from the upper limit of the Outer Pṛthagjanas to the lower limit of those below the ranks of Good Destinies who had not even entered the Path.

The degree of seriousness for the transgressions constituted the determining factor for the differences among the ranking of the three grades. But Hui-yüan does not draw clear distinctions among the three grades, due, as he admits, to the difficulty of ranking people who have not yet entered the Path.

We must therefore reject the traditional view of orthodox Pure Land writers that Hui-yüan ranked *all* nine grades as Āryapudgala.[89] Even by the orthodox Pure Land Buddhist usage of the term "Āryapudgalas," Hui-yüan assigned to the three grades those who were clearly not Āryapudgalas, such as those below the rank of Good Destinies.

Hui-yüan intended the ranking of the nine grades to encourage practitioners and devotees to aspire to higher grades of rebirth. But he does not discuss the reasons for placing the nine grades in the framework of the more traditional Buddhist Path, especially when the hierarchy among the nine grades was quite explicit in the *Kuan-ching.* The evident hierarchy of the nine grades in the sutra could have adequately motivated the Pure Land aspirants to be reborn in a higher grade.

One plausible reason may be that Hui-yüan's ranking attempted to gain a wider appeal by using a better known, established category of the Buddhist community, especially of his scholar-monk colleagues and students. This was necessitated because prior to the year 550 C.E. the *Kuan-ching* did not enjoy wide circulation among the Buddhist commentators. Not only was the *Kuan-ching* a relatively obscure text, but also the category of nine grades was virtually unknown.[90] Among the existent Buddhist literature available in Hui-yüan's time, the only reference to a categorical division of nine-grades appears in the *Mahāvibhāṣā-śāstra.*[91] Hui-yüan knew of this category for he discusses it in his *Mahayana Encyclopedia.*[92] There is, however, no evidence that this category was well-known. Further, there is no compelling reason to believe that this *Mahāvibhāṣā* reference had any influence on Hui-yüan's ranking of the nine grades, since the *Mahāvibhāṣā* grades are not referred to collectively as the "nine grades" and, more importantly, have nothing to do with rebirth in the Pure Land.

In contrast, the Bhūmi category to which Hui-yüan assigned the two highest grades commanded wide recognition within the 'Hui-kuang lineage." Hui-kuang, Fa-shang, and Ling-yü, for example, wrote commentaries on at least one of the two texts that dealt at length with the Bhūmi ranks, the *Avataṃsaka-sutra* and Vasubandhu's *Daśabhūmika-śāstra.* The Lineage and Practice of Resolution stages to which the lowest of the high grades was assigned, are discussed in the *Ti-ch'ih ching,* another popular and widely circulated sutra of Hui-yüan's time, especially among Hui-yüan's circle.[93]

Further, these ranks are frequently discussed throughout the *Mahayana*

*Encyclopedia.* In fact, "rank" (*wei*) makes up one of the standard exegetical categories Hui-yüan employs in explaining many entries.[94] For example, Hui-yüan explicates the meaning of "five wisdoms" through these five categories: (1) characteristics, (b) esssence, (c) affliction and non-affliction, (d) rank, and (e) person. In explaining the five wisdom based on rank, Hui-yüan mentions the same stages as employed in the *Commentary* ranking of the nine grades of rebirths: Inner and Outer Pṛthagjanas, the Bhūmis, and Lineage.[95] These ranks are further employed in numerous other entries of the *Mahayana Encyclopedia,* such as *dhāraṇī* and six *pāramitās.*[96] Since the *Mahayana Encyclopedia* is believed to reflect the mainstream doctrinal position and concerns of the Buddhist community in north China during the early and mid-sixth century, their occurrence in this text indicates their general acceptance and utilization during Hui-yüan's time.[97]

As previously noted, Hui-yüan's *Commentary* marks the oldest known work to rank the nine grades, especially since Ling-yü's 'lost' commentary is nowhere mentioned in connection with the ranking of the nine grades. Though a more definitive answer requires further study, undoubtedly Hui-yüan played a key role in promoting, if not in initiating, this practice. The ranking of the nine grades in the context of the traditional Path is found in virtually every surviving subsequent commentary on the *Kuan-ching.* The following is a synopsis of the rankings in the major works:

1. Chi-tsang's commentary: Bodhisattvas of sixth Bhūmi (highest of high and middle of high grades) and first Bhūmi (lowest of high); those who attain Hinayana Āryapudgala ranks (middle grades); those who attain Mahayana effects (low grades).[98]
2. The Tun-huang manuscripts by an anonymous author: the last mind in the Ten-Transferences stages, the Ten-Understandings and Ten-Practices stages, and the Ten-Faiths stages (the high three grades); *uśmagata* and *murdhān* stages, General and Specific *smṛtyupasthāna,* and Five [Meditations] for Terminating [the Perversions of] the Mind (the middle three grades); Pṛthagjanas who raise the Bodhi mind, who break the Five Precepts and who perform unvirtuous acts (the three low grades).[99]
3. Chia-ts'ai's *Pure Land Treatise*: the first mind of the Ten Understanding stages, the first mind of the Ten-Faiths stages, and the entire Pṛthagjanas of Good Destinies prior to the Ten-Faith stages (the three high grades); Hinayanists of the latter four of the Seven Skillful Means, those of the former three of the Seven Skillful Means, and the entire Pṛthagjanas of the Good Destinies

from those who have accepted the Five Precepts up to those of the Seven Skillful Means (the three middle grades); the entire Pṛthagjanas who commit evil, such as Ten Evils and Five Grave Offenses (all three low grades).[100]

4. The *Chih-i Commentary*: from Lineage to Practice of Resolution stages (equal Ten-Understandings to Ten-Transferences stages) (the three high grades); Ten-Faiths stages and below (the three middle grades); the entire Pṛthagjanas (the three low grades).[101]
5. The *Shan-tao Commentary*: (see listing above)[102]

While the list above reveals the extent of the discussion surrounding the ranking of the nine grades within the general Buddhist framework, Hui-yüan's ranking is most often cited in subsequent discussions. In his *Pure Land Treatise,* Chia-ts'ai observes that the practice of ranking the nine grades had been going on "since of old." He considered Hui-yüan the representative figure among those who had engaged in the ranking and even refers to him as the "Eminent Dharma Master [Hui-]yüan." Throughout the ranking of the nine grades, Chia-ts'ai cites Hui-yüan and utilizes his ranking as his chief reference.[103]

A partially reconstructed commentary of the *Kuan-ching* ascribed to Lung-hsing quotes extensively from the *Commentary.*[104] Not only does it quote the *Commentary* more often than any other extant Chinese writing, but also quotes the section on Hui-yüan's ranking in its entirety.[105] As another indication of the stature of Hui-yüan's ranking, Lung-hsing cites a certain Dharma Master Li (*Li fa-shih*) whose ranking of the middle and low grades agrees with that of Hui-yüan.[106] In his *Shih ching-t'u ch'ün-i lun,* Hui-kan lists some of the rankings of the nine grades. While he does not identify by name the proponents of the rankings, the first one discussed on the three high grades coincides with Hui-yüan's.[107]

By employing a better known, established set of categories, Hui-yüan set a precedent for subsequent commentators. More than anyone else's, his ranking system became regarded by these commentators as the standard. This practice of ranking the nine grades effectively legitimized the nine grades and, in turn the *Kuan-ching* itself, as an object of exegesis for writers. The number of treatises other than the commentaries on the *Kuan-ching,* which either offered their own views on the ranking or reported on this subject, reflects the importance that exegetes attached to the ranking.[108] The *Kuan-ching* was brought from the wings to center stage for the commentators of the Sui and early T'ang period. It attracted the attention of a large number of commentators, among whom many, such as Chi-tsang, have never been considered Pure Land Buddhists.

This interest in the ranking system challenges the often cited reason for the sudden popularity of the *Kuan-ching* in the second half of the sixth century and early seventh century, namely, that the message of the *Kuan-ching* was in keeping with the arrival of the Last Period of Dharma (*mo-fa*).[109] The interest in the ranking of the nine grades may well account for the attention devoted to this sutra.

# Chapter Six

## Impact On The *Shan-tao Commentary*

### Background

In assessing Tao-ch'o and Shan-tao's roles in the development of Pure Land Buddhism, Yuki Reimon writes:

> The various forms of the sinified new Buddhism that emerged in the Sui-T'ang period had three common aims. First, their Buddhist teaching had to be accessible to the practice of contemporary Chinese. Second, the teaching had not only to be accessible to practice but also be qualitatively sound. Since there would be no value to the teachings if they were not up to the standards of Indian Buddhism, [their proponents strove] to make them of even higher quality so as to be not inferior [to Indian Buddhism]. Third, the teaching had to be in accord with the Buddha's original intent.
>
> Among the Pure Land proponents of the Sui-T'ang period, Tao-ch'o was the first to attempt to make Pure Land Buddhism a teaching for the Chinese. But when compared to other new Buddhist forms such as T'ien-t'ai and Hua-yen, his Pure Land teaching completely fulfilled the first of the above three points but the success level of the second and third points was progressively lower from point two to point three. . . .
>
> Shan-tao's calling was to take Tao-ch'o's understanding of the "contemplation on the Buddha through oral recitation of the name" and to complete points two and three above. . . . This was accomplished through the *Shan-tao Commentary.*[1]

Thus, in Yuki's view, Shan-tao was responsible for authenticating Pure Land Buddhism as a teaching that was the equal of Indian Buddhism and in keeping with the original teaching of the Buddha. He accomplished this through his commentary on the *Kuan-ching,* the *Shan-tao Commentary.* But this would be a fair assessment of Shan-tao's role only in the context of orthodox Pure Land Buddhism, but not necessarily in the larger context of Pure Land Buddhism.

In the context of Pure Land Buddhism, the findings of this study suggest it was Hui-yüan, rather than Shan-tao, who played a vital and crucial role in fulfilling Yuki's points two and three, namely, authenticating the Pure Land teaching of the *Kuan-ching* in the context of both Indian Buddhism and the original intent of the Buddha. As argued in chapter 4 of this study, Hui-yüan's *Commentary* greatly contributed to placing the sutra in the formal "mainstream" commentarial tradition of latter sixth century Chinese Buddhism. Compiled about one hundred years after the *Commentary,* the *Shan-tao Commentary* applied a framework that was already operative in Hui-yüan's *Commentary.* In other words, Shan-tao wrestled with many of the same questions and issues found in the *Commentary.* Shan-tao, moreover, even agreed with Hui-yüan on many points, and when he did disagree, he regarded Hui-yüan's position as the standard on the subject.

While Shan-tao strove to validate his position by citing sutra and treatise passages of Indian masters, nonetheless, he completely neglected justifying either the validity or importance of the *framework* of issues and doctrinal categories structuring his outlook. But since it had become an accepted standard by his time, Shan-tao did not feel compelled to justify this framework. Moreover, as argued in earlier chapters, the *Commentary* contributed to this standardization by authenticating within the Indian Buddhist context the issues and categories that made up much of this framework. Examples of the standardization include the placement of the sutra within Buddhist literature (discussed previously in chapter 4), the various causal practices for rebirth including oral recitation and visualization (chapter 5), and the ranking of the nine grades of rebirth (chapter 5). Some writers have alluded specifically to Hui-yüan's impact on Shan-tao. For example, Agawa Kantatsu has listed those doctrinal points that Shan-tao and the early masters of the Jodo School adopted from the *Commentary.*[2] None of these scholars, however, has adequately described the precise character of Hui-yüan's influence on Shan-tao.

Shan-tao adopted some of the issues and categories of Hui-yüan's *Commentary* as the framework for expounding his own views. Since it is this chapter that sets forth Shan-tao's basic interpretation of the *Kuan-ching,* this chapter attempts to document this by focusing on the first fascicle of the *Shan-tao Commentary,* the "Kuan-ching hsüan-i fen." In discussing the four issues below, special attention will be paid to their role in facilitating Shan-tao's elevation of oral recitation to a primary form of practice in the orthodox Pure Land soteriological scheme.[3]

## The *Kuan-ching*'s place among the Buddhist scriptures

Shan-tao presents his views in seven sections, which he calls the "seven gates" (*ch'i-men).*[4] The third of the seven gates states:

> The third [gate] explains how the import [of the sutra] is not the same and whether a teaching is Mahayana or Hinayana. Like in the *Vimalakīrti-sūtra,* the inconceivable liberation is the import. Like the *Large [Prajñāpāramitā] Sutra,* the wisdom about emptiness is the import. As these examples show, [the sutra imports] are not the same. With regard to the *Visualization Sutra* (*Kuan-ching*) now under discussion, the Buddha-visualization *samādhi* is its import; the Buddha-contemplation *samādhi* is also its import. To singlemindedly direct one's wish to be reborn in the Pure Land is its essence.
>
> With regard to "whether the teaching is of Mahayana or Hinayana," it is asked, "In which of the two Piṭakas is this *Visualization Sutra* contained, and in which of the two teachings is [this Sutra] included?" It is answered, "This *Visualization Sutra* now under discussion is contained in the Bodhisattva Piṭaka and included in the sudden teaching."[5]

Although Shan-tao does not mention the source of these categories, undoubtedly he adopted three of Hui-yüan's five-essentials: (1) the Bodhisattva or Śrāvaka Piṭaka, (2) the gradual or sudden teaching, and (3) the main import.[6] The two sutras that Shan-tao cited in his discussion of the main import, the *Vimalakīrti* and *Large Prajñāpāramitā,* not only are the same but also are set forth in the same order as Hui-yüan's list of sutras. Shan-tao also adopted as his fourth gate the "five kinds of speakers," which corresponds to Hui-yüan's fifth essential. Shan-tao explains:

> The fourth [gate] explains the differences among speakers. All the sutras are preached by no more than five kinds of beings: 1) the Buddha, 2) the [Buddha's] saintly disciples, 3) the hermits, 4) the spirits and gods and 5) the transformed beings. Here, this sutra is preached by the Buddha himself.[7]

Hence, among the five-essentials, the only one that Shan-tao did not adopt was the fourth essential, the "differences in sutra titles."[8]

The first two essentials are utilized as *p'an-chiao* classifications and are the only *p'an-chiao* classifications to be found in this work. Shan-tao not only adopted Hui-yüan's categories but also agreed with Hui-yüan on these points, as he placed the *Kuan-ching* among the Bodhisattva Piṭaka and the sudden teaching. Concerning the next essential, the main import, Shan-tao again agreed with Hui-yüan as he cited the "*samādhi* of Buddha-visualization." But he adds to it the "*samādhi* of Buddha-contemplation," which was not found in Hui-yüan's scheme.

Tao-ch'o, Shan-tao's teacher, begins his *An-le chi* with a section entitled the "First Great Gate," which includes nine subsections called the "gates." The fourth of these subsections elucidates the import of the sutras, in which "Buddha-visualization" is considered the main import of the *Kuan-ching.* He further cites four of the sutras mentioned by Hui-yüan, the *Nirvāṇa, Vimalakīrti, Prajñāpāramitā* and *Ta-chi ching* (*Mahāsaṃnipāta*). He ascribes the same import as Hui-yüan to all except the first one, to which he assigns Buddha nature (*fo-hsing*) instead of nirvana. Other than this one minor difference, the category of the main import conforms to Hui-yüan's third essential, suggesting that Tao-ch'o also based this subsection on Hui-yüan's category.[9]

As mentioned above, Shan-tao departed somewhat from Hui-yüan by his addition of "*samādhi* of Buddha-contemplation" to "*samādhi* of Buddha-visualization" as main import of the *Kuan-ching.* While previous discussons on this subject have made much of this addition, they have been centrally preoccupied with establishing the primacy of contemplation, that is, oral recitation over visualization.[10] Consequently, this has accentuated the difference between Hui-yüan's and Shan-tao's positions, while virtually neglecting that the "*samādhi* of Buddha-visualization" constitutes a major aspect of the sutra's teaching for both writers.

Shan-tao's term "Buddha-contemplation" (*nien-fo*) included a wide range of practices such as "recollection" (*i*), "listening" (*wen*), and "oral recitation" (*ch'eng*).[11] Thus, it is not limited strictly to "oral recitation" as many previous writers have claimed.[12] Nevertheless, Shan-tao's understanding of oral recitation does not come under the rubric of "contemplation." Consequently, the claim that his addition of "*samādhi* of Buddha-contemplation" proves Shan-tao's high estimation of oral recitation as a Pure Land practice seems plausible. Yet while orthodox Pure Land Buddhism may traditionally assume the primacy of Buddha-contemplation (meaning "oral recitation" of Buddha Amitābha's name) over Buddha-visualization as the main import in Shan-tao's doctrinal scheme, this cannot be assumed without further study.[13]

Shan-tao's fourth issue, the five kinds of speakers, virtually accords with Hui-yüan's fifth essential:

| Hui-yüan: | Shan-tao:[14] |
|---|---|
| Buddha himself (*fo-tzu*) | Buddha (*fo*) |
| sagely disciples (*sheng ti-tzu*) | sagely disciples (*sheng ti-tzu*) |
| holy recluses (*shen-hsien*) | celestial recluses (*t'ien-hsien*) |
| celestial spirits (*t'ien kuei-shen*) | spirits (*kuei-shen*) |
| apparitional beings (*pien-hua*) | apparitional beings (*pien-hua*) |

Tao-ch'o also listed the same category in his *An-le chi.*[15] Both Shan-tao and Tao-ch'o's lists are much closer to Hui-yüan's than to a very similar list in the *Ta chih-tu lun.*[16] This, in addition to the fact that Tao-ch'o and Shan-tao did not acknowledge the *Ta-chih-tu lun* as a scriptural source, suggests that they adopted the list from Hui-yüan rather than directly from the *Ta-chih-tu lun.*[17]

| *Ta chih-tu lun*: | Hui-yüan: | Tao-ch'o: | Shan-tao: |
|---|---|---|---|
| Buddha himself | Buddha himself | Buddha himself | Buddha |
| Buddha's disciples | sagely disciples | sagely disciples | sagely disciples |
| recluses | holy recluses | celestial beings | celestial recluses |
| heavenly beings | celestial spirits | holy recluses | spirits |
| apparitional beings | apparitional beings | apparitional beings | apparitional beings |

The differences between Shan-tao's and Tao-ch'o's lists do not indicate that Shan-tao borrowed from his teacher, Tao-ch'o. Kashiwabara has suggested Shan-tao appropriated this category from Tao-ch'o, but it appears more likely that Hui-yüan was the source rather than Tao-ch'o.[18] This possibility derives from the degree of similarity between the two lists, the strongest evidence being that the order of the third and fourth groups (recluses and spirits) is the same in Hui-yüan's and Shan-tao's lists but reversed in Tao-ch'o's list. Apparently, Hui-yüan served as the model for Shan-tao even more than his own teacher on this point.

In sum Shan-tao's writing incorporates four categories that match four of Hui-yüan's five-essentials. It also appears that Hui-yüan's essentials served as the source for Shan-tao's categories. Hence, Shan-tao, the most celebrated orthodox Pure Land master, adopted categories from Hui-yüan primarily to place the *Kuan-ching* within the general corpus of Buddhist literature, in which the first two essentials served as a form of *p'an-chiao* classification. Not only did Shan-tao adopt Hui-yüan's framework but also he agreed with him on effectively every point regarding these four-essentials.

## Meditative and non-meditative good acts

Hui-yüan's *Commentary* is the earliest known text to employ the terms "meditative good act" (*ting-shan*) and "non-meditative good act" (*san-shan*), terms used, respectively, to refer to the visualizations and the three purified acts.[19] These terms become standard nomenclature in the subsequent commentarial tradition of the *Kuan-ching*. They appear, for example, in the Chi-tsang's commentary and the *Chih-i Commentary.*[20] The

*Shan-tao Commentary* was no exception in this regard, but Shan-tao applied them differently from Hui-yüan, as he explains:

> Question: What are "meditative good acts"? What are "non-meditative good acts"?
>
> Answer: The [first] visualization on the sun up to and including the thirteenth visualization is called "meditative good acts." [The practices concerning] the threefold meritorious acts and the nine grades (fourteenth, fifteenth and sixteenth visualizations) are called "non-meditative good acts."[21]

Shan-tao only considers the first thirteen visualizations meditative good acts, while the last three visualizations and the three meritorious acts (purified acts) comprise the non-meditative good acts. Despite this disagreement with Hui-yüan's position, Shan-tao still adopted Hui-yüan's two terms without any change in their meaning. They differed only in their application.[22]

Orthodox Pure Land scholars have made much of these different applications. They submit these differences as evidence for Shan-tao's elevation of oral recitation to a primary Pure Land practice.[23] Shan-tao discusses oral recitation only in reference to the nine grades of the fourteenth through the sixteenth visualizations. By distinguishing the practices associated with the nine grades as "non-meditative good acts" from the other visualizations, which he regarded as "meditative good acts," he accorded oral recitation an independent status. This qualitative distinction was further strengthened, as Shan-tao explains:

> The sixth section clarifies that the people for whom the [teaching] was taught were Vaidehī and others.
>
> Question: By whom were the two good acts of the meditative and the non-meditative requested?
>
> Answer: The gate of the meditative good acts was requested by Vaidehī, while the gate of the non-meditative good acts was taught by the Buddha himself [without anyone requesting].[24]

For Shan-tao, the non-meditative good acts were taught by the Buddha without being requested by anyone, which differed from the meditative good acts (the thirteen visualizations) taught in response to Vaidehī's request. In so doing, Shan-tao further enhanced the independent status of the non-meditative good acts. This shifted the emphasis from Hui-yüan's treatment of Buddha-visualization, that is, of meditative good acts, as the main import of the sutra, to Shan-tao's. The latter treatment accorded greater importance to non-meditative good acts by adding Buddha-contemplation to Buddha-visualization as one of the two main imports of the sutra. Further evidence for the greater independence of the non-meditative good acts appears in his dedication of two of the chapters in the *Shan-tao Commentary,* naming them, the "On the Meaning of Meditative Good Acts of the Main Section of the Visualization Sutra: Fascicle Three" and the "On the Meaning of Non-meditative Good Acts of the Main Section of the Visualization Sutra: Fascicle Four."

In Shan-tao's scheme, oral recitation constituted one of the main practices of the non-meditative good acts. Shan-tao stated at the outset of the fourth chapter on non-meditative good acts:

> There are two [aspects] with regard to these meaning [of non-meditative good acts]. The first [aspect] clarifies the three meritorious [acts] as the correct cause. The second clarifies the nine grades as the correct practice.[25]

With regard to the second aspect, the correct practice, Shan-tao recognizes five kinds: (1) chanting of the three sutras, the *Kuan-ching, A-mi-t'o fo ching,* and *Wu-liang-shou ching,* (2) mentally perceiving, visualizing and recollecting Amitābha's land, (3) worshipping Amitābha, (4) oral recitation of the Buddha's name, and (5) praising and offering. Each one of the so-called Five Correct Practices must be carried out with the same "single-minded concentration."[26]

These Five Correct Practices are further divided into essential and auxiliary action. Essential action is "to contemplate with singleminded concentration on the name of Amitābha," while the auxiliary is "to worship, chant, etc."[27] As discussed in the previous section, if Shan-tao did indeed include oral recitation under the category of contemplation on the Buddha, it follows that Shan-tao regarded oral recitation as an essential action, not simply an auxiliary action.

This discussion has presented the process by which Shan-tao, as Yuki argued above, ranked oral recitation as equal with, if not greater than, visualization in importance and credibility. Although Shan-tao differed from Hui-yüan in his application of the terms of meditative and non-meditative good acts, he nonetheless retained the same categories. Contrary to Yuki's statement, the doctrinal standard that Shan-tao observed was not that of Indian Buddhism but that of his predecessor, Hui-yüan. On one occasion Shan-tao solicited the authority of a passage from the *Avataṃsaka-sūtra.* But he did not go outside the framework of meditative and non-meditative good acts, a framework that was Chinese not Indian.

Shan-tao probably adopted these categories since they were employed by virtually all of the extant *Kuan-ching* commentaries. Shan-tao was compelled to adopt them because they were in vogue and thereby allowed him to "plug into" an already established exegetical framework. The retention of this structure enhanced the credibility of his own position, which in his case involved the elevation of oral recitation to a vital Pure Land practice.

**The ranking of the nine grades**

In analyzing the significance of Shan-tao's ranking of the nine grades, Yuki states:

> In contrast to the Masters (Hui-yüan, etc.) who ranked the nine grades as Āryapudgalas, Shan-tao ranked all nine grades as Pṛthagjanas. The fact that Shan-tao regarded the non-meditative good acts [associated with the nine grades] as a teaching initiated by the Buddha [without anyone requesting him as in the case of the meditative good acts] stemmed from Shan-tao's conviction that the rebirth of the Pṛthagjanas is in keeping with the Buddha's original message. From the standpoint of the independence of the gate of Buddha-contemplation (i.e. oral recitation) in Chinese [Buddhism], it was inevitable that [Shan-tao] regarded all [nine grades] as Pṛthagjanas, and it was this assertion that was at the root of the difference in the [divergent] opinion [concerning the ranking of the nine grades.][28]

Yuki, thus, sees a close relationship between Shan-tao's ranking of all nine grades as Pṛthagjanas and his elevation of oral recitation to a legitimate, independent practice in its own right. In short, because he regarded the *Kuan-ching* as a teaching solely for the Pṛthagjanas, it follows that he would give greater credence to oral recitation, a practice more fitting the capabilities of the Pṛthagjanas.

Shan-tao devoted the majority of the first chapter in the *Shan-tao Commentary* to the ranking of the nine grades. Much of it criticizes the ranking that he attributes to the Masters, understood to mean, among others, Hui-yüan's Chih-i and Chi-tsang. As the ranking is clearly Hui-yüan's, presumably Shan-tao had him in mind when he criticized the Masters. In the sixth of the first chapter's seven sections, "the reconciliation of the differences among the sutras and treatises (*shih-hui ching-lun*)," Shan-tao elucidates in four subsections his position on the ranking of the nine grades.

The first subsection sets out, in Shan-tao's words, to "elucidate the Dharma Masters' understanding of the nine grades." In doing so he rather accurately describes Hui-yüan's position on the assigned ranks. The description, however, includes additions to Hui-yüan's original statement. These additions accentuate the higher ranking of Hui-yüan's scheme in contrast to that of Shan-tao's.[29] As the first of such examples, for the middle of the middle grades he lists only the "Inner Pṛthagjanas" whereas Hui-yüan had also included the lower "Outer Pṛthagjanas."[30] In mentioning only the higher of the two groups, Shan-tao gives the impression that Hui-yüan ranked this grade higher than he actually did.

Another example is his addition of the title "Bodhisattva" to the lowest of the high grades, "*Bodhisattvas* from the ranks of Lineage up to the first Bhūmi."[31] While the rank assignment is accurate, Hui-yüan never referred to those of this grade as "Bodhisattvas" in his description: "Those of the Lineage and Practice of Resolution stages are said to be of the lowest of the high grades."[32] Similarly, Shan-tao describes those of the three upper grades as "all being of the rebirth ranks of the Mahayana Āryapudgalas."[33] Hui-yüan, however, never described them as "Mahayana Āryapudgalas."[34] Such an appellation also does not correctly reflect Hui-yüan's understanding of the lowest of the high grades, for, as discussed in the previous chapter, Hui-yüan regarded the Lineage and Practice of Resolution ranks as Pṛthagjanas, not Āryapudgalas.[35]

In the second subsection, which he calls the "refutation based on principles," Shan-tao directly criticizes what he perceives as Hui-yüan's unduly high ranking of the upper three grades. He objects to the great discrepancy between, on the one hand, the fourth Bhūmi and above, the first Bhūmi and above, and the Lineage stages and above (the ranks to which Hui-yüan assigned the upper three grades) and, on the other hand, the Pṛthagjanas for whom he believes the sutra was taught. In contrasting the superior capabilities of these Bodhisattvas and Bodhisattva-candidates with those of the Pṛthagjanas, Shan-tao cites passages from the *Avataṃsaka-sutra* and the *Ta chih tu lun.* According to the *Avataṃsaka-sutra,* the Bodhisattvas above the first Bhūmi have the "body of Dharma-nature" and the "body of transformation" that can be created at will in the realm of *saṃsāra.*[36] He then asks why these adepts need "to be so worried as to rely on the Pṛthagjana Vaidehī's request [for Buddha's teaching] to seek rebirth [in the Pure Land]."[37] The Pure Land teaching, Shan-tao asserts, is like an urgent rescue of a drowning person rather than the safe remove of one standing on the bank.[38]

Shan-tao in the third subsection presents his own ranking of the nine grades. In discussing each of the remaining eight grades, he first mentions Hui-yüan's ranking as a point of contrast that serves as a straw man for his subsequent argument. He then sets forth his own ranking, which is discernably much lower. In order to support his ranking, Shan-tao quotes a passage from *Kuan-ching* on the three kinds of beings who belong to the highest of the high grade.

> The Masters state that persons of the highest of the high grade are Bodhisattvas who are above the fourth Bhūmi and below the

> seventh Bhūmi. [If that is true] why then did the *Kuan-ching* state that the three kinds of sentient beings will gain rebirth? Who are the three [kinds of beings]?
>
> The first is of those who *can only* maintain the precepts and cultivate compassion. The second is of those who, neither can maintain the precepts nor cultivate compassion and *can only* recite the Mahayana [sutras]. The third is of those who neither can maintain the precepts nor recite the sutras and *can only* contemplate on the Buddha, Dharma, Sangha, etc.[39] (emphasis added)

But careful comparison of the citations with the original passages of the *Kuan-ching* discloses some discrepancies between the two. The emphasized words from the quoted passage above demarcate Shan-tao's addition of a phrase "can only" (*tan-neng*) to the description of each of the three groups. This effectively accentuates the inferior capability of the people involved. The original *Kuan-ching* passage reads:

> The first [group] is of those with the mind of compassion who do not kill and observe the various precepts and practices. The second is of those who recite the Mahayana Vaipulya scriptures. The third is of those who cultivate the six-fold contemplations and transfer [the merit] to vow to be reborn in that Buddha country.[40]

He does not cite Indian treatises as scriptural authority for his ranking. The only sutra mentioned, the *Avataṃsaka-sūtra,* simply refers to an earlier quotation in the second subsection discussed above.[41] His main argument either quotes or summarizes the relevant *Kuan-ching* passages for each of the grades and then stresses Hui-yüan's higher ranking. These arguments do not stem from any firm doctrinal basis, but simply from Shan-tao's basic premise that the Pṛthagjanas of his day should identify with the nine grades in order to arouse faith and attain birth in the Pure Land.

In the fourth subsection Shan-tao cites ten passages from the *Kuan-ching* to support his assertion that the *Kuan-ching* was meant for Pṛthagjanas rather than Āryapudgalas. His citations responded to a question that challenged Shan-tao's views as too subjective and without scriptural support. He then appeals to ten passages advancing his own assertion that the Buddha preached to the Pṛthagjanas. This, however, is an inappropriate argument against Hui-yüan, for he, as seen in chapter 5, agreed with Shan-tao on this point.

As is evident from the above, Shan-tao's ranking of the nine grades proceeds entirely in the context of Hui-yüan's ranking. While he criticizes it, it nevertheless serves as the reference point for his own ranking. In fact Shan-tao never once questions the validity of ranking the nine grades.

### The Pure Land classification

One of the major issues that preoccupied the exegetes of Pure Land scriptures concerned the question of whether Amitābha's Pure Land was either a lower Transformed-land (*hua-t'u*; *nirmāṇa-kṣetra*) or a higher Rewarded-land (*pao-t'u*; *saṃbhoga-kṣetra*). Shan-tao maintained that it was a Rewarded-land as he explains in the *Shan-tao Commentary:*

> Question: Is the pure country of Amitābha a Rewarded or a Transformed[-land]?
>
> Answer: It is a Rewarded[-land] and not a Transformed[-land]. How is this known? It is as explained in the *Mahāyānābhisamaya-sūtra,* "The Sukhāvatī in the Western Quarter and Buddha Amitābha are [,respectively,] Rewarded-Buddha and Rewarded-land."[42] Yuki describes the significance of Shan-tao's position:
>
> By taking the position that all five groups of beings can enter [the Pure Land] by the power of the Buddha's vow, Shan-tao revealed a religious stance which was accessible to all people. By advocating the idea that [Amitābha's Sukhāvatī Pure Land] is a Rewarded-land and not a Transformed-land, Shan-tao revealed the superiority of the religious content of his position. We cannot ignore the fact that in his assertion we find the basic element for the independence of Chinese Buddhism.[43]

Yuki, thus, finds evidence for "the independence of Chinese Buddhism" in Shan-tao's elevation of the Pure Land to a Rewarded-land. Yet, it is Hui-yüan, who provides the earliest known classification that allowed a pure land to be classified as a Rewarded-land. His classification of the pure lands into three categories is believed to be one of the earliest, if not the earliest, known attempts by a Chinese Buddhist to subsume three distinct categories of pure lands under one scheme. The three categories of pure lands are delineated in the "Chapter on the Concept of Pure Land" in his *Mahayana Encyclopedia.* Hui-yüan discusses the three categories from the different perspectives of the characteristics (*hsiang*) and of the cause (*yin*).[44]

The first perspective of characteristics contains: (1) Pure Lands of Phenomena (*shih ching-t'u*), (2) Pure Lands of Form (*hsiang ching-t'u*), and (3) Pure Lands of True Reality (*chen ching-t'u*). The second perspective based on cause is comprised of: (1) the Land of Perfect Response (*yüan-ying t'u*; *nirmāṇa-kṣetra*), (2) the Land of True Reward (*shih-pao t'u*;

*saṃbhoga-kṣetra*) and (3) the Land of Dharma-nature (*fa-hsing t'u*; *dharma-kṣetra*).[45]Both of the three-fold pure land classifications advanced the idea of pure land over the two-fold pure land scheme espoused by T'an-luan.[46] Hui-yüan, it appears, based his three-fold classification of the pure lands on the three-body (*trikāya*) formulations of the Yogācāra tradition.[47]

In the first classification based on characteristics, Hui-yüan included Amitābha's Sukhāvatī in the lowest category, "Pure Land of Phenomena." He reserves the Pure Lands of Phenomena for the Pṛthagjanas, thus conforming with his views in the *Commentary* that regarded the teaching of the *Kuan-ching* to be for the Pṛthagjanas. Decorated with jewels and adornments, these lands are sought by Pṛthagjanas, who are attracted by 'worldly' values. Accordingly, this category of pure lands is attained through defiled pure actions. While such actions correctly aspire for rebirth in the pure land, they embody intentions distorted by the worldly allurements of the pure lands. The size of these pure lands is limited and different for all aspirants and accords with the degree of zeal exhibited during their religious practice. The adornments of the pure land also depend on the kind of adornments envisioned by the aspirants during their practice.[48]

There are two kinds of Pure Lands of Phenomena: those of the (1) heavenly beings (*deva*), and (2) places such as that of Amitābha's Sukhāvatī. The difference between the two lies in the nature of the practitioner's intention and the quality of religious practice involved in attaining rebirth. With regard to the former, the Pṛthagjanas, who are reborn there, practice pure actions with the intent to attain some form of existence. They are still attached to the idea of rebirth in some higher level of existence. Consequently, they gain rebirth in one of the heavens of the Realm of Desire (*kāma-dhātu*) or Realm of Form (*rūpa-dhātu*). The second subgroup of Pure Lands of Phenomena differs from the first in that its aspirants seek to transcend the Three Realms. Hence, the Pure Lands that they attain, such as Amitābha's Sukhāvatī and the Realm of Fragrances (*chung-hsiang chieh*) discussed in the *Vimalakīrti-sūtra,* are not located within the Three Realms.[49]

Next the Pure Lands of Form differ from the Pure Lands of Phenomena in that they are reserved for the Śrāvakas, Pratyekabuddhas and Bodhisattvas. Like the Pure Land of Excellence (*miao ching-t'u*) mentioned in the ninety-third chapter of the *Ta chih tu lun,* these pure lands also lie beyond the Three Realms. Since the three groups of practitioners have overcome defilement through meditation, their pure lands result from non-defiled actions and are not limited to a particular location.[50]

The Pure Lands of Form comprise two kinds of pure lands. This first kind designates the realm of rebirth for Śrāvakas and Pratyekabuddhas. The diverse lands of this realm arise from practices based on benefiting the practitioner alone. Like the Formless Realm of Peace and Cessation, this realm is serene and formless. In contrast, the second kind among the Pure Lands of Form is attained by Bodhisattvas whose practices benefit others. This second type does not constitute a resting place like the first realm of the Śrāvakas and the Pratyekabuddhas. Rather it effects the salvation of others. Accordingly, the pure lands of this realm correlate with the needs of those to be saved.[51]

Thirdly, the Pure Lands of True Reality are reserved for the Bodhisattvas of the Bhūmis and the Buddhas. Because their practices are undefiled, this category of pure lands attains permanence. Further, because there is no conditioned thought, the lands occur without form. As the practice for attaining them is without attachment, these lands lack any specific locus.[52]

The standpoint of "cause" defines the second set of pure land categories. Hui-yüan discusses Rewarded-land from the standpoint of cause as follows:

> Before manifesting the Land of Dharma-nature, the Bodhisattvas relentlessly cultivate the inexhaustible practices of true reality (*dharmadhātu*). By means of the power generated by the merits from these pure practices, the Bodhisattvas decorate the boundless realm of the pure true reality with an immeasurable variety of adornments. This realm is named the "Land of True Reward" (*saṃbhoga-kṣetras*).[53]

This Rewarded-land differs from the True-land (in this formulation, "Land of Dharma-nature"), the true reality or the land of original nature. If the True-land were analogous to gold itself, the Rewarded-land would be the ornamental work wrought from it. Also, Bodhisattvas cannot behold the True-land, since only Buddhas can perceive it. While Rewarded-land exhibits definite shapes and colors in its adornments, the True-land is like space, unobstructive, unmoving and without possessions.[54]

When compared to the Transformed-land, however, the Rewarded-land is considered a land of reality in the same category as the True-land. If Rewarded and True-lands were like pure jewels, the Transformed-land would be a multifarious manifestation according with the capacities of the sentient beings who attain it. Given this perspective based on the cause that establishes the pure lands, Hui-yüan explains that the Transformed-land occurs without any cause of its own, since it emanates from the ultimate source, that is, from the true reality or True-land. Hui-yüan likens Transformed-land to a shadow that exists on account of the shape of an object.[55]

Hui-yüan's definition of Rewarded-land essentially conforms to Shan-tao's. Like Hui-yüan, Shan-tao saw a Rewarded-land as a reward for practices accomplished by a Bodhisattva. In response to the question about assigning Amitābha's Pure Land to a Rewarded-land, Shan-tao cites the *Wu-liang shou-ching* and summarizes: "When Bhikṣu Dharmākara was at Buddha Lokeśvararāja's place, practicing the Bodhisattva path, he made forty-eight vows." Shan-tao then concludes, "Now that Dharmākara has attained Buddhahood, he is a Rewarded-body."[56] Shan-tao's argument implies that because the Buddha is a Rewarded-body, the land that he presides over is also a Rewarded-land. This does not differ from Hui-yüan's description of this land, which results from the merits accumulated through the pure actions of the Bodhisattvas.

While they agree on the definition of a Rewarded-land, they disagree on the identification of Amitābha's Sukhāvatī Pure Land. As seen above, Hui-yüan regarded Sukhāvatī as a Transformed-land, while Shan-tao considered it a Rewarded-land. Hui-yüan based his reasoning on the low capability of the Pṛthagjanas, for whom Amitābha's Sukhāvatī was established. In other words, with Pṛthagjanas as a criterion, Hui-yüan determined Sukhāvatī to be a Transformed-land in keeping with his previously discussed definition of Transformed-land as a land for those of low accomplishments. Shan-tao, in contrast, sought in the vows of Dharmākara/Amitābha the efficient cause for both the establishment of the Pure Land itself and the rebirth of the Pṛthagjanas in that land. When asked how the lowly Pṛthagjanas, characterized by defilements and hindrances, could be reborn in a Rewarded-land when it was difficult even for the Hinayana Āryapudgalas, Shan-tao responded:

> If we were to discuss the defilements and hindrances of sentient beings, then it would certainly be difficult for them to aspire [to the Pure Land]. It is precisely because of the reliance upon the Buddha's vow as efficient cause that those of the five vehicles are all able to enter [the Pure Land].[57]

Despite these differences regarding the status of the Pure Land, Shan-tao nevertheless employed a classification that appeared for the first time among the extant texts in Hui-yüan's *Mahayana Encyclopedia.* This is not to say that Shan-tao adopted the classification *directly* from Hui-yüan. The category of Rewarded-land enjoyed circulation during his era, as seen in the writings of Tao-ch'o, Chia-ts'ai, [K'uei-]chi and its She-lun proponents.[58] But from the standpoint of both Pure Land Buddhism and Chinese Buddhism, Hui-yüan's coinage of the "Rewarded-land" constitutes the first known case that antedated its adoption by any of the orthodox Pure Land figures.

## Observation

This account of these four issues demonstrates that Shan-tao intended to authenticate his doctrinal position within the context of the categories of Hui-yüan's *Commentary* rather than, as Yuki asserted, directly within the categories of Indian Buddhism. His emphasis on oral recitation seems to confirm this. No compelling support can be summoned for Yuki's claim that Shan-tao consciously set out to authenticate his position in the context of Indian Buddhism. Moreover, Shan-tao not only knew about Hui-yüan's views but also, consciously or unconsciously, worked within that very framework established by Hui-yüan. In sum, the orthodox Buddhism that finally authenticated his understanding of the *Kuan-ching* derived from Hui-yüan rather than from India.

Biographically speaking, Shan-tao apparently had other exposure to Hui-yüan's interpretation of the *Kuan-ching* than that of the *Commentary.* Shan-tao trained for a few years at the Wu-chen Monastery on Chung-nan Shan near Ch'ang-an. This monastery was built by the followers of Ching-yeh (564–616), who was a direct disciple of Hui-yüan. When Shan-tao visited this monastery soon after 633 (the year of his ordination), there were monks residing at the monastery such as Fa-ch'eng (563–640), Hui-yüan (597–647, not Ching-ying Hui-yüan) and Fang-ch'i, who had good reasons for being scholars and/or practitioners of the visualization practices taught in the *Kuan-ching.*[59] Quite likely, Shan-tao's training at this monastery, founded by a direct disciple of Hui-yüan and composed of monks involved with the *Kuan-ching,* provided him with an opportunity to become familiar with Hui-yüan's thought.

A cursory investigation of the impact of the *Commentary* on the remaining three chapters of the *Shan-tao Commentary* reveals further evidence of Hui-yüan's influence on Shan-tao, notably in the content and format of the line by line exegesis to which the latter three chapters are devoted. For example, Shan-tao's exegesis of the opening line of the *Kuan-ching* closely resembles that of Hui-yüan's.[60] Also, the interpretation of the "eight kinds of virtues," which describe the water of the fifth visualization, is the same.[61] Many of the exegetical terms that are ascribed to the divided sections also follow those used by Hui-yüan: "general encouragement," "general conclusion," and "benefits."[62] A better assessment of Hui-yüan's impact on Shan-tao must await future research on these and other topics in the remaining chapters of the *Shan-tao Commentary.*

# Chapter Seven

## Conclusion

The *Commentary*'s contribution to Pure Land Buddhism lies in successfully transforming the *Kuan-ching* into a legitimate object of study among the scholastics of the late sixth century and early T'ang period. Contrary to Yuki Reimon's crediting of this achievement to Shan-tao, Hui-yüan instead stands as the person more responsible for "authenticating" the Pure Land teaching within the context of Indian Buddhism. Hui-yüan accomplished this by constructing an acceptable doctrinal framework that placed the teachings of the *Kuan-ching* within a wider Buddhist context. It served as a basic referent for subsequent commentaries, as in the case of the first chapter of the *Shan-tao Commentary.* When the *Shan-tao Commentary* was compiled, there was little need to explain or justify its categories and issues, because in large part they had already gained legitimacy within the commentarial tradition of the *Kuan-ching.*

An examination of the five-essentials reveals that Hui-yüan selected a relatively obscure sutra and treated it like such major Mahayana sutras, as the *Nirvāṇa-sūtra* and the *Vimalakīrti-sūtra.* He compiled the *Commentary* in the so-called *shu* format, which conformed to the orthodox exegetical style of his time. The ranking of the nine grades within the traditional Buddhist Path system brought the practices and the soteriological scheme of the *Kuan-ching* into a more traditional Buddhist framework.

Hui-yüan treated the three texts, the *Kuan-ching,* the *Wu-liang shou-ching,* and the *Rebirth Treatise,* as a set. This set later came to be regarded by orthodox Pure Land Buddhists as canonical. Hui-yüan attempted, more than T'an-luan, a thorough reconciliation of the apparent discrepancies among these texts. Hui-yüan interpreted the three as representing a unified position and, therefore, dismissed differences among them as superficial. Since he believed they expressed a single teaching, it can be assumed that Hui-yüan's *Commentary* bears witness to the existence of a contemporary Pure Land tradition. Hui-yüan recognized Pure Land texts as compatible in content and constitutive of a distinct form of Buddhism. His surviving commentaries regarded only the *Kuan-ching* and the *Wu-liang shou-ching* as sutras expressly taught for the Pṛthagjanas.

Such a development taking place outside the "boundaries" of orthodox

Pure Land Buddhism challenges the assumptions of previous scholarship. Pure Land Buddhist activities among the non-orthodox Pure Land Buddhists manifest greater vitality than previously reported particularly among those of the 'Hui-kuang lineage,' to which Hui-yüan belonged. Hui-yüan and Ling-yü, another major figure in this lineage, wrote the earliest known commentaries on the *Kuan-ching* and *Wu-liang shou-ching.* Ling-yü is further credited with a commentary, though now lost, on the *Rebirth Treatise,* whose date of compilation approximates the oldest surviving commentary and celebrated canonical text of orthodox Pure Land Buddhism, the *T'an-luan Commentary.* Hui-yüan's *Commentary* contains the earliest instance of the shorter titles *Wang-sheng lun* and *Ta-ching* for *the Rebirth Treatise* and the *Wu-liang shou-ching,* respectively. Both of these titles became common for orthodox Pure Land Buddhists in China as well as in Japan.

While more definitive studies are required, a strong possibility exists that these texts, especially the *Rebirth Treatise,* served as scriptural authority for the devotional and soteriological needs of the members of this lineage. Such a possibility runs counter to the traditional scholarly image of this lineage. It also questions the validity of commonly labeling Chinese Buddhists of this period as either exclusively 'academicians' or 'practitioners.' There is, thus, room for future investigation into the relationship between scholarly pursuits and religious practice.

Also, several previous assumptions about Hui-yüan's views were discovered to be unfounded, especially those positions previously considered a monopoly of orthodox Pure Land Buddhism. Contrary to explicit claims by orthodox Pure Land writers, Hui-yüan did recognize oral recitation as a legitimate causal practice for rebirth. Hui-yüan advocated a type of visualization intended specifically for the Pṛthagjanas, not for the Āryapudgalas as the orthodox writers assert. Their distortions of Hui-yüan's position are rooted in the semantic differences for the term "*fan-fu*" (*bon-pu/bonbu*; Pṛthagjana) as used by Hui-yüan and orthodox Pure Land tradition. The orthodox proponents also mistakenly believe that Hui-yüan interpreted the *Kuan-ching* to be a sutra taught for the Āryapudgalas rather than for the Pṛthagjanas. But Hui-yüan not only disclaimed the Āryapudgalas but advocated the Pṛthagjanas as the rightful "audience" of the *Kuan-ching* teaching.

The *Commentary* exerted a substantial and enduring influence on later commentaries of the *Kuan-ching*. Previous scholarship has already documented the debt of the *Chih-i Commentary* to the *Commentary* with respect to its content, which borrowed wholesale from entire sections of the *Commentary.* Since the *Chih-i Commentary* and its sub-commentaries comprise a major stream within the commentarial tradition of the *Kuan-ching* in China and Japan, they expanded the exposure of the *Commen-*

*tary* and thus the latter's impact on subsequent commentaries of the *Kuan-ching.*

Besides its influence on the *Chih-i Commentary,* that the commentaries compiled in the early T'ang period looked to the *Commentary* as the standard commentarial work on the *Kuan-ching*, is reflected in their categories and issues that they adopted. Nowhere was this more evident than in the ranking of the nine grades of rebirth. Even treatises other than commentaries on the *Kuan-ching* dealt with this issue.

As it structured the first fascicle of Shan-tao's *Shan-tao Commentary* more extensively than previously reported, the *Commentary* more substantially affected the orthodox Pure Land Buddhists than is conventionally acknowledged. While earlier studies have made generalized references to its influence, this study has documented the content and the manner of this influence. While prior studies focused on the differences between the two, this enquiry finds that, despite Shan-tao's criticism of Hui-yüan's views, he worked within an exegetical and doctrinal framework established largely by Hui-yüan. Since this framework had gained acceptance and legitimacy by Shan-tao's time, Shan-tao needed neither to justify the legitimacy nor to explain the meaning of the categories and issues that he raised in his *Shan-tao Commentary.* Moreover, by extension it could be argued that he chose to articulate his doctrinal position, which rests on the centrality of the vow of the Buddha based on the *Wu-liang shou-ching,* through a commentary on the *Kuan-ching* rather than one on the *Wu-liang shou-ching.* He did so precisely because the commentarial tradition of the *Kuan-ching* offered a more established and, thereby, a more effective framework for communicating his views.

The above findings also question the traditional practice of sharply demarcating orthodox from non-orthodox Pure Land Buddhism, often referred to as the "Gate of Pure Land Path" and the "Gate of the Path of the Sages," respectively. Those characteristics previously believed to be the monopoly of orthodox Pure Land Buddhism turn out, in fact, not only to have parallels but also to have antecedents outside this group. The recognition of oral recitation as a legitimate causal practice, the employment of the shorter titles for two of the Pure Land scriptures, and the view that the *Kuan-ching* was for the Pṛthagjanas demonstrate this wider currency. Moreover, it was Hui-yüan, rather than the orthodox Pure Land proponents, who wrote the oldest extant commentaries on the *Kuan-ching* and the *Wu-liang shou-ching.* The impact of his work on Tao-ch'o's *An-le chi* and especially on the *Shan-tao Commentary* attests to the need for reassessing the conventional views of this early stage of Pure Land development.

The findings of this study have implications for understanding the emergence of Pure Land Buddhism. Orthodox writers have customarily cited the arrival of the Last Period of Dharma (*mo-fa*) as the major reason for the popularity of the *Kuan-ching* as an object for both religious devotion and scholarly study. In their view, Vaidehī's plight narrated in the sutra found a sympathetic ear among those experiencing similar fates amidst the political and economic turmoil of the second half of the sixth century in northern China. Moreover, since modern proponents of this theory believe the *Kuan-ching* was the sutra most instrumental in generating interest in Pure Land teaching, the belief in the Last Period of Dharma is thus regarded as the major factor in the emergence of Pure Land Buddhism as a whole.

This study failed to find any evidence of concern for this eschatological doctrine of the Last Period of Dharma in the *Commentary,* the *Wu-liang shou-ching i-shu* or Hui-yüan's other commentaries. Since Hui-yüan's *Commentary* played a vital role as a pace-setter for some of the major textual and doctrinal issues within the subsequent commentarial tradition of this sutra, questions must be raised about the widely held assumption that the doctrine of the Last Period of Dharma explains the popularity of this sutra and the rise of Pure Land Buddhism. This, however, does not reject the Last Period of Dharma as a factor in the emergence of other forms of Pure Land Buddhism on the popular level. Rather, it bears only on the role of the *Kuan-ching* and on its commentarial tradition.

The popularity of the *Kuan-ching* among its commentators derives from the sutra's categories and issues, and particularly from its ranking of the nine grades. Its appeal lay in the framework that the *Commentary* was largely instrumental in establishing. As indicated by the extent of its adoption, this framework gained acceptance from the "orthodox" standpoint both in terms of its exegetical format and in that of its doctrinal foundation. In this process, a minor sutra used primarily for liturgical purposes in the first hundred years or so after its translation became an object of formal commentaries written by eminent scholar monks of the caliber of Hui-yüan, Ling-yü, Chi-tsang and Shan-tao. Its subsequent popularity so endured that, assuming Sato's suggestion is correct, the *Chih-i Commentary* on it was compiled around the year A.D. 700 by members of his lineage. As they could not justify the lack of a commentary on such an important sutra by their master, they fabricated one.

The popularity of the *Kuan-ching* should be considered as one possible factor in understanding the relationship between the so-called Maitreya cult and Amitābha cult during the Sui and early T'ang. No clear explanation yet exists for the gradual increase in the number of Amitābha images and the decrease in that of Maitreya images, in the caves of Northern China from the period spanning the Nan-pei Chao (420–581 C.E.) to around 700 C.E. of the T'ang period.

If this reflected an actual ascendency of the Amitābha cult over the Maitreya cult, it may be that the former found a following among the commentators and ecclesiastically highly placed monks who took an interest in the *Kuan-ching* precisely for the reasons suggested above. The Maitreya cult, on the other hand, could not claim to have a sutra with such a following. While the Maitreya cult may have been more successful in the beginning, it could not sustain its earlier successes without the strong support of the clergy and a firm doctrinal foundation that would appeal to a wider Buddhist framework. This is not to imply that the Maitreya cult was totally ineffective on these points, for a commentary on a Maitreya sutra is attributed to [K'uei-]chi. But no sutra in the Maitreya cult captured the imagination and interest of so many exegetes as did the *Kuan-ching*.

# Part II

# Translation of the Commentary

## General notes for the translation

1. ( ) = page numbers of the *Sutra*
2. [ ] = page numbers of the *Commentary*
3. *Sutra* = *Kuan-ching*
4. This translation is of the *Taishō* text (no. 1749). Two manuscripts of the *Commentary* from the Taishō University Library, Tokyo, (nos. 1153.223.1 and 1153.228.2–1) were consulted.
5. "Pure Land" refers specifically to Amitābha's Sukhāvatī, while "pure land" is a generic reference.

## Synopsis of the *Kuan-ching*

The sutra begins with a prologue of the story of King Ajātaśatru and his parents, former King Bimbisāra and Lady Vaidehī. Upon learning from Devadatta about his father's failed attempt to kill him at birth, Ājataśatru imprisons Bimbisāra with the intent to starve him to death. Lady Vaidehī, however, succeeds in keeping Bimbisāra alive by secretly feeding him during his visits. When Ajātaśatru discovers his mother's clandestine activity, he also imprisons her out of extreme anger. Deeply distressed by her son's actions and her own circumstances, Vaidehī turns to Śākyamuni Buddha for instruction on gaining rebirth in another realm without any suffering. The Buddha then through his transcendental powers illuminates the countless realms in the ten quarters of the universe. Vaidehī selects Amitābha's Sukhāvatī as the realm of her choice.

The Buddha proceeds to expound the required practices for aspirants' rebirth. They include the "three purified acts" that are ethical in nature, for example, the caring for one's parents and teachers, the adherence to precepts, and the reciting of the Mahayana sutras. The Buddha then leads Vaidehī and others to see Amitābha's realm and, in that process, to attain the Insight of Non-arising of *dharmas*.

Concerned for the future beings, who will not have the benefit of Buddha's direct instruction, Vaidehī inquires about the methods for their rebirth. In response, the Buddha instructs her in the sixteen kinds of visualization. The first thirteen begin with the visualization of the setting sun in this Sahā world, then moves to the physical features in Sukhāvatī realm such as the ground, trees and lakes, and concludes with the features of Buddha Amitābha and his attendants, Bodhisattvas Avalokiteśvara, and Mahāsthāmaprāpata. The last three visualizations have as their object the people of the nine grades of rebirths, the level of their spiritual attainment, the quality of their death-bed welcome, and the length of time spent in Sukhāvatī before hearing the Dharma and attaining complete enlightenment. This section on the visualizations, which is four times longer than the prologue section, comprises the main body and the primary aim of this sutra.

In the epilogue, which is one-third the length of the prologue, Vaidehī attains the Insight of Non-arising, while her five-hundred female attendants are prophesized by the Buddha about their imminent rebirth.

# The Commentary on the Sutra of Visualization on the Buddha of Immeasurable Life

## Part One
## by
## Śramaṇa Hui-yüan of Ching-ying Monastery

*Translator's note: Hui-yüan divides the *Sutra* into three parts: preface, main body, and conclusion. The preface section includes discussions on the (1) five-essentials, (2) explanation of the title of the sutra, and (3) division of the sutra. The five-essentials comprise a set of *p'an-chiao* classifications through which Hui-yüan attempts to determine the status of the *Sutra* within the corpus of Buddhist literature. The five essentials concern (1) the teaching as Mahayana or Hinayana, (2) the teaching as limited, gradual or sudden, (3) the main import of a sutra, (4) the differences in the titles of various sutras, and (5) the differences in the speakers of sutras.

With regard to this *Sutra,* I shall in the opening section first elucidate the five-essentials (*wu-yao*) and afterwards explain its title: "What are the five-essentials?" [173a1–3]

First, one ought to know whether the teaching (*chiao*) is Mahayana or Hinayana, since the [Buddhist] teachings are divided into two Piṭakas (collection of writings), namely, the Śrāvaka Piṭaka (*sheng-wen tsang*) and the Bodhisattva Piṭaka (*p'u-sa tsang*). Those that teach the Śrāvaka method are called "the Śrāvaka Piṭaka," while those that teach the Bodhisattva method are called "the Bodhisattva Piṭaka." In distinguishing the meaning [of the two sets of terms] in accordance with the usual explanation, this *Sutra* is to be included among the Bodhisattva Piṭaka. [173a4–6]

Second, one ought to know whether the teaching is limited (*chü*), gradual (*chien*) or sudden (*tun*). The Hinayana teaching is called "limited." The Mahayana teaching entered by way of Hinayana is categorized as "gradual." The Mahayana teaching that is not entered by way of Hinayana is called "sudden." This *Sutra* is the Dharma wheel of the sudden teaching (*tun-chiao*). How does one know this? It is known because this *Sutra* was taught specifically for Vaidehī, who, as will be explained below, was a Pṛthagjana (*fan-fu*; an ordinary being below the stage of Āryapudgalas).[1] Since it is taught for the sake of Pṛthagjanas and not entered by way of Hīnayana, this teaching is known as the "sudden teaching."[173a6–10]

Third, one ought to know the main import (*tsung-ch'ü*) of a sutra. The main imports that the various sutras espouse differ. For example, for the *Nieh-p'an ching* (Sutra on Nirvana, henceforth, *Nirvana Sutra*), nirvana is its main import; for the *Wei-mo ching* (Sutra on the Questions of Vimalakīrti, henceforth, *Vimalakīrti Sutra*), the inconceivable liberation is its main import; for the *Ta-p'in ching* (Great Perfection of Wisdom Sutra; *Mahāprajñāpāramitā-sūtra*) and other [wisdom sutras], wisdom (*prajñā*) is their main import; for the *Hua-yen* (Flower Garland Sutra; *Avataṃsaka*), the *Fa-hua* (henceforth, *Lotus Sutra*), the *Wu-liang-i* ([Sutra of] Immeasurable Meaning) and other [sutras], concentration (*samādhi*) is their main import; for the *Ta-chi ching* (Great Collection Sutra; *Mahāsaṃnipāta-sūtra*) and other [sutras], esoteric formulae (*dhāraṇī*) are their main import. Thus, their main imports are not the same, and for this *Sutra* the Buddha-visualization *samādhi* (*kuan-fo san-mei*) is its main import. [173a10–15]

Fourth, one ought to know that the titles (*ming*) of sutras are not the same; the sutras bear distinct and different titles. Sometimes they are based on doctrine (*fa*) as in the case of the *Nirvana Sutra, Pan-jo ching* (Perfection of Wisdom Sutra; henceforth, *Prajñāpāramitā Sutra*), and so forth; sometimes they are based on persons (*jen*) as in the case of *Sa-ho-t'an t'ai-tzu ching* (Sutra on Prince Sa-ho-t'an)[2]; sometimes they are based on analogy (*yü*) as in the case of the *Chin-kuang-ming* (Sutra of Golden Light), *Ta-yün ching* (Sutra of the Great Cloud), and so forth; sometimes they are based on physical objects (*shih*) as in the case of the *K'u-shu ching* (Withered Tree Sutra)[3], and so forth; sometimes they are based on location (*ch'u*) as in the case of the *Chia-yeh-shan-ting ching* (Mt. Gayā Pinnacle Sutra)[4] and so forth; sometimes they are based on time (*shih*) as in the case of the *Shih-ching* (Sutra on Time), and so forth; sometimes both person and doctrine constitute the title as in the case of *Sheng-man ching* (Sutra Expounded by Queen Śrīmālā; henceforth, *Śrīmālādevī Sutra*)[5] and so forth; in some, physical objects and doctrine are both mentioned in the title as in the case of the *Fang-teng ta-chi-ching* (Expansive Sutra of Great Collection]) and so forth; in some, doctrine and analogy are expressed together as in the case of the *Dharma Lotus Sutra* and *Fa-ku ching* (Dharma Drum Sutra). As the above examples show, [the sutra titles] are not the same. Here in this *Sutra,* both person and doctrine comprise its title; "Buddha" is the person in the title, and "Discourse on the Visualization of the [Buddha of] Immeasurable Life" is the doctrine in the title. [173a15–23]

There are, in all, four kinds of sutras that list persons in their titles. The first mentions the speaker, as in the *Vimalakīrti Sutra* and *Śrīmālādevī Sutra.* The second mentions the interlocutor as in the *Mi-le wen ching* (Sutra on the Questions of Maitreya). The third mentions the person to whom the sutra is taught, as in the *Sutra on Prince Sa-ho-t'an.* The fourth mentions the person for whose sake the sutra is taught, as in the *Yü-yeh ching* (Sutra on Yü-yeh)[6] and *Hsü-mo-t'i nü ching* (Sutra on Woman Hsü-mo-t'i).[7] Here in this *Sutra,* the character "Buddha" denotes the speaker. [173a23–b1]

Fifth, one ought to know about the differences among the speakers (*shuo-jen*). The sutras give discourses in five general ways, as has been described by Nāgārjuna: first, by the Buddha himself, second, by [Buddha's] sagely disciples, third, by holy recluses, four, by celestial spirits, and five, by apparitional beings.[8] Of these five kinds of sutras, this *Sutra* is that taught by the Buddha. The above points of discussion are known as the five-essentials. [173b1–4]

Translator's note: Hui-yüan proceeds to explain the title of the *Kuan-ching,* dividing the explanation into two sections: the one on the speaker and the other on the doctrine. The former focuses on the term "*Buddha*" and the latter on the "*Sutra on the Visualization of the* [*Buddha*] *of Immeasurable Life*".

I shall next explain its title. The first character "Buddha" indicates the speaker and is translated as "the enlightened" (*chüeh*). There are two meanings of "the enlightened." The first meaning, "enlightened perception" (*chüeh-ch'a*), combats the hindrances of affliction (*kleśāvaraṇa*). Such matters as the damages caused by [the hindrances of] affliction are like those caused by thieves. The Buddha is known as "the enlightened" because only by means of enlightened knowledge of the Sage (Buddha) is one not subjected to the damages [caused by the hindrances of afflictions]. This first meaning is like the explanation found in the *Nirvana Sutra.* The second meaning, "enlightened awakening" (*chüeh-wu*), combats the hindrances of knowledge (*jñeyāvaraṇa*). Such matters as obscuration due to ignorance are like those of sleep. [The Buddha] is known as "the enlightened" because the wisdom of the Sage is a total perspicacious great awakening like the awakening from sleep. [173b4–9]

Two kinds of ignorance are to be combated. The first is the nature-fettering ignorance that deludes and covers up true nature. Because the Buddha has eliminated that kind of ignorance and has awakened to the principle of true nature, he is known as "the enlightened." The second kind of ignorance concerns the objects [of the senses] for it prevents clear comprehension of such objects. Because the Buddha has eliminated that kind of ignorance and has understood the three categories of *dharmas* (the fundamental elements of existence)—the entire virtues, non-virtues, and so forth, he is known as "the enlightened."[9] Thus, the *Ti-ch'ih* (Treatise on the Bodhisattva Stages; *Bodhisattvabhūmi*) states:[10]

> He is called the "Buddha," for he was enlightened to the impartiality of the meaning of the categories of meritorious, non-meritorious and non non-meritorious. [173b10–15]

He is called the "Buddha" because he became enlightened on his own, then enlightened others and brought the practices for enlightenment to full fruition. "He was enlightened on his own" distinguishes him from the Pṛthagjanas; "enlightened others" means he differs from the two vehicles [i.e., the Pratyekabuddhas and Śrāvakas]; "brought the practices for enlightenment to full fruition" displays his differences from the Bodhisattvas. Therefore, he alone is called "the Buddha." [173b15–17]

I shall next bring up the topic of the doctrine that is expressed [in the title of this *Sutra*]. The character "Discourse" [in the title] refers to the [Buddha's act of] orally proclaiming [the teaching]. "Visualization" refers to the restraining of thoughts and the inspecting [of the auspicious marks of the Buddha], while "Immeasurable Life" refers to the Buddha to be visualized. [173b17–18]

There are two kinds of visualization of the Buddha: first, the True-body visualization (*chen-shen kuan*) and, second, the Response-body visualization (*ying-shen kuan*). To visualize the Buddha as the body of the impartial Dharma gate is the "True-body visualization." In contrast, to visualize the Buddha as the body of the Tathāgata, who shares [characteristics] with a worldly body, is called the "Response-body visualization." [173b18–21]

The visualization of the True-body is as taught in the "Chapter on Seeing Akṣobhya [Buddha]" of the *Vimalakīrti Sutra.* which states:

> To visualize the true form of the body and to visualize the Buddha are the same. I visualize the Tathāgata that does not come from the previous period, depart for the subsequent period, or dwell in the present. [173b21–24][11]

[Hence, the meaning is] as described above.

To summarize, (visualization requires the practitioner) to completely sever all [deluded] forms and to be fully endowed with virtues. The complete severance of all [deluded] forms does not allow even of a form. With the full endowment of virtues, the practitioner does not lack even one moral good. Even though one possesses all moral goods, they are of the same essence and are distinguished only in terms of virtues. This is like space that is without obstruction, immovable and without the marks that are distinguished between 'this' and 'that.' Since there are no marks that are distinguished between this and that, the faculties of the [thirty-two primary] marks and the [eighty secondary] auspicious marks all pervade the Dharma-realm like the ten characteristics of the ocean, which are of the same essence and that are all pervasive.[12] Since [the auspicious marks of a Buddha] pervade everywhere and the eye functions as a gate [to these marks], the faculties of primary and secondary auspicious marks as well as the Buddha lands and the entire sentient beings [who inhabit them] are all encompassed completely in a single eye. The same holds true for visualizing any of the remaining primary and secondary marks. [173b24–c2]

The Response-body visualization is as explained in the *Kuan fo san-mei ching* (Sutra on the Buddha-visualization *Samādhi*):

> To mentally grasp the form and marks of the Buddha and to restrain thoughts and to inspect [the marks] is called [collectively] the "Response-body visualization."

There is a beginning (*shih*) and an end (*chung*) of the Response-body visualization. Having come to know about the existence of innumerable Buddhas in the realms of the ten directions through hearing the Bodhisattva Piṭaka, one restrains thoughts, investigates and makes the mind perspicacious. In this way, the vision derived through unrefined pure-faith (*chu ching-hsin chien*) is called the "beginning." To go in person for an audience [with the Buddha], through great supernatural powers, or to be reborn and to gaze closely and make offerings is [collectively] called the "vision derived from true reality" (*chen-shih chien*); this constitutes the end [of the Response-body visualization]. [173c2–8]

There is also a beginning and an end with regard to True-body visualization. To attain the vision derived from unrefined pure-faith by hearing the [teachings from] the Bodhisattva Piṭaka, to know the Dharma-body (*dharmakāya*) of the Buddha and to restrain and inspect the mind are together called the "beginning." To eliminate deluded thoughts and to be internally in accordance with enlightenment are said to be the "end" [of the True-body visualization]. The *Sutra* expounds upon a visualization which, as a form of Response-body visualization, derives from unrefined pure-faith. [173c8–11]

Within the Response-body visualizations are the general (*t'ung*) and the specific (*pieh*) [visualization], as explained in the *Sutra on Buddha-visualization Samādhi.* To grasp the Buddha's marks in a general manner, to visualize and inspect them and to be settled [on the marks] without [distinguishing] this from that [mark] are collectively called the "general" visualization. On the other hand, to visualize and analyze [individual

Buddhas] such as Maitreya and Akṣobhya are together considered a specific visualization. What this *Sutra* discourses upon is the specific visualization, namely, a specific visualization of the Buddha of Immeasurable Life (*Amitāyus*) of the western quarter. [173c11–14]

Similarly, there are the general and the specific with regard to the names of the Buddhas. "Tathāgata," "Arhat" and "All-knowing," and so forth are general names. In contrast, Śākyamuni, Maitreya, Akṣobya Buddhas, and so forth are specific names. There are numerous kinds of specific names. Some are based on a clan, such as Kāśyapa and Śākyamuni. Others are based on the physical body, such as Body-honoring Buddha and Body-bestowing Buddha. Some are based on sounds and voices, such as the Buddha of Exquisite Sounds and the Buddha of Exquisite Voices. Others involve light and brilliance as in the Buddha of Exquisite Light and the Buddha of Universal Brilliance. Some are based on internal virtues such as the Buddha of Virtues and the Buddha of Wisdom. Others are based on analogy, of which there are numerous kinds. Others are based on life span. The Buddha being visualized in this *Sutra* is named after his span of life. [173c14–21]

Among those [distinguished] in terms of life span, there are True (*chen*) and Response (*ying*) Buddhas. The true Buddhas, like space, are absolute and inexhaustable. Some of the Response-body [Buddhas] have long life spans, while others are short. The Buddha now under discussion here [in this *Sutra*] is a Response and not a True Buddha. Thus, the *Kuan-yin shou-chi ching* (Sutra on the Avalokiteśvara Prophecy) states:

> Even though the life span of the Buddha of Immeasurable Life is extremely long, it will in the end be exhausted. It should, therefore, be known as a Response Buddha. Because the life of this Buddha is extremely long and [appears to be] limitless, the Pṛthagjanas and those of the two vehicles cannot possibly comprehend it. This Buddha is, therefore, called "Immeasurable," but since his life span is, in actuality, limited it is referred to as "Life" [as in "Life" of "the Buddha of Immeasurable Life"]. [173c21–26][13]

The question is asked, "Since this *Sutra* is concerned not only with visualizing the Buddha but also with visualizing the land (*kṣetra*), [Bodhisattva] Avalokiteśvara, [Bodhisattva] Mahāsthāmaprāpta, the nine grades of rebirth, and so forth why limit the title [of this *Sutra*] to 'Visualizing [the Buddha of] Immeasurable Life'?" [173c26–28]

The Buddha was singled out because the primary [concern of the *Sutra*] is that of visualizing him. Further, the visualization of the Buddha was singled out, since the inclusion of all the other objects in the title was impossible. [173c28–29]

The character "ching" in the foreign country is known as "*hsin-to-lo*" (sutra), which in translation means "stem" or "thread." The words of the Sage can penetrate the various teachings, just as a stem can pierce a flower. Consequently, it was metaphorically named "stem" and is called "ching" (meaning "warp") since it can support the woof, just as a stem can pierce a flower. The characteristics of the two being similar, it was named "ching." If we rely on its secular reading, "ching" means "permanent" because, as a teaching, one Dharma has existed constantly having been transmitted from antiquity to the present. [173c29–174a4]

*Translator's note: In this section, Hui-yüan adheres to the contemporary practice of dividing the text.

The entire text of this *Sutra* is divided into three parts, which are called "preface" (*hsü*), "main body" (*cheng*), and "conclusion" (*t'ung*). From the beginning to "World Honored One, what [evil past] conditions caused you also to be a relative of Devadatta?" (340c27–341b16) comprises the preface. From "I only request that you describe for me in detail a place where there are no sorrow" and below (341b16–346b5) comprises the main body. From "Ānanda asked the Buddha,[6] what shall we name this sutra?'" and below [to the end of the text] (346b5–21) comprises the conclusion. Because any instructions [by the Buddha] must[14] have a reason, the Buddha first revealed the preface. Then, the Buddha revealed the main body so as to expound correctly the teaching based on the foregoing preface. On completing the teaching that he desired to be transmitted to future generations, the Buddha then praised its superior qualities, and encouraged its study and propagation for later. He, thereby, revealed the conclusion. [174a4–10]

*Translator's note: Hui-yüan elucidates the two sections of the preface.

First, while divided into many sections, the passages of the preface have essentially only two basic meanings, the preface for initiating the teaching (*fa-ch'i hsü*) and the preface for demonstrating trust (*ch'eng-hsin hsü*). The term "initiating" (*fa-ch'i*) refers to [the activities of] the Buddha, who when he is about to deliver a sermon, first sets the time and the place and assembles the crowd through supernatural powers. To generate [a set of activities in preparation] for what is to be taught is the "initiating." As this initiation serves as the background for delivering a sermon, this section is called "the preface for initiating the teaching." [174a10–14]

As for the term "preface for demonstrating trust," Ānanda in desiring to transmit the Dharma to future generations initially proclaimed to the sentient beings, "I have thus heard the Dharma from the Buddha." Be cause it demonstrates the necessity to trust [in the teaching], it is called "demonstrating trust." As this demonstration of trust provides the reason for transmitting the *Sutra,* this section is called the "preface for demonstrating trust." [174a14–16]

> *Translator's note: Hui-yüan's exegetical format for a section generally includes two stages. He first divides and discusses the meaning (*i*) of the major subsections. He, then, engages in a more detailed division of the passages (*wen*). He now begins the second stage.

"Now that the meaning [of the two kinds of preface] has been clarified, how are the passages to be divided?" The first passage "Thus I have heard" (340c29) clearly carries the meaning of demonstrating trust. [The following passage] "One day the Buddha . . ." (340c29) carries both meanings. If the original intention of this last passage is taken as initiating the teaching, then it would be deemed as the [preface for] "initiating the teaching." As Ānanda's introductory remarks [of "Thus I have heard"] demonstrate the credibility of the *Sutra,* that may be regarded as "demonstrating trust." However, the passages [of the entire preface] include both meanings, and one should, therefore, not choose one meaning over another. The sense of right or wrong by whimsical human emotion cannot be fully applied for all times. [174a17–20]

> *Translator's note: An extensive discussion ensues about the initial passage of the *Sutra,* "Thus I have heard." Hui-yüan regards this passage as the preface for demonstrating trust and discusses it from three points of view.

There are three gates (*san-men*) to be distinguished in our understanding of the meaning of the initial passage ("Thus I have heard"), which clearly is meant to demonstrate trust: first, to understand the phrase "Thus I have heard" as an answer [to the questions to be asked below], second, to see it as establishing the intentions [of the *Sutra*], and, third, to simply explain the phrase "Thus I have heard." [174a20–22]

As for "the answer" (first of the three gates), [it is in response to the following questions]. "Why do we find the phrase 'Thus I have heard' at the beginning of sutras?" Because sutras are the teachings of the Buddha. "Why did the Buddha teach?" Because Ānanda requested it. "Why did Ānanda request it?" Because Aniruddha (the first of Buddha's ten great disciples) instructed him to do so. "Why did Aniruddha instruct him?" Because he saw that Ānanda's mind was grieving. "Why was Monk Ānanda grieving?" Because Ānanda realized that Tathāgata's complete nirvana (*parinirvāṇa*) was imminent. [174a22–26]

The Buddha was about to enter complete extinction as he lay between the twin Sāla trees with his head facing north. Filled with grief over Buddha's imminent extinction, Ānanda cried out "Why am I unable to overcome [this grief]!" Thereupon, Aniruddha explained to Ānanda:

> "You are the transmitter of the Dharma, why do you not inquire of the Buddha about the worldly matters for the future? What benefit is there in merely lamenting!"

Ānanda responded, "My mind is presently too sunken in grief to know what to ask." Aniruddha, then, instructed Ānanda in the four topics to be asked of the Buddha:

> "First, you should ask, 'who will the monks have as their teacher after Buddha's death?' Second, you should ask, 'what will the monks rely on to exist after Buddha's death?' Third, you should ask, 'how are we to live together with evil-natured monks?' Fourth, you should ask, 'what phrase ought to be placed at the beginning of all sutras?'"

Having been so instructed and his mind somewhat clearer [than before], Ānanda inquired of the Buddha. [174a26–b5]

> The Buddha complied and answered him:
>
> "As to your question 'who will the monks have as their teacher,' they should rely on the Prātimokṣa (Rules of conduct) as their teacher. Even if I were alive in this world, my answer would not be any different. Because the Prātimokṣa consists of precepts which the monks cultivate, I explain it as your 'teacher'."
>
> As to the question, "what will the monks rely on?" they ought to rely upon the Four Mindfulness (*catuḥ-smṛtyupasthānāḥ*). What are the Four Mindfulness? They refer to the monks meditating on their inner body (*kāya*), cultivating the meditation of the body and very diligently and single-mindedly eliminating worldly passions. In this manner, one meditates on the outer body, and the inner and outer body; the same holds for sensation (*vedanā*), the mind (*citta*), and the *dharmas*. These are, then, said to be the places in which the monks rely. The *Sutra,* therefore, states, "If one dwells in the Four Mindfulness, it is referred to as 'one's own realm, unbound by Māra (the Evil One).' If, on the other hand, one dwells in the Five Desires, it is referred to as, 'someone else's realm where one is bound by Māra'."[15]
>
> As to the question, "how the monks will live together with evil-natured monks?" the Brahma punishment stick (*Brahma-daṇḍa*) will keep them in line. If the mind is to be settled, [the Buddha] teaches one to separate

oneself from sutras [that expound the extreme positions] of existence or of nonexistence. "*Brahma-daṇḍa*" is a foreign term, but here in this country it is known as "silently not exchanging words."[16]

As to the question, "what phrase ought to be placed at the beginning of all sutras?" one ought to place phrases such as "Thus I have heard." Consequently, at the beginning of this *Sutra* is the phrase, "Thus I have heard." [174b5–17]

Secondly, I shall next describe the intentions for establishing the phrase "Thus I have heard" (second of the three gates). "Based on what teaching did the Buddha originally place this phrase to produce trust among sentient beings? How can the characters '*ju shih*' (meaning "thus" or "in such a way") produce trust?" It can do so because Ānanda himself believed in the words of the Buddha and adhered to the words of the Buddha. Just as if the words were spoken by the Buddha himself, so do these words cause other sentient beings to produce trust in the same way. "How can the characters "wo-wen" ("I have heard") produce trust?" Had Ānanda, being a deficient person himself, have said "This Dharma was taught by me," many people would have been skeptical. But because he said he heard the Dharma from the Buddha, all people believed in it. Thus, to produce trust is [to be understood] in this manner. [174b17–22]

"What significance is there in producing trust?" Trust is the initial gate for entering the Dharma and plays a vital role in taking up the Dharma. Whenever one is to enter the Buddha Dharma, it is first necessary to awaken trust in the Dharma. It is for this reason that the sutras and treatises state:

> Unlike a person with hands who can reach out to the place of rare jewels and grab them as he wishes, one without hands is unable to obtain anything. Trusting [in the Dharma] is like this.

Therefore, if a person entering the Buddha Dharma possesses the hand of the trusting mind, he would then be able to grasp at will the jewels of Buddha Dharma. However, if one has no trust, there would be nothing to obtain. Therefore, one should awaken [trust]. [174b22–27]

As for the third (of the three gates in the preface for demonstrating trust), I shall now explain the meaning of the phrase, "Thus I have heard." In the past, people understood the character "*ju*" ("thus" or "similar") in many ways. As we now discuss it formally, there are two ways of understanding it. One way of understand is in terms of the teaching (*fa*), and the other is in terms of the person (*jen*). [174b27–c1]

In terms of the teaching, [the opening *Sutra* phrase] says "similar" [or "thus"] because the Buddha's words which Ānanda conveyed are similar to [previous] teachings. What the Tathāgata taught are teachings that were all previously proclaimed. He taught principles that were similar to the principles [which were previously taught], taught objects similar to the objects [which were previously taught], taught causes similar to [the previously taught] causes, and taught effects similar to [the previously taught] effects. Such being the case for all that he taught, it is rendered "similar." The phrase "similar teachings" (*ju-fa*) must be regarded as correct from the point of view of the principles. Consequently, as distorting the teachings is wrong, the "similar teachings" is deemed correct. [174c1–5]

In terms of the person, it says "similar" [or "thus"] because what Śākyamuni taught was similar to all the previous Buddhas. Since discrepant explanations are wrong while similar explanations are correct, [the *Sutra*] says "Thus [I have heard]." [174c5–7]

It is said "*I* have heard" because [the phrase] "I have heard" refers to Ānanda explaining for the sake of future beings the teaching which he has digested himself. "Why did he say 'I' when he actually heard it with his ear?" Granted [this *Sutra*] could have specified the actual sense faculty involved, all faculties are functions of the self [or "I"]. Since it is the principal element [of anything] that is revealed in its description, [the *Sutra* in this case] stated "*I* have heard." [174c75–9]

The question is asked, "Since no 'person' is recognized in the Buddhist teaching, where is the principal element on which [the *Sutra*] stated, 'I have heard'?" [174c9–10]

Even though there is no fixed principal element according to the teaching, that does not mean, however, that there is no idea of a governing function that is provisionally named. It is, therefore, possible to claim, "I". For this reason, the *Nirvana Sutra* states:

> "Four soldiers make up an army, and even though there is no fixed principal element, it is still possible for each soldier to proclaim, '*My* army is brave, strong and superior to others.'"(174c10–13]

[What your question raises] is the same as in this [analogy].

The question is asked, "Why does Ānanda who has realized the status of the Āryapudgalas still speak of a 'self' like the Pṛthagjanas?" [174c13–14]

Even though Ānanda also speaks of a self, this is not used in the same way as the Pṛthagjanas. How are they not the same? It is as explained by Nāgārjuna:

> There are three ways of speaking about the self. The first speaks of a self based on the perverted view [of the self] (*ātma-dṛṣṭi*); this refers to the Pṛthagjanas who claim that the self exists, since the passions derived from perverted views have not yet perished and the perverted view of the self exists. The second speaks of a self based on

pride (*māna*); this refers to those [at the stages of] Trainers who claim that the self exits, since even though the passions derived from perverted views are eliminated, passions derived from pride as well as from self pride still remain. The third claims an existence of the self in accordance with the ways of the world; this refers to those [at the stage of] Non-trainers whose perverted views and pride are eliminated, but for the purposes of propagation he proclaims the self in accordance with the ways of the world." [174c14–20]

Thus, here in this case, when Ānanda assembled the teaching [of the Buddha] he dwelt in [the saintly stage of] Non-trainers, having eliminated perverted views and pride. Only in order to propagate in accordance with the ways of the world, did he speak of the self. His case, therefore, is unlike that of the Pṛthagjanas. [174c20–21]

The question is asked, "The truth of non-self is the supreme teaching; why didn't Ānanda teach non-self in this supreme sense, rather than teach the self in accordance with the ways of the world?" [174c21–23]

The teaching must be so presented in order to instruct sentient beings who regard the self as real. If he did not speak of the self, on what basis will he be able to distinguish one person from another and make the people understand the teaching? Thus, those [in the stage of the Non-trainers] and the Buddhas speak about the "self" in refering to themselves for the purpose of instructing the people. [174c23–25]

*Translator's note: Hui-yüan turns to a discussion on the *Sutra* passages, "At one time, Śākyamuni Buddha was staying on Mount Gṛdhrakūṭa in Rājagṛha with a large assembly of twelve hundred and fifty Bhiksus. There were also thirty-two thousand Bodhisattvas led by the Dharma Prince, Mañjuśrī. At that time, in the great city of Rājagṛha, there was a prince named Ajātaśatru. . . ." (340c29–341a3ff) Hui-yüan regards this set of passages as the preface for initiating the teaching and discusses it by dividing it into five sections.

Even though [the *Sutra* passage] "At one time . . ." (340c29) carried two meanings (the two kinds of preface discussed earlier), since the prior section dealt entirely with the preface for demonstrating trust, I shall from this point concentrate on the preface for initiating the teaching. [174c25–27]

There are two locations involved with this part, and its passages are divided into five sections. As for the two locations, the first begins with the 'preface for initiating the teaching at different locations'; the Buddha resided on Vulture Peak but later appeared miraculously at the King's palace to instruct [Vaidehī]. The second location, which begins with the passage, "The Buddha disappeared from the Vulture Peak . . ." (341b9) constitutes the 'preface in which the [Buddha] himself goes to [assist in] the instruction.' This makes this *Sutra* and the *Śrīmālādevī Sutra* very much alike [on the point of the Buddha assisting someone else to teach the Dharma], and no such example is found among other sutras. [174c27–175a1]

The five sections into which this part is divided are as follow: first, "At one time" describes the time of the instruction; second, "the Buddha" reveals the fact that he is the person in charge of the instruction; third, "[When the Buddha] was staying at Rājagṛha . . ." describes the location of the instruction; fourth, "with a great [assembly] . . . ," which indicates the physical arrangement of the assembled followers; fifth, "At the time in the great city of Rājagṛha . . ." (341a2) describes the events leading up to the instruction. [175a1–4]

First, people have understood the meaning of "At one time" differently and have always been ready to destroy [each other's opinion]. A formal discussion here renders the morning (*ch'en*) at which the instruction took place "time" (*shih*). The Buddha during his lifetime gave instructions at various times; in order to simplify all the different times, this *Sutra* stated "At one [time]" (*i-shih*). This phrase is similar to what the *Nirvana Sutra* states:

> I at one time resided at Kapilavastu. I at one time resided at Rājagṛha. I at one time resided on the bank of River Ganges. I at one time resided in a cemetery.[17]

One should not interpret the meaning of [the phrase] differently from the way the Buddha understood it. [175a4–9]

As for the third section on the location of the instructions, "Rājagṛha" is the one most generally mentioned. This ancient city where numerous kings have resided is, thus, known as the "City of the Kings" (Rājagṛha). "Gṛdhrakūṭa" is specifically mentioned throughout the sutras and is translated as the "Peak of Spirits and Vultures." It was called the "Peak of Spirits and Vultures" because many spirits of ascetics as well as vultures dwelt on this peak. Since numerous vultures dwelt on this peak and the contour of the peak itself resembled a vulture's head, it was also translated as the "Vulture Head Peak." The *Sutra* stated, "the [Buddha] resided," to denote the places visited during his missionary travels. Although the truth-body is impartial and in reality without any identification [with any one location], [the sutras] specified a location only in order to teach; hence, the *Sutra* stated, "the [Buddha] resided." "For what reason did the *Sutra* go out of the way to say he resided at *this* [particular] location?" The reason for this is as explained in the *Fa-hua lun* (Dharma Flower Treatise):

> Only in order to reveal the supreme teaching was it specified that [Buddha] resided "here." As Rājagṛha was supreme among the cities and Vulture Peak the most excellent among the five mountains, the teaching [expounded there] is most exemplary. [175a9–19]

In the fourth section on the assembly, the Śrāvakas are seated in the front [of the assembly] while the Bodhisattvas are in the back. Most sutras are the same in this regard. "But why is this so?" There are three reasons for this. [175a19–20]

The first reason is the 'distinction based on proximity' (*chin-yüan fen-pieh*). Since the Śrāvakas are always emulating the Tathāgata, the sutras describe them as following closely behind the Buddha and lined up in the front of the assembly. Because the Bodhisattvas are different, they shall be discussed later. "Why are the Śrāvakas so close to the Tathāgata?" There are two reasons for this. First, it is said that the Śrāvakas are slightly inferior in intelligence and have yet to consummate the teachings of the Path. Even though they have obtained the fruit of the Āryapudgalas, they have ceased to progress further, for they are caught up in the mechanism of decorum and constantly in need of the Buddha to teach them; therefore, they mostly stayed close to the Buddha. For this reason, the Tathāgata up until the time he [died] in the Sāla Grove always regulated them through the precepts. As stated in the *Nirvana Sutra,* the Buddha regulated the Śrāvakas, for example, by prohibiting the eating of meat. In contrast, because the Bodhisattvas are profound, have consummated the teachings of the Path and no longer avail themselves of the teachings of the Buddha, they do not need to stay close to the Buddha. Secondly, because the Śrāvakas are still concealed from the Buddha's enlightenment and are deeply indebted to the Buddha for their having transcended the ranks of Pṛthagjanas to become Āryapudgalas, they constantly follow the Buddha to serve and honor him. In contrast, because the Bodhisattvas out of feelings for others travel about to teach and thus do not settle down in one place, they do not stay close to the Buddha. This discussion has been the first distinction based on proximity. [175a20–29]

The second [reason] is the distinction based on physical appearance (*hsing-hsiang fen-pieh*). As the Śrāvakas look dignified, well disciplined and respected by all the people in the world, they lined up in the front. In contrast, since the physical appearances of the Bodhisattvas are not fixed [as in the case of the Śrāvakas] in accordance with [the differing conditions faced in giving] instruction, they appeared in the rear of the assembly. This is as stated in a sutra, "When one summer [Bodhisattva] Mañjuśrī spent the retreat in three separate locations [in violation of the rules],

Mahākāśyapa reprimanded and punished him." This poignantly makes the point being made here. [175a29–b3]

The third [reason] is the distinction based on virtue (*te fen-pieh*). There are, as taught by Nāgārjuna, two kinds of teachings. One is the secret teaching, according to which the Bodhisattvas, being of superior virtue, should rightfully be in the front, while the Śrāvakas being of inferior virtue should, in principle, be in the back. The second kind is the revealed teaching. Since the Śrāvakas and Pratyekabuddhas have exhausted afflictions in the same way as the Buddha, they line up in the front. However, since the Bodhisattvas reveal themselves to Pṛthagjanas according to the conditions necessary for instructing them, they have not yet destroyed afflictions. If the people heard that the Bodhisattvas had lined up in front of the Arhats, they would be dismayed. The Bodhisattvas, therefore, lined up in the rear. Here in the *Sutra,* based on the revealed teaching, the Śrāvakas lined up in the front and the Bodhisattvas appeared in the back. [175b3–9]

In regards to the assembly of Śrāvakas, the first word [in section four] "with" (in "with a great assembly of . . .") means that the Śrāvakas are physically with him (the Buddha); hence the *Sutra* said "with." The phrase "great Bhikṣus (monks)" (*ta pi-ch'iu*) refers to this assembly. "Great" in the foreign countries is known as "*mahā.*" This is translated in three ways. The first is rendered "many" as in 'congregation of many people,' thus the meaning of the *Sutra* passage reads "an assembly of many." The second is rendered "superior" as in 'superior to other paths.' The third is rendered "great" as in 'extensively endowed with high virtues.' [175b9–12]

*Translator's note: In discussing the five meanings of the term "Bhikṣu," Hui-yüan says the first meaning ("fearful of Māra") is based on the first character (*pi*). The second ("mendicant") and third ("pure existence") meanings are based on both the first and the second characters (*pi* and *ch'iu*). The fourth ("pure observance of the precepts") and fifth ("destroying evil") are based on the second character (*ch'iu*).

The term "Bhikṣu" is another foreign word, and its meaning when translated in this country encompasses five meanings. The first meaning is "fearful of Māra." It is so said, since when Bhikṣus are about to leave their worldly existence, they dread doing battle with Māra. Thus, the *Sutra* states, "[The Bhikṣus are] fearful of Māra." "What makes the Bhikṣus become terrified when leaving their worldly existence?" They become terrified because Māra's nature is to abuse and terrify others who are superior to him and to fear Bhikṣus who, like him, instruct people to leave their [worldly] realm. Therefore, the Bhikṣus are frightened of Māra. As espoused in the *Nirvana Sutra,* this first meaning is expressed by the first [character of the phrase, "fearful"]. [175b12–17]

The second meaning is "mendicant priest." They are called "mendicant priests," because having abandoned their worldly existence and being without any possessions, they beg for alms for their livelihood. The third meaning is "pure life."[18] Because they lead a proper life, beg for alms and stay away from the teachings of improper life, it is rendered "pure life." For the last two meanings (second and third), their respective meanings were expressed by both [of the two characters].[19] [175b17–20]

The fourth meaning is "pure observance of the precepts," for the Bhikṣus diligently observe the precepts without transgression. The fifth meaning is "destroying evil," since the observance of the precepts destroys and separates one from evil. These last two meanings (fourth and fifth) are so designated because of the last character. [175b20–22]

When there is more than one, it is called an "assembly" (*chung*) [as in the *Sutra* passage, "assembly of one thousand two-hundred fifty great Bhikṣus."] The *Sutra* phrase "together with one-thousand two-hundred fifty [Bhikṣus]" indicates their number. "Why is it that the sutras most often mention this figure of 'one thousand two-hundred fifty Bhikṣus'?" It is because when the Buddha first realized the Path, he first brought to deliverance the three Kāśyapa brothers and their group of disciples that totalled one thousand. Gradually they came to the Buddha at Rājagṛha where he brought to deliverance Śariputra and Mahāmaudgalyāyana along with their group of disciples that numbered two-hundred fifty, thus, bringing the total to one-thousand two-hundred fifty [as in many of the sutras]. These sages, once steeped in darkness, were first delivered by the Buddha as they abandoned the wrong teaching and took refuge in the correct teaching; the debt they owed to the Buddha was so enormous that they constantly followed and honored him. This accounts for the huge number in the assembly. [175b22–28]

*Translator's note: Having discussed the Bhikṣus, Hui-yüan proceeds to discuss the Bodhisattvas who are also in the assembly.

From this point the *Sutra* discusses the Bodhisattvas. The term "Bodhisattvas" indicates a separate group [from that of the Bhikṣus]. In foreign countries, this term is formally rendered "P'u-t'i sa-to," but the translation is abbreviated so that it is simply rendered "P'u-sa"; here in this country, it is translated as "beings of enlightenment (*bodhi*)" (*tao chung-sheng*). "P'u-t'i" is rendered "enlightenment" and "sa-to" is rendered "beings." This group of people has personally pursued enlightenment, and they nurture others once their enlightenment is realized. They are thus called "beings of enlightenment."[20] [175b28–c1]

"If such is the case, all the Śrāvakas and Pratyekabuddhas also pursue enlightenment, actualize enlightenment in the same manner and nurture others. Why then is this [Bodhisattva group] the only one that is singled out to be called, "Bodhisattva" [in the sense of 'beings of enlightenment']?". [175c1–3]

The term "sages" has a general and a specific meaning. In its general meaning, it applies uniformally. Therefore, the *Nirvana Sutra* states:

> Those up to the rank of the Stream-winner are also called "Bodhisattvas," since they seek [to realize] the wisdom of exhaustion (*kṣaya-jñāna*)[21] and the Insight of Non-arising of *dharmas.*[22] They are referred to as "aspiring to become Buddhas," since they have been perfectly enlightened to both the common path and the uncommon path.[23] Those up to the rank of the Buddhas are also called "Stream-winners," since they cultivate realization of non-affliction and the reversal of the cycle of birth and death. [175c3–8]

In order to divide the sages, this group alone is called the "Bodhisattvas." "In equally dividing the sages, why is it that only this group is singled out to be called the 'Bodhisattvas'"? There are three reasons for this. The first reason is the distinction based on one's desired outcome that accords with one's wishes. Since only this group expected the great enlightenment (*bodhi*) while others did not seek [the same goal], only they are called the "beings of enlightenment." It is for this reason that the *Daśabhūmika-śāstra* (Treatise on the Sutra of Ten-stages) states, "Because they are firmly determined to attain the great enlightenment, they alone are called 'Bodhisattvas'." Hence, [our first] reason accords exactly with this [sutra passage]. [175c8–12]

The second reason is the distinction based on the desired principle that accords with one's understanding. The Pṛthagjanas dwell in [their attachment to] existence, while those of the two vehicles (Śrāvakas and Pratyekabuddhas) cling to [their attachment to] nonexistence. Both existence and nonexistence depart from the middle and are not in accord with the middle path. Consequently, they cannot be called the "beings of enlightenment." The Bodhisattvas differ in that they have abandoned both existence and nonexistence and accord with the middle path. [175c12–15]

The third reason is the distinction based on practice. Entrance to the Buddhist way has generally three approaches: teaching, understanding, and practice. The teaching is shallow, understanding is profound, but the practice is supreme. The Śrāvakas (*sheng-wen*), with weak faculties, follow the teaching and are so named; "*sheng*" (voice) means "teaching."

Since they are enlightened by 'eating' voices, they are called "*sheng-wen* (those who hear voices.") The Pratyekabuddhas (*yüan-chüeh*) are superior [to the Śrāvakas], and since they follow understanding, they are so designated; "*yüan* (conditioned nature) means "understanding." Since their enlightenment is based on interpretation, they are called "*yüan-chüeh* (those who are enlightened through correct understanding of the conditioned nature of existence)." The Bodhisattvas are supreme because they are so called based on practice. This practice is none other than the so-called enlightenment based on the benefit for oneself and the benefit for others; as they are able to accomplish enlightenment of both benefits—for the self and for others, they are called the "beings of enlightenment." For this reason, the *Bodhisattvabhūmi* states:

> Śrāvakas and Pratyekabuddhas are able to save only themselves, while the Bodhisattvas, being different, save themselves and others, and are called "those of the superior enlightenment." Because they are of superior enlightenment, they are called "beings of the enlightenment." [175c15–23]

As for the "thirty-two thousand," this indicates the number [of the Bodhisattvas present in the assembly]. Because Mañjuśrī is at the head [of the Bodhisattva group], the *Sutra* placed his name there and also named him in order to distinguish the superior from the inferior [among the Bodhisattvas]. Mañjuśrī means "exquisitely virtuous." [175c23–25]

*Translator's note: An extensive discussion ensues concerning the fifth section, which Hui-yüan saw as describing the background for the expounding of the *Sutra.* He divides the section into subsections, mini-sections, segments, phrases, etc.

From this point on the *Sutra* describes the fifth section concerning the events leading up to the instruction. There are two subsections. The first subsection describes the incarceration of Bimbisāra by his son and the dispatch by Tathāgata of people (his disciples) to explain the teaching on his behalf. The second subsection includes the passages "When Ajātaśatru asked the guard . . . ," (341a14) which describes Vaidehī's imprisonment by her son and how the Tathāgata himself went there to assist in the instruction. [175c25–28]

"Why is it fitting in the former case to dispatch someone, while in the latter case the Buddha himself went?" In the former case, the Buddha himself did not go because Bimbisāra requested simply to hear the teaching and so it was sufficient just to send anyone to give the instruction. In contrast, Buddha himself had to go in the latter case because Lady

Vaidehī sought rebirth in the Pure Country (*ching-kuo*), and instruction on the Pure Land could not be given by anyone but the Buddha. [175c28–176a3]

"Why bring up this evil and atrocious event [as a preface for] initiating the instruction?" This was to demonstrate that this world is extremely evil and detestable and to make people abandon and turn their backs on it. Even parents and their own flesh and blood children are endangering and harming each other, so how much worse the situation is among strangers! Thus, in desiring to make others similarly aspire for the Pure Land, Vaidehī explained to the Buddha, "I only request that you describe for me a place where there are no sorrows and where I should be reborn. I no longer wish to remain in the Jambūdvīpa, this defiled and evil world "(341b17).[24] The above discussion is an overview of the events leading up to the instruction. [176a3–7]

The passages of the first subsection are further divided into four mini-sections. The first mini-section describes how Bimbisāra was incarcerated by his son (341a3). The second mini-section, "The first lady of the country, named Vaidehī . . . ," (341a5) relates how Lady Vaidehī secretly offered food to the King to nourish his body. The third mini-section is from "Having finished rinsing his mouth . . ." (341a8) to the explanation of the teaching by the sagely disciples, which thereby, console the King's heart (341a13). The fourth section, "Twenty-one days having passed in this way . . . ," (341a18) which describes how the King did not die for many days on account of his eating and listening to the teaching. [176a7–11]

In regards to the first mini-section, "At that time in the great city of Rājagṛha there lived a prince named Ajātaśatru" (341a2) indicates the person who imprisoned his father. The phrase "at that time" refers to when the Buddha resided in the city of Rājagṛha. "The great city of Rājagṛha" is the place where he (Ajātaśatru) was born. "There was a prince" refers to a person with a broken finger. "Ajātaśatru" indicates a name to be avoided, and in this country it is translated "Unborn Hatred." Prior to the birth of this child, a physiognomist predicted that when the child was born he would most certainly harm his father. For this reason he came to be called an "Unborn Hatred."[25] [176a12–17]

"Following instructions of the evil friend Devadatta, [Ajātaśtru] . . . ," (341a3) describes the conditions that lead up to Ajātaśatru imprisoning his father. This event is the same as that explained in a sutra. That is to say, Devadatta was Buddha's younger cousin (on the father's side) and an older blood brother of Ānanda. After leaving his household existence, Devadatta cultivated and attained the Five Transcendental Powers[26] and requested that Ajātaśatru be his lay-supporter (*dānapati*). He also went to the Buddha one day and sought to take away the Buddha's disciples, saying, "World Honored One, you are getting on in your years. It is best that you hand your disciples over to me, and I shall instruct them." The Buddha scolded him:

> Śāriputra and Maudgalyāyana possess supernatural powers and great wisdom. Why should I not hand over my disciples to them, rather than to you who is ignorant and will end up eating your own words?

Greatly angered[27] by what he heard, Devadatta went to Ajātaśatru to disclose to him the conditions surrounding Ajātaśatru's [malicious] injury on the day of his birth and encouraged him to destroy his father. Ajātaśatru, then, proclaimed:

> By becoming the king myself, I shall kill Gautama; and after becoming the Buddha, I, as both the new King and the new Buddha, will change the world so that the world will not be an undesirable place.

For these reasons, Ajātaśatru generated the intent to destroy his father, and, thus, the *Sutra* stated, here, "Following the instructions of the evil friend Devadatta, Ajātaśatru. . . ." [176a17–27]

What follows depicts Ajātaśatru's imprisonment of his father. "He arrested his father . . ." (341a4) means he imprisoned him. "He prohibited all officers [from seeing him] so that no one was able to approach the King" (341a5) means the King was isolated and could not see anyone. "From what reason of his past life did King Bimbisāra have to meet with such peril?" The reason is as stated in the *Nirvana Sutra:*

> Bimbisāra in his past life was also a king. One day, traveling through the Vipula Mountains on a deer hunt, he found himself sadly without a catch. In meeting up with an ascetic, the king decided to chase him on horseback, and in the end he ordered him killed. The ascetic as he was about to die made a malevolent vow, "I vow to return in my next life and just as you have destroyed me today, I shall mentally and verbally destroy you."

That ascetic is today Ajātaśatru; the king who ordered the murder of the ascetic is King Bimbisāra. King Bimbisāra has, therefore, returned at this time to be destroyed by Ajātaśatru. [176a27–b5]

What follows below is the second mini-section, which relates how Lady Vaidehī secretly offered food to the King to nourish his body. This mini-section first describes how the Lady offered food and later how the King ate it. Regarding the former, the first phrase "the first lady of the country, named Vaidehī" (341a5) points out the person [who offered food]. She is also the actual mother who gave birth to Ajātaśatru. "She venerated the great King" (341a6) indicates her deep respect for him. She offered him food because of her respect for him, which is why the *Sutra* went out of its way to mention it (her respect for the King). "She washed and purified . . ." (341a6) means her body [pasted with honey and ghee mixed with corn flour] was offered as food. That the King ate the food is self-evident (the second part of this mini-section), [and thus does not require further explanation]. [176b5–10]

The third mini-section follows below and accounts for how the sages (Buddha's disciples) instructed the King in the teaching so as to console him. This mini-section first relates how King Bimbisāra initiated the request [for a teacher]. "At that time, Maudgalyāyana . . ." (341a11) means that the sage came over [to the King] to explain the teaching. Concerning the request, the first phrase "having rinsed his mouth" concludes the preceding section and initiates the following section (*tieh-ch'ien ch'i-hou*).[28] "Putting his hands together and duly paying respects," is a bodily action for making a request of the Buddha. Because he wanted the Tathāgata to feel pity for him and to communicate the teaching, he made the bodily show of respect. "He then uttered . . ." (341a9 ) indicates that Bimbisāra made an oral request to Maudgalyāyana. "Great Maudgalyāyana, you are my good friend" (341a10) means he wanted him to come. "I request that you, with compassion for me, initiate me in the Eight Precepts" (341a10)[29] means that the King sought pity and that Maudgalyāyana was to initiate him in the Eight Precepts. With regard to the sage's explanation, the *Sutra* first describes how Maudgalyāyana responded to the earlier oral request by initiating him in the Eight Precepts. "Flying as fast as a falcon or an eagle, he arrived at the King's place,"(341a11) is the response to the earlier bodily action requesting his good friend to come. "Day after day he initiated the King in the eight precepts" (341a11) is the oral initiation responding to the earlier request for the precepts. [176b10–17]

"What are the Eight Precepts?" They are: (1) to refrain from killing, (2) to refrain from stealing, (3) to refrain from sexual misconduct, (4) to refrain from telling a lie, (5) to refrain from drinking liquor, (6) to refrain from singing and dancing, cultivating performing skills, or going to see or to hear performances, (7) wearing perfume, scented clothing, and other ornaments on the body, (8) to refrain from sleeping on a high, large bed, and (9) to refrain from eating after mid-meal. [176b17–21]

"These add up to nine. How can you call them Eight Precepts?" If based upon the *Abhidharma* (canonic commentarial) literature, the two precepts for prohibiting the wearing of perfume, scented clothing, and the sleeping on high beds are treated as one and the same precept under 'ornaments and raised dwelling'; thus, they are called the "Eight Precepts." If based on *Ch'eng-shih [lun]* or *Ta-chih [tu] lun,* the first eight are precepts, while the last one is abstinence.[30] When abstinence and precepts are combined they are called the "Eight Precepts and Abstinence." The meaning of 'Eight Precepts and Abstinence' is as explained extensively in the *Separate Treatise* (i.e., the *Mahayana Encyclopedia*) which delineates this subject in detail.[31] Bimbisāra had the monks initiate him, because the householders also observe these Eight Precepts, which are basically instructions, meant for the world-renouncer. [176b21–26]

The following states that the Tathāgata was requested to come in person, but he, instead, sent someone else to give the instruction. The reason for Buddha himself not going is as previously explained. "Why did the Buddha select and send Pūrṇa to give the instructions?" Among the disciples he selected and sent Pūrṇa because he was the most skillful at opening up the people's heart [to the teaching]. [176b26–29]

The following is the fourth mini-section, which depicts how by eating [the food that Lady Vaidehī secretly brought in] and by listening to the teaching, Bimbisāra did not die for many days. The descriptions that are revealed in [this mini-section] are self-evident. [176b29–c1]

*Translator's note: Having completed the discussion of the four mini-sections of the first subsection, Hui-yüan proceeds to the second subsection which contains four mini-sections of its own. The mini-sections are further divided into segments, which in turn are divided either into "sentences" (*chü*) or into "passage segments" (*wen-ch'ü*).

What follows below from this point [in the *Sutra*] constitutes the second subsection, which relates the confinement of Lady [Vaidehī] by her son and the arrival of the Buddha to assist in the teaching. There are four mini-sections. The first discloses the son's confinement of the Lady. The second, "When Vaidehī was imprisoned . . . ," (341b2) indicates how Vaidehī requested the Buddha because of her confinement. The third, "Before she even raised her head . . . ," (341b7) reports the arrival of the Buddha and his disciples in response to her request. The fourth, "When Vaidehī saw the World Honored One . . . ," (341b13) relates how Vaidehī broke down out of despair when she saw the Buddha. [176c1–5]

The first mini-section has three further segments. The first segment describes how King Ajātaśatru wanted to destroy his mother. The second, "At that moment, a minister . . ." (341a21) states that the ministers persuaded [King Ajātaśatru not to kill his mother] and, that they, thereby, did not comply [with the King's wishes]. The third is "the King ordered the officers . . . ," (341b1), which signals that the King with his anger not totally abated, placed his mother under confinement. [176c5–7]

The first segment has three sentences. First, "Ajātaśatru asked the guard" means he was asking, "Where is King Bimbisāra now?" Second, "the guard" means the person who gave an account of [Bimbisāra's state]. Third, "The King [Ajātaśatru] on hearing what the guard said became enraged" means he then wanted to destroy his mother. [176c7–9]

The first sentence, "In hearing these words" exhibits the reason for his (Ajātaśatru) anger. "Enraged with his mother . . ." means he verbally scolded and rebuked his mother; he called his father a criminal and his mother an accomplice, and blamed the monks for being evil persons. What these words reveal is self-evident. "He then grabbed a sword . . ." make evident that he personally wanted to destroy his mother. This concludes the first segment. [176c9–12]

The second segment in which the ministers do not comply [with the King's wishes] by advising [the King not to kill his mother] has four passage segments: (1) the ministers advising and not complying, (2) the King being terrified, (3) Jīvaka again advising, and (4) on hearing about the Buddha, the King releasing his mother. [176c12–14]

In the first passage segment, the *Sutra* first indicates the advisors (the ministers). "Paying proper respects to the King . . ." (341a22) discloses the manner in which the two ministers advised the King. "When the two grand ministers stated these words . . ." (341a26) describes how the two having finished advising withdrew themselves. The [role of] advisors is self-evident [and requires no explanation.] In regard to their advice, their observance of proper respects was that of 'bodily advice,' and their speaking, and so forth to the King was that of 'oral advice.' As to what [the two ministers said to the King], they first revealed how the present case [with King Ajātaśatru] differed from the past; ever since the first Kalpa there had been innumerable evil kings, but none had ever destroyed his own mother. "King, if you now [kill your mother] . . ." (341a24) describes to the King how the present case differed from any past cases, and that were he now to destroy his mother, he would "bring disgrace upon the military class." "We cannot bear [to hear] . . ." (341a25) demonstrates that they themselves[32] detested evil. "We cannot bear to hear of it" means that they cannot bear to hear of it in their own minds. "But were he to kill his mother, it would be the eyes that would see the killing. What words would be heard?" "We cannot bear to hear" refers to the stories that would circulate among the people of the world. "It would not be suitable to live here" (341a26) means the ministers themselves would not live there. The above discussion has completed the [topic of the ministers'] advice, and the following discussion describes their manner of leaving [King Ajātaśatru's presence]. [176c14–21]

"With their speech concluded" (341a26) connects the previous section of the *Sutra* and initiates the subsequent section. "Holding down their swords, they stepped backwards and withdrew [from the King's presence]"

(341a27) aptly describes the departure of the ministers from the premises. The ministers turned their backs on the King in fear of the impending danger [that they believed would descend upon the King for his actions]. Because the sword is to protect oneself, it is necessary to hold it down when stepping back to withdraw [from the premises]. The above discussion has dealt with the minister's advice. [176c21–24]

The second passage segment on the topic of the King being alarmed follows below. "Ajātaśatru became terrified" (341a28) means his heart was frightened. On seeing the two ministers withdraw by holding their swords down, the King became alarmed by this strange conduct; consequently, he became terrified. "The King announced to Jīvaka . . ." (341a28) indicates the verbal words that were then asked. Fearful that they had turned their backs on him to side with his father, the King then asked "Will you not be friendly to me?" [176c24–27]

"Jīvaka replied . . ." (341a28) is the third passage segment; Jīvaka again advises the King as before, "Be rational and do not injure your mother." These were Jīvaka's words of advice. [176c27–28]

"The King on hearing this . . ." (341a29) is the fourth passage segment, which relates how the King released his mother on account of the advice. "On hearing these words" means the King heard the words of Jīvaka's repeated advice. "The King repented and sought their support" (341a29) means he repented for his earlier transgressions. This "repentance" is for the earlier transgression of wanting to destroy his mother. Because the King did not kill his mother on account of the request of the two ministers, the *Sutra* said "He sought their support." The King then threw down the sword and stopped himself from destroying his mother" (341a29) means he put a stop to an imminent crime; he put an end to the killing. [176c28–177a3]

The above four passage segments make up the second segment [of the first mini-section of the second subsection], which concerned the two ministers advising the King and how they did not comply [with the King's desire]. [177a3–4]

"The King ordered . . ." (341b1) constitutes the third segment that describes Ajātaśatru's confinement of his mother due to his festering anger. With his festering anger unabated and fearful that his mother would again offer food to King Bimbisāra, King Ajātaśatru ordered her confined. From "Ajātaśatru asked the guard" (341a14) down to this point (341b2) comprises the first mini-section [of the second subsection], which detailed Vaidehī's confinement at the hands of her son. [177a4–7]

What follows below this point, the second mini-section, gives an account of Vaidehī's request for the Buddha due to her confinement. In other words, she requested the Tathāgata to send his disciples to her so that she might have an audience with them. This mini-section has three segments: (1) from when she is about to make the request to the first paying of proper respects (341b2–3), (2) "Spoke these words . . ." (341b3), which initiates her formal request, (3) "After speaking these words, in grief" she wept . . ." (341b6), which records that after making her request, she again paid proper respects. [177a7–10]

In the first segment, the initial phrase "Vaidehī being thus confined" makes the transition from the previous section and initiates the following section. "Stricken with sorrow and grief" (341b2) describes her troubled mind. "Facing towards Gṛdhrakūṭa . . ." (341b3) describes the proper respects of her bodily action; the paying of proper respects is none other than requesting with the body. [177a10–12]

With regard to the third (but should read "second"; the text is in error) segment that initiates the formal request, "World Honored One, in former times you always sent Ānanda to come and comfort me" (341b3) brings up the past so as to compare it with the present in hope that the Buddha would not fail to send [Ānanda this time again]. "I am now in sorrow and grief . . ." (341b4) reveals how Vaidehī sought to make the present the same as the past [when conditions for her were better]. "I am now in sorrow and grief" reveals how deeply she was suffering. "World Honored One, you being so majestic and important, in no way will I be able to see you," (341b5) means that she did not presume to expect the Buddha himself to come. "I pray that you send [Maudgalyāyana] . . . ," (341b5) is a request [to the Buddha] to send his disciples so that "she may have an audience with them" (341b6). "Why did Vaidehī seek to see Maudgalyāyana and Ānanda?" She chose to see them, because Maudgalyāyana came from a good family and Ānanda, the Buddha's attendant, always accompanied him. Moreover, she sought to see both, because staying confined at the back of the palace, it proved disadvantageous to choose to see only one. "What did she seek to see?" Vaidehī grew weary of this evil realm and sought rebirth in the Pure Land. She wanted the two disciples to mourn her situation, to convey her intentions, and to request the Buddha [for instructions regarding her rebirth in the Pure Land]. Such were the reasons for her seeking to see them. [177a12–21]

With regard to the third segment, "Having uttered these words, in grief she shed tears like rain" (341b6) reports how Vaidehī looked to Buddha for sympathy. "Facing towards the Buddha in the distance, she paid him proper respects" (341b6) indicates the person to whom she wished to make the request. Having already paid proper respects she once again repeated it here to display her deep concern [about her predicament and what she was about to request]. [177a21–22]

The third mini-section follows below this point and reveals how the

Buddha and the two disciples came quickly in response to her request. Regarding this, the first phrase "Before she even raised her head" (341b7) shows how quickly the sages came. Because her condition was deemed very serious, the sages rushed to her side before she raised her head. "At that time . . ." (341b6) reveals how the sages hurried to her. "At that time the Honored One resided on Gṛdhrakūṭa" (341b7) indicates where the sages resided. "The Buddha understood the thoughts that Vaidehī had on her mind" (341b7) indicates Buddha's understanding of Vaidehī's inner mind. "The Buddha ordered Great Maudgalyāyana and Ānanda to go" (342b8) constitutes a verbal order. "The Buddha also disappeared from Gṛdhrakūṭa and appeared in the King's palace" (341b10) demonstrates that the Buddha went in person. In order to respond quickly to Vaidehī's thought of deep reverence [for himself and his disciples], the Buddha ordered his disciples to go to the palace [by traversing] through the sky. Then, the Tathāgata himself disappeared from Gṛdhrakūṭa and appeared at the palace. Because it was difficult to traverse on the ground to the recesses of the palace where Vaidehī was confined, the Buddha performed this [miraculous] transformation. "Why did the Tathāgata himself go when Vaidehī earlier sought to see just his disciples?" It was made necessary for the Buddha himself to go, since the revelation of the Pure Land can neither be accomplished nor its difficulties be fully explained by anyone other than the Buddha. [177a23–b4]

What follows below this point constitutes the fourth mini-section, which clarifies how on account of meeting with the sages, Vaidehī expressed her grief and sorrow. This mini-section discusses first her meeting [with the Buddha] and later her grief and sorrow. [177b4–5]

Regarding the meeting, "When Vaidehī raised her head after paying proper respects" (341b10) describes the occasion of her meeting; "she saw the Honored One . . ." (341b10 ) clearly states whom she was meeting. As the Buddha and his disciples were all eminent [religious] persons, the worldly protocols had to be avoided when meeting them. Because the palace chamber [where Vaidehī was confined] was not an appropriate place for instruction, the Buddha and the disciples remained in the sky. [177b5–8]

The following describes her grief and sorrow. "On seeing the Buddha" (34b13) makes the transition from what had earlier been observed. "She discarded her ornaments and prostrated herself on the ground" (341b13) manifests a bodily karmic action stemming from severe distress. "She inquired of the World Honored One" (341b14) displays a verbal karmic action stemming from resentment and grief. "World Honored One, what evil karmic action did I commit in my previous life to give birth to this evil child?" (341b14) evinces how a transgression committed in her previous life had brought on this grief. "World Honored One, what conditions caused you to be a relative of Devadatta?" (341b15) questions the Buddha's possible motive for [coming to see Vaidehī]. The former phrase expresses the grief she was feeling over her evil son, while the latter phrase conveys her resentment of the Buddha for once having had an evil disciple [like Devadatta]. This resentment stemmed precisely from Devadatta telling Ajātaśatru [about the secret surrounding Ajātaśatru's past], so that the latter committed evil deeds [on his parents]. [177b8–14]

*Translator's note: Having discussed the preface, Hui-yüan now comments on the section about the main purport of the *Sutra.* Compared to the preface and the conclusion, the main section is the longest. The four subsections divide along what Hui-yüan calls the "general" and "specific," where the former refers to pure lands in general while the latter deals specifically with Sukhāvatī and Buddha Amitābha.

Part two follows below and elucidates the main purport (*cheng-tsung*) of the *Sutra.* The passages of this part have four sections: (1) There is Vaidehī's general request (*t'ung-ch'ing*), (2) "At that time, the World Honored One emitted light from between his eyebrows . . ." (341b2) is the Buddha's general revelation (*t'ung-hsien*), (3) Vaidehī saying to the Buddha, "Even though the Buddha lands are pure . . ." (341b27) is her specific request (*pieh-ch'ing*), and (4) "The World Honored One, then, smiled gently . . ." (341cl) is the Tathāgata's specific revelation (*pieh-hsien*). [177b14–17]

Section one has four subsections: (1) There is her seeking of rebirth in a pure country; (2) "I no longer enjoy this corrupt and evil realm of Jambūdvīpa . . ." (341b17) relates how she had come to detest this defiled land; (3) "Now, World Honored One, prostrating on all five limbs before you . . ." (341b19) describes how she repented from destroying the evil causes about which she had earlier expressed detestation; and (4) "I only wish that the sun-like Buddha teach me. . . ." (341b20) describes how she inquired into the good causes about which she had earlier requested. [177b17–20]

Regarding the first subsection, "I only wish" (*wei-yüan*) (341b16) bears the meaning of "concentrated search." Because Vaidehī sought Buddha with a concentrated mind, the *Sutra* stated, "I only wish." "The place where there are no sorrow" (341b16) relates clearly the object of her search. Being peaceful, the Pure Land is appropriately named "the place where there are no sorrows." "[Place] where I should be reborn" (341b17) expresses what she seeks to do. [177b20–23]

The second subsection, which describes the object of her detestation, "I do not wish to live in this corrupt and evil world of Jambūdvīpa," (341b17) constitutes a general statement about what she detested. "I do not wish to live in the Jambūdvīpa" constitutes one gate and reveals the pain stemming from her resentment and hurt. "I do not wish to live in this corrupt and evil world" constitutes the other gate and reveals how she detested the pain of evil Destinies of the Sahā World-realm.[33] This "corrupt and evil . . ." specifically shows what she detested and also describes the above two gates. From this point to "there is much accumulation of evil" (341b18) discloses the reasons for Vaidehī's earlier statement, "I no longer wish to live in this corrupt and evil world." This section describes the suffering that results from belonging to the three [evil] Destinies.[34] This is the reason for her statement on no longer desiring to live in this corrupt and evil place. In summarizing the above discussion, "this corrupt and evil realm" refers to this Sahā World-realm which is, indeed, a corrupt and evil place. [177b23–29]

"Filled with hells, beasts and hungry ghosts" describes the existence [in the Sahā realm] of the results of the evil paths of the three Destinies. "Ti-yü" (underground prison) in the foreign countries is rendered by "*niraya*" (or "naraka"). The *Tsa-hsin [lun]*[35] (*Treatise on the Heart of Collected Abhidharma*) explains that because the word means "that which cannot be enjoyed," it was rendered as "underground prison." The *Ti-ch'ih lun* explains that because it means "something to be completely detested," it was rendered as "*naraya*." All of these, however, are not the correct definitions because they explain [psychologically] in terms of the detesting mind. In discussing this correctly, it is a prison below the ground. On account of its being the place where transgressors receive their retributions, it is called the "underground prison." [177b29–c5]

The *Tsa-hsin [lun]* explains that "beasts" (*ch'u-sheng*) was rendered "beasts" as a secondary meaning. This merely describes its characteristics (*hsiang*) but does not clarify the meaning (*i*) of the term.[36] "What is then the true meaning of the term?" The basis for so naming lies in its meaning as "domesticated [animals]." As all the people of the world domesticate these beings in order to use them for labor or to eat them as food, they have [primarily been understood] to mean "domesticated living beings" [rather than as "beasts"]. [177c5–8]

Regarding the term "hungry ghosts" the *Tsa-hsin [lun]* explains that they were called "hungry ghosts" on account of their immense craving. This again merely describes the characteristics and does not clarify the meaning of the term. The correct understanding of the term's meaning is as follows. Being starved and thirsty, they are called "hungry"; being ethereal, cowardly and very much dreaded, they are called "ghosts." [177c9–11]

Since [each of] the three thousand lands [in the Sahā World-realm] alike contain these evil Destinies, the *Sutra* states "[the Sahā realm is] filled with [hell-beings, etc.]" (341b18) "There is an accumulation of much evil" (341b18) refers to the causes of evil paths. Because there is no one to prevent evil from happening the *Sutra* speaks of "much," or because evil is constantly occurring, it again speaks of "much." Taking life, stealing, being unchaste, and so forth contradict the principles and are detrimental to other beings; hence they are explained as "evil." "Collection" is that which is referred to as "accumulation" [in the *Sutra* passage]. [177c11–13]

That this corrupt world contained the future causes and effects of evil was the reason that Vaidehī did not wish to live in it. "I pray that I do not in the future either hear evil voices or see evil people" (341b18) reflects her earlier statement, "I do not wish to live in Jambūdvīpa." That the Jambūdvīpa contained evil practices and evil people was the reason that she did not wish to live in Jambūdvīpa. On account of evil practices in her previous life, she encountered evil people in this life. "Evil practices" is expressed [in the *Sutra*] as "evil voices." To pray that she will not hear evil voices means she does not *want* to hear evil voices; how much more is the case for not wanting to meet in the future beings who have committed grave acts such as Ajātaśatru and others, who are the very people [the *Sutra*] calls "evil people." The meaning of "I pray that I do not see evil people" is to be understood in the same way [as in the case with not wanting to hear evil voices]. The crimes that Ajātaśatru and others committed are referred to as "evil" in the *Sutra.* This evil grave act is referred to as the "evil voices." To pray that she will not hear evil voices means that she does not *want* to hear; how much more so with regard to not wanting to meet evil people. Those who commit grave acts are referred to as "evil people" [in the *Sutra*]. What [Vaidehī] wished no longer to see has been the object of her detestation, which subsection two elucidated above. [177c13–22]

The third subsection follows below this point and treats how she repented in order to destroy the evil causes of which she had earlier expressed her detestation. "Now, World Honored One, prostrating on all five limbs before you" (341b19) describes the means for expressing repentance. Both hands, two feet and the forehead constitute the five parts of the body [which must touch the ground]. Because utilizing the five parts of the body for homage expresses respect for the essence of Dharma, the *Sutra* spoke of "prostrating herself on the ground." "I repent (*ch'an-hui*) and ask for your mercy," (341b20) properly depicts her repentance. Because she looked to the Buddha to grant mercy and to hear her expression of repentance, the *Sutra* stated, "I ask for your mercy." "*Ch'an-mo*" (a transliteration of *kṣama*) is a foreign term, meaning "to feel regret for one's transgressions." Because a foreign and a Chinese term were juxtaposed [to make a compound term], the *Sutra* states, "I repent (*ch'an-hui*).[37] [177c22–27]

"When did Vaidehī commit the crime for which she is now seeking repentance?" It is said to have been in a past life. "Under what condition did Vaidehī know that she had transgressed in her past life, for which she now seeks repentance?" She realized it when she gave birth in this life to an evil child who now confines her. By taking the result and examining the cause, it became clear that she had committed a crime in her past life. Because she feared that the retribution for her criminal act had not been exhausted in the present life and that she would still be affected by it in the future, she felt compelled to repent so as to destroy [the evil causes]. [177c27–178a2]

The fourth subsection follows below this point, in which Vaidehī inquires about the good causes for which she had earlier aspired. "I only wish of the sun-like Buddha" (341b20) points to the person from whom the answer is being sought. Since the Buddha is able to destroy the darkness of the ignorance of sentient beings, just as the sun eliminates darkness, the *Sutra* says, "the sun-like Buddha." "Please instruct me to perceive the place where one can be reborn by performing purified acts" (341b20) clearly describes the object of her request. The rest of the exquisite Buddha lands are also places of refuge attained by performing totally good acts. They were, therefore, called "the places where one can be reborn by performing purified acts," and it was such a place of purified action that [Vaidehī requested when she beseeched the Buddha,] "Please instruct me to perceive." [178a2–7]

Section two follows below this point. In response to Vaidehī's request, the Tathāgata performed a general revelation wherein he completely manifested the entire Buddha lands. With regard to this, the *Sutra* states, "the Buddha emitted rays from between his eyebrows" (341b21). The Tathāgata had between his eyebrows a white curled hair that was white as snow and slightly over eleven feet in circumference.[38] From this hair between the eyebrows a light was emitted into the sky, and it revolved in a right (clockwise) swirl like a Vaiḍūrya gem (lapis lazuli).[39] The Buddha emitted the light from this auspicious mark. [178a7–11]

Next, the *Sutra* describes how the light, which illuminated all the immeasurable number of Buddha lands, returned to rest on Buddha's head and then was transformed into a golden platform. (341b21) The *Sutra* then describes how the Buddha fully revealed on the platform immeasurable number of Buddha lands for Vaidehī to see. [178a11–12]

The question is asked, "Since Vaidehī wished to be reborn specifically in Sukhāvatī, why did the Buddha not simply reveal that particular country, instead of a general revelation of all the Buddha lands?" [178a12–13]

Had the Buddha not performed a general revelation, there would have been no comparative basis enabling the Buddha not only to reveal the land of Amitābha as the most supreme of all but also to enhance its profound bliss. Therefore, he first performed the general revelation. [178a13–15]

Section three follows below this point and describes Vaidehī's specific request. In specifically requesting rebirth in Sukhāvatī, Vaidehī said to the Buddha, "All these Buddha lands are also pure and radiant with rays of light," (341a27) which refers to the Buddha's earlier general revelation. "I now wish to be reborn in the Realm of Utmost Bliss, the place of Buddha Amitābha" (341b28) identifies what she was seeking. "[World Honored One,] I only wish that you instruct me to think (*szu-wei*) and to concentrate (*cheng-shou*)"[40] (341b29) states the causes for actualizing the object of her request. Thought and concentration can be distinguished into two gates. The first distinguishes the meditative (*ting[-shan*]) and the non-meditative (*san[-shan*]). The three purified acts (*san ching-yeh*) (to be discussed below) are the non-meditative mind that involves thinking and calculating and is thus called "thinking." But the sixteen correct visualizations are explained as "concentration." The second [of two gates] is based on the meaning of the sixteen correct visualizations. The first two visualizations are called "thinking," while the remaining fourteen visualizations, from the 'visualization of the ground' (number three) are performed on the basis of a settled [mind] and are, thus, explained as "concentration." [178a15–22]

Section four follows below this point and relates the Tathāgata's specific revelation. There are two subsections: (1) the Buddha emits rays from his body to benefit King Bimbisāra (341c2); and (2) the Buddha gives a sermon on the Dharma to benefit Lady Vaidehī (341c5). [178a22–24]

In the first subsection, the *Sutra* first describes how the Buddha's light illuminated the King and how the King was subsequently benefited. Since the King had earlier become a Stream-winner, the *Sutra* now says, "He made progress to become a Non-returner."[41] (231c4) [178a24–25]

In the [second subsection in which the Buddha] benefits Lady Vaidehī, those passages from the Buddha first giving the sermon (341c5) to those where, upon completion of these utterances, Vaidehī and the five hundred women attendants obtained [Insight of] Non-arising [of *dharmas*] (346a27), describes how Vaidehī was benefited. [178a25–27]

The first part [of the second subsection, that is, the Buddha's sermon] has four mini-sections. The first mini-section briefly indicates that Amitābha's place is "not far from here." (341c5) The second mini-section, "You must restrain [your thoughts] . . . ," (341c6) constitutes general encouragement for visualization-inspection. The third mini-section, "I shall explain for you in detail the analogies," (341c6) reveals the characteristics as well as the benefits of the explanation. The fourth mini-section, "Those who desire to be reborn in his country, shall cultivate the three meritorious acts . . . ," (341c8) correctly explains the acts necessary for rebirth. [178a27–b1]

In the first mini-section, "You should know that Amitābha Buddha dwells not far from here" means that his land is [only] ten thousand times a hundred million lands away; hence the *Sutra* stated "not far."[42] [178b1–2]

The second mini-section on the general encouragement of the visualization, "You should visualize his country" (341c6) shows how the Buddha encouraged visualization of the dependent rewards (*i-pao*), while "[You should visualize] those in the Pure Land, who have accomplished purified acts," indicates the Buddha's encouragement of the visualization of the main reward.[43] In other words, [the main reward refers to] the Buddha, the Bodhisattvas, the people of the three [highest][44] grades of rebirth and so forth, who are called "those who have accomplished the purified acts." [178b2–5]

The third mini-section begins with "I shall now explain for you in detail the analogies" (341c6); it reveals the characteristics of the explanation. The following is referred to as "analogies," since the descriptions of the sun, water, and so forth as well as of the iconographical images of the Buddha and Bodhisattva in this realm (Jambūdvīpa) approximates those in that realm (Amitābha's land). "And the Buddha will bring [to rebirth] . . ." (341c7) describes the benefits of the explanation. Precisely since the explanation benefited Vaidehī and other Pṛthagjanas, the *Sutra* states, "And the Buddha will bring to rebirth in the western realm all Pṛthagjanas who desire to cultivate the purified acts." (341c7) [178b5–9]

The passages of the fourth mini-section are distinguished into two parts. The first instructs the cultivation of the three kinds of purified acts, that is, the non-meditative good acts (*san-shan*) for rebirth. The second part is "The Buddha spoke to Ānanda [and Vaidehī] . . ." in which the Buddha instructs them to cultivate the sixteen correct visualizations, that is, the meditative good acts (*ting-shan*) for rebirth. [178b9–11]

In the first part, the *Sutra* begins with general encouragement for the cultivation of visualization, then enumerates them separately, and ends with a general conclusion and a praise. The passage "Those who desire rebirth in that land should cultivate the three meritorious acts" (341c8) is the general encouragement. The first gate concerns the specific [enumerations], and is a teaching that is common to the Pṛthagjanas. The second is a teaching that is common to those of the two vehicles, while the third is strictly a Mahayana teaching, which is not in common [with the Hinayanists]. [178b11–14]

Regarding the first gate, the *Sutra* first describes how to perform the meritorious acts. "To filially support [one's parents] and respectfully serve teachers and elders" (341c9) are conducts that honor one's superiors. "Be of a compassionate heart and do not kill" (341c10) are conducts of compassion towards one's inferiors. "To cultivate the Ten Virtuous Acts (*shih shan-yeh*)" (341c10) is a practice of calm (*śamatha*).[45] The bodily [virtuous acts] eliminate the three heresies, while the verbal [virtuous acts] separate oneself from the four transgressions, and the mental [virtuous acts] destroy the three evils; these make up the Ten Virtuous Acts.[46] They are to be understood according to the *Separate Treatise,* which discusses this subject in detail. [178b14–18]

The second gate, "To observe the three refuges" (341c10) constitutes the precept for the householders; this [observance of the three refuges] also comprise the Ten Precepts of the novice monks.[47] The meaning of the Three Refuges is to be understood according to the *Separate Treatise,* which discusses it in detail.[48] "To maintain all the precepts and not to violate the rules of decorum" (341c10) stipulates the precepts for the world-renouncers. Not committing the Four Grave Transgressions refers above to "maintaining the precepts," while freeing oneself from the light transgressions was explained above as "[not violating] the rules of decorum."[49] Also, freeing oneself from an evil nature refers above to "maintaining the precepts," that is to say, to free oneself completely from killing, stealing, sexual acts, and so forth. Freeing oneself from the light transgressions refers above to "not violating the rules of decorum," that is to say, to free oneself completely from the transgressions of partaking of alcoholic drinks, and so forth [178b18–23]

In the third gate, the *Sutra* first admonishes the cultivation of benefiting oneself (*tzu-li*) and later describes the [cultivation] of benefiting others (*li-t'a*). The former, that is, benefiting oneself, "They should generate the mind aspiring for *bodhi* (enlightenment)" (341c11) explicates how to generate the vow. "*Bodhi*" is the fruit of Buddhahood [as the culmination of the Buddhist] path, and it is rendered "*bodhi*" in explaining [the nature of] its perfect comprehension. To generate the thought for a firm direction [towards the attainment of *bodhi*] is "to generate the mind [aspiring for *bodhi*]." As it is important, the *Sutra* discussed it, saying in effect [to the practitioner], he should also obtain what the Buddha obtained in a similar manner. The meaning of the *bodhi* mind is to be understood according to the *Separate Treatise,* which enumerates it in detail. "To firmly believe in the principle of cause and effect" elucidates the cultivating of faith. "To study and chant the Mahayana sutras" (341c12) elucidates the cultivating of understanding. Because practice can transport [the practitioner], it is regarded as a vehicle. Vehicles are distinguished into three. The one that the Buddhas ride is called the "great [vehicle]," since the other two vehicles cannot surpass it. The preceding constitutes the discussion on the benefit for oneself. Now, "to encourage and persuade the practitioners" (341c12) comprises the benefiting of others. [178b23–c1]

The above has been the specific enumeration [of the three purified acts], the following is the general conclusion and praise. "These three items are called the 'purified acts'" (341c12) states the general conclusion. "The Buddha said to Vaidehī, 'Do you not know that these three kinds of acts are the purified acts which are the true causes for the enlightenment of all the Buddhas of the three periods (the past, present and future)?'" (341c13) expresses the words of praise. [178c1–4]

In regards to the meditative good acts for rebirth, the visualizations are distinguished into sixteen kinds: (1) visualization of the sun, (2) visualization of water, (3) visualization of the ground, (4) visualization of the trees, (5) visualization of the lake, (6) unified visualization of the entire storied-pavilions, trees and lakes, and so forth, (7) visualization of the flower throne, (8) visualization of the images of the Buddha and Bodhisattvas, (9) visualization of the Buddha-body, (10) visualization of Avalokiteśvara, (11) visualization of Mahāsthāmaprāpta, (12) visualization of one's own rebirth, (13) [visualization that] randomly describes the Buddhas and Bodhisattvas, (14) visualization of the rebirth of the highest grades, (15) visualization of the rebirth of the middle grades and (16) visualization of the rebirth of the lowest grades. [178c4–9]

The first seven visualizations of the sixteen are the dependent rewards, while the latter nine visualization gates are the main rewards. The earlier *Sutra* statement of "You must carefully visualize that land" (341c6) refers to these first seven visualizations, while "you must visualize those who have accomplished the purified acts" (341c6) refers to the latter nine visualizations. The distinctions of the visualizations are as enumerated above. [178c9–12]

Now with regard to the passages [on the visualizations], the first six visualizations are to be discussed together as a set, while the latter ten visualization gates are to be counted as another set. The [seventh] visualization on the flower throne should actually be discussed with the first six, but is included in the latter [nine] because it functions to initiate the [subsequent] visualizations of the Buddha. The passages on the first six visualizations have three segments: (1) Buddha's ordering of sanctioned instruction,[50] (2) Vaidehī's request, and (3) the Tathāgata's instruction. [178c12–16].

The first segment has five subsegments: (1) As a general response to Ānanda and Vaidehī, the Buddha ordered them to hear his sanctioned instruction (341c15–17); (2) "Excellent [Vaidehī!] . . ." (341c17) is a specific response in which the Buddha praised Vaidehī for her earlier perceptive question [on rebirth in the Pure Land]; (3) "Ānanda, . . ." (341c17) is a specific response in which the Buddha encouraged Ānanda to remember [his words] and to instruct others; (4) "I, the Tathāgata, will now . . ."

(341c18) states how the Buddha himself revealed the benefits of what he is about to instruct; and (5) "Vaidehī, you are a Pṛthagjana . . ." (341c23) discloses the characteristics of the instruction the Buddha is about to teach. [178c16–19]

In the first subsegment, the Buddha first speaks to two persons (Ānanda and Vaidehī), ordering them to listen critically and to consider carefully his words. "To be critical" is similar [in meaning] "to judge." "Carefully" (in the above context) means "well." The following describes how the Buddha invoked sanctions and gave instruction: "I, the Tathāgata, will now expound the purified acts for the sake of sentient beings of the future who will suffer from the plunderers, that is, blind passions."(341c15–17) Because blind passions harm, they are referred to as the "plunderers." Since blind passions generate the Five Evils (*wu-o*) and elicit the production of such matters as the Five Pains (*wu-t'ung*) and the Five Burnings (*wu-shao*), the *Sutra* spoke of suffering.[51] The Buddha gave instruction on the purified acts in order to conquer this suffering. He instructed the six kinds of visualizations beginning with the one on the sun [with the same intent] as when he gave instruction on the purified acts. [178c19–25]

In subsegment two, "Excellent (*shan-tsai*), Vaidehī!" are words of general praise. "Excellent" (*shan*) is synonymous with "well" (*hao*), while "*tsai*" is its auxiliary word. "You have done well to ask about this" (341c17) indicates the object of Buddha's praise. The Buddha fully reveals the acts for rebirth in the Pure Land and praises Vaidehī because of Vaidehī's previous request. [178c25–27]

In subsegment three, the Buddha first ordered Ānanda to remember his words and later ordered Ānanda to instruct extensively for the sake of others (341c17). [178c27–28]

In subsegment four, "I, the Tathāgata, will now" (341c18) identifies the instructor, while "instruct Vaidehī, and so forth" (341c19) indicates the persons to be instructed. [Buddha] will now instruct Vaidehī but will into the distant [future continue] to instruct all sentient beings of the future. The intention of the Sage is universal.[52] "To visualize the Realm of Utmost Bliss in the western direction" (341c19) expresses the topic of instruction. Within the first six visualizations, the Buddha has yet to instruct Vaidehī to visualize people as objects, for he has only talked about visualizing the Land of Utmost Bliss. [178c28–179a3]

"With Buddha's power . . ." (341c20) describes the benefits of visualization. There are three kinds of such benefits: (1) One sees because of the Buddha's power. Because one sees the land clearly, the Buddha states, "It is like seeing one's face in a clear mirror." (341c21)) By the power of Buddha's teaching and the supernatural powers, one can see the land; (2) From seeing the land, the mind rejoices; (3) "At that time . . ." (341c22) describes how with joyful mind for seeing the land, Vaidehī obtained the Insight of Non-arising [of *dharmas*]. [The *Sutra* says that Vaidehī] obtained the Insight of Non-arising because the apprehension of the non-substantiality of the *dharmas* follows from the realization that the [Pure] land is manifested by the mind. The Insight of Non-arising is a truth principle, and the mind of wisdom that rests on this principle of truth is called the "Insight of Non-arising." [179a3–8]

There are, specifically, five kinds of Insight, as explained in the *Jen-wang ching.*[53] The first is the Suppression Insight (*fu-jen*). It is named the "Suppression [Insight]," since in the ranks of Lineage and the Practice of Resolution one trains to visualize the *dharmas,* thereby, enabling the suppression of passions.[54] The second is the Faith Insight (*hsin-jen*). It is named "Faith Insight," since in the second and third Bhūmis the mind of faith in the truth principle of Non-arising is firmly established. The third is the Accordance Insight (*shun-jen*). It is named "Accordance Insight," since in the fourth, fifth, and sixth Bhūmis one destroys forms and enters [the realm of] suchness in strict accordance with the Insight of Non-arising. The fourth is the Insight of Non-arising. It is named the "Insight of Non-arising," since in the seventh, eighth, and ninth Bhūmis one realizes the real and frees oneself from form. The fifth is the Insight of Cessation (*chi-mieh jen*). It is named the "Insight of Cessation," since in the tenth Bhūmi and above one destroys form completely, and the once confused mind attains ultimate cessation and realizes the great nirvana. The Insight of Non-arising, which is discussed here in this *Sutra,* refers to the fourth gate above. The passages, which proclaim the attainment of the Insight of Non-arising by Vaidehī and others, point precisely to this matter. [179a8–16]

In subsegment five, "The Buddha saying to Vaidehī, 'You are a Pṛthagjana,'" (341c23) refers to her capabilities. "You are unable to see far," (341c23) reveals what Vaidehī is incapable of. Vaidehī is in reality a great Bodhisattva (*ta p'u-sa*). At this encounter, "She obtained the Insight of Non-arising" reveals how [the Buddha] knew that she was not of the small [vehicle] (Hinayana) but that she manifested as a Pṛthagjana. "Your mental thoughts are inferior, etc." clearly indicates that she was incapable. "Your mental thoughts are feeble and inferior" (341c23) state that her mind was unable to shine upon the distant [Pure] Land. "You have not yet obtained the divine eye" (341c23) describes how her eyes could not see far enough to see the [Pure] Land. "The Tathāgatas possess various skillful means to enable you to see" (341c24) describes what has already been indicated. This reveals in outline form the characteristics [of what the Buddha is about to teach]. To teach Vaidehī and others to visualize such objects as the sun and water of this realm (Sahā) enables them to know about the other realm (Pure Land), for which reason the *Sutra* stated,

"The Tathāgatas possess various skillful means to enable you to see." Up to this point [the *Sutra* has discussed] the first [of three segments on the first six visualizations], that is, the Buddha's sanctioned instructions. [179a16–24]

The second segment on Vaidehī's request for instruction follows below this point. "Vaidehī said to the Buddha, 'by the power of the Buddha I have seen that country'" (341c25) means that [Vaidehī] received the Buddha's caring and shows that she had personally seen the land. Vaidehī's ability to see the Land within the pillar of Buddha's rays, as previously discussed, is called the "vision based on Buddha's power" (*fo-li chien*). "'When the Buddha dies . . .'" (341c26) is Vaidehī's request [for a teaching] for the sake of others. "'After your (Buddha's) death, how can sentient beings who are defiled, evil and non-virtuous . . .'," (341c26) states that they possess evil causes. [179a24–27]

"Defilement" here refers to the Five Defilements. What are the five? First is said to be the Defilement of Life, because the reward in terms of [longevity] of life is greatly shortened. The second is the Defilement of Sentient Beings, as none among them practices [the Dharma]. The third is the Defilement of Blind Passions, because the fetters greatly increase. The fourth is the Defilement of Perception, that is to say, when people slander and do not trust each other. The fifth is the Defilement of the Period, because of famines, epidemics, and wars. Since these five all defile and disturb the pure mind, they are called "Defilements." "Evil" here refers to the Five Evils. The five are killing, stealing, engaging in sexual misconduct, lying, and partaking of alcoholic drink. "Non-virtuous" here refers to the Ten Non-virtuous Acts. These ten are comprised of the three bodily, four spoken and three mental transgressions. It is possible for the Five Evils alone to represent [what the *Sutra* meant when it said], "[sentient beings who are] defiled, evil and "non-virtuous." [179a28–b5]

"Beings, who are tormented by the Five Sufferings (*wu-k'u*)," (341c26) explains that they are beset by the effects of suffering. The *Large Sutra* (*Wu-liang-shou ching*) states, "The Five Pains and the Five Burnings are the Five Sufferings."[55] "What are the Five Pains?" The Five Pains are committed by persons who engage in killing, stealing, lying, sexual misconduct, or in the partaking of alcoholic drinks; as such people present danger [to the country and its citizens] the king punishes them according to the law. "What are the Five Burnings?" The Five Burnings are so called, because, as previously discussed, those who commit the Five Evils will fall into the lowest three Destinies to receive the poisons of suffering. In the statement, "How will they be able to see Amitābha's Realm of Utmost Bliss?" (341c27) Vaidehī makes the formal request [for the Buddha's instruction]. [179b5–10]

What follows below this point is segment three, in which the Buddha gives instruction. With regard to this, I shall first explain the meaning of pure land and afterwards comment on the passages. The meaning [of pure land] is as explained in the *Separate Treatise*.[56] As for the passages [of this segment, the *Sutra*] first teaches the visualization of the [setting] sun causing the practitioners to be aware of the proper direction [of the Pure Land to the west]. The subsequent five [visualizations] instruct her on the visualization of the adorned features of the Land. [179b10–13]

The sun visualization entails three subsegments: (1) [Buddha's] general encouragement for visualization, (2) instruction, and (3) conclusion. "You and the sentient beings must perceive the western quarter with a concentrated mind" (341c28) is the general encouragement. "How is it to be done . . . ?" (341c29) is the instruction. "How" denotes a question. "To perceive . . ." is the [actual] instruction. "All sentient beings, if not born blind, have sight and can see the setting sun" indicates the objects to be visualized. "You should focus your perceived thoughts . . ." (342a1) is the formal instruction on the visualization-inspection (*kuan-ch'a*).[57] "This is [the visualization on the sun] . . ." (342a4) is the conclusion. [179b13–16]

The passages of the second visualization are divided into four subsegments. The first enumerates the features (*hsiang*) of the visualization. The second, "This is . . . ," (342a19) is the conclusion. The third, "When this perception is completed . . ." (342a19) reveals the completed features (*ch'eng-hsiang*) of the visualization. The fourth, "A perception such as this is called "unrefined vision" (*ts'u-chien*) . . ." (342a23) summarizes the capabilities [of the practitioners]. [179b16–19]

There are four phases in the first subsegment: (1) forming the perception of the water, (2) mentally transforming water into ice, (3) mentally transforming ice into Vaiḍūrya stones, and (4) visualizing the Vaiḍūrya forming the expansive ground. The last phase (four) has three subphases: (1) visualizing the Vaiḍūrya [ground] as brilliant and transparent both within and without, (2) seeing the jeweled pillars supporting the ground from below, and (3) seeing the various adornments above the ground. There are four kinds of adornments. First, the ground is crisscrossed with a multitude of jewels. Second, these jewels emit assorted lights, which form [a pedestal on which there are] numerous storied-pavilions. Third, there are numerous flowered banners on both sides of the storied-pavilions. Four, there are on top of these flowered banners, numerous musical instruments playing melodious sounds. The rest (subsegments two through four) should all be easily understood [without explanation]. [179b9–24]

The passages of the third visualization are divided into five subsegments. First, it describes the visualization features that are seen, based on what the *samādhi* called, the "perception of the ground." Second, "This is . . ." (342a24) forms the conclusion. Third, "The Buddha spoke [to Ānanda] . . ." (342a26) encourages Ānanda to remember [the teaching] and to instruct others. Four, "If you visualize . . ." (342a27) describes the benefits of the visualization. Five, "To perform this visualization . . ." (342a29) distinguishes the correct from false visualizations. [179b25–27]

The passages of the fourth visualization on the trees are divided into three subsegments. The first subsegment summarizes the previous segment and begins the next subsegment in order to initiate the visualization. The second subsegment describes the features of the visualization. The third subsegment concludes it (the passages on this visualization). Being self-evident, these passages should be understood [without explanation]. [179b27–29]

The passages of the fifth visualization, of the water, are divided into three subsegments: (1) general [encouragement to] initiate [the visualization], (2) enumeration of the features of the visualization, and (3) its general conclusion. The water of Eight Excellent Qualities are clear, odorless, light, cool, glossy, delicious, appropriate whenever one drinks it, and free of diseases. These are the eight. "Clear" is the sense object of form, "odorless" is the object of smell, "light, cool, glossy" are the object of touch, "delicious" is the object of taste, and the last two are objects of *dharmas*. [179b29–c4]

The sixth gate, which follows below this point, comprises the unified visualization (*tsung-kuan*). Its passages are divided into four subsegments: (1) enumeration of the features of the visualization, (2) its general conclusion, (3) description of the benefits of the visualization, and (4) distinction of the correct from wrong visualization. The first subsection has four phases. The first visualizes the jeweled, storied pavilions; the second visualizes the trees; the third visualizes the ground; and the fourth visualizes the jeweled lake. In the visualization of the storied pavilions, the Buddha first instructed them to visualize the storied pavilions, and then to visualize the numerous musical [instruments hanging in suspension] above the storied pavilions and up in the sky; he in the end concluded with instruction on the features [of the visualization] and named them the "unrefined vision." [179c4–8]

*The Commentary on the Visualization Sutra part one* end

# The Commentary on the Sutra of Visualization on the Buddha of Immeasurable Life

## Part Two
## by
## Śramaṇa Hui-yüan of Ching-ying Monastery

*Translator's note: Having completed the first six visualizations, Hui-yüan turns his discussion to the latter ten visualizations.

The passages on the latter ten visualizations are divided into four segments. In the first segment, the Buddha ordered Ānanda and Vaidehī to listen to his sanctioned instruction and encouraged them to transmit and preserve the teaching. In the second segment, because the Buddha encouraged Vaidehī to seek the vision [of the Pure Land], the Buddha had Buddha [Amitābha] and Bodhisattvas [Avalokiteśvara and Mahāsthāmaprāpta] appear together. In the third section, on account of the visualization [of the Buddha and Bodhisattvas], Vaidehī gave homage [to the Buddha], and on receiving the Buddha's power with deep respect, Vaidehī made the request [for Buddha's instruction] for the sake of future beings. In the fourth section, the Tathāgata in response to her request gave instruction on the methods involved in the last ten visualizations. [179c12–16]

There are three subsegments to the first section. In the first subsegment the Buddha ordered the two (Ānanda and Vaidehī) to listen and encouraged them to think about [what he was about to teach]. In the second subsegment, Buddha's sanctioned instruction on the method of eliminating suffering was referred to as the "method for eliminating suffering," because through visualization one destroys his evil karma, abandons this (Sahā world-realm) and is reborn there (in the Pure Land). In the third subsegment, the Buddha encouraged them to preserve and to instruct others. [179c16–18]

The second segment describes first the manifestations of the Buddha and the Bodhisattvas and later the incomparable majestic light. The third segment describes first how Vaidehī, because of her vision [of Amitābha Buddha and Bodhisattvas, made possible by the Buddha] paid homage [to the Buddha]; it next recounts how due to the reception of Buddha's power, the objects to be observed in the visualizations were manifested as if they actually existed; and lastly it reports how Vaidehī made the request for the sake of future beings. The meaning of the passages being self-evident, it should be understood [without further explanation]. [179c18–21]

*Translator's note: Hui-yüan further divides the ten visualizations into four groups.

In the fourth segment, in which the Buddha gives instructions on the ten visualizations, there are four groups within these ten visualizations. The first five visualizations (seventh to eleventh) of the first group have the visualization of the Buddha and Bodhisattvas as a common feature; the next group, comprised of one gate (the twelfth), is a visualization of one's own rebirth (*tzu wang-sheng kuan*); the next group, comprised also of one gate (thirteenth), again explains a visualization of the Buddha and Bodhisattvas; the last three (fourteenth to sixteenth of group four) delineate the visualizations of the rebirth of others (*t'a sheng chih kuan*). [179c21–23]

Of the first set of five visualizations (seventh to eleventh), its first gate engages in the visualization of the Buddha's throne. The next gate engages in the visualization of the three images of the Buddha [Amitābha] and the two Bodhisattvas. The last three gates engage in the visualizations of the True-body of the Buddha and the two Bodhisattvas. [179c23–25]

The passages on the first mentioned visualization (the seventh) of the throne are divided into six subsegments. The first describes the features of the visualization. The second, "This is . . ." (343a10), constitutes the conclusion. The third, "Ānanda . . ." (343a11), elucidates the cause by which this throne was established, that is to say, [Bhikṣu] Dharmākara's vow power. The fourth, "If you wish to . . ." (343a12), again reveals the prescriptions of the visualization. The fifth, "Those who completes this perception . . ." (343a15), describes the benefits of the visualization. The sixth, "To engage in this visualization . . ." (343a16), distinguishes the correct from wrong visualizations. Being self-evident, the meaning of the passages should be understood [without further explanation]. [179c25–180a3]

The passages on the visualization (the eighth) of the images [of the Buddha and the two Bodhisattvas] are divided into four subsegments. The first describes the features of the visualization. The second, "Then compare it with the sutras . . ." (343b9), distinguishes the correct from wrong visualizations. The third, "This is . . ." (343b11), forms the conclusion. The fourth, "Those who perform this [visualization] . . ." (343b13), explains the benefits of the visualization. [180a3–5]

There are four mini-segments in the first subsegment [on the features of the visualization]. The first is the simplified visualization (*lüeh-kuan*), where one visualizes only the images of the Buddha and the Bodhisattvas. The second, "When this perception is accomplished . . ." (343b4), identifies an accomplished feature (*ch'eng-hsiang*) of the visualization.[1] The third, "[Under] each tree . . ." (343b5), describes the comprehensive visualization (*kuang-kuan*), where one visualizes the images of the Buddha and two Bodhisattvas under each tree. The fourth, "[When] these features [of the visualization] are accomplished . . ." (343b7) also reveals an accomplished feature of the visualization. [180a5–8]

In the first mentioned simplified visualization, one first visualizes the image of the Buddha and afterwards visualizes and inspects the images of the two Bodhisattvas. In the visualization of the image of the Buddha, one is first encouraged to visualize the Buddha and to do what the Buddha has revealed, and then afterwards to visualize correctly the image [of the Buddha]. In encouraging [Ānanda and Vaidehī] to visualize the Buddha, the *Sutra* first explains the meaning of the Three Buddha-[bodies], and afterwards explicates the meaning of the passages. The meaning [of the Buddha-bodies] is to be understood in accordance with the *Separate Treatise*.[2] Of these [three Buddha-bodies], what is being visualized here [in this *Sutra*] is the Response-body.[3] [180a8–12]

There are three segments to the passages [on the eighth visualization]. The first segment concludes the previous [visualization] (seventh) and initiates the subsequent [visualization] (eighth) and, thereby, constitutes an introduction: "After you have gained the vision of the previously [-instructed] objects, you should next perceive the Buddha" (343a18). The second segment, "Why? Because . . ." (343a19), sets forth the reasons for encouraging [Vaidehī to engage in the visualization. The third segment, "Therefore, you must single-mindedly restrain your thoughts . . . ," (343b22) concludes [with the Buddha] encouraging [Ānanda and Vaidehī] to visualize and to inspect them. [180a12–14]

With regard to the second segment [of the passage mentioned above], the question "Why?" inquires subtly about [the nature of] the introductory section [to this eighth visualization]. The Buddha-body emanates from the [human] mental function, because of which Buddha encouraged them to perceive it. The Buddha encouraged its perception in response to the *Sutra* statement, "The Buddha as the Dharma-realm Body enters the mind of each sentient being" (343a19). "Therefore, . . ." (343a20) describes how the Buddha as [the product of] mental perception is none other than the principle of the previously mentioned Buddha entering the mind of the sentient beings. [180a14–18]

*Translator's note: Hui-yüan comments on the well-known *Sutra* passage, "The mind is the Buddha; the mind becomes the Buddha," which attracted the attention of later commentators.

There are four phrases (subsegments) [in the *Sutra*] concerning the above principle [of the Buddha entering the mind of each sentient being]. The first phrase reveals that "the mind is the Buddha" (*hsin shih fo*). When Śākymuni Buddha earlier said, "Therefore, [you should single-mindedly] . . ." he was encouraging Ānanda and Vaidehī to avail themselves of the former (the mind), to reveal the latter (the Buddha). Because this Buddha as Dharma-body (*dharmakāya*) enters the mind of each sentient being, the *Sutra* said, "When you visualize the Buddha in your mind, this mind is none other than the [thirty-two] marks of perfection and [eighty minor] marks of excellence." (343a20) The second phrase reveals that "the mind becomes the Buddha" (*hsin tso fo*) and completes the previously mentioned phrase, "the mind is," [which is part of the phrase "the mind is the Buddha"]. The third phrase, "*This* mind is the Buddha" (*shih hsin shih fo*), consummates the previously mentioned first phrase ("the mind is the Buddha").[4] The fourth phrase, "The universal wisdom of the Buddhas is produced from the perception of the mind," (343a22) concludes the previously mentioned second phrase ("the mind becomes the Buddha"). [180a18–22]

"Why did the *Sutra* say, '[the mind] *becomes* [the Buddha]' and '[the mind] *is* [the Buddha]'?" There are two meanings [answering this question], each of which will be distinguished. The first meaning is distinguished into the beginning and ending of the Buddha-visualization; the cultivation in the beginning was referred to as "to become," while the completion [of the cultivation of the visualization] in the end was referred to as "is." The second meaning is distinguished into the present and future with regard to the [earlier discussed principle of] the Dharma-body of the Buddhas and the self being of the same substance (*t'i*). When one visualizes the Buddha, what appears in the mind is the substance of the Dharma-body of the Buddhas; this is precisely what the Buddha meant when he stated, "the mind is the Buddha." In contrast, to hope for one's future result by visualizing one's rebirth there [in the Pure Land] is what the Buddha meant when he stated, "the mind becomes the Buddha." The above discussion has been the second segment, which has explained the reasons for the encouragement. [180a22–27]

What follows below is segment three [of the passages dealing with the eighth visualization] that concludes [with the Buddha] encouraging [Ānanda and Vaidehī] to visualize and inspect. "Therefore" (343a22) means the Dharma-body of the Buddhas has entered the mind of each sentient being, on account of which [the *Sutra* admonishes] "You should single-mindedly restrain your thoughts and visualize Buddha Amitābha."[5] [180a27–29]

The number of Buddha's epithets are innumerable, but I shall, in brief, point out four kinds. "Fo" is an epithet for Buddha, whose meaning is as previously explained. (173b4–17) "To-t'o-a-chia-tu" refers to the epithet "Thus-come" (Tathāgata); he is called "Thus-come" because by availing himself of the path of *thusness* he has *come* to establish the perfect enlightenment. As for "A-lo-ho" (Arhat), he is called "Worthy of Worship." He is called "Worthy of Worship" because the Buddha in severing [ignorance and passion] through wisdom has qualified himself to be worshipped. In the foreign language, three appellations are mutually understood to mean "Arhat": (1) "Al-lo-ho" means "one worthy of worship"; (2) "Al-lo-han" means "one without rebirth" or "one without attachment"; (3) "A-lu-ho" means "killer of the plunders [of passions]." Here, we have chosen the first meaning. "San-miao san-fo-t'o" is translated as "one who is perfectly true, perfectly awakened." The character "*san*" is rendered "perfectly"; the character "*miao*" is rendered "true"; the character "*san*" is again rendered "perfectly"; the characters "*fo-t'o*" is rendered "awakened." [180a29–b7]

In the context of my earlier statement "[When Ānanda and Vaidehī are] encouraged to visualize the Buddha and do what the Buddha has revealed [and afterwards they are properly encouraged to visualize the image]" [see 180a9–10], this *Sutra* states "To perceive the Buddha" (343a24) refers to the phase "first perceive the image" down to the phase "[afterwards] they are properly encouraged to visualize the image." The meaning of the passages is self-evident and should be understood [without further explanation]. With regard to my earlier statement, "First visualize the Buddha's image, then afterwards visualize and inspect the images of the two Bodhisattvas" means to perform first [the visualization of] the two seats and afterwards to visualize properly and inspect the images of the two Bodhisattvas. [180b7–10]

The subsegment [one] up to this point has dealt with the simplified visualization.[6] The rest of the segment [on the eighth visualization] is similar to what has been explained. The meaning of these passages is self-evident, and should be understood [without further explanation]. [180b10–11]

There are four segments to Buddha-body visualization (the ninth visualization): (1) concludes the previous [eighth visualization] and initiates the subsequent [ninth visualization]; (2) extensively discusses the visualization; (3) "This constitutes . . ." (343c8), which is the conclusion; and (4) distinguishes correct from wrong visualizations. [180b11–12]

In segment two there are four subsegments: (1) extensively discusses the features of the visualization; (2) "For to see these objects is to see all the Buddhas of the ten quarters. . . ." (343b28) describes the benefits of the visualization; (3) "In order to visualize the Buddha of Immeasurable Life, begin with one of the auspicious marks or of the secondary marks. . . ." (343c4) again discusses the proper conduct[7] of the visualization; and (4) "Once you have seen the Buddha of Immeasurable Life, will immediately see the Buddhas of the ten quarters. . . . ," (343c7) again discusses the benefits of the visualization. [180b12–15]

In subsegment one, the Buddha first gave instruction on specific [visualizations.]. "Those sentient beings who contemplate the Buddha [of Immeasurable Life] are embraced and are not abandoned . . ." (343b26) is the general conclusion to [Buddha's] encouragement. [180b15–16]

The prior [section on specific visualization] has three mini-segments: (1) visualizing the form of the Buddha's body; (2) "The height of the Buddha's body . . ." (343b17) visualizes its size; (3) "In the rays . . ." (343b21) visualizes the number [of transformed Buddhas in the rays]. Section one is to be thus understood. [180b17–18]

The sentences on visualizing the size of the Buddha's body (mini-segment two) are further divided into five phases. The first phase visualizes the size of the body whose "height is six hundred thousand *nayutas* of *koṭis* of *yojanas*, as innumerable as the sands of Ganges."[8] (343b17–18) The second phase focuses on the size of the white tuft mark, which is like that of Mt. Sumeru; Mt. Sumeru is three million three hundred sixty-thousand *li*[9] high, and so are its vertical and lateral dimensions. The height of the Buddha's white tuft mark is, in actuality, more than five times that of [Mt. Sumeru]. The third mini-segment calls for one to visualize the size of the eyes, which is like that of the four great oceans. [180b18–22]

"One must grant that the size of the white tuft and the eyes is surpassed by that of the body, as the measurement of the body is very great. However, the body surpasses its white tuft and eyes by only a small measurement. How can this be?" [180b22–24]

Generally, those people of the world whose bodies are five *ch'ih* (1.79 meter) have eyes that are one *ts'un* (.0358 meter), so that the body does not surpass the length of the eyes by more than fifty to sixty times. The same holds true for the Buddha as well. The eyes of the Buddha of Immeasurable Life are as large as the four great oceans. Since the length and width of one ocean are eighty thousand *yojanas,* the four oceans combined would be three-hundred thirty-six thousand *yojanas.*[10] [180b24–28]

"If the Buddha's body surpasses its eyes by fifty to sixty times as you claim, it would not exceed one-hundred times even if we assumed the maximum ratio. How is it that the Buddha's body, which is in height as many *yojanas* as six-hundred thousand times *nayutas* of the sands of the River Ganges, is determined to be only six-hundred thousand times *nayutas* of *yojanas* long in comparison with the eyes?"[11] [180b28–c1]

Perhaps, the translator inserted by mistake the characters *"heng-ho sha"* (sands of Ganges River). If the body is actually as many *yojanas* as six-hundred *nayutas* of *koṭis* high, the white tuft and the eyes would then be far too small in comparison to the body. This must be a mistake on the part of the translator. The measured size of the bodies of Avalokiteśvara and Mahāsthāmaprāpta have not yet been determined in comparison to the measured length of the Buddha's body. [180c1–5]

The fourth [of five phases of mini-segment two] visualizes the size of the bodily rays, of which where each emitted ray from the hair pores is the size of Mt. Sumeru. The fifth phase [visualizes] the size of the circular rays, which are the size of ten billion Three-thousand Worlds. [180c5–6]

The sentences of mini-segment three, which describes the number [of the transformed Buddhas in the rays], are further divided into five phases. The first describes the number of transformed Buddhas: "in the circular rays there are transformed Buddhas numbering in the hundreds of millions of *nayutas,* innumerable as the sands of River Ganges" (343b21). The second phase discusses the number of attendants: "each of the manifested Buddhas has as attendants an innumerable number of [manifested] Bodhisattvas" (343b22). The third phase describes the number of auspicious marks: "[the Buddha of Immeasurable Life] has eighty-four thousand auspicious marks" (343b23). The fourth phase reports the number of secondary marks: "each auspicious mark has eighty-four thousand secondary marks" (343b24). The fifth phase refers to the number of rays: "each secondary mark has eighty-four thousand rays" (343b25). The above has been a discussion on the specific visualizations [encouraged by the Buddha]. [180c6–12]

"Sentient beings who contemplate on the Buddha . . ." (343b26) constitutes the general conclusion on [the Buddha's] encouragement [when he admonished,] "Sentient beings who contemplate on the Buddha will be embraced and not be abandoned" (343b26). "Rays, auspicious marks, secondary marks and transformed bodies cannot be fully explained by words" (343b27) concludes this section by attesting to their [immeasurably] large numbers. "But by simply recollecting . . ." (343b27) are words of encouragement. This concludes the first subsegment [on the features of the ninth visualization]. [180c12–15]

The following is the second subsegment on the benefits of the visualization; it has three mini-segments to it. The first describes how on seeing Buddha Amitābha, one also sees the bodies of all the Buddhas. The second mini-segment describes how on seeing the body of Buddha Amitābha, one also sees the Buddha's mind. The third mini-segment is the conclusion encouraging one to visualize and inspect. [180c15–18]

The first subsection has three sentences. The first states that "a person who sees these objects—the auspicious marks of the body of the previously mentioned Buddha Amitābha—also sees all the Buddhas in the ten quarters" (343b28). Because the substance of the Buddhas is the same, when one sees one Buddha, he also sees all Buddhas. The second sentence expresses how "on account of seeing the bodies of all the Buddhas, he also attains the '*samādhi* of Buddha-contemplation' (*nien-fo san-mei*) (343c28)." The third sentence, "To engage in this visualization . . . ," (343c29) concludes the section by revealing the benefits. [180c18–21]

The second mini-segment has three sentences. The first sentence describes "when one sees the body, he also sees the Buddha's mind" (343c1). Since the body arises on account of the mind, when one is able to see the body, one is also able to see the mind. Also, since mental thoughts are transformed and illuminated on account of seeing the body, one is able to see the mind. [180c21–24]

*Translator's note: Hui-yüan begins a long discussion on the *Sutra* phrase, "great compassion." He makes a distinction between small compassion (which he first explains) and great compassion which, in his view, is espoused by the *Sutra*. In the exercise of great compassion, a Bodhisattva is free from making distinctions unlike in the case of small compassion and is natural and spontaneous in his actions.

The second sentence, "The Buddha's mind is none other than the great compassion and commiseration . . . ," (343c2) depicts the characteristics of the Buddha's mind. This is called the "unconditioned compassion" (*wu-yüan tz'u*), which embraces all sentient beings. This mind of compassion and commiseration is distinguished into great and small. When one makes distinctions (*fen-pieh*) based on certain conditions, it is called "small." In contrast, when mental thoughts are totally destroyed so that there are no distinctions to be made with regard to sentient beings, one naturally manifests actions to benefit them; this is categorized as "great." [180c24–27]

With regard to small compassion, there are three kinds. The first is the "[compassion] conditioned by sentient beings" (*chung-sheng yüan)*, in which [the Bodhisattva] in desiring to grant them happiness, desires to extricate them from their suffering. [180c27–28]

The second [of the small compassions] is the "[compassion] conditioned by the Dharma" (*fa-yüan*) in which [the Bodhisattva] practices compassion and commiseration in perceiving that in sentient beings there is neither self nor person but simply *dharmas* of the five aggregates that are produced and destroyed. "How can one practice compassion when there is no self or no person?" It is possible as the *Vimalakīrt-sūtra* explains, "It is called 'compassion' because [a Bodhisattva] in thinking about the sentient beings teaches the Dharma for the sake of sentient beings in accordance [with their needs and capacity]." Also, the Bodhisattva practices compassion and commiseration, because in thinking about the sentient beings he sees that they are bound by [the false notions of] 'self' and 'person' due to delusion and are to be deeply pitied. "If there are no sentient beings, for whom will the Dharma be taught, and on whom will [the Bodhisattva] contemplate as bound by the false notion of self?" The sutra states, "[That sentient beings] do not exist, simply means that the nature of a person does not exist" It is not that sentient beings do not exist in the illusory sense or in terms of a provisional name; hence, we can speak of Bodhisattvas thinking that the beings are indeed fettered [by false notions]. [180c28–181a5]

The third [of three compassions] is the "unconditioned [compassion]." In perceiving that the aggregates (*skandhas*) are empty and that ultimately nothing exists, [the Bodhisattva] practices compassion and commiseration. "Since *dharmas* do not exist, how can you speak of 'practicing compassion'?" There are two meanings to this compassion. First, in thinking about sentient beings, one teaches the Dharma for the sake of sentient beings in accordance [with their needs and capability]; because this is the ultimate principle by which happiness is made available to the people, it is called "compassion." Second, [the Bodhisattva] practices compassion and commiseration because in thinking about sentient beings, who by delusion are bound to the [false notion] that *dharmas* exist, are, therefore, to be deeply pitied. [181a5–9]

"Since *dharmas* do not exist, where would a person exist and yet still teach [the Dharma]?" In answer to your question, [our contention is] based on the Bodhisattva's own mind, which does not see persons or *dharmas* as ultimately real. Since [the Bodhisattva] does not see *dharmas* [as ultimately real] there is nothing to teach. Since [the Bodhisattva] does not see persons [as ultimately real], there is no one to teach [the Dharma]. Thus, a sutra states, "In the impartiality of the Dharma-Realm the Buddhas do not save sentient beings." This idea is aimed at sentient beings who, in looking at Bodhisattvas, see the Bodhisattvas as existing independently of themselves. However, if on hearing the Bodhisattva explain that persons and *dharmas* do not ultimately exist, they abandon delusion, adopt the real and identify with what is to be obtained, then it can be said [as was earlier] that "The Bodhisattvas espouse the doctrine that persons and *dharmas* do not exist." Thus, a sutra has stated, "When I am forced to make distinctions regarding sentient beings, I teach that the Buddhas do save sentient beings." [181a9–16]

The above three compassions are based on [the Bodhisattvas'] cultivation of perception [concerning the plight of sentient beings], and the three are generally referred to as the "small [compassion]." [181a16–17]

The great immeasurable mind (great compassion) also has three kinds. The first is the "[compassion] conditioned by sentient beings," where even without the mind considering the conditions of the sentient beings [as in the case with small compassion], [the Bodhisattva] automatically manifests benefits. Thus, the *Nirvana Sutra* said, "I do not actually go [to them] but the power of virtuous faculties stemming from compassion enables sentient beings to see matters such as this." The second is the "[compassion] conditioned by the Dharma," where even without the mind perceiving the *dharmas* [as in the case with small compassion], the mind automatically shines universally upon the *dharmas*, just as the sun shines on all creatures without discrimination. The third is the "unconditioned [compassion]," where even without the mind perceiving [the emptiness of the five aggregates] as in the case [with small compassion], [the Bodhisattva] naturally dwells with ease in the equality of the ultimate principle. [181a17–22]

Here, this *Sutra* espouses [compassion] conditioned by sentient beings of the great compassion. Hence, the *Sutra* states, "With unconditioned compassion, the Buddha embraces [all] sentient beings" (343c2). The above second section (= sentence) has discussed the characteristics of the Buddha's mind. [181a22–24]

The third sentence, "Those who have engaged in visualization will upon abandoning this body for the other [realm will be reborn before the Buddhas] . . ." (343c2) describes the benefits of visualization. This has been the second mini-segment, which has concerned the topic of seeing the Buddha's mind. [181a24–25]

"Thus, those with wisdom . . . ," (343c4) comprises the third mini-segment, which concludes the encouragement to visualize and inspect. [181a25–26]

Up to this point this has been the second subsegment, which has detailed the benefits of visualization. [181a26]

"To visualize the Buddha of Immeasurable Life, begin with one of the auspicious marks . . ." (343c4) forms the third subsegment, which again describes the proper conduct relative to the visualization. The fourth subsegment, "Once you have seen the Buddha of Immeasurable Life, you see immediately the countless number of Buddhas of the ten quarters, and so forth" (343c7) again reveals the benefits of visualization. This has been segment two, which has extensively discussed the features of this visualization. [181a26–29]

Segment three is the general conclusion. Segment four distinguishes wrong from correct visualizations. Because the meaning of the passages is self-evident, it should be understood without [further explanation]. [181a29]

Next, the passages on visualizing Avalokiteśvara (tenth visualization) are distinguished into six segments: (1) concludes the preceding [set of passages] and initiates the following; (2) the statement, "This Bodhisattva . . ." (343c12) extensively discloses the features of the visualization; (3) the statement, "This is . . ." (344a9) is the conclusion; (4) the statement, "Buddha said [to Ānanda] . . ." (344a11) describes the benefits of the visualization; (5) the statement, "If there are . . ." (344a14) again reveals the prescriptions of the visualization; (6) the statement, "To have engaged in this [visualization] . . ." (344a16) distinguishes wrong from correct visualizations. [181b1–3]

Segment two has ten features of the visualization: (1) visualizing the features of the body, (2) visualizing the features of the head, (3) visualizing the circular rays, (4) visualizing the jeweled crown, (5) visualizing the features of the face, (6) visualizing the features of the white tuft, (7) visualizing the ornaments, (8) visualizing the features of the hands, (9) visualizing the features of the feet, and (10) the statement, "The rest of his [body] . . . ," (344a8) which refers to the rest of the features that point to the same features as those of the previously discussed Buddha [Amitābha]. [181b3–7]

In visualizing the body (the first feature), one first visualizes the measurements of the body. The length of the body of the previously discussed Buddha [Amitābha] was in height as many *yojanas* as six-hundred thousand *nayutas* of *koṭis* of the sands of River Ganges [180b29], while [the *Sutra* states,] "The length of this Bodhisattva in height is as many *yojanas* as eight-hundred thousand *nayutas* of *koṭis* of the sands of River Ganges" (343c12). Afterwards, one visualizes on the color of the body, which is like purple-gold. [181b7–10]

Visualizing the head (the second feature) is self-explanatory. In visualizing the circle of rays emanating from him (the third feature), three sentences are to be distinguished: (1) those visualizing the number of transformed Buddhas within the rays emanating from the Bodhisattva Avalokiteśvara; (2) those visualizing the number of attendants for each of these transformed Buddhas; (3) those visualizing the bright rays emanating from the form-body (*se-shen*) of these transformed Buddhas (*hua-fo*). The sentient beings of the five destinies are all manifested in the rays.[12]

In visualizing the jeweled crown (fourth feature), one first visualizes the jeweled crown, and afterwards visualizes the number of transformed Buddhas on the crown. With regard to the fifth gate [among the ten features], one visualizes his "face whose color is like Jāṃbūnada gold" (343c19). There are five sentences to be distinguished about visualizing the features of the white tuft (sixth feature): (1) those visualizing the color of the white tuft, which is like the seven jewels; (2) those visualizing the rays of the white tuft; (3) those visualizing and inspecting the number of the transformed Buddhas in the rays emanating from the white tuft; (4) those visualizing the number of attendants for these transformed Buddhas; (5) those visualizing the miraculous manifestations produced by these transformed Buddhas. "[These Buddhas and Bodhisattvas] appear freely, filling the realms of the ten quarters . . ." (343c22) concerns the visualization of the ornaments (seventh feature), hands (eighth), feet (ninth), and so forth. As the meaning of the passages regarding [these sets of visualization] is self-evident, it should be understood [without further explanation]. [181b10–18]

What follows below are the remaining four segments: the general conclusion, the benefits of the visualization, the prescriptions of the visualization and the distinction of wrong from correct visualizations. As the meaning of the passages [for these segments] is self-evident, it should be understood [without further explanation]. [181b18–19]

The passages on the visualization of Mahāsthāmaprāpta (eleventh visualization) are distinguished into five segments: (1) initiates the discussion in general terms; (2) describes the features of the visualization; (3) concludes the discussion in general terms; (4) the statement, "will eliminate [the evil karma accumulated during] countless [kalpas] . . . (344b10) describes the benefits of the visualization; (5) the statement, "When this visualization is completed . . ." (344b12) concludes in general terms the accomplished prescriptions of the two visualizations of Avalokiteśvara and Mahāsthāmaprāpta. [181b19–21]

The passages of the second segments are distinguished into seven subsegments: (1) the visualizing of the features of the body; (2) the visualizing of the jeweled crown; (3) the visualizing of the tuft; (4) the visualizing of the jeweled pitcher; (5) the sentence, "The remaining [features of the body] . . ." (344a29) refers to the remaining features, which are the same as those of Avalokiteśvara; (6) in the *Sutra* statement, "When [this Bodhisattva] moves . . . ," (344b1) one visualizes the feature of his movements; (7) in the *Sutra* statement, "When he sits down . . . ," (344b3) one visualizes the feature of him sitting down. [181b21–24]

In the first visualization [of the body], one first visualizes the measurement of the body as in the case of Avalokiteśvara, and afterwards one visualizes the rays [emanating from] the body; regarding the [latter visualization], one first visualizes the breath of the rays. [181b24–26]

Secondly, "[Sentient beings] who have connections . . ." (344a21) elaborates the benefits of visualizing the rays, of which there are four. The first benefit is stated in the *Sutra*, "[Sentient beings] who have connections and see the rays emanating from each hair pore of this Bodhisattva will also see the rays of all the Buddhas of the ten quarters" (344a21). Since the substance of the Dharma-body of this Bodhisattva and all the Buddhas is the same, one who sees the rays of this Bodhisattva will also see the rays of all the Buddhas. The second benefit is in the *Sutra* statement, "Therefore, . . ." (344a23), which concludes by praising his name, which the *Sutra* called "Unlimited Rays." The third benefit is in the *Sutra* statement, "[With the rays of] wisdom . . ." (344a24), which explains the benefits of the rays. It relates that the rays illuminate all sentient beings and enables them to separate from the three evil destinies and obtain the highest power of the Buddha. The fourth benefit concludes with the praise of his name, which the *Sutra* named "Mahāsthāmaprāpta" (344a25). [181b26–c2]

Next, as the meaning of the first five visualizations [on the jeweled crown, tuft, jeweled pitcher, remaining features and his movement] is self-evident, it should be understood [without further explanation]. As for visualizing the features of his sitting down (the seventh visualization), one is first encouraged to visualize how "When [Mahāsthāmaprāpta] sat down, all [the Buddha lands] shook and trembled" (344b3), and later to visualize what the *Sutra* describes, namely, "the duplicate bodies of countless Buddhas, Avalokiteśvara and Mahāsthāmaprāpta all converge [on Sukhāvatī] to proclaim the excellent Dharma" (344b5). The foregoing was segment two, which has extensively discussed the features of the visualization. [181c2–5]

Segment three is the general conclusion. Segment four reveals the benefits of the visualization. Segment five concludes in general terms the accomplished prescriptions of the two visualizations of Avalokiteśvara and Mahāsthāmaprāpta. As the meaning of the passages [of these segments] is self-evident, it should be understood [without further explanation]. [181c5–6]

Since these two [visualizations of the two Bodhisattvas] are mutually dependent, they are here concluded together in general terms; they have been treated together among the "visualizations of the Buddhas and Bodhisattvas." [181c6–7]

Following is the gate on the visualization of one's own rebirth (twelfth visualization), which has five segments: (1) the perception of [one's own] rebirth; (2) the passage, "... in accordance with the twelve [divisions of sutra] ..." (344b19), which concerns the prescriptions of its visualization; (3) the statement, "After you have seen this ..." (344b20), which reveals the capability [of the practitioners]; (4) a generalized conclusion; and (5) describes the benefits of the visualization, which calls for the "[countless number of] manifested [bodies] of Buddha [Amitāyus] and the [two] Bodhisattvas to come constantly to the place [of the practitioners]" (344b22). [181c7–10]

The first segment has seven subsegments: (1) perception of [one's own] rebirth; (2) perception of [oneself] sitting cross-legged [in the lotus flower]; (3) perception of the flower being closed; (4) perception of the flower being opened; (5) perception of [what the *Sutra* states,] "there will be rays illuminating your body when the flower opens up" (344b17); (6) perception in which the eyes open; and (7) perception of seeing the Buddha and Bodhisattva and hearing the Dharma. [181c10–13]

As the meaning of the remaining sections (two through five) is self-evident, it should be understood [without further explanation]. [181c10–13]

The following is a gate (thirteenth visualization) that repeats the description of the visualization of the Buddha and of the [two] Bodhisattvas (which was previously discussed under eighth visualization). "Why was it necessary to repeat?" It was necessary because the visualization of the Buddha and the Bodhisattvas discussed earlier could not be fathomed by the lowest among the Pṛthagjanas; hence, this is repeated to teach [all] Pṛthagjanas to visualize and inspect [the images]. The visualization shall be first discussed and later concluded. [181c13–16]

The discussion section first describes the visualizing and inspecting of the Buddha's body and later the visualizing [and inspecting] of the [bodies of the] Bodhisattvas. There are six segments in the section on visualizing the Buddha. The first segment properly teaches one to visualize and inspect "the sixteen-foot image standing above the waters of the lake" (344b26). The image represents Buddha Amitābha, and the lake water represents the lapis lazuli ground [of the Pure Land]. [181c16–18]

The second segment, "As [explained] earlier ...," (344b26) clarifies the reasons why it was necessary to teach [again] the visualization of the image [of the Buddha]. As previously stated, the *Sutra* statement, "the Buddha's body is limitless [in size]" (344b26) is not something that can be fathomed by Pṛthagjanas; thus, the [Buddha] taught them to visualize the image. [181c18–20]

The third segment, "However, [on account of the power] of that [Buddha's], ...," (344b27) describes how those Pṛthagjanas, who visualize the image, are certain to accomplish [the visualization], and produce in other people the desire to cultivate [the visualization]. On account of the power of the Tathāgata's original power those who engage in the visualization are certain to accomplish [the visualization]. [181c20–21]

The fourth segment, "Those who simply perceive, . . . ," (344b28) depicts how those who visualize receive numerous benefits and offer encouragement to people to visualize and inspect. The *Sutra* thus explains, "Just by visualizing the image of the figure, they obtain immeasurable merit; how much more so for those who visualize the Buddha's body!" (344b28) [181c21–23]

The fifth segment, "A-mi-t'o . . . ," (344c1) details how the object of visualization is sometimes large and at other times small, but is at all times of the same Buddha body. It wipes away the doubts of sentient beings and produces in people the desire to cultivate visualization. "Why do sentient beings have doubts?" They have them because earlier they had heard that the Buddha's body was extensively great and immeasurable but now they hear of visualizing a [body that is extremely] small. Hence, they doubt that it is the Buddha's body and cannot respect the small body of the Buddha. Therefore, in feeling the necessity to wipe away any vestiges of doubt, the Buddha clarified that all [bodies] are of the Buddha, and, thereby, generated in them the renewed desire [for the cultivation of visualization]. [181c23–26]

The sixth segment, "What is manifested . . . ," (344c2) describes how the great and small bodies, which are manifested despite their differences, are the auspicious and secondary marks of the form-body and do not differ from the earlier marks; they, therefore, prevent people from engaging in different visualizations. On hearing that large and small bodies are all of the same Buddha-body, people now go around saying, "We can engage in the various forms of visualization and still attain visualization and inspection." But it is in order to prevent [people from engaging in] heterodox visualizations that the [Buddha] explained as he did above. [181c26–29]

What follows below is the visualization of Bodhisattvas. In this regard, the *Sutra* first states, "The physical features of the Bodhisattva Avalokiteśvara and Mahāsthāmaprāpta are the same in all respects" (344c4). On account of this sentiment, beings find it difficult to distinguish the two. "By simply visualizing . . ." (344c5) instructs people to distinguish the two. "By simply visualizing the marks on the head" (344c5), one immediately recognizes the difference between the two. This visualization of the head is not that of the hands and feet. There is a transformed Buddha on top of the head of Avalokiteśvara, and there is a jeweled pitcher on top of the head of Mahāsthāmaprāpta. Thus, by visualizing the two heads, one immediately recognizes the difference between the two. "These two Bodhisattvas assist Buddha Amitābha" (344c6) reveals how these two

Bodhisattvas assist the Buddha in instructing and in greatly benefiting the people by enabling them to engage in visualization. [181c29–182a6]

The following concludes [the discussion of this visualization]. Since these Buddha and Bodhisattvas are visualized and inspected together, the *Sutra* calls it "composite (*tsa*) [visualization]." [182a6]*

*Translator's note: Hui-yüan discusses the last three visualizations on the nine grades of rebirth in two main parts, analysis and explanation of the passages. The analysis part is divided into six sections or "gates", of which the first focuses on the celebrated ranking of the grades.

The following three visualizations (fourteenth, fifteenth, and sixteenth visualizations) are to be consolidated into the same category as visualizations of the 'rebirths of other [people],' in which one visualizes the features involved in the rebirths of the nine grades of people. "Why does one visualize them?" They are visualized in order to make the people of the world know that they can ascend to higher grades or descend to lower grades depending on their [causal] acts for rebirth and that they can cultivate and be reborn [in the higher grade]. For this reason, the *Sutra* encourages this set of visualizations. [182a7–9]

I will first elucidate this [set of visualizations] through six gates and afterwards explain the passages. The six gates are those which (1) rank these people, (2) delineate the causes [of their rebirth], (3) describe the fact that the Buddhas seen in the past are not the same, (4) describe the fact that there are differences when they reach there [in the Pure Land] for rebirth, (5) reveal the fact that there are distinctions in the benefits to be obtained when they are reborn there, and (6) reconcile [the inconsistencies among] the sutras and commentaries (*śāstras*). [182a9–12]

The first gate that ranks people has three groups, when roughly divided, and nine groups, when divided in detail. Roughly divided, the three are high, middle, and low. Those Mahayanists of the rank of Lineage and above are of the high grade. Those Hinayanists of the ranks of Pṛthagjanas up to the Āryapudgalas, who maintain the precepts without violation, are of the middle grade. Mahayanists of the rank of Outer Pṛthagjanas, who have committed evil karma, are of the low grade.[13] [182a12–15]

Of the finely divided nine grades, the high category has three grades that are known as "highest of the high, middle of the high, and lowest of the high." Those Mahayanists of the fourth Bhūmi and above are of the highest of the high grade. They are the Bhūmis of the [Insight of] Non-arising, since one obtains the Insight of Non-arising immediately upon being reborn there [in the Pure Land]. In reality, it normally takes longer to obtain Insight of Non-arising, but this *Sutra* has those of superior [capabilities] in mind when it says, "[they] obtain [Insight] immediately [upon rebirth]."[14] [182a15–19]

Those Bodhisattvas of the first, second and third Bhūmis who have obtained Faith Insight are of the middle of the high grade. It is because of this that the *Sutra* states that they obtain the Insight of Non-arising one small Kalpa[15] after being reborn there. In reality, it actually takes two or three Kalpas to obtain [the Insight of Non-arising from these levels]. But this *Sutra* is speaking in a superior context when it says, "one [small] Kalpa." [182a19–22]

A question is asked: "The *Ti-ch'ih [ching]* states that it requires one great Uncountable (*asaṃkhya*) Kalpa[16] to go from the first Bhūmi to the eighth Bhūmi. Why is it that this *Sutra* states it only requires one small Kalpa to obtain the Insight of Non-arising?" [182a22–24]

There are three reasons for understanding [this alleged discrepancy]. The first reason is that the time spans of the Kalpas are not the same; for example, the *Avataṃsaka-sūtra* states:

> One Kalpa in the Sahā realm is equivalent to only one day and one night in [the Pure Land of the Buddha of] Immeasurable life, while one Kalpa in the [Pure Land] is equivalent to countless and unlimited number of Uncountable Kalpas in the Sahā realm.

Because the *Ti-ch'ih [ching]* is based on this [*Avataṃsaka-sūtra,*] it stated that one great Uncountable Kalpa is required to reach the eighth Bhūmi. However, because this *Visualization Sutra* refers to the longer Kalpa in the land of Amitābha, it states that one obtains the Insight of Non-arising in just one Kalpa. [182a24–28]

The second reason lies in the difference of the standpoint for stating the view of the two sutras. The one great Uncountable [Kalpas] that the *Ti-ch'ih* says it takes to reach the eighth Bhūmi is stated from the point of view of someone in the first Bhūmi. In contrast, the one small Kalpa that the *Visualization Sutra* maintained is required to reach the [seventh Bhūmi] of Non-arising proposed from the point of view of one at the final stage [of the first, second, and third Bhūmis when] the Faith Insight is obtained. This final stage at which one obtains the Faith Insight is the third Bhūmi. Had this *Sutra* been speaking from the point of view of the first Bhūmi [and not from the third as it does], it, indeed, would not have been able to say that one obtains the [Insight of] Non-arising in just one [small] Kalpa. [182a28–b3]

The third reason lies in the distinction of levels to be reached. The level that the *Ti-ch'ih* says is reached in one great Uncountable Kalpa is the eighth Bhūmi. In contrast, the level at which the *Visualization Sutra* says one obtains the Insight of Non-arising in one small Kalpa is the seventh Bhūmi; this is because [traditionally] one obtains the Insight of Non-arising for the first time at the seventh Bhūmi. This concludes the section on the middle of the high grade, which is as discussed above. [182b3–5]

Those of the Lineage and Practice of Resolution stages are of the lowest of the high grade. This is based on the *Sutra* explanation that those of this grade require three small Kalpas to obtain the Wisdom of the Hundred Teachings (*pai-fa ming*) upon reaching the first Bhūmi.[17] [182b5–7]

A question is asked, "The *Ti-ch'ih* states it takes one great Innumerable [Kalpa] to reach the first Bhūmi from the Lineage stages. Why is it that the *Visualization Sutra* says that one reaches the first Bhūmi after only three small Kalpas?" [182b7–8]

In responding, [I say] it is so because the lengths of Kalpa are not the same. Because the *Ti-ch'ih* is based on the short Kalpa of this Sahā realm, it states that one reaches the first Bhūmi only after one large Uncountable Kalpa. [On the other hand,] because the *Visualization Sutra* is [speaking] in terms of Kalpas that are longer [in actual length], it states that one reaches the first Bhūmi in three small Kalpas. [182b8–11]

A question is asked, "The *Ti-ch'ih* says the time it takes to reach the first Bhūmi from the Lineage stage is one great Uncountable Kalpa, and another great Uncountable Kalpa to reach the eighth Bhūmi from the first Bhūmi. Why is it that this *Sutra* proclaims here that those of the middle of the high grade take only one small Kalpa to obtain the [Insight of] Non-arising and similarly proclaim that those of the lowest of the high grade take only three small Kalpas to reach the first Bhūmi?" (182b11–14]

In reality, the two positions you raise are nearly the same. My earlier statement that those of the middle of the high grade spend one small Kalpa in obtaining the Insight of Non-arising was made from the point of view of those at the final stage [of the first three Bhūmis] at which Faith Insight is obtained.[18] Similarly, my earlier statement that those of the lowest of the high grade spend only three small Kalpas in reaching the first Bhūmi was made from the point of view of those at the initial stage [of Lineage and Practice of Resolution] in which the Suppressive Insight is obtained.[19] This first [set of statements] is virtually the same [in its argument]. Also, the earlier proclamation that it takes only one small Kalpa to obtain the Insight of Non-arising was so stated in terms of the seventh Bhūmi in which the Insight of Non-arising is first obtained rather than in terms of the stages past [the seventh Bhūmi where the Insight would be more fully developed].[20] The latter statement that it takes three [small] Kalpas to reach the first Bhūmi was [not] stated in terms of those reaching stages past [the first Bhūmi].[21] This second [set of statements] is virtually the same [in its argument]. [182b14–20]

The capabilities of the three [grades of] people of the high category are roughly as [just discussed above].[22] [182b20]

There are also three grades to the middle category that are highest of the middle, middle of the middle, and lowest of the middle. "What are the levels of their capabilities?" [182b20–21]

Those of the first three [Āryapudgala] fruits [of attainment] among the Hinayanists are of the highest of the middle grade, since upon being reborn in the Pure Land they immediately obtain Arhatship.[23] In reality, it actually takes longer to obtain Arhatship, but this *Sutra* stated, "obtains immediately," speaking in a superior context. [182b21–24]

A question is asked, "Are Arhats reborn or not reborn [in a pure land]?" [182b24]

This *Sutra* does not say they are reborn, since Arhats [by definition] are not reborn again. [182b24–25]

A question is asked, "Nāgārjuna states the Arhats also are reborn in a pure land, since a pertinent passage [from Nāgārjuna's writing] states, 'There are subtle pure lands (*miao ching-t'u*) which are beyond the three realms and where the term 'blind passions' do not even exist.' These Arhats will be reborn there, and once there they listen to the *Lotus Sutra.* How can you, therefore, say that the Arhats are not reborn there?" [182b25–27]

There are two interpretations for understanding [this passage by Nāgārjuna]. The first explains in terms of the Arhats of deluded teaching. Those of deluded teaching cling to Hinayana and are confused about Mahayana teaching. When these people of deluded teaching abandon their present body comprised of the [five] aggregates, they enter extinction without remainder before taking on any other physical form. [Another group, in contrast,] after staying an inconceivably larger number of Kalpas in Nirvana without remainder, perceive in their mind the thought of being reborn, and then are reborn in a pure land to take on physical form and listen to the Dharma. Nāgārjuna based himself on the latter [group of Arhats] in his view that [all Arhats] are reborn in a pure land. This *Sutra,* on the other hand, refers to the former [group of Arhats], on account of which it says [all Śrāvakas] are not reborn. [182b27–c3]

The second interpretation explains in terms of the Arhats of non-deluded teaching. Arhats who understand Hinayana and know Mahayana are called "[Arhats of] non-deluded teaching." Upon death, they immediately take on physical form and listen to the Dharma. But they are not reborn in any pure land. "What is the meaning of this?" There are coarse and subtle lands among the pure lands. A coarse pure land is a place mixed with Hinayanists, but a subtle pure land is only for Mahayanists. [182c3–6]

Further, coarse lands are generally for the rebirth of Pṛthagjanas whose life-spans are limited and subject to transmigration.[24] The subtle lands, however, are only for Āryapudgalas who are capable of creating their bodies at will in the realm of transmigration.[25] The country of Buddha Amitābha is among the coarse pure lands. There are also subtle lands, but this *Sutra* does not address them. The *Avataṃsaka[-sutra]* further discusses this point:

> The Arhats of non-deluded teaching, after exhausting their passion and defilement, seek the Mahayana teaching whole heartedly, and are reborn in a subtle land but not in a coarse country.

Basing his views on the subtle land, Nāgārjuna stated that the Arhats are reborn in a pure land. On account of this he said [as mentioned earlier], "There are subtle pure lands which are beyond the three realms and where the term 'blind passions' does not even exist, and where Arhats are reborn." In contrast, the *Visualization Sutra* is concerned only with a coarse pure land and, therefore, does not say that the Arhats are reborn; [to say otherwise] would constitute a biased statement [deviating from its basic premises]. Those of the first three Āryapudgala fruits are of the highest of the middle grade. [182c6–13]

Those of the two categories of Pṛthagjanas, the Inner and Outer, prior to the [Path of] Insight (*darśana-mārga*) who earnestly uphold the pure precepts and seek to escape transmigration (*saṃsāra*) are of the middle of the middle grade. The *Sutra* says after being reborn there and listening to the Dharma for seven days, they obtain the Stream-winner stage; then after half a Kalpa they become Arhats. In reality, it takes longer to listen to the Dharma to obtain the [Āryapudgala] fruits; the *Sutra* said "seven days and a half a Kalpa" because it spoke from a superior context. [182c13–16]

Those worldly Pṛthagjanas prior to the Path of Insight, who cultivate the remaining worldly virtues and seek to escape transmigration, are of the lowest of the middle grade. This follows from the *Sutra* statement that after spending one small Kalpa they become Arhats. In reality, it actually takes longer to become Arhats, but the *Sutra* is speaking in a superior context. [182c16–19]

This concludes the middle category, which is as discussed above. [182c19]

The lowest category also has three grades, highest of the low, middle of the low, and lowest of the low. The three grades are divided according to the degree of transgressions (*kuo*) committed among those who have initiated training in the Mahayana teaching. Since they are yet with a rank on the Path (*tao*; *mārga*), it is difficult to discuss their ranking. [182c20–22]

The distinction of the people [aspiring for rebirth] are as discussed above; the first gate (of the six gates) is concluded. [182c22]

I will next discuss the causes (the second of six gates). In this regard, first the relevant characteristics will be distinguished, and later people will be discussed. What are the relevant characteristics? The sutras explain them differently. The *Larger Prajñāpāramitā Sutra*[26] advocates wisdom (*prajñā*) and regards wisdom based on emptiness as the cause [for rebirth]. By eliminating the obstruction of karmic evil through cultivation of wisdom based on emptiness, he desires to be reborn in the pure land and is immediately reborn there. [182c23–25]

According to the *Nirvana Sutra,* the entire set of good deeds provides the causes for rebirth in the pure land. While they are too numerous to be listed in detail, there are roughly four main causes. The first cause is the cultivation of the precepts, which call for one to separate themselves completely from the Ten Evil Acts, and to cultivate the Ten Virtuous Acts to observe the pure precepts and not to commit any grave offense. Such people will cease [committing evil deeds], dwell [in good deeds], and gain rebirth in the pure land. The second cause is the cultivation of generosity, which calls for one to widen roads, dig wells, plant orchards, provide medical care and medicine for the sick, build monks' quarters, make offerings to those who observe the precepts and preach the Dharma, cast images, build stupas or make various kinds of offerings. Such people [who cultivate this generosity] will gain rebirth. The third cause is the cultivation of wisdom. Those who copy down one fascicle or even one verse [of a sutra], hear and recite aloud [the sutras] and preach for the sake of others will gain rebirth in the pure land. The fourth cause is the protection of the Dharma. Those who protect the true Dharma and do not criticize the Vaipulya (Mahayana) [sutras] will gain rebirth in the pure land. These and others serve as causes enabling rebirth in all the [pure lands], so that those who seek to be reborn in Sukhāvatī should cultivate them. [182c26–183a5]

According to *Vimalakīrti-sūtra,* the eight teachings constitute the cause for rebirth. This sutra, thus, states, "If one acquires the eight teachings and carries out [these teachings that lead to] no distress, one will be reborn in the pure land." "What are the eight teachings?" The first teaches benefiting sentient beings without expecting anything in return. This is compassion. The second teaching assumes, in their behalf, the suffering and afflictions of all the sentient beings. This is commiseration. The third is to bestow [on sentient beings] all the virtues that have been performed. This is joy. Because joy eliminates jealousy, one performs virtues and bestows them all on others. The fourth is to maintain a non-discriminate mind towards [all] sentient beings and to be unhesitantly humble towards even those of inferior status. This is equanimity. Because equanimity entails rejecting both hatred and affection and treating equally both the despised and the revered, it is unhesitantly non-discriminating. The above four [teachings] have been for the benefit of oneself, but the next four benefit others. [183a5–12]

The fifth is to feel affection towards Bodhisattvas just as one does for the Buddha, to hear a sutra that has not yet been heard and to have no doubts, to awaken in one's mind faith and respect for the object of one's training, and to awaken respect for people and produce faith towards the Dharma. The sixth is not to concede to the Śrāvaka [teaching], to oppose other [forms of] training, and to disperse the obstructive mind. The seventh is not to be envious of the offerings made to others and not to exalt one's own benefits, by subduing and controlling his mind [beset by such thoughts]. Also, one is to bring to rest his defiled mind, which seeks objects of gratification. The eighth is to be constantly vigilant towards one's own faults and not to accuse others of shortcomings. One continuously cultivates virtues with singleness of mind and raises the mind by concentration on the matters to be cultivated. These constitute the eight causes for rebirth in all of the pure lands, so that those seeking rebirth in [Amitābha's] Sukhāvatī should cultivate them. [183a12–19]

According to the *Rebirth Treatise,* the five gates comprise the causes. The first is the gate of worship. One recites the name, physically worships Buddha Amitābha, and seeks to be reborn in his country. The second is the gate of praise. One praises the wisdom of brilliant light and all the virtuous qualities of Buddha Amitābha. The third is the gate of aspiration. One aspires to be reborn in his country and cultivates what Buddha Amitābha practiced and accomplished. The fourth gate is the gate of visualization and inspection, of which there are three categories: first, visualizing the adornments that are the virtuous qualities of that country, second, visualizing the adornments that are virtuous qualities of that Buddha, and third, visualizing the adornments that are the virtuous qualities of the Bodhisattvas. Each category carries numerous meanings, but we can not enumerate them here. The fifth is the gate of transference. One cannot abandon suffering beings but make the transference [of virtues] the primary [practice]. It is by transferring his accomplished virtues and by bestowing them to sentient beings that all will be reborn together in that land. [183a19–26]*

*Translator's note: Hui-yüan's views on the *Sutra's* discussion of the causes are surprisingly comprehensive and, contrary to traditional interpretation, includes oral recitation. See chapter 5 of the study for details.

"According to the *Visualization Sutra,* there are also numerous causes, of which there are roughly four categories. The first cause is rebirth by cultivating visualization (*hsiu-kuan*). The sixteen visualizations are distinguished, as discussed above. The second cause is rebirth by cultivating [pure] acts (*hsiu-yeh*). There are three kinds of pure acts as previously explained. [183a26–28]

The third cause is rebirth by the cultivation of the mind (*hsiu-hsin*); there are three kinds of mind as the following passages explain. The first is the sincere mind (*ch'eng-hsin*); "sincere" means "real." Because one initiates practice without false [reasons] and seeks to depart [this world] with the real mind, it is called the "sincere mind." The second is the deep mind (*shen-hsin*); one longs for and is extremely anxious and desirous to be reborn in that country. The third is the mind that aspires for rebirth by transferring merit (*hui-hsiang fa-yüan chih hsin*). To seek without any particular expectation is explained as "aspiration" (*yüan*), while to seek in presumption of a favorable [result] is explained as "transference" (*hui-hsiang*). There are two kinds of aspirations. First, one aspires to be reborn in that country and, two, one aspires to see that Buddha. What one accomplishes is what one practices. The above has been [a discussion on] the third cause, that is to say, rebirth by cultivating the mind. [183a28–b5]

The fourth cause is devotion (*kuei-hsiang*), on account of which one is reborn; this cause is explained in the following passages. Even though one does not engage in the practices himself, a virtuous friend[27] gives him instructions on the names of the Buddha, Dharma, and Sangha,[28] or praises Buddha Amitābha by explaining his virtues, or praises [the virtues of] Avalokiteśvara and Mahāsthāmaprāpta, or praises the exquisite and supreme phenomena of that land. By single-minded devotion, one gains rebirth. As forms of devotion, those who contemplate (*nien*), worship (*li*), praise (*t'an*) or recite his (Buddha Amitābha) name (*ch'eng-ch'i-ming*) shall all gain rebirth. [183b5–9]

The relevant characteristics of the causes are as discussed above. The following discusses [the causes] from the point of view of people (*jen*). The statements in the sutras on this subject are not the same. According to the *Wu-liang-shou ta ching* (Large Sutra on [Buddha of] Immeasurable Life), people are divided roughly into three grades, respectively, based on their causes. [183b9–10]

Those of high grade rebirth became monastics (*śramaṇa*), having abandoned their family and rejected [the life of] desire. They have raised the mind set on enlightenment (*bodhicitta*), have single-mindedly contemplated the Buddha of Immeasurable Life, have cultivated various virtues and aspired to be reborn in that country. They have, therefore, gained rebirth. Those of middle grade rebirth did not become monastics and were unable to cultivate virtuous deeds extensively. They have, however, raised the mind set on enlightenment and have single-mindedly contemplated the Buddha of Immeasurable Life. They have cultivated the meritorious virtures to a limited extent, observed fasting and precepts [of the householders], built images, erected *stūpas,* made various offerings and aspired for rebirth in that country. They have, therefore, gained rebirth. Those of low grade rebirth have not performed virtuous deeds, but have raised the mind set on enlightenment, have single-mindedly contemplated the Buddha of Immeasurable Life in as little as ten moments of thought, have heard the preaching of the profound Dharma, have rejoiced in serene faith, and have harbored no doubts and aspired with sincere mind for rebirth in that land. They have, therefore, gained rebirth. [183b10–18]

This *Sutra* discusses the people, having distinguished them into nine grades. The *Sutra* first comments on those of the high category (or upper three grades), all of whom similarly cultivated the Mahayana practices as causes [for their rebirth in the Pure Land]. This group is further distinguished into [three] subgroups. [183b18–20]

The first such group is the highest of the high grade of rebirth; those of this group first raise the three minds: (1) the sincere mind, (2) deep mind, and (3) the mind that aspires [for rebirth] by transferring merit. Next, they cultivate the three [pure] acts: (1) "to possess the mind of compassion and refrain from killing" (344c14) is the first act; (2) "to observe the precepts" (344c14) is the second act; and (3) "to recite the Mahayana [sutras] and cultivate the 'six kinds of mindfulness'"[29] (344c14) is the third act. Lastly, they transfer these virtues in desiring to be reborn and are, [in the end,] immediately reborn. [183b20–24]

Those of the middle of the high grade of rebirth must also first raise the three kinds of mind; I shall not discuss them here, since they are the same as those elucidated above. What follows below [in regards to the rest of the section on the three minds] is also similar to those above. Next, they cultivate the three acts. Since "to possess the mind of compassion and refrain from killing" and "to maintain precepts" are similar to the previous section, I shall also not discuss them here. They are, however, unable to uphold, recite or cultivate the Mahayana teaching. They are only able to be resolute[30] with regard to the highest truth and deeply believe in the [principle of] cause and effect. This last point should be regarded as being included in the third pure act. Lastly, they transfer these virtues in wanting to be reborn and are, [in the end,] immediately reborn. [183b24–28]

Those of the lowest of the high grade of rebirth also first raise the three kinds of mind, which are similar to those above. Next, they cultivate the three [pure] acts. The first act, "possessing a compassionate mind and refraining from killing, and observing the precepts," is the same as before. They are not able to uphold, recite or understand the meaning of the Mahayana teaching. They are only able to believe in the [principle of] cause and effect and to cultivate the causes. This belief is none other than the third pure act mentioned above. [183b28–c3]

The high category is as [discussed] above. [183c3]

Next, I shall discuss those of the middle category, all of whom practice the causes by cultivating the Hinayana [teaching]. However, they gain rebirth, because in the very end they generate the mind-set on enlightenment and contemplate the Buddha Amitābha. This category is further distinguished into three groups. [183c3–5]

Those of the highest of the middle grade of rebirth are persons of the first three [Āryapudgala] fruits in the Hinayana ranking. They possess all the saintly virtues, though these *Sutra* passages do not elaborate them and, instead, merely discuss the persons involved. They observe various precepts and practices; this is similar to the second pure act mentioned above. Lastly, they transfer these virtues in wanting to be reborn and are [in the end] immediately reborn. Those of the middle of the middle [grade of] rebirth observe the eight precepts for one day and one night, or observe the novice (*śramaṇera*) precepts for one day and one night, or observe the complete set of precepts of the monks for the same duration. This also is the second pure act mentioned above. Lastly, they transfer the virtues in wanting to be reborn and are [in the end] immediately reborn. Those of the lowest of the middle [grade of] rebirth filially attend their parents and carry out the moral virtues of the world. This then is the first pure act mentioned above. When the life [of a person belonging to this grade] is about to end, a virtuous friend expounds for him the things concerning the bliss of the land of Buddha Amitābha as well as those of the forty-eight aspirations of [Bodhisattva] Dharmākara. With sincere mind, serene faith and the desire for rebirth, they are immediately reborn. The middle category is as [discussed] above. [183c5–13]

Next I shall discuss those of the low category. These people in their past lives encountered and cultivated the Mahayana teaching. Thus, it is expounded in the *Large Sutra,* "These people raised the mind set on enlightenment. . . . In hearing the preaching of the profound Dharma, they attained serene faith without any doubt."[31] In their present life, they have, under appropriate conditions, committed various evil karma. For this reason, this *Sutra* has focused on and revealed their transgressions. Even though they have committed this evil karma in this life, through the power of devotion revealed to them by the virtuous friend, they are able to gain rebirth. This group is further distinguished into [three] subgroups. [183c13–17]

Those of the highest of the low grade of rebirth have in this life committed minor karmic evil. A virtuous friend explains to them the names of Mahayana sutras and instructs them to recite the name of the Buddha Amitābha. On account of having destroyed the [effects of] karmic evil [by following the instructions of the virtuous friend], they are reborn. Those of the middle of the low grade of rebirth have in this life committed major karmic evil. However, the virtuous friend praised the virtues of Buddha Amitābha, whereby they rejoiced and attained serene faith. On account of having destroyed the [effects of] karmic evil, they are reborn. Those of the lowest of the low grade of rebirth have in the present life committed karmic evil such as the Four Heavy Transgressions and the Five Grave Offenses.[32] The virtuous friend instructs them to recite the name of Buddha Amitābha. So, with the sincere mind, they recite the name of their voices uninterrupted for as little as ten moment of thoughts; they thereby destroy the effects of their karmic evil and are reborn. [183c17–22]

I have elucidated the causes as discussed above, and the second gate is now concluded. [183c22–23]*

*Translator's note: In this third gate, Hui-yüan focuses on the differences in the Buddha bodies.

Next I shall describe how in the past [the people of the grades] saw the Buddha differently. The Buddha embodies Three-bodies: (1) True-body (*chen-shen*), which is also called the "Dharma[body]" (*fa [-shen]*) and "Rewarded[-body] (*pao[-shen]*),[33] (2) Response-body (*ying-shen*), in which the Eight Characteristics are manifested and accomplished, and (3) Transformed-body (*hua-shen*), which is manifested in accordance with the capacity [of the devotees]. [183c23–25]

According to the *Large Sutra,* those of the high grade see the Buddha in its Response-body as it comes to receive them [for the Pure Land]. Those of the middle grade see the Transformed-body. Those of the low grade see in their dreams [a body that] cannot be determined to be either a Transformed or a Response-body. As the True-body is eternally tranquil, without any appearances by which it might receive [the devotees to the Pure Land], it is not discussed here [in the sutra]. [183c25–27]

According to this *Visualization Sutra,* those of the three grades of the high category all see the Buddha both in its Response and Transformed bodies that come to receive them. That some among this category see the Transformed-body either as smaller or greater degree than others serves to distinguish the differences [among the three grades of the category]. Those of the highest of the high category see countless manifested Buddhas. Those of the middle of the high category see one thousand of them. Those of the lowest of the high category see five-hundred of them. Among those of the three grades of the middle category, some see, while others do not, the Buddha. Those of the two grades, highest of the middle and the middle of the middle, see the Buddha, but not those of the lowest of the middle grade because of their inferior practices. [183c27–184a2]

A question is asked, "The *Large Sutra* states that those of the middle grade all see the Buddha. Why then does this *Sutra* say some see the Buddha while others do not?" [184a3–4]

This can be explained as follows. The *Large Sutra* made a statement about the general characteristic [of the upper grade]; based on the majority of those in the group, it said those of the middle category all see the Buddha. But this *Sutra,* having divided the grades in greater detail, says there are some who see the Buddha and others who do not. Those who do see, see only the Response-body of the Buddha but not the Transformed-body since they are inferior to those of the previous [group, the high category who saw both the Response and the Transformed]. Among those of the three grades of the low category, some see while others do not. Those of the highest of the low and of the middle of the low see the Buddha, but those of the lowest of the low see only the lotus flower. [184a4–7]

A question is asked, "The *Large Sutra* states that those of the low category are not able to see the Buddha. Why then does this Sutra say there are those who do see the Buddha among the low category?" [184a7–8]

This can be explained as follows. This *Sutra* describes how to cultivate the practice of visualization, as the visualization destroys the effects of karmic evil. Those of the low category who see the Buddha, even though they see the Buddha at the end, see only its Transformed-body, since they are inferior in capacity to the previous group (the middle category). [184a8–10]

A question is asked, "The *Large Sutra* states those of the high category see only the Response-body, those of the middle category see only the Transformed-body and those of the low category see in their dreams a body of the Buddha that cannot be determined as either a Transformed or a Response-body. Why then does this *Sutra* say those of the high category see both the Response and the Transformed, those of the middle category see the Response and those of the low category see the Transformed?" [184a10–13]

This can be explained as follows. This *Sutra* describes how to cultivate the practice of visualization and how through visualization the mind is illuminated. This being so, those of the high category see both the Response and the Transformed, those of the middle see the Response and those of the low see the Transformed. Since the *Large Sutra* does not describe the practice of visualization, it is not the same as [this *Sutra* in its description of the accomplishment of the respective categories.] [184a13–15]

This concludes the third gate. [184a15]*

*Translator's note: In the fourth gate, Hui-yüan discusses the differences in the length of time between death in this world and rebirth in the Pure Land. All Pure Land aspirants are not immediately reborn upon reaching the Pure Land, but spend varying lengths of time in the lotus flower depending on their past accomplishments. There is, thus, a distinction made between "reaching" (*chih*) the Pure Land and being "reborn" (*wang-sheng*) in the Pure Land.

Next I shall discuss the differences in the lengths of time required to be reborn in that land. The lengths of time of rebirth are different for each of the three high categories. For those of the highest of the high grade of rebirth, the flower opens immediately after they reach the Pure Land, so that they do not spend any length of time [in the flower]. Those of the middle of the high grade of rebirth spend overnight before the flower opens. Those of the lowest of the high grade of rebirth spend one day and one night before the flower opens. [184a15–20]

The length of time for rebirth for those of the three middle categories is also different. For those of the highest of the middle grade of rebirth, the flower opens immediately upon reaching the Pure Land, as in the case of the highest of the high grade. "Why is this so?" It is because among the Hinayanists, it is the Āryapudgalas who are [included in this group to be] reborn. Even though their actions are inferior [compared to the Mahayana Āryapudgalas], because they are without passion and have purified their mind, the flower opens immediately upon reaching the Pure Land.[34] Those of the middle of the middle grade of rebirth spend seven days before the flower opens up. As for those of the lowest of the middle grade of rebirth, the *Sutra* passage does not elaborate but simply comments, seven days after rebirth they meet the sages (Avalokiteśvara and Mahāsthāmaprāpta Bodhisattvas) and hear the Dharma [taught by them]. [184a20–22]

The length of time of rebirth for those of the three lowest categories also varies. Those of the highest of the low grade of rebirth spend forty-nine days, at the end of which the flower opens. Those of the middle of the low grade of rebirth, with the retributions of their karmic evil being very heavy, spend six Kalpas before their flower opens. Those of the lowest of the low grade of rebirth, the obstruction from their karmic evil being extremely heavy, spend twelve great Kalpas before their lotus flower opens up. Because the gravity of their karmic evil determines the length of time necessary for rebirth, they will deserve to be admitted into the Dharma only if they purify and cultivate the mind. [184a22–26]

The division of the length of time [for rebirth] is as discussed above. This concludes the fourth gate. [184a26–27]*

*Translator's note: Hui-yüan in the fifth gate elaborates on the benefits obtained in the Pure Land according to the ranking.

I shall next reveal the distinctions seen in the benefits attained after rebirth in the Pure Land. Among those of the three [grades of] the high categories the attained benefits are different. Those of the highest of the high grade of rebirth attain the Insight of Non-arising immediately upon reaching there (Pure Land), for the [Insight of] Non-arising is attained in the seventh Bhūmi. In reality it actually takes much longer to attain this insight, but the *Sutra* has said so in a superior context. Those of the middle of the high grade of rebirth spend one small Kalpa in the Pure Land before attaining the Insight of Non-arising. The *Sutra* has again made the statement in a superior context with regard to those of this group who will spend some time in the Pure Land before attaining the insight. Those of the lowest of the high grade of rebirth spend three small Kalpas before they can dwell in the first Bhūmi. [184a27–b2]

The benefits attained by those in each of the three grades of the middle category are also different. Those of the highest of the high grade of rebirth attain the fruit of the Arhats immediately upon rebirth there. Again, [in actuality more time is required to attain the fruit, but the *Sutra*] has made the statement in a superior context. Those of the middle of the middle grade of rebirth spend seven days, after which they attain the stage of Stream-winner; after half a Kalpa, they attain the Arhat stage. Those of the lowest of the middle grade of rebirth spend one small Kalpa before they attain the Arhat stage. [184b2–6]

The benefits attained by those in each of the three grades of the lowest category are also different. Those of the highest of the low grade of rebirth spend ten small Kalpas before attaining the first Bhūmi, since they were initially of the Good Destinies.[35] Those of the middle of the low grade of rebirth spend six Kalpas in the lotus flower before hearing the Dharma to generate the mind set on enlightenment (*bodhicitta*). Those of the lowest of the low grade of rebirth spend twelve great Kalpas in the flower before hearing the Dharma and generating the mind set on enlightenment. These people of the low category had the proper nature for generating the mind set on enlightenment because they previously cultivated the Mahayana teaching in their former lives. It is for this reason that [all three grades of the low category] similarly generated the mind of Mahayana. [184b6–10]

The topic of their attaining the benefits in the Pure Land is as discussed above. This concludes the fifth gate. [184b10]*

*Translator's note: In the sixth gate Hui-yüan attempts to reconcile the doctrinal differences between the *Sutra* and the other two major Pure Land scriptures.

The next topic for discussion is the sixth gate, which reconciles the sutras and commentaries. [184b10–11]

A question is asked, "According to texts such as the *Rebirth Treatise*, it is stated that those with the nature of the two vehicles do not attain rebirth [in the Pure Land]. Why then does this *Sutra* advocate that those of the middle category train in the Hinayana [teaching] and attain rebirth?" [184b11–12]

This can be explained as follows. One cannot attain rebirth in the right location, where Buddha Amitābha and Bodhisattvas dwell, by only cultivating Hinayana practices. The devotees are required to sow the seeds of Mahayana by availing themselves of the Mahayana teaching at the end of their lives so as to generate the mind set on enlightenment; only by so doing, will they gain rebirth. Hence, the *Large Sutra* states, "Those of the two vehicles generate the mind set on enlightenment." Because the position of the *Rebirth Treatise* on this matter is based on the [status of those of the two vehicles] at the end [of their lives], it stated that those with the nature of the two vehicles are not reborn. On the contrary, because this *Sutra* is concerned with the beginning [with the opportunities to make the conversion to Mahayana], it stated that those of the middle category, who once trained in the Hinayana teaching, will also gain rebirth [in the Pure Land]. [184b12–16]

A question is asked, "If in order to attain rebirth, it is necessary to avail themselves of the Mahayana teaching at the end of one's life and to generate mind set on enlightenment, then should he not realize the fruits of the Mahayana path? Why is it that he attains only the fruits of Hinayana?" [184b16–18]

This can be explained as follows. Even though these people converted to avail themselves of the Mahayana teaching at the end of their lives, upon reaching that country and hearing about suffering and impermanence they understood according to the original [Hinayana] teaching and initially realized the Hinayana fruit due to their extensive training in the

Hinayana. But having availed themselves of Mahayana teaching at the end of their lives in order to generate the Mahayana mind, they, after attaining the Hinayana fruit, will not dwell there but definitely return to enter the Mahayana [path]. [184b18–21]

A question is asked, "According to texts such as the *Rebirth Treatise*, it is stated that women and those with deficient faculties are not reborn [in the Pure Land]. This *Sutra*, however, speaks of Vaidehī and her five-hundred female attendants all being reborn. How do you account for this?" [184b21–23]

That can be explained as follows. When the commentary states that women and those with deficient faculties do not attain rebirth, they are referring to *after* rebirth in the Pure Land. There are no women in the Pure Land because those who are reborn in that country have pure rewards and are freed from desires. Because the physical rewards of those reborn are supreme, none has a deficient faculty there. If these persons under discussion only possessed virtuous minds, then [Buddha Amitābha's Sukhāvatī] would not be distinguished from all the other [pure lands]. [184b23–26]

A question is asked, "The *Large Sutra* states that those who commit the Five Grave Offenses do not attain rebirth. This *Sutra,* on the other hand, says those who commit the karmic evil of the [Five] Grave Offenses do attain rebirth. What is the reason for this?" [184b26–28]

There are two reasons explaining this. The first reason involves the distinction based on people. There are superior and inferior people among those who commit the Grave Offenses. Those below the rank of Good Destinies, who are constantly wallowing [in a state where they] commit the Grave Offenses, are "inferior" people. Those in the ranks of Good Destinies, who commit the Grave Offenses after being confronted with conditions [ripe for committing such offenses], are "superior" people. These superior people such as secular kings may commit Grave Offenses, but they invariably feel deep repentance, causing the effects of their karmic evil to dissipate and thereby allowing them to attain rebirth. Because this *Sutra* is concerned with this group, it states that those of the five Grave Offenses also attain rebirth. In contrast, inferior people commit Grave Offenses but do not show deep repentance, so that they cannot attain rebirth. Because the *Large Sutra* is concerned with this latter group, it states that those who commit grave offenses are not reborn. [184b28–c4]

The second reason is based on the distinction of practice. Among the practices performed by those who have committed these Grave Offenses, there are the meditative [virtues] and the non-meditative [virtues]. The *samādhi* of Buddha-visualization is called "meditative." The cultivation of the other virtuous faculties is called "non-meditative" virtue. The power of non-meditative virtues is weak and cannot eliminate the grave effects of the karmic evil of the Five Grave Offenses, thereby, not allowing practitioners to attain rebirth. Because the *Large Sutra* is concerned with this [latter non-meditative group], it stated that they are not reborn. The power of meditative virtue is strong and can erase the effects of karmic evil, thereby, allowing the attainment of rebirth. Because this *Sutra* describes visualization, it states [those who have committed even the Five Grave Offenses] are reborn [in the Pure Land]. [184c4–8]

The distinction [based on the six gates] is as discussed above. [184c8]*

*Translator's note: Having completed his analysis of the section on the nine grades of rebirth based on the six gates, Hui-yüan begins his exegesis of the passages from the same section.

Next I shall explain the passages. First, I will explain the visualizations of the three grades of people of the high category. The three grades will be discussed first and be concluded in general terms afterwards. [184c9–10]

Concerning the highest of the high grade, I shall first raise [the main issues], then discuss them and lastly offer a general conclusion. This discussion has three segments: (1) the description of the causes, (2) the passage, "When they are reborn in that country, these people . . . " (344c17), which remarks on the causes that consummate rebirth, and (3) the statement, "After being reborn in that country, they see the Buddha . . ." (344c25), which comments on the acquisition of benefits upon rebirth. [184c10–13]

In describing the causes, I shall first discuss the mind and afterwards the practice. With regard to the mind, the *Sutra* statement, "If those who aspire to be reborn in that land generate the three kinds of mind . . . ," (344c10) indicates the general import [concerning the mind]. The *Sutra* distinguishes the names of [each of the three minds]. "What [are the three]?" (344c11) questions [this distinction]. The passages that follow will discuss it. "Sincerity" is the "real mind." To perform practice without falsity is called the "sincere mind" (344c11). To seek rebirth with a genuine [intention] is also called the "sincere mind." The "deep mind" (344c12) means an "extremely earnest mind." To perform practice in extreme earnestness is called the "deep mind." To seek to leave [for the Pure Land] in extreme earnestness is also called the "deep mind." [184c13–17]

"Transferring merit to generate [aspiration for rebirth]" (344c12) is the mind that seeks to leave [for the Pure Land]. To seek rebirth by cherishing one's merit is called "transference." It is generally said that because one directs (*hui*) his merit towards (*hsiang*) the great enlightenment (*bodhi*) or directs his merits towards rebirth in that land, it is called "transference" (*hui-hsiang*) (i.e. "to direct" "towards"). The meaning of transference is to be understood as discussed extensively in the *Separate Treatise;* it is discussed there in great detail. To seek in a straightforward manner (as contrasted with transference) is said to be "aspiration" (*yüan*). Because one aspires for the great enlightenment or aspires for rebirth in that [land], it is called "aspiration." [184c17–21]

The *Sutra* statement, "Those who possess the three minds will with certainty be reborn in that country" (344c12) is the general conclusion. [184c22–23]

As for performing practice, the *Sutra*'s first statement, "Again, [by performing] the three kinds [of practices], [sentient beings] will gain rebirth" (344c12) indicates the general import. Next the *Sutra* lists the names; it first asks questions and afterwards lists them. These three [practices], as previously discussed, are the three kinds of pure acts. "Compassionate mind and non-killing" (344c14) are [collectively] the first pure acts. Previously, when I discussed the first act, I described how [those performing the first act] cared for their parents, honored their teachers and elders, and with a compassionate mind refrained from killing and cultivated the ten virtues. Here, however, I shall point out only the compassionate mind as the rest are omitted and not discussed. "To observe the precepts" (344c14) is the second pure act in the earlier passage. "To recite the Mahayana sutras and to generate the aspiration" (344c14) are the third pure act in the earlier passage. "To transfer . . ." (344c15) applies to all three previous pure acts. "They aspire to be born in that country. [By performing these acts] for one to seven days" (344c15) describes their capacity for cultivation. [184c23–29]

"They gain immediate rebirth" (344c16) concludes the cultivation and describes their benefits. The preceding has described the causes. [184c29]

In the second segment on the cause that consummates their rebirth, Tathāgata Amitābha, [Bodhisattva] Avalokiteśvara, and others come to welcome them since this group of people make great effort [to be reborn]. "When the practitioner sees [the Bodhisattvas praise him], he rejoices . . ." (344c23) describes his rebirth in that land. [185a1–2]

There are three subsegments of the third segment on the benefits of rebirth. The first is being reborn in that country, seeing the Buddha, listening to the Dharma, and obtaining the Insight of Non-arising. The second is serving extensively the various Buddhas and receiving prophecies from them. The third is returning to the original country and obtaining the esoteric formula (*dhāraṇī*), that is to say, the gate of the supreme esoteric formula. "This is called . . ." (345a4) is the conclusion. [185a3–5]

I shall next look at the middle of the high grade. I will first raise [the main issues], then discuss them and lastly conclude in general terms. There are again three segments to the elucidation. The first segment describes the causes. The second segment deals with the causes[36] that consummate rebirths. The third segment is on the benefits acquired after being reborn. [185a5–7]

With regard to the causes (in the first segment), the initial words "They do not necessarily uphold the Vaipulya (Mahayana) sutras" (345a5) point out how this [group] differs from the former [group, the highest of the high grade]. "They fully understand and accomplish . . ."[37] (345a5) correctly discusses the causes. "With this aspiration . . ." (345a7) indicates the resource they apply in seeking rebirth. The same holds true here as in the case of the middle of the high grade where the three kinds of mind, compassion, and observance of the observance of the precepts were discussed (p.184b24ff); being the same it will not be discussed. [185a7–10]

The first part of the second [segment on the causes which consummate] rebirth sets forth how they (Buddha Amitābha and Bodhisattvas) come to welcome people. "A practitioner sees himself seated on a [purple-] golden pedestal . . ." (345a11) depicts this person's rebirth in that land. "After spending one night, the [petals of the lotus flower] opened" (345a14), revealing the time [required for] rebirth. [185a10–12]

The passages of the third segment on the benefits have also three subsegments: (1) obtaining benefits after being reborn there, (2) extensively serving the many Buddhas and cultivating concentration (*samādhi*), and (3) after spending one small Kalpa in that country, one obtains the Insight of Non-arising and receives prophecy in the presence [of each Buddha]. With regard to the benefits obtained after being reborn there, "The body [of the practitioner] turns into a color of gold" (345a14) is the supreme primary reward (*cheng-pao*). "Under his feet there is another lotus flower" (345a14) is the supreme secondary reward (*i-pao*). "The Buddha and Bodhisattvas emit rays to shine [upon the practitioner] . . ." (345a15) describes how they serve as supreme virtuous friends. "Due to what was cultivated in previous [lives], and so forth (345a16) is the supreme Dharma to be listened to. "Stepping down from the [purple-] golden pedestal, he bows and praises the Buddha . . ." (345a17) is the supreme practice to be generated. "After spending seven days, etc." is the supreme [goal] to be accomplished. [185a12–18]

I shall next discuss the lowest of the high grade. Again I shall first raise [the main issues] and then discuss them in three [segments]: (1) the causes, (2) the rebirth, and (3) the description of the benefits to be obtained. [185a18–19]

With regard to the causes, the segment does not describe how [people of this grade] fully comprehend the import of their meaning, which demonstrates that this group is inferior to the previous group. "[Those of this grade] also believe in the [principle of] cause and effect" (345a22) correctly discusses the cause. Those with this belief are like those in the previous group, and, therefore, [are to be understood] according to the previous statement. "With these virtues . . ." (345a23) remarks on the resolve they apply in seeking rebirth. [185a19–21]

In the second segment on rebirth, the *Sutra* first relates how they (Buddha and Bodhisattva) come to welcome the practitioner. "When he sees these things . . ." (345a27) characterizes his rebirth in that country. "After spending one day and one night, the lotus flower opens" (345a29) discloses the time involved in the rebirth. Being inferior to the previous group, this group requires one day and one night before the flower opens. [185a21–23]

The [third segment] on the benefits also has three subsegments. The first is rebirth in that country and obtaining the benefits of seeing the Buddha and hearing the Dharma. The second is serving extensively the many Buddhas and hearing the Dharma from them. The third is spending three small Kalpas in that country and obtaining the gate of the hundred teachings[38] and dwelling in the Stage of Rejoicing. [185a23–26]

The above is referred to as "rebirths of the high category, the fourteenth visualization." This constitutes a general conclusion. [185a26]

I shall next look at the rebirth of the people of the middle three grades, and discuss the first two grades separately and afterwards offer general conclusions. [185a26–27]

Concerning the separate discussions, I shall first look at the rebirth of the highest of the middle grade; next raise [the main issues]; then discuss them and lastly conclude. The discussion of the causes has three segments: (1) the discussion of the causes, (2) the causes that consummate their rebirth, and (3) the acquisition of benefits after being reborn. [185a27–29]

As for the causes, the initial words "the Five Precepts" and "the Eight Precepts" require the precepts for the householders, while "cultivate and carry out the precepts" (345b9) are the precepts for those who have renounced the householder existence. These describe what is to be cultivated and regulated. "They do not commit the Five Grave Offenses and are without various other transgressions" (345b10) conveys how they are free of transgressions. "With these virtues . . ." (345b10) indicates the resolve they apply to seeking rebirth. The second segment on the causes [that consummate rebirths] first describes how they (Buddha and Bodhisattvas) come to welcome him, [the practitioner]. "The practitioner sees . . ." (345b11) remarks on his rebirth in that country. "When the lotus flower opens" (345b16) reveals the time required for rebirth, because this is a rebirth of an Āryapudgala, the flower opens up immediately. [185a29–b5]

In the third segment on the benefits, one listens to the Dharma after the lotus flower opens and later obtains the fruits of the path. "To obtain Arhatship" (345b17) is called "non-rebirth" or also "non-attachment."

The cause is absent in non-attachment, while the result is destroyed in non-birth. The Three Knowledges (*san-ming*) are generally said to be [the recollection of one's] previous past, divine sight, and the extinguishing of one's impurities; these are the Three Knowledges. The Six Transcendental Powers (*liu-t'ung*) are generally said to be the transcendental power of bodily [levitation], divine sight, divine ear, [knowledge of] the mind of others, [recollection of one's] previous past and the extinguishing of one's impurities; these are as extensively discussed in the *Separate Treatise*. [185b5–9]

The Eight-fold Emancipation (*pa chieh-t'uo*) is also referred to in the sutras as the Eight Abandonments (*pa-pei*). "What is the meaning of the term?" Internally, there exist characteristics of the forms, and externally, one visualizes the forms to be one. One's own body is called "internal," and another's body is called "external." When the forms in the context of one's own body have yet to be extinguished or destroyed, it is called the "visualization of internal existence" (*nei-yu kuan*). When the internal and external are [visualized to be] all completely impure, it is called the "forms of external visualization" (*wai-kuan se*). [185b9–12]

"With regard to this, both the internal and the external exist together, but why do you say that only the internal exists?" (185b12–13]

The internal forms exist in the beginning but do not exist at the end. Because our point of reference is the end when [the forms] do not exist, we explained that they exist in the beginning. The first three emancipations do not destroy external forms, and, thereby, it is not only [the internal forms] that exist in the beginning. Because of this, we have not said that the external forms exist [all the time].[39] [185b13–15]

"In this gate, one visualizes both the internal and external forms to be all completely impure. Why is it that you only speak of visualizing the external?" [185b15–16]

This conceals the visualization[40] and reveals the name. The previous internal forms have revealed existence but conceal the appellations of visualization. Now, the external forms reveal the visualization but conceal the name. Internally, there are no form characteristics, while externally, one visualizes the forms to be two. Imagine one's own body in its deceased form, where the insects eat and the fire burns up the form; this is referred to as the "non-existence of the internal." One visualizes and analyzes all external forms to be completely impure. These two previous kinds [of visualization] are none other than visualizations of the impurities. [185b16–21]

The emancipation through pure form is the third [of the Eight-fold Emancipation]. With regard to internal and external forms, one eliminates the skin and flesh and visualizes only the white bones. The previous three are the visualizations of the forms. The locus of emptiness (*śūnyatā*, the locus of consciousness, the locus of the absence of existence and of emancipation based on non-thought processes comprise the last four. Added to the previous [three] these make seven in all. The Āryapudgalas have obtained the four concentrations of the locus of emptiness, which are then explained as the [latter] four emancipations. The emancipation of total annihilation is the eighth emancipation; the so-called concentration of total annihilation (*nirodha-samāpatti*) is this eighth emancipation. This topic is to be discussed in detail as extensively [discussed] in the *Separate Treatise*. [185b21–26]

I shall next look at middle of the middle grade by first raising [the main issues], discussing them and at the end arriving at a general conclusion. There are three segments to the discussion. The first describes the causes. The second, "Imbued with the fragrance of the precepts . . . ," (345b21) discusses the causes that consummate rebirth. The third, "When the [lotus] flower is opened . . . ," (345b27) concerns the benefits that accrue on rebirth in that country. In the second segment on the [causes that consummate] rebirth, they first come to welcome the practitioner. "The practitioner sees himself seated on a lotus flower . . ." (345b25) describes his rebirth in that country. "After spending seven days, the lotus flower opened" (345b27) reveals the duration [required] for rebirth. [Those of this group,] being inferior to those of the previous [groups,] spend seven days in the flower before it opens up. [185b26–c2]

I shall next look at the lowest of the middle grade, by first raising in general [the main issues], then discussing them and at the end arriving at a conclusion. There are three segments to this discussion. The first describes the causes; the second deals with the causes that consummate rebirth; the third describes the benefits obtained on rebirth in that country. [185c2–4]

There are two kinds of causes. The first is the virtue of the practice of worldly people who filially care for their parents. The second is when at the end of one's life, having heard the virtuous teacher extoll that country and also heard Dharmākara's forty-eight aspirations, he aspires for happiness and desires for rebirth. In the second segment on the causes [that consummate their rebirth], practitioners are directly reborn with the Buddha coming to welcome them because the practices of this group of people are inferior [to those of the previous groups]. In the third segment on the benefits, practitioners do not visualize or see the Buddha because the practices of this group of people are inferior; to obtain Arhatship they hear instead the Dharma from Avalokiteśvara and Mahāsthāmaprāpta. This group is called the "lowest of the middle grade," and I now conclude specifically the discussion on the lowest of the middle grade.[185c4–8]

The above [three groups] are called the "middle category," and I now generally conclude the discussions of the middle grades. [185c8–9]

I shall next look at the people of the three lowest grades. Since this category of people dwells at the ranks of Good Destinies and below, it is difficult to know their capabilities [based on the Path system]. Also, each of the three groups of people of this group will also be discussed separately and later be concluded together. [185c9–11]

In separately [discussing each of the three grades,] I shall first look at the highest of the low rebirth. Once again, I will first raise in general [the main issues], then discuss them and at the end arrive at a conclusion. There are four segments to the discussion. The first discloses the transgressions of karmic evil. The second, "When one's life is about to end . . . ," (345c12) comments on the virtuous causes [for their rebirth]. Because listening to the sutra destroys karmic evil and reciting the Buddha's [name] eliminates evil, they attain rebirth. The third, "At that time, the Buddha dispatched transformed Buddhas . . . ," (345b16) describes how one is reborn. In this regard, the transformed [Buddhas and Bodhisattvas] come to welcome him. "After these words were spoken, the practitioner sees . . ." (345b19) describes how by following the transformed [Buddhas and Bodhisattvas] one is reborn in that country. "After spending forty-nine days the lotus flower opened" (345b21) remarks on the span of time required for rebirth to take place. Because karmic evil was light, the flower opened in just forty-nine days. The fourth [segment], "When the flower opened the great compassionate Avalokiteśvara [and Mahāsthāmaprāpta] emitted light . . . ," (345b22) describes the benefits obtained by those of this grade who are reborn there. In this regard, the *Sutra* first details how Avalokiteśvara first preaches for them the highly profound sutras and later remarks on how those people who hear the Dharma resolutely believe and generate the mind [set on enlightenment] and obtain the path. [185c11–19]

I shall next look at the middle of the low grade, by first raising in general the main issues again, then discussing them, and at the end arriving at a conclusion. There are four segments to the discussion. The first reveals their karmic evil. The second, "Such a person of karmic evil as this will [fall into hell] because of his evil acts . . . ," (346a1) sets forth the virtuous causes. On account of hearing the Buddha's virtues and the precepts, wisdom, and so forth [which the Buddha accomplished], one destroys his evil acts. The third [segment], "The fire of hell transforms into [cool] breeze . . . ," (346a6) relates how one is reborn. With regard to this, the transformed Buddha [and Bodhisattvas] come to welcome him. "As in a single-thought moment . . ." (346a7) [describes how] one is subsequently transformed and reborn. "In six Kalpas the flower opens" (346a8) reports the duration [required] for rebirth. Since the karmic evil is grave, the flower does not open for six Kalpas. The fourth [segment], "Avalokiteśvara and Mahāsthāmaprāpta preach the Dharma for him . . . ," (346a9) [describes] the benefits obtained by him once reborn in that [country];

he raises the mind [set for enlightenment upon hearing the Dharma. [185c19–25]

I shall next look at the lowest of the low grade, by again first raising in general the main issues, then discussing them and arriving at a conclusion. There are four segments of the discussion. The first relates their karmic evil. "Those who commit evil acts" (346a13) is mentioned as the general [import]. The Five Grave Offenses, and so forth are specific [imports]. The Five Grave Offenses are patricide, matricide, killing an Arhat, destroying the harmony among the monks, and drawing blood from the Buddha's body. [185c25–29]

A question is asked, "As stated in the *Large Sutra* those who commit the Five Grave Offenses are not reborn. Why is it that here those who commit the Five Grave Offenses are also reborn?" (185c29–186a1]

It is so because the two sutras do not concern the same persons. If a person has not planted any roots for acquiring the path in his previous lives, he will in the present life commit offenses and would have no recourse for rebirth at the end of his life. However, even if in confronting certain conditions one has committed karmic evil such as the Five Grave Offenses, the Four Heavy Transgressions or the Vilification of Dharma, he will invariably produce deep repentance like the secular kings and be also reborn because he has previously [in his past lives] awakened the mind-set on enlightenment. This is also true for those of the Good Destinies of Mahayana, who have committed the Five Grave Offenses, the Four Heavy Transgressions, and the Vilification of Dharma. The meaning of the term "ten evils" is as enumerated above. "Those who posses non-virtues" (346a13) are those who possess [karmic evil of] the Four Heavy Transgressions, and so forth. The above has discussed the first [segment] and has revealed the evil acts [committed by those of this grade]. [186a1–6]

The second segment, "Like these people of karmic evil who fall [to the evil Destinies of existence] on account of their evil acts . . ." (346a13) discusses their virtuous causes. There are two subsegments. The first adversely points out people's failings,[41] while the second, "The virtuous teacher says . . . ," (346a17) reveals their attainments. There are two sentences concerning the failings (subsegment one): (1) "They fall into hell on account of their evil acts"; and (2) "At the end of one's life . . . a virtuous teacher expounds the teaching, but one has no leisure to contemplate the Buddha" (346a15). Leisure is similar to "unoccupied time." Because there is no unoccupied time to contemplate the Buddha, the *Sutra* said, "He does not have leisure to [contemplate the Buddha]." There are two sentences concerning the attainments [subsegment two]: (1) The virtuous teacher expounds the teaching to encourage one to recite the Buddha's name so as to manifest the ten moments of contemplation (346a18);

and (2) "By reciting the [name of the] Buddha, he eliminates with every moment of thought the karmic evil of eighty *koṭi* Kalpas of birth and death" (346a19). This concludes the second segment on virtuous causes. [186a6–13]

The third segment, "At the end of one's life one sees a golden lotus . . . ," (346a21) [comments on how one] is reborn [in that country] by availing oneself of a virtuous [teacher]. Concerning this, the *Sutra* first describes how one sees the lotus flower, then obtains rebirth and lastly realizes his rebirth in that country. It takes twelve great Kalpas for the flower to unfold. On account of his extremely heavy karmic evil, it takes twelve great Kalpas for the flower to open. [186a13–16]

The fourth segment, "Avalokiteśvara and Mahāsthāmaprāpta with [voices of] great compassion . . . ," (346a18)) describes the benefits obtained after rebirth in that country. [186a16–17]

The general conclusion [for this section on the lowest of the low grade of rebirth] is self-evident [and, thus, no further explanation is needed]. [186a17]

The above discussion has fully explained the three kinds of pure acts and the sixteen correct visualizations. [186a17]

What follows below describes the benefits. The benefits are distinguished into three sections: (1) Vaidehī and the five-hundred female attendants who saw the Country of Peace and Happiness as well as the Buddha and the Bodhisattvas, and acquired the Insight of Non-arising; (2) The five-hundred female attendants who raised the mind-set on enlightenment and aspired for rebirth in that country, and the Buddha who explained that all would attain rebirth; and (3) Heavenly beings who raised the mind [set on enlightenment]. [186a18–20]

With this, the main import [of the Sutra] is concluded. [186a21]*

*Translator's note: The *Commentary* concludes with the discussion of the third part, the transmission.

What follows below describes the transmission, of which there are two sections: (1) transmission at the royal palace, and (2) "[The Buddha] walked [through the sky] . . ." (346b18) concerns transmission at Mount Gṛdhrakūṭa. [186a21–22]

The former section has four subsections. The first enumerates the name [of the *Sutra*] and how the teaching is to be remembered. The second subsection, "Practice this [*samādhi*] . . . ," (346b9) relates how Maudgalyāyana and others heard the Dharma and greatly rejoiced. In the first subsection, Ananda first began with a question; "what should the title of this *Sutra* be?" (346b5) is a question concerning its title. Up to now the meanings expressed about the titles have not been uniform. What should the meaning of this *Sutra* be? "How should the essence of this teaching be received and remembered?" (346b6) inquires into the protocols for receiving [the *Sutra*]. How should the ultimate essence of this teaching be received and remembered? The Buddha answers [this question] below. This *Sutra* is called "Visualizing on the [Land of] Extreme Bliss, Buddha of Immeasurable Life, Avalokiteśvara and Mahāsthāmaprāpta," or also called "Purifying of karmic [hindrances] and being reborn in the presence of various Buddhas" (346b7); this is in response to the first question [on the title of the *Sutra*]. "You should accept and remember, and do not forget" (346b8) responds to the latter question [as to how one should receive and remember the essence of the teaching]. "Do not forget" means "to remember." [186a22–29]

The following is the second [of the four subsections on the transmission at the royal palace] and describes the benefits derived from cultivation. With regard to this, the *Sutra* first sets forth the practices. [Through cultivation of the] earlier[-discussed] sixteen *samādhis* of the gate of visualization, one acquires great benefits, that is, "in this body one sees those Buddha and Bodhisattvas" (346b9). "If a good man or a good woman simply hears the name" (346b10) describes the benefits of contemplating the Buddha and Bodhisattva. "By simply hearing the names of [the Buddha and] two [Bodhisattvas], one eliminates the karmic evil of immeasurable [Kalpas of birth and death]; how much more so if the person is mindful [of the same Buddha and Bodhisattvas]" (346b10) relates the great benefits that a Bodhisattva acquires. Since inferior [forms of practice were] mentioned [first], how much greater [are the benefits for] superior [practice]. [186a29–65]

"If one contemplates the Buddha . . ." (346b12) describes how one acquires great benefits by contemplating the Buddha. "Whoever contemplates the Buddha is a white lotus (*puṇḍarīka*) among men" (346b12) displays his excellence. Because while the lotus is most excellent and this person is like this [flower], he is called a "*puṇḍarīka*."[42] "Avalokiteśvara and Mahāsthāmaprāpta will be his excellent friends" (346b13) demonstrates the excellence of his friends. [186b5–7]

"Sitting at the place of enlightenment (*bodhi-maṇḍa*)" (346b14) locates where the supreme [enlightenment] was attained. "Place" is similar to "locus." The locus where enlightenment was attained is called the "place of enlightenment," just as a place that grows wheat is called "the place of wheat." In this way, all are discussed in accordance with [the Buddha's] instruction [based on the enlightenment]. Because Buddha attained Buddhist enlightenment under the Bodhi tree, that location is called the "place of enlightenment." Since [the Buddha] occupied this [place] in attaining Buddhahood, it is called the "seat." (186b7–10]

The teaching relies on reality to discuss the meaning [of the seat] in order to teach the comprehensive and the limited. The "comprehensive" is where the virtues of all the practices of a Bodhisattva produces the fruit of Buddhahood; this is called the "place of enlightenment" as discussed in the *Vimalakīrti-sūtra.* The "limited" is where at the end of the diamond-*samādhi* (*vajra-samādhi*), one produces for himself Buddha's virtues; this is called the "place of enlightenment." The meaning [of the reference in the *Sutra* to] the "seat" was based on attaining the fruit [of enlightenment]. [186b10–14]

"He is reborn into the family of the Buddha" (346b14) refers to the superior [group] into which he will enter and is also called the "locus that is relied upon." The inconceivable Dharma of the Buddha is the locus where the Buddha dwells and is called the "family of the Buddha." One who belongs to the first Bhūmi or above enters the family of the Buddha, and in relying on this, he carries out the practices and is said to "be reborn in the family of the Buddha." [186b14–16]

The third subsection encourages one to remember the *Sutra.* The fourth subsection discusses how the practitioners heard and rejoiced [in the teaching]. The passages [to these subsections] are self-evident. [186b16–17]

In the second [of the two transmissions], the Buddha first walked through the sky and returned to Gṛdhrakūṭa; in order to increase their respect and to have sentient beings honor and follow his word, the Buddha appeared in this manifestation. Ānanda, then, expounded the teaching, and, in the end, the heavenly beings, the Nāgas and others rejoiced upon hearing [the teaching], paid proper respects [to the Buddha] and departed. [186b17–19]

*The Commentary on the Sutra on the Visualization of the Buddha of Immeasurable Life part two* end

# Appendix 1: Rankings of the Buddhist Path (*mārga*)

## Mahayana Ranks According to Hui-yüan

| Bhūmis | Ten-Bhūmis | Āryapudgalas |
|---|---|---|
| Practice of Resolution (*adhimukticaryā*) | Ten-Transferences | Inner Pṛthagjana (*nei-fan*) |
| Lineage (*gotrabhū*) | Ten-Practices<br>Ten-Dwellings (or Understandings) | |
| Good Destinies | Ten-Faiths | Outer Pṛthagjanas (*wai-fan*; *bāhyaka-pṛthagjana*) |

----------------------------------------Beginning of the Path----------------------------------------

Good Destinies

Those who have not yet
entered the Path
and those who have
committed transgressions
e.g. Five Grave Offenses,
Four Heavy Transgressions,
Vilification of the Dharma[1]

## Traditional Buddhist Ranks

| | | |
|---|---|---|
| Āryapudgala (sage) | Arhat (worthy one) | Non-trainer (*aśaikṣa*) |
| | Non-returner (*anāgāmin*) | Trainer (*śaikṣa*) |
| | Once-returner (*sakṛdāgāmin*) | |
| | Stream-winner (*srotāpanna*) | |
| Pṛthagjana (ordinary seeker) | | |

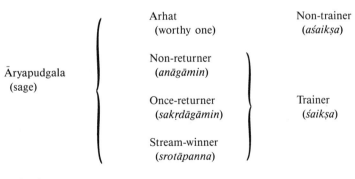

## Mahayana Bhūmi Stages Compared to Non-Mahayana Ranks

| *Non-Mahayana* | | *Mahayana* |
|---|---|---|
| Arhat | Non-trainer Path | Tenth Bhūmi |
| ("Worthy One") | (*aśakṣamārga*) | Ninth Bhūmi |
| | | Eighth Bhūmi |
| Non-returner | | Seventh Bhūmi |
| (*anāgāmin*) | Practice Path | Sixth Bhūmi |
| | (*bhāvanāmārga*) | Fifth Bhūmi |
| Once-returner | | Fourth Bhūmi |
| (*sakṛdāgāmin*) | | Third Bhūmi |
| | | Second Bhūmi |
| Stream-winner | Insight Path | First Bhūmi |
| (*srotāpanna*) | (*darśanamārga*) | |

1. Hui-yüan's basic views on Mahayana ranks are expressed in the *Mahayana Encyclopedia, T* 44.1851.810b15–c5, 811b13–15, 811c25–29, 813c4–5; *Commentary, T* 37.1749.182c20–22.

# Notes

## Introduction

1. Kenneth Ch'en, *Buddhism in China: A Historical Survey* (Princeton, New Jersey: Princeton University Press, 1972), pp. 342–350.

2. See Selected Bibliography section below for details.

3. For Hōnen, see his *Senchaku hongan nembutsu-shū, T* 2608.83.2c6–7; For Shinran, see his *Ken jōdo shinjitsu kyōgyōshō mon'rui, T* 2646.83.600b13–26.

4. *Bukkyō-gaku kankei: Zasshi ronbun bun'rui mokuroku* (Kyoto: Nagata bunshodō, 1975), pp. 168–176. See, for example, the section of Japanese articles on Chinese Pure Land written between 1960 and 1974.

5. Lu-shan Hui-yüan, Shan-tao and Fa-chao are among the seven patriarchs of the Lotus Society. *Fo-tsu t'ung-chi, T* 2035.49.260c–264a. Pu-tu's (Yüan period) *Lu-shan lien-tsung pao chien* also includes the above three and T'an-luan. *T* 1973.47.321c–324a.

6. One of the earliest references, if not the earliest, to Lu-shan Hui-yüan by a Pure Land commentator appears in Chia-ts'ai's *Pure Land Treatise* (compiled sometime early in the second-half of the seventh century), in which he is listed among the eminent Pure Land practitioners. *T* 1963.47.90c28. There is, however, no evidence of Hui-yüan's influence on the doctrinal position expressed in the *Pure Land Treatise*. Ogasawara Senshu, nevertheless, argues that the association continued to exist on Mt. Lu and had influence on the development of Pure Land Buddhism through the T'ang and into the Sung period. Ogasawara Senshu, *Chūgoku jōdokyoke no kenkyū* (Kyoto: Heirakuji shoten, 1951), pp. 17–21.

7. For example, see Ogasawara, Ibid., pp. 7–9; Ch'en, *Buddhism in China,* p. 107. Their findings suggest that Hui-yüan was set up as 'founder' of the Sung lineages as an attempt by their compilers situated in southern China to enlist Hui-yüan for his name value, as Hui-yüan continued to be revered in south China even eight hundred years after his death.

8. See Tsukamoto Zenryu. *Tōchūki no jōdokyō* (1933, Reprint. Kyoto: Hōzōkan, 1975), p. 256.

9. The notion of "apocryphal sutras" was expressed early in Chinese Buddhist history, for example, Tao-an's list of twenty-six "apocryphal sutras" in the *Ch'u san-tsang chi chi.* *T* 2145.55.38b7–c16. Seng-yu's own list of twenty more sutras beyond Tao-an's is found in the same catalogue. Ibid., 38c17–39b15.

10. They include the *Sui-yüan shih-fang wang-sheng ching* (*T* 1331.21.527c–532b), the *Ching-tu san-mei ching* (*ZZ* 1.87.4), the *Shan-wang huang ti ching* (not extant; see *Bussho,* 6: 370a), the *Wei wu san-mei ching* (not extant; see *Bussho,* 11: 114b), and the *Shih wang-sheng ching* (*ZZ* 1.87.4). Cf. Makita Tairyo, *Gikyō kenkyū* (Kyoto: Kyoto daigaku jinbun kagaku kenkyūjo, 1976), p. 11.

11. *T* 1958.47.19a15–17. See preceding note for references to the two sutras.

12. *T* 1959.47.24c7–8, 25b4–8 (*Shih wang-sheng ching*); 25b29–c6 (*Ching-tu san-mei ching)*; 25c15 (*Wei-wu san-mei ching*). *T* 1980.47.447c14–18 (*Shih wang-sheng ching*).

13. Essays on apocryphal sutras regarding Pure Land Buddhism are few, and no serious study exists that deals specifically with Pure Land Buddhism. See Mochizuki Shinko, *Jōdokyō no kigen oyobi hattatsu* (Tokyo: Kyōritsu-sha, 1930), pp. 215–216; Todo Kyoshun, "Zendō kyōgaku ni okeru gikyōten—toku ni *Jūōjōkyō* o megutte," *Ōryō shigaku* 3 and 4 (1977): 319–337.

14. The *Taishō shinshū daizōkyō* editions of these texts are, respectively: *T* 1960.47, *T* 1961.47, *T* 1966.47, and *T* 1967.47. Though the *Ching-t'u shih-i lun* is attributed to Chih-i (538–597), scholars are now generally of the opinion that it is a much later work, compiled sometime in the period 695 to 774 C.E. For a summary of scholarship concerning the authorship of this text and its English translation, see Leo Pruden, trans. "*The Ching-t'u lun Shih-lun,*" *Eastern Buddhist* 6-1 (May, 1973): 126–157.

15. *Nien-fo ching, T* 1966.47.127c20–128c29; *Ching-t'u shih-i lun, T* 1961.47.78a2–b2, 79b17. Among examples of the questions that were posed in the latter text is one presumably by a Ch'an adherent:

> Being empty, the nature of the *dharmas* is originally without arising and is equanimous and tranquil. But now you have abandoned this and seek birth in the Western Pure Land of Amitābha. How could it not go against the truth? Moreover, the *[Vimalakīrti*-sūtra] says, "If one seeks the Pure Land, first purify the mind, because when the mind is pure the Buddha Land is pure." (*T* 475.14.79a2–4)

16. The importance of the *Shan-tao Commentary* to the Japanese Pure Land Buddhists can be traced to Hōnen's personal salvation, which he credits to his reading of a passage from this text. Shinran included Shan-tao as one of the three Chinese patriarchs and quoted extensively from Shan-tao's works.

17. *Bussho,* vol. 2, p. 199a–b.

18. For the list, see chapter 3 below. Authors whose commentaries did not survive include Ling-yü (518–605), Hui-ying (d. 600) and Fa-ch'ang (567–645).

19. For the *Larger Sukhāvatīvyūha Sutra,* there are five extant Chinese recensions: *T* 360, 361, 362, 363, 364, and two for the *Smaller Sukhāvatīvyūha Sutra: T* 366 and 367. For a detailed discussion of the extant as well as of the lost recensions of the two sutras, see Fujita Kotatsu, *Genshijōdo shisō no kenkyū* (Tokyo: Iwanami shoten, 1970), pp. 13–115.

20. Mochizuki, *Chūgoku jōdokyōri-shi* (1942. Reprint. Kyoto: Hōzōkan, 1964), p. 90; Yamaguchi Koen, *Tendai jōdokyō-shi* (Kyoto: Hōzōkan, 1967), p. 125; Etani Ryukai, "Zui-tō jidai no kangyō kenkyū shikan," *Tsukamoto Festschrift,* p. 125; Nogami Shunjo, *Chūgoku jōdokyō-shi,* (Kyoto: Hōzōkan, 1981), p. 197.

21. Etani, "Zui-tō jidai no kangyō kenkyū shikan," p. 125; Fujiwara Ryosetsu, *Nembutsu no kenkyū* (Kyoto: Nagata bunshodō, 1957), p. 215.

22. Etani Ryukai, *Jōdokyō no shin kenkyū,* pp. 55–61. As support Etani cites the strong possibility that Wŏn'gwang (d. 630) studied with Hui-yüan in Ch'ang-an and that he brought back to Korea the Pure Land ideas associated with or similar to Hui-yüan's. Wŏn'gwang had an influence on Chajang, who resided at the same monastery, the Hwangnyong-sa, following Wŏn'gwang. As for Wŏnhyo, he too resided at the same monastery, and Etani finds influence of Hui-yüan's Pure Land thought in his writings. Ŭisang's commentary on the *A-mi-t'o ching* is lost, but he was also a resident of Hwangnyong-sa and claimed among his main disciples Ŭijŏk. Ŭijŏk's reconstructed commentary on the *Wu-liang-shou ching* reveals Hui-yüan's influence. The extant work of Pŏbwi and Hyŏnil also shows Hui-yüan's influences.

23. Ibid., pp. 56–57; Inouye Mitsusada, *Nihon jōdokyō seiritsushi no kenkyū* (Tokyo: Yamakawa shuppansha, 1956), p. 431.

24. *T* 1819.40. Its full title is the *Wu-liang-shou ching yu-po-t'i-she yüan-sheng chieh-chu,* and is a commentary to a treatise attributed to Vasubandhu (*T* 1524.26). T'an-luan is also credited with two shorter works, the *Tsan a-mi-t'o fo chi* (*T* 1978.47), and the *Lüeh-lun an-le ching-t'u i* (*T* 1957.47). The former is a poem in praise of the virtues of Buddha Amitābha and the Pure Land. The latter, whose authorship by T'an-luan has been questioned, is regarded as a synopsis of his *Wang-sheng lun-chu* without any new contributions beyond the latter work. See Leo Pruden, "A Short Essay on the Pure Land," *The Eastern Buddhist,* 8-1 (May, 1975): 74–95.

25. Such representative articles are: Etani, "Zui-tō jidai no kangyō kenkyū shikan," pp. 125–135; Yuki Reimon, "Kangyōsho ni okeru zendō shakugi no shisōshi teki igi," *Tsukamoto Festschrift,* pp. 907–924; Fukagai Jiko, "Zendō to Jōyōji-eon," *Tōyōgaku ronshū* (Kyoto:Hōyū shoten, 1979), pp. 1265–1280.

26. See *T* 1753.37.247c22, 248b7, 249a7.

27. Rei'ō, *Bussetsu kanmuryōjukyō kōki* in *Shinshū zensho,* vol. 5, pp. 1–298. For a modern explanation of the twenty-two points, see Yuki, "Kangyōsho ni okeru zendō shakugi," pp. 907–924.

28. Ohara Shojitsu, *Zendō kyōgaku* (Kyoto: Nagata bunshodō, 1974), pp. 61–65; Fujiwara, *Nembutsu shisō,* pp. 214–215 (partial listing of the twenty-two points); Yuki, ibid., pp. 907–924.

29. *T* 1745.37.

30. The only article that gives adequate coverage is Agawa Kantatsu, "Jōdo resso yori mitaru jōyō," in *Imaoka kyōju kanreki kinen ronbunshū,* edited by Taisho daigaku jodogaku kenkyukai (Tokyo: Taishō daigaku jōdogaku kenkyū, 1933), pp. 830–891. The article lists and compares Hui-yüan's doctrinal points derived from his *Wu-liang-shou ching i-shu* and the *Commentary* with positions of orthodox Chinese Pure Land masters such as Shan-tao and masters of the Japanese Jōdo School.

31. *T* 1753.37.247c22–249c9.

32. Ibid., p. 247b22–c8.

33. Ibid., p. 251a8–9. To a question as to how "inferior beings" with obstructions of defilement are able to be reborn, it is answered, " . . . on account of entrusting in the Buddha's vow which becomes the efficient condition."

34. T'an-luan's espousal of the efficacy of Buddha's vow is evident in the description of the "path of the easy practice" (*i-hsing tao*), which he defines with the phrase "the power of the Buddha's vow" (*fo-yüan li*). (*T* 1819.40.826a6–7) The Buddha's vow has received much attention in Japanese scholarship, influenced, no doubt, by Hōnen and especially Shinran, who rejected the efficacy of any effort on the part of the aspirant and, instead, stressed absolute entrusting (*shinjin*) in the vow.

35. Nobuo Haneda, "Dōshaku zendō nisshi no kangyō gebon-kan hikaku," *Shinran kyōgaku* 37 (1980): 76–81. Some basic differences between the two are: (1) Tao-ch'o ranked the lowest of the low grade as Ten-Faith stages while Shan-tao ranked the same grade much lower; (2) Tao-ch'o accepted the efficacy of good deeds performed in past lives while Shan-tao rejected it as nonexistent; and (3) Tao-ch'o advocated raising the mind-set on enlightenment (*bodhicitta*) in this life but Shan-tao relegated it to after death in the Pure Land.

36. The highly touted reference to Shan-tao's Five Correct Practices by the orthodox writers is not fully supported by Shan-tao's own writing. For detailed discussion, see chapter 6 below, notes 11–14.

**Notes Chapter 1**

1. Cf. Fujita, *Genshijōdo shisō,* p. 3; Mochizuki Shinko, *Chūgoku jōdokyōri-shi,* (Kyoto: Hōzōkan, 1934), p. 1.

2. For reference to the two sutras, see note 19 of the introduction above. The cosmos at the time of the emergence of Pure Land teaching included countless numbers of world-realms of which 'our' Sahā was one and Sukhāvatī was another. The Sahā realm consists of Mt. Meru at the center with seven concentric mountain ranges along with a surrounding wall of iron. Seas fill the regions between the mountain ranges. Four continents lie in each of the four quadrants of Mt. Meru, of which the southern Jambūdvīpa, was regarded as the continent of India. Further, three Realms (*loka*) of Desire (*kāma*), Form (*rūpa*) and Formless (*arūpya*) exist vertically with Mt. Meru as their focus. For details, see Randy Kloetzli, *Buddhist Cosmology* (Delhi: Motilal Banarsidass, 1983), pp. 23ff.

3. See introduction, note 19. These are the basic themes shared by all the extant versions.

4. See Fujita, *Genshijōdo shisō,* pp. 507–511. According to Fujita, there is one occurrence of the term "*ching-t'u*" in the *Wu-liang-shou ching* (*T* 360.12.267b25), but it is in reference to Buddha-lands in general and not specifically to Sukhāvatī. This is the only appearance of the term in these early versions of the Pure Land sutras prior to Hsüan-tsang's translation of the *Smaller Sukhāvatīvyūha Sutra* (*T* 367.12), which contains numerous occurrences of this term even in its title. But, its Sanskrit manuscript (though not the same version from which the Hsüan-tsang made his translation) does not show any occurrences of the Sanskrit equivalent of the term "pure land," thereby, leading Fujita to suggest that Hsüan-tsang during translation inserted the term "*ching-t'u*" where no Sanskrit original existed.

The "pure land" reflects a concept associated with the Mahayana Bodhisattva practice of "purifying the Buddha land" (*buddhakṣetra-pariśuddhi*; *buddhakṣetra-pariśodhana*; *kṣetraṃ pariśodhayati, etc.*). "Purification" in this context refers to the spiritual process of leading all beings dwelling within the Bodhisattva's realm to enlightenment. This idea finds clear expression in such early Mahayana sutras as the *Aṣṭasāhasrikā-prajñāpāramitā, Lotus, Daśabhūmika* and *Vimalakīrtinirdeśa.*

As for the adjective-noun compound term "pure land" (*ching-t'u*) Kumārajīva was apparently one of the first to adopt this term in his Chinese translation. In his translation of the *Vimalakīrti-sūtra* Kumārajīva adopted this term on twenty occasions. The Tibetan counterpart for three of these instances is "*saṅs rgyas kyi shiṅ yons su dag pa*" (purification of Buddha land), while that for the remaining seventeen is "*saṅs rgyas kyi shiṅ*" (Buddha's land). Thus, Kumārajīva appears to have adopted the term "pure land" as a gloss translation for these terms associated with the Mahayana concept of "purifying the Buddha land" alluded to above.

5. *T* 1819.40.829a24. See Fujita, *Genshijōdo shisō,* pp. 506–511; Hirakawa, "Jōdokyō no yōgo ni tsuite," in *Bukkyō ni okeru jōdoshisō,* ed. Nihon bukkyō gakkai (Kyoto: Heirakuji shoten, 1977), pp. 2–11.

6. *T* 1819.40.843a18.

7. *T* 1958.47.13c6.

8. Ibid., pp. 4b27–28; 4c20, 22.

9. *T* 1979.47.428b3.

10. The term "Pure Land teaching" also is formed in *Hsi-fang yao-chüeh shih-i t'ung-kuei* attributed to [Kue-]ch'i (632–82) (*T* 1964.47.104b25), and "Pure Land sect or import" (*T* 1965.47.119b20) is referred to in the *Yusim allakto* attributed to Wŏnhyo. However, these texts must be treated with caution since the authenticity of their authorship has been questioned by modern scholars. See Mochizuki, *Jōdokyō no kenkyū,* (Tokyo: Nihon tosho sentā, 1977), pp. 466–480 (for the former work ascribed to [Kue-]ch'i), and Etani, *Jōdokyō no shin kenkyū,* pp. 76–84 (for Wŏnhyo's work).

11. B. N. Mukherjee, "A Mathura Inscription of the Year 26 and of the Period of Huvishka," *Journal of Ancient Indian History,* vol. 11 (Calcutta: University of Calcutta, 1979): 82–84.

12. Gregory Schopen, "The Inscription on the Kuṣān Image of Amitābha and the Character of Early Mahāyāna in India," *Journal of the International Association of Buddhist Studies* 10–2 (1987): 119.

13. *Sung kao-seng chuan, T.*2061.50.890b1–c15.

14. Gregory Schopen, "Sukhāvatī as a Generalized Religious Goal in Sanskrit Mahāyāna Sūtra Literature," *Indo-Iranian Journal* 19 (1977):177–210.

15. Fujita, *Genshijōdo shisō,* pp. 222–257. Also, most of the early translators of Pure Land texts were from Central Asia or North India. Fujita also makes the case that the luxurious depictions of Sukhāvatī may reflect the opulence of the mercantile class, resulting from active trading in the region with Rome and the Hellenistic world.

16. These past Buddha names are found, for example, in a sutra from the Long Āgama section (*T* 1.1.10b16–17); this sutra corresponds to *Mahāpadāna-suttanta* (Dīgha-nikāya 14). J. Takasaki reports that inscriptions from the Aśokan period mention offerings to Buddha Koṇāgamana (Kanakamuni). Takasaki suggests that since the names of the Buddhas vary according to schools, the concept of the seven past Buddhas was established prior to the sectarian divisions that were at least well under way by Aśokan period. See Jikido Takasaki, *An Introduction to Buddhism,* Rolf W. Giebel trans. (Tokyo: Tōhō Gakkai, 1987), pp. 59–60.

17. Takasaki, *An Introduction to Buddhism,* p. 61.

18. Yabuki, *Amidabutsu no kenkyū* (Tokyo: Heigo shuppansha, 1911), pp. 118–125. For an excellent treatment on Maitreya, see Alan Sponberg and Helen Hardacre, eds. *Maitreya, the Future Buddha* (Cambridge: Cambridge University Press, 1988).

19. *Majjhima Nikāya* (Pali Text Society) i, pp. 190–191; *Itivuttaka* (PTS), p. 91; *Saṃyutta Nikāya* (PTS) iii, p. 120.

20. Teresina Rowell, "The Background and Early Use of the Buddha-kṣetra Concept," *The Eastern Buddhist* 4-2 and 3 (March, 1935): 426–431. Fujita, *Genshijōdo-shisō,* pp. 361–376. Randy Kloetzli, *Buddhist Cosmology,* pp. 91–111. S. Z. Aung and C. A. F. Rhys Davids, *Points of Controversy: Kathāvatthu* (London: Pali Text Society, 1915), p. 355.

21. See Fujita, *Genshijōdo shisō,* p. 366. *Mahāvastu* I, pp. 123–124, III, p. 342. Buddhaghosa and Yaśomitra both corroborate this in their *Katthāvatthupakaraṇaṭṭhakathā,* p. 190 and *Abhidharmakośa-vyākhyā,* p. 338, 1. 22, respectively.

22. Mayeda Sengaku, *Genshibukkyō-seiten no seiritsushi kenkyū* (Tokyo: Sankibō-busshorin Publishing Co., Ltd., 1964), pp. 588–590. Mayeda summarizes the findings of previous scholarship on the date of compilation of the *Kathāvatthu.* While most Western scholars have accepted the traditional view that the work was compiled during the time of King Aśoka, Japanese scholars in general have asserted that the original sections were compiled during Aśoka's time but that additions continued at least through the second century B.C.E.

23. Cf. Fujita, *Genshijōdo shisō,* p. 360 1: *Dīgha-nikāya* II, p. 225; III, p. 114; *Majjhima-nikāya* III, p. 65, etc.

24. Cf. ibid., pp. 357–358, 360 3. *Bodhisattvabhūmi,* edited by U. Wogihara, pp. 92:8–93:5; *Yu-chia-shih ti-lun, T.*1579.30.499c.

25. Cf. Rowell, "Buddha-kṣetra Concept," pp. 232–237.

26. From *Nidānakathā,* p. 64 as cited in Rowell, "Buddha-kṣetra Concept," p. 236.

27. A. L. Basham, "The Evolution of the Concept of the Bodhisattva," in *The Bodhisattva Doctrine in Buddhism,* ed. Leslie Kawamura (Ontario, Canada: Wilfrid Laurier University Press, 1981), pp. 44–47. Cf. Teresina Rowell, "Buddha-kṣetra Concept," p. 426.

28. Cf. Rowell, "Buddha-kṣetra Concept," pp. 426–427.

29. Kajiyama Yuichi, *Satori to ekō* (Tokyo: Kōdansha, 1983), pp. 168–184. The Theravādins also shared a similar concept of benefit but expressed it by other terms, for example, by "*ādiśati*" (to direct, offer). For example, there is a story from a sutra of merchants who offer clothes because they take pity on a naked female hungry ghost. But the hungry ghost tells the merchants to offer the clothes to the monks who will then direct the merit accrued from that virtuous act to her. Upon doing so, the merchants found the female hungry ghost garbed in a beautiful garment.

30. T. W. Rhys Davids, trans. *The Questions of King Milinda* Part I (1890; reprint ed., New York: Dover Publications, Inc., 1963), pp. 148–149. For Davids, this work was compiled "at or little after the beginning of the Christian era," (ibid.,

p. xi) while Mayeda moves up the compilation date of the 'original form' of this work to mid-first century B.C.E. Mayeda, *Genshibukkyō-seiten,* p. 615.

31. *T* 1521.26b27–28.

32. Fujita, *Genshijōdo shisō,* pp. 287, 304.

33. Ibid., pp. 306–309.

34. Ibid., pp. 287–291, 304. The exact original term for the transliteration is still unclear. While foregoing any conclusions, Fujita suggests that the original was derived from dropping either the final syllable or vowel from "Amitābha" or "Amitāyus."

35. Ibid., pp. 262–273. E. J. Eitel (1838–1908) was probably the earliest to advocate this position, and others include P. Carus, S. Beal, L. A. Waddell, S. Levi, P. Pelliot, J. Przyluski, A. Bareau, H. de Lubac, L. de La Vallée Poussin, É. Lamottee, A. Grünwedel, and A. B. Keith.

36. Fujita, *Genshijōdo shisō,* pp. 273–278.

37. Ibid., pp. 280–282.

38. Mochizuki, *Jōdokyō no kenkyū,* pp. 69–71; Yabuki, *Amidabutsu no kenkyū,* pp. 63ff.

39. Fujita, *Genshijōdo shisō,* pp. 322–334. For example, in the *Mahāparinibbāna-suttanta* the Buddha states, "Ananda, if I wish I would be able to live for one Kalpa or longer than a Kalpa." (*Dīgha-nikāya* II, p. 102–121, especially p. 103) The light theme is seen, for example, "Among the radiance the Truly Enlightened One is the best; this light is unsurpassed." (*Saṃyutta-nikāya* I, p. 15)

40. Cf. ibid., p. 333. *I-pu-tsung lun-lun, T*2031.49.15b29–c1.

41. Ibid., p. 333. Another Chinese version of the same work translates this corresponding phrase as "light is immeasurable and life is immeasurable." *T* 2032.49.18b14.

42. Ibid., pp. 466–468, 471–473.

43. Sugiyama Jiro, *Gokurakujōdo no kigen* (Tokyo: Chikuma shobō, 1984), pp. 150–167.

44. Fujita., *Genshijōdo shisō,* pp. 469–471.

45. Ibid., 285, 355.

46. This text, *Shih-chu p'i-p'o-sha lun,* is the earliest known text to mention oral recitation in relation to Amitābha, "Those who wish to go [to the Buddha lands] to attain the non-retrogressive state should with deep respect hold and recite their names." (*T*1521.26.41b13–14)

47. The text reflects more the contents of stage two. This work exists only in one Chinese translation, and some modern scholars have questioned Nāgārjuna's authorship. For example, Richard Robinson and Willard Johnson, *The Buddhist Religion: A Historical Introduction* (Belmont, California: Wadsworth Publishing Company, 1970), pp. 89, 138–140 suggest that this work is a Central Asian or Chinese forgery. Then there is a view that these passages on recitation did not exist in the original but were actually Kumārajīva's textual interpolations. See Kagawa Koyu, "Shōmyō shisō no keisei," *Indogaku bukkyōgaku kenkyū,* 11-1 (1963): 45–46.

48. *T* 365.12.342c28–346a26. Controversy also surrounds the compilation of this sutra. See chapter 3.

49. Fujita, *Genshijōdo shisō,* pp. 122–123, 132. The compilation probably took place in Central Asia, reflecting prevailing practices in India and Central Asia. Cf. chapter 5 below.

50. Ibid., 343b29.

51. In fact, the vision of Amitābha Buddha is mentioned as one of the accomplishments in association with the Pratyutpanna-samādhi. *T* 417.13.899a10–14.

52. See below note 5 in chapter 3.

53. Julian Pas, "Shan-tao's Interpretation of the Meditative Vision of Buddha Amitāyus," *History of Religion,* 14-2 (November, 1974):96–116.

54. *T* 12.343a20–21.

55. Ibid., 345c10–346a26.

56. Komaru Shinji, "Kanmuryōjukyō to shōmyōshisō," *Bukkyō shisō no shomondai* (Tokyo: Shunjūsha, 1985), pp. 430. Komaru notes the *Mahāvastu* passage to be from page 245 in the edition by E. Senart.

57. Ibid., p. 435ff.

58. The Sankrit title is uncertain. Its full title of the Chinese translation is the *Wu-liang-shou ching you-po-t'i-she yüan-sheng chi* (The Verses on the Vow to be Reborn and the Instructions on the Sutra of the Buddha of Immeasurable Life), *T* 1524.26. For a full translation and study of this text, see Minoru Kiyota, "Buddhist Devotional Meditation: A Study of the *Sukhāvatīvyuhopadeśa,*" Minoru Kiyota, ed. *Mahayana Buddhist Meditation Theory and Practice* (Honolulu: University of Hawaii Press, 1978), pp. 249–296. See chapter 3 for a discussion of its title.

59. The references to recitation appear *T* 1524.25.231b15, 233a12.

60. Ibid., pp. 232c3, 233a17–18.

61. Cf. Fujita, *Genshijōdo shisō,* p. 143. *Ta chih tu lun, T* 1509.25. There are numerous references to Amitābha, pp. 93a, 115c, 127a, 134b, 221b, 276a, 302b–c,

309a, 311c, 342a–b, 343a, 418a, 529c, 708c, 712a. For *Daśabhūmika-sūtra* commentary, *T.*1521.26.26b, 42c, 43a–b, 45a, 64c.

62. Ibid., p. 41a13–b6.

63. *T* 1592.31.103b17–20. References are found also in other Chinese translations, pp. 121b, 141b, 292b. Tibetan translation, Peking edition, no. 5549, 6, 112, p. 225–4–2ff.

64. For example, in Vasubandhu's commentary to the *Mahāyānasaṃgraha, T* 1595.31.194b8–9. References are found also in other Chinese translations, pp. 292a and 346a. Tibetan translation, Peking edition, no. 5551, vol. 112, p. 290–1–1ff.

65. *T* 1525.26.233a17–25.

66. *T* Ibid., pp. 231a14, 232a3–9.

67. Fujita, *Genshijōdo shisō,* pp. 141–164.

68. Jikido Takasaki, *A Study on the Ratnagotravibhāga (Uttaratantra),* series Orientale Roma 32 (Roma: Istituto Italiano Per Il Medio Ed Estremo Oriente, 1966), pp. 390.

69. Fujita, *Genshijōdo shisō,* pp. 339–341.

70. Ibid., pp. 23–62. The two translations are found in *T* 362.12 and 361.12, respectively.

71. There are four surviving recensions of the Chinese translation. *T* 416.13, 417.13, 418.13, and 419.13.

72. *T* 2103.52.351b20–23.

73. *T* 417.13.899a10–14.

74. *T* 2122.53.616b15–c1. See Tsukamoto Zenryu, "Shina jōdkyō no tenkai," *Shina bukkyō shigaku* 3–3 and 4 (Dec. 1939):13.

75. *T* 50.395b25–c1.

76. See Ch'en, *Buddhism in China,* p. 66; Erik Zürcher, *The Buddhist Conquest of China,* (Leiden: E. J. Brill, 1959), p. 125.

77. *T* 2103.52.196b25–c9. The translation is by Zürcher, *The Buddhist Conquest,* p. 128.

78. *T* 2102.52.29c19–33b11.

79. *T* 2059.50.358c22ff. Cf. Zürcher, *Buddhist Conquest.,* pp. 219–220.

80. See Mochizuki, *Chūgoku jōdokyōri-shi,* pp. 49–50.

81. See Tsukamoto Zenryu, "Shina jōdokyō no tenkai," p. 20.

82. Fujita, *Genshijōdo shisō,* pp. 62–77.

83. Ibid., pp. 69–70.

84. Ibid., pp. 104–112.

85. Ibid., pp. 116–133.

86. *Kao-seng chuan, T* 2059.50.380c13–14.

87. Ibid., 381c12–16.

88. *T* 1763.37.377–611.

89. Todo Kyoshun, *Muryōjukyōronchū no kenkyū* (Kyto: Bukkyō bunka kenkyūjo, 1958), pp. 3–8.

90. *T* 1958.47.14b9–16.

91. See *T* 2060.50.497c17.

92. See note 24 of introduction for references to his three works. The earliest Chinese reference attributing this work to T'an-luan is found in Chia-ts'ai's *Pure Land Treatise* (*T* 1963.47.97c13–14). Cf. Leo Pruden, "A Short Essay on the Pure Land," *The Eastern Buddhist* 8-1 (May, 1975): 74–95.

93. *Further Biographies, T* 2060.50.470a13–c15.

94. *Pure Land Treatise T* 1963.47.98b6–11; *T* 2060.50.684a12–13.

95. *Lu-shan lien-tsung pao chien. T* 1973.47.322a23–b23.

96. *T* 2646.83.600b13–26.

97. *T* 1819.40.826b7–8.

98. Ibid., 843a18.

99. See Roger Corless, "T'an-luan: Taoist Sage and Buddhist Bodhisattva," in *Buddhist and Taoist Practice in Medieval Chinese Society,* David W. Chappell ed. (Honolulu: University of Hawaii Press, 1987), pp. 36–45.

100. *T* 1819.40.835c8–13.

101. See Hsiao Ching-fen, "The Life and Teachings of T'an-luan" (Ph.D. dissertation, Princeton Theological Seminary, 1967), pp. 20–23.

102. *T* 2060.50.470.

103. Ibid., p. 826b7–9.

104. Tao-ch'o's *An-le chi,* though not in the standard commentarial form, is essentially a commentary on the *Kuan-ching.*

105. See notes 24 and 25 in chapter 3.

106. *T* 2060.50.470c3–5.

**Notes Chapter 2**

1. Yuki Reimon, "Chūgoku bukkyō no keisei," edited by Miyamoto Shoson, et al. *Kōza Bukkyō IV: Chūgoku bukkyō* (Tokyo: Daizō shuppan, 1967), pp. 79–104; idem., "Zui-tō no chūgoku-teki shin bukkyō soshiki no ichirei to shite no *Kegon hokkai kanmon* ni tsuite," *Indogaku bukkyōgaku kenkyū* 6 (1958): 276–281; Kamata Shigeo, *Chūgoku bukkyō shisōshi kenkyū* (Tokyo: Shunjūsha, 1968), pp. 260, 353–354.

2. As an example of modern works that regard Hui-yüan as a member of the Ti-lun School, see: Mochizuki, *Chūgoku jōdokyōrishi,* p. 89; Ocho Enichi, *Chūgoku bukkyō no kenkyū,* vol. 3, p. 163; Fujiwara Ryosetsu, *Nenbutsu no kenkyū,* p. 154. For examples of his purported affiliation with the She-lun school, see the next note.

3. As an example of references to Hui-yüan's affiliation with the She-lun School, see Hirose Takashi, *Kangyōsho ni manabu: gengibun ni* (Kyoto: Hōzōkan, 1980), pp. 341–342. It appears that his purported She-lun affiliation stems from the first fascicle of the *Shan-tao Commentary* in which Hui-yüan's position as well as that of the *She ta-ch'eng lun* (*Mahāyāna-saṃgraha*) is criticized in the same context. Despite the fact that Hui-yüan had little or nothing to do with the context of the *She ta-ch'eng lun,* Hui-yüan came to be associated with this treatise and the 'school' that developed around it. The point of contention in the *She ta-ch'eng lun* concerns the idea of "intended for a later time" that regarded the Pure Land practice of "Buddha-contemplation" as merely preliminary which, by itself, does not lead to enlightenment or even rebirth in the Pure Land. For Shan-tao's defense against *She ta-ch'eng lun*'s criticism, see *T* 1753.37.249c10–250b10.

4. Among Chih-i's writings, see *T* 1777.38.527b16, 25. Among Chi-tsang's writings, see *T* 1716.33.704c4; *T* 1824.42.126c5.

5. Yoshizu Yoshihide, "Jironshi to iū kōshō ni tsuite," *Komazawa daigaku bungakubu kenkyū kiyō* 31 (1973):307–323.

6. *Further Biographies,* p. 490a10–18.

7. See below for a complete listing of Hui-yüan's writings. The surviving works from the northern dynasties, other than those of Hui-yüan, are commentaries on the following sutras and treatises: *Avataṃsaka-sūtra* by Hui-kuang (*T* 2756.85), *Daśabhūmika-śāstra* by Fa-shang (*T* 2799.85), *Avataṃsaka-sūtra* by Ling-pien (*ZZ* 1.93.5), *Avataṃsaka-sūtra* by Ling-yü (*ZZ* 1.88.1), *Ta chih tu lun* by Hui-ying (*ZZ* 1.74.3 and *ZZ* 1.87.3), *Rebirth Treatise* by T'an-luan (*T* 1819.40) and *Awakening of Faith* by T'an-yen (*ZZ* 1.71.3). Of these, only T'an-luan's treatise

is a complete work. See Ocho Enichi, *Chūgoku bukkyō no kenkyū,* vol. 3 (Kyoto: Hōzōkan, 1979), p. 159.

8. Hui-yüan's commentary on the *Śrīmālādevī-sūtra* (*ZZ* 1-30-4) is profusely quoted in Chi-tsang's commentary on the same sutra, the *Sheng-man pao-k'u* (*T* 1744.37). See Fujieda Akira, "Shōmangyō gishō," *Shōtoku taishi shū,* Nihon-shisō taikei 2 (Tokyo: Iwanami shoten, 1975), pp. 489, 541 10; Yoshizu, "Jironshi to iū kōshō ni tsuite," pp. 212–213; Fujii Kyoko, "Pelliot Ch. 2091 *Shōman giki* kange zankan shahon ni tsuite," *Shōtoku taishi kenkyū* 13 (1979): 27–37.

9. Yoshizu Yoshihide, "Eon Daijōkishinron gisho no kenkyū," *Komazawa daigaku bukkyōgakubu kenkyū-kiyō* 34 (1976): 169, 21; idem, "Daijōgishō hasshikigi kenkyū," *Komazawa daigaku bukkyōgakubu kenkyū-kiyō* 30 (1972): 157 9.

10. Hui-yüan's commentary on this sutra is reportedly quoted and criticized in Chih-i's commentaries on the same sutra (*ZZ* 1-27-5 to 1-28-2) and Chi-tsang (*T* 1781.38). See Yoshizu, "Daijōgishō hasshikigi kenkyu," p. 157, 10.

11. This is the focus of this study, particularly chapter 6.

12. See above, note 8.

13. Yoshizu Yoshihide, "Daijōgishō no seiritsu to jōyōji eon no shisō (1)," *Sanzō* 165 (1978):3.

14. Kamata Shigeo, *Chūgoku bukkyō shisō-shi,* pp. 318–326, 354.

15. *T* 1851.44. Yoshizu alludes to the impact that this treatise had on the writings of later writers including Chi-tsang, Chih-i, Kue-ch'i, Chih-yen, Fa-tsang, Ch'eng-kuan. See Yoshizu Yoshihide, "Daijōgishō no seiritsu to jōyōji eon no shisō (1)," pp. 2–3.

16. Ocho, *Chūgoku bukkyō,* vol. 3, p. 163.

17. Kamata's article (in *Chūgoku bukkyō shisō-shi*) is probably the first modern work to attempt to treat more than one doctrinal point. Yoshizu Yoshihide of Komazawa University has been the most prolific writer on Hui-yüan, whose studies have been published in numerous articles that number over twenty and mostly appeared during the 1970s (see Bibliography below).

Some examples of articles on specific topics based on the *Mahayana Encyclopedia* are: Fukushima Koya, "Jōyōji eon no shikan shisō," *Tōhōgaku* 36 (1968): 15–28; Fukihara Shoshin, "Jōyōji eon no bussho-setsu," in *Hokugi bukkyō no kenkyū* ed. Ocho Enichi (Kyoto: Heirakuji shoten, 1970):203–260; Takahashi Koji, "Eon to zendō no busshin-ron," in *Zendō kyōgaku no kenkyū,* ed. Bukkyō daigaku zendō kyōgaku kenkyūkai (Kyoto: Tōyōbunka shuppan, 1980): 79–96.

18. Kamata, *Chūgoku bukkyō shisōshi,* p. 306. Kamata contrasts Hui-yüan with the likes of T'an-luan of the Pure Land tradition, Hui-wen and Hui-szu of the T'ien-t'ai tradition, and Tu-shun or the Hua-yen tradition, all of whom were

meditators. He suggests this difference led to the latter group becoming founders of new schools, while Hui-yüan never gained equivalent status. Ocho Enichi concurs because he views Hui-yüan and Chi-tsang as two individuals who were more compromising in their doctrinal assertions and less attuned to the conditions of the time, as contrasted with Chih-i and Hsin-hsing. See Ocho Enichi, *Chūgoku bukkyō,* vol. 3, p. 146.

19. Kamata, *Chūgoku bukkyō shisōshi,* pp. 353–354.

20. *Further Biographies,* p. 491c14–15.

21. *Further Biographies,* pp. 489c26–492b1. *Kuang-hung ming-chi, T* 2103.52.153a27–154a9. *Fo-tsu t'ung-chi, T* 2035.49.358b20–c8. *Fo-tsu li-tai t'ung-tsai, T* 2036.49.557a15–c12.

22. For an excellent study on this persecution, see Tsukamoto Zenryu, "Hokushū no haibutsu ni tsuite," *Tōhō gakuhō, Kyoto* 16 (1948): 29–101; 18 (1950): 78–111; reprinted in *Idem, Gisho shakurōshi no kenkyū* (Kyoto: Bukkyō-bunka kenkyūsho shuppan, 1961), pp. 359–478; *idem,* "Hokushū no shūkyo haiki-seisaku no hōkai," *Bukkyō shigaku* 1 (1949): 3–31.

23. *Kuang hung-ming chi,* p. 153c23–27.

24. Ibid., p. 153a29–b9.

25. Ibid., p. 153b10–14.

26. Ibid., p. 153b10–c22

27. Confucianism, Buddhism, and Taoism.

28. Traditionally, Emperor Ming, inspired by a dream, sent for Buddhist missionaries who translated the first sutra in Loyang in A.D. 67. Though the historicity of this story is now questioned, there is other evidence for the presence of Buddhism in China in the first century A.D.

29. The three traditional emperors of ancient China are most often said to be Fu-hsi, Shen-nung, and Huang-ti, or T'ien-huang, Ti-huang, and Jen-huang.

30. Righteousness, humanity, loyalty, considerateness, and sincerity.

31. The message here appears to be that one needs writings in order to know about the truths that they convey. The two are indispensible just as mother and father are for a child.

32. Ch'in-chin is traditionally considered the "original home" of China, while Lu lies outside. Its people and customs have borne the brunt of many jokes and much ridicule for their unsophisticated ways.

33. According to the traditional burial order (*chao-mu hsü*), the original ancestor is in the center, with the second, fourth, and sixth generations buried to its left (*chao*) and the third, fifth and seventh to its right (*mu*).

34. The five are the Books of *Poetry, Rites, History,* and *Change,* plus the *Spring and Autumn Annals.*

35. Based on the early Buddhist cosmology, Jambūdvīpa is the continent on which Śakyamuni Buddha emerged and where Buddhism prospers. The four oceans surround Jambūdvīpa. Cakravartin is a sagely, universal monarch like Emperor Aśoka.

36. The reference to Maudgalyāyana is based on the *Yu-lan-p'en ching* (*T* 685), while that of the Buddha on *Ching-fan-wang pan-nieh-p'an ching* (*T* 512).

37. Ibid., p. 153b15–c22

38. *Further Biographies,* p. 490c20–29. Ando Toshio has proposed a possible reason for Hui-yüan's dauntless stand against the mighty Chou Emperor. The *Nirvāṇa-sūtra* served as a scriptural basis of Mahayana precepts during the period of *mo-fa* for several of the major *Nirvāṇa-sūtra* scholars in the north, Ling-yü, T'an-yen, Fa-shang, and Hui-yüan. They were proven scholars and lecturers of the *Nirvāṇa-sūtra,* and all overtly refused to submit to the demands of the Northern Chou rulers during their persecution of Buddhism. See Ando Toshio, "Hokugi nehangaku no dentō to shoki no shironshi," in *Hokugi bukkyō no kenkyū,* ed. Ocho Enichi, (Kyoto: Heirakuji shoten, 1970), pp. 192–194.

39. *Further Biographies,* p. 490c29–491a3.

40. Ibid., p. 491a15–16, c7–12.

41. Ibid., p. 491c14–15.

42. Ibid., p. 491a5–6. The "Bodhisattva monks" refer to the one-hundred twenty of the former monks whom Emperor Hsüan in 580 handpicked and placed in the Chih-hu Monastery to carry out their Buddhist practices sponsored by the state. They differed from the past clergy in that they were allowed to grow their hair. The Bodhisattva monks, however, were short-lived as the new group was abolished in June of the following year. See Kamata, *Chūgoku bukkyō shisōshi,* p. 303.

43. *Further Biographies,* p. 491a3–20.

44. Ibid., p. 491a21–27.

45. Ibid., p. 491a28–b28.

46. Ibid., p. 491C17–19. For an overview of the records and catalogues listing works attributed to Hui-yüan, see Sato Tetsuei, "Jōyōji eon to sono mugagi," in *Muga no kenkyū,* edited by Ryukoku daigaku bukkyōgakubu (Kyoto: Hyakkaen, 1977), p. 98.

47. Some modern scholars interpret "*shou-kuan*" to mean both the *Wu-liang-shou ching* and the *Kuan-ching,* but it would be inconsistent with the practice of

this record to list the names of the sutras by two characters. The former sutra appears in the catalogue which follows.

48. *T* 2183.55.1147B14, 1148C23, 1150c17, 1153B14, 1156b5, 1158c26. Ocho Enichi mentions *Fa-hsing lun* by Hui-yüan in this catalogue, but I have been unable to locate it. See his *Chūgoku bukkyō no kenkyū,* vol. 3, p. 154.

49. Of the ten fascicles, only the second half of the third, the first half of the fourth, and the second half of the fifth fascicles have survived.

50. The last six fascicles have not come down to us.

51. The second half is missing. Fortunately, however, Tun-huang manuscripts (Pelliot ch. 2091 and Pelliot ch. 3308) corresponding to most of the missing second half have been discovered. See Fujieda Akira, "Hokuchō ni okeru shōmangyō no denshō," *Tōhō gappō, Kyoto* 40 (1969): 342–345.

52. The last of the five categories, entitled the "Assorted Dharmas" totalling six fascicles, have not survived.

53. *T* 2060.50.497c14–28. Ling-yü's works include a commentary on the *Kuan-ching,* as will be discussed in chapter 3 below.

54. *Further Biographies,* pp. 488a3–489c25, especially 489c23–25. His only surviving work is a commentary on the *Awakening of Faith* (*ZZ* 1.71.3; only the first fascicle survives.)

55. Hirai Shun'ei, *Chūgoku hanya shisō-shi kenkyū* (Tokyo: Shunjusha, 1976), pp. 354–357. As Hirai points out, there is no assurance that all of the works attributed to Chi-tsang were actually his; the authenticity of authorship of part of such a major work as the *Ta-ch'eng hsüan-lun,* traditionally associated with Chi-tsang, has been called into question. When the nonextant works that are attributed to Chi-tsang are counted, they total a staggering thirty-four works and over one-hundred sixty-one fascicles. See Ocho Enichi, *Chūgoku bukkyō,* vol. 1 (Kyoto: Hōzōkan, 1958), pp. 153–154.

56. See Yoshizu, "Eon daijōkishinron-gisho no kenkyū," p. 167 2. According to Yoshizu, Mochizuki was one of the earliest to question Hui-yüan's authorship. See Mochizuki Shinko, *Daijōkishin no kenkyū* (Tokyo: Kanao bun'eidō, 1921).

57. Yoshizu, "Eon daijōkishinron-gisho no kenkyū," pp. 151–152. The reference to a "Dharma Master Hui-yüan" occurs in *T* 1843.44.192b28–29.

58. Ibid., pp. 151–152. Yoshizu's arguments, however, in my view fail to convince. His strongest argument rests on the parallels between this work and others attributed to Hui-yüan. But even this can be explained were the author a disciple familiar with Hui-yüan's thought. In particular, the occurrence of the phrase "Dharma Master Hui-yüan" strongly argues against Hui-yüan's authorship. To merely attribute this to a later insertion lacks cogency.

59. Tsujimori Yoshu, "Daijōgishō kaidai," *Kokuyaku issaikyō* Shoshu-bu 13, 362–366.

60. Ibid., p. 364. Tsujimori does not, however, tell us why Hui-yüan named this work "*Ta-ch'eng i-chang*" if it were indeed based on the *Tseng-shu fa-men* of his teacher, Fa-shang. In my view this can be explained by noting that several other works with the same title were written prior to and during Hui-yüan's time in the northern dynasties. These include those of Tao-p'ing and T'an-wu-tsui's of Northern Wei, followed by the those of the 'Hui-kuang lineage,' the same Fa-shang as above and Ling-yü. This being the case, it could very well be that Hui-yüan obtained the title from the *Mahayana Encyclopedia* of his teacher Fa-shang, or that even Hui-yüan's *Mahayana Encyclopedia* was actually his teacher's.

61. According to Sato's calculations, Hui-yüan defers explanation to the *Mahayana Encyclopedia* on hundred forty-three occasions within his surviving commentaries on: (1) the *Ch'ih-ti lun* (11 times), (2) the *Daśabhūmika-śāstra* (38), (3) the *Nirvāṇa* (32), (4) *Vimalakīrti* (39), (5) the *Śrīmālādevī* (6), (6) the *Wu-liang shou-ching* (8), and (7) the *Kuan-ching* (9). Sato, "Jōyōji eon to sono mugagi," pp. 100–101.

62. *Further Biographies,* p. 491c15.

63. Ibid., p. 491c17.

64. Ibid., pp. 492a5, 10. Cf. Yoshizu Yoshiei, "Daijōgishō no seiritsu to jōyōji-eon no shisō (2)," *Sanzō* 166 (1978): 3.

65. Fujieda Akira, "Hokuchō ni okeru shōmangyō no denshō," p. 344. Fujieda's suggestion is based on his impression of Hui-yüan's biography in the *Further Biographies* that this text was written during his days in Yeh (ca. 538-553). However, the year 572 falls during his residence in Ch'ing-hua monastery and not during his days in Yeh as Fujieda states.

66. Kamata Shigeo, *Chūgoku-bukkyō shisō,* p. 353.

67. As this area is not the primary objective of this study, I am basing much of the discussions on earlier studies by Kamata Shigeo and Yoshizu Yoshihide.

68. *T* 1851.44.483a12–29.

69. Hui-kuang's *p'an-chiao* theory is reported by Chih-i's in his *Fa-hua yen-hsüan* (T1716.33.801b12–15).

70. The "three treatises" probably refer to: (1) the *Chung-kuan lun (Madhyamaka-śāstra)*, (2) the *Shih-erh-men lun* (*Dvadaśamukha-śāstra*), and (3) the *Pai-lun* (*Śataka-śāstra*). These treatises constituted the primary object of study for the so-called San-lun school.

71. Hui-yüan also makes a minor innovation in his characterization of each of the four doctrines as "Doctrine that establishes nature," and so forth. (the first

column) Such characterizations are not found in Hui-kuang's scheme as reported by Chi-tsang.

72. Elucidated for example in Ti-kuan's *T'ien-t'ai szu-chiao i, T* 1931.46.774c9ff. See *Nakamura,* pp. 362–3.

73. *T* 1851.44.483b8–23. He also cites the *Śrīmālādevī-sūtra* that advocates both "womb of emptiness" (*śūnya-garbha*) and "womb of non-emptiness" (*aśūnya-garbha*), which correspond respectively to the third and fourth doctrines.

74. Ibid., 583a22–27.

75. Kamata, *Chūgoku-bukkyō shisōshi,* p. 321.

76. According to Yoshizu, the scriptures associated with the Asaṅga-Vasubandhu Yogācāra teaching—with which the members of the 'Hui-kuang' lineage primarily worked—provided the basis for Hui-yüan's critical view of the concept of emptiness as espoused in the Mādhyamika-related texts translated by Kumārajīva. These two streams of thought are reflected in the two Mahayana doctrines in his scheme. See Yoshizu Yoshihide, "Jōyōji-eon no kyōhanron," *Komazawa daigaku bukkyōgaku kenkyūkiyō* 35 (1977): 216.

77. *T* 1851.44.483b22.

78. Ibid., 483b23–27; See Yoshizu, "Jōyōji-eon no kyōhanron," p. 214.

79. Ibid., pp. 216–217.

80. *T* 2799.85. (1) 764b7; (2) 764b7–8; (3) 771c11; (4) 771c11, 772a28–29; (5) 771c11–12.

81. *T* 1851.44.524b26–525a1.

82. *T* 1851.44.524c19–21.

83. *T* 1851.44.486b19–24. According to the notes in the *Taishō* page where this passage appears, the scriptural sources for the four citations are respectively: (1) the *Daśabhūmika-sūtra* fourth fascicle (*T* 287.10) or the *Hua-yen ching* 26th fascicle (*T* 278.9), (2) the *Hua-yen ching* 26th fascicle, (3) the *Pu-tseng pu-ch'ien ching* (*T* 668.41), and (4) the *Sheng-man ching* (353.12).

**Notes Chapter 3**

1. *T* 365.12. The earliest catalogue to record Kālayaśas' authorship is the *Fa-ching lu* (compiled in 593) from the Sui period. This entry was adopted by virtually all subsequent catalogues. The *Biographies of Eminent Monks* (compiled in 519) by Hui-chiao also recognized Kālayaśas as the translator, thereby, constituting the oldest extant text in support of Kālayaśas' translation of the *Kuan-ching.* This, however, does not mean there are no reasons to question Kālayaśas'

role. For example, a few catalogues instead list Dharmamitra (356–442) as the translator, and the *Ch'u san-tsang chi chi*—the earliest surviving catalogue, hence, older than the *Fa-ching lu*—lists this *Kuan-ching* in its fourth section, the "Records of miscellaneous sutras by anonymous translators." These reasons, however, are not compelling enough to reject the ascription of Kālayaśas as the translator. See Fujita, *Genshijōdo shisō,* pp. 116–118.

2. See Fujita, *Genshijōdo shisō,* pp. 121–122.

3. A good summary of this subject appears in Fujita Kotatsu, *Genshijōdo shisō,* pp. 116–136. Much of this section is based on the findings reported in this work.

4. Ibid., p. 122. For the names of the proponents of the two camps, see below in their respective section.

5. Ibid., p. 121. In keeping with the practice of modern Japanese scholarship on the subject, Fujita recognizes five sutras as 'visualization sutras.' As a common theme, they espouse the cultivation of visualization, as seen in the character *kuan* that appears in each title. They were all translated at about the same time during the first half of the fifth century. The other four 'visualization sutras' are: (1) *Kuan fo san-mei hai ching* translated by Buddhabhadra (*T* 642.15), (2) *Kuan p'u-hsien p'u-sa hsing-fa ching* translated by Dharmamitra (*T* 277.9), (3) *Kuan hsü-k'ung-tsang p'u-sa ching* translated also by Dharmamitra (*T* 409.13), and (4) *Kuan mi-le p'u-sa shang-sheng tou-shuai-t'ien ching* by Chü-ch'ü Ching-sheng (*T* 452.14).

6. For a biographical account of Chü-ch'ü Ching-sheng, see *T* 2145.55.106b22–c18 and *T* 2059.50.337a4ff. For Dharmamitra and Buddhabhadra, the other translators of the visualization sutras, and their ties with Central Asia, see *T* 2145.55.104c29–105b16 for Dharmamitra and *T* 2145.55.103b27–104a28. Cf. Fujita, *Genshijōdo shisō,* pp. 123–124.

7. Ogasawara Senshu, "Kōshōkoku no bukkyō kyōgaku," *Tsukamoto Festschrift,* p. 141. Cf. Fujita, *Genshijōdo shisō,* p. 123.

8. Fujita, *Genshijōdo shisō,* pp. 124–125. For the suggestion regarding the colossal Buddha image of Bāmiyan, see Nakamura Hajime, "Jōdo sanbukyō no kaisetsu," *Jōdo sanbukyō,* vol. 2 (Tokyo: Iwanami shoten, 1964), p. 206. For the proposal regarding the tenth visualization, see Ono Genmyo *Daijō bukkyō gei jutsushi no kenkyū* (Tokyo: Kanao-bun'endō, 1927), pp. 33–34; idem., *Bukkyō no bijutsu to rekishi* (Tokyo: Kanao-bun'endō, 1937), pp. 98–99.

9. Fujita, *Genshijōdo shisō,* p. 125.

10. Ibid., pp. 125–126.

11. Ibid., pp. 126–131. Regarding the "forty-eight vows of Bhikṣu Dharmākara" in the *Kuan-ching* (p. 345c3–4), such a phrase does not appear in the *Wu-liang-shou ching* and thus constitutes a descriptive phrase in reference to the vow section comprised of 48 vows (*T* 360.12.267a–269b). The passage regarding the

opening titles of the twelve divisions of Mahayana appears in the *Kuan-ching* (p. 345c13)

12. Ibid., p. 132.

13. Yamada Meiji, "Kangyō kō - Muryōju-butsu to Amida-butsu," *Ryūkoku daigaku ronshū* 48 (1976): 76–95.

14. Yoshizu Yoshihide, "Kyōritsuron-inyō yori mita daijōgishō no seikaku," *Komazawa daigaku bukkyō-gakubu ronshū* 2 (1971): 128–132. Yoshizu lists the sutras that are quoted in the *Mahayana Encyclopedia.* While the *Wu-liang-shou ching* is listed, the *Kuang-ching* is not.

15. *T* 2059.50.343c18–19.

16. Ibid., 405c21.

17. Ibid., 402a24–28.

18. This caution stems from the fact that the variant reading for "Kuan ching" in both cases—Fa-lin and T'an-hung—is "Kuan *yin* ching" according to the manuscripts of the three editions of the Sung, Yüan and Ming as well as of the old Sung edition. This would then mean that the sutra referred to here was a sutra on Avalokitesvara, not the *Kuan-ching.*

19. *T* 1819.40 (T'an-luan's commentary) and *T* 1524.26 (Vasubandhu).

20. *T* 1819.40.831c5 (corresponds to p. 342c23ff of *Kuan-ching*), 29 (343b17ff), 832a8 (343a19ff), 833c27 (346a12), 834a15 (346a13ff), 19 (346a13ff), b14 (343a13–19). None of these citations is exactly like the corresponding sutra passages.

21. In regards to the term "*ten contemplations*" found in the last sutra citation (834b14ff), T'an-luan explains that it does not mean ten *times* or *moments,* but a state of mental concentration, which he calls the "ten consecutive contemplations." He then conjectures to suggest that this "ten contemplations" (which the *Kuan-ching* states leads to rebirth in the Pure Land) can be realized through the recitation of the name of Amitābha. See Fujiwara, *Nembutsu no kenkyū,* pp. 141ff.

22. Fujiwara, *Nembutsu no kenkyū,* p. 148; Mikogami Eryu, *Ōjōronchū kaisetsu,* p. 250; Morimitsu Jusaburo, "Chūgokushisō-shi ni okeru zendō no chi'i," in *Zendō kyōgaku no kenkyū,* edited by Bukkyō daigaku zendō kyōgaku kenkyūkai (Kyoto: Tōyō bunka shuppan, 1980), pp. 11–12.

23. *T* 1963.47.97c11–14.

24. The earliest extant catalogue to list this work, Fa-ching's *Chung-ching mu-lu,* is "*Wu-liang-shou lun chi chu-chieh* in one *chüan* by Shih T'an-luan." (*T* 2145.55.148a21) Tao-hsüan's *Nei-tien lu* comments, Śramaṇa T'an-luan compiled a *Lun chu-cheih.*" (*T* 2149.55.221b9) This note, however, appears in the wrong place next to an entry of a *Wu-liang-shou ching* translated by An Shih-kao, one of the alleged lost texts of the *Larger Sukhāvatīvyūha Sutra.* The rest of the major cata-

logues up to the end of the T'ang do not list this work. They list, however, Vasubandhu's treatise on which T'an-luan wrote the commentary.

25. Kogatsuin Jinrei, *Jōdoronchū kōgi* (Kyoto: Hōzōkan, 1974), p. 3.

26. Ibid., pp. 3–4. Chikō in the mid-eighth century wrote the earliest known Japanese commentary on T'an-luan's work.

27. This assessment is partly attributable to the fact that T'an-luan appears not to have had direct disciples. That practically nothing is known about T'an-luan's direct disciples implies that he did not nurture a cadre of direct disciples who transmitted his teachings. Even Tao-ch'o, whom the Pure Land writers generally consider T'an-luan's disciple, never met T'an-luan. He was born ten years after T'an-luan's death and was reportedly forty-eight years old before he was inspired by an epigraphic inscription about T'an-luan. See *Further Biographies,* p. 593c16–20. Chia-ts'ai in his *Pure Land Treatise* says Tao-ch'o abandoned his studies to pursue Pure Land teaching in the fifth year of the Ta-yeh Era (609) of Sui period. *T* 1963.47.98b11–12.

28. *T* 1963.47.87b1–2ff.

29. Hui-kan's *Shih ching-t'u ch'un-i lun* cites an opinion on the ranking of the nine grades that matches that of Hui-yüan without mentioning his name (*T* 1960.47.67b15–c17). Also the commentary on the *Kuan-ching* attributed to Chih-i, but now thought to be apocryphal as will be discussed below, borrowed heavily from the *Commentary.* Further, Hui-yüan's name and passages are cited in a partially reconstructed commentary on the *Kuan-ching,* which Etani ascribes to Lung-hsing (655–712?). See Etani, *Jōdokyō no shin kenkyū,* 351–491. For a detailed discussion on this text, see Etani Ryukai, "Koshitsusho ryūkō no kanmuryōjukyōki no kenkyū," *Indogakubukkyō* 8-1 (1960): 84–92. Among Japanese writings, Hui-yüan's views appear in Genshin's (942–1017) *Ōjō yōshū* (*T* 2682.84) and *Anyōshō* (*T* 2686.84).

30. *T* 2179.55.1137c9. This entry of the *Commentary* differs from the present *Taishō* edition on some points: (1) is *"i-chi"* not *"i-shu"* as in the *Taishō* edition, (2) is only one and not two *chüans,* and is (3) "Ching-ying" not "Hui-yüan." See *Bussho,* vol. 5, p. 264b–265a for textual information concerning the catalogues.

31. For the catalogues of the other schools, see *T* 2177, 2178, 2180, 2182.55.

32. *T* 2183.55.1150c26. This entry differs from the *Taishō* edition on the following two points: (1) is simply *"shu",* not *"ching i-shu",* and (2) is one, not two *chüans* (fascicles).

33. Lewis Lancaster, *The Korean Buddhist Canon: A Descriptive Catalogue* (Berkeley: University California Press, 1979), p. xiii.

34. Yüan-chao's sub-commentary, *Kuan wu-liang-shou ching i-shu, T* 1754.37.280a14, 285c25. Mochizuki reports of Ŭich'ŏn receiving the vows from Yüan-chao. Mochizuki, *Chūgoku jōdokyōrishi,* p. 367.

35. Nogami Shunjo, *Chūgoku jōdokyō-shi,* pp. 74–76. Later in the book, however, he states that the dating of the *Commentary* is not known: p. 197. The *mo-fa* comprises the third period in a progressively deteriorating evolution after the death of the historical Buddha. The first period, the Period of True Dharma, lasts 500 years, followed by the Period of Counterfeit Dharma for 1,000 years, with the Last Period of Dharma lasting 10,000 years. According to this theory, the Last Period of Dharma was believed to begin 552 C.E. counting from the Buddha's demise in 949 B.C.E. In the first period, both the teaching and enlightened persons existed, but in the second period only the teaching could be found; in the third period even the teaching disappeared. The belief in the arrival of the Last Period of Dharma contributed in part to the popularity of new Buddhist formulations including those of the Three Stage school and some strands of Pure Land movement.

36. The citations for the *Nirvāṇa-sūtra* are 175a7, 25, b16, c5, 176a29, 181a18, 182c26, and for the *Ch'ih-ti ching-lun* 173b13, c21, 177c2, 182a22, 26, 28, b3, 7, 9, 11.

37. Yoshizu Yoshihide, "Dai jōgishō no seiritsu to jōyōji eon no shisō," (2), pp. 2–3. His suggestion that Hui-yüan began to concentrate on the study of the *Nirvāṇa-sūtra* during his residence at Ch'ing-hua Monastery is based on the many students who studied with Hui-yüan during this period and later became experts on the *Nirvāṇa-sūtra.*

38. See chapter 4 below, for further discussion of the "five essentials."

39. Since the *Wu-liang-shou ching* is also mentioned by name in the *Commentary,* it is not possible to determine the order of their respective compilation. Applying the argument mentioned above (see above note), the *Commentary* would have been compiled later. A more detailed study is needed to clarify the chronological relationship between these two Pure Land sutras.

40. Mochizuki, *Chūgoku jōdokyōri-shi,* p. 90; Yamaguchi Koen, *Tendai jōdokyō-shi,* p. 125; Etani Ryukai, "Zui-tō jidai no kangyō kenkyū shikan," p. 125; Nogami, *Chūgoku jodōkyo-shi,* 197.

41. *T* 2060.50.497c17.

42. Makita Tairyo, *Chūgoku bukkyō-shi,* vol. 1 (Tokyo: Daitō shuppansha, 1981), p. 245. This epigraphic text is entry 21 in a catalogue of the rubbings of the rock inscriptions from Ho-nan Pao-shan stored in the Jinbunkagaku kenkyusho at Kyoto University. This text is dated 632, making it an older biographical source for Ling-yü than the *Further Biographies* whose compilation did not begin until 645.

43. The possibility of error in this instance derives from the failure of the *Further Biographies* to list the *Wu-liang-shou ching* among Ling-yü's writings.

44. However, this would be the case only in the assumption that the epigraphic account had made an error so that it actually referred to a commentary on the *Kuan-ching* rather than to one on the *Wu-liang-shou ching.* But even if the account were not erroneous, given the affinity of the subject matter of the two

sutras, it would not be unreasonable that a commentary on the *Kuan-ching* was compiled close to the time of his commentary on the *Wu-liang-shou ching.* But no available evidence firmly refutes claims for the *Commentary* as the first commentary on the *Kuang-ching.* Nonetheless based on the above findings the possibility must be left open that Ling-yü wrote a commentary on the *Kuan-ching* earlier than Hui-yüan.

45. *T* 2760.85.249b–253a.

46. Mochizuki, *Chūgoku jōdokyōri-shi,* pp. 129–130.

47. The concept of "intended for a later time" is one of the four intentions found in the Buddha's discourse: (1) equality, (2) later time, (3) different meaning, and (4) *pudgala* (beings). See *Bukkyō-gaku jiten,* p. 12c. The four intentions appear in Asaṅga's *She ta-ch'eng lun* (*T* 1593.31.121b10–18) and Vasubandhu's commentary (*T* 1597.31.346a8–18).

48. *T* 2760.85.252c18. The quoted opinion ranks the highest of the high grade of rebirth as the Bodhisattvas of the sixth Bhūmi. The same opinion is expressed in the Chi-tsang's commentary. (*T* 1752.37.244c13) It should be noted that this particular ranking—sixth Bhūmi—is a unique view which is not found in any other ranking of this grade and which, thereby, strengthens the odds that this opinion belongs to Chi-tsang.

49. *Bussho,* vol. 2, pp. 183–205, especially pp. 199–200.

50. See note 58 below.

51. See Ishida Mitsuyuki, "Fragmented Copied Manuscripts of the *Wu liang shou ching kuan tsan-shu,*" *Monumenta Serindica* I (1958): 14–15.

52. Mochizuki, as discussed earlier, feels Ling-yü was the author of this work. See Mochizuki, *Chūgoku jōdokyōrishi,* pp. 129–130.

53. See Sato, *Tendai daishi no kenkyū* (Kyoto: Hyakkaen, 1961), p. 595.

54. Etani Ryukai, *Jōdokyō no shin kenkyū,* pp. 171–189. The primary text from which the quotations were retrieved was an eleventh century Japanese work, *Anyōshō* by Genryūkoku (1004–1077), which Etani himself discovered in 1933 on Mt. Hiei.

55. Ibid., pp. 341–350.

56. Ibid., pp. 351–391. For an earlier but more complete discussion of this work, see Etani Ryukai, "Koshitsusho ryūkō no kanmuryōjukyōki no kenkyū," pp. 84–92.

57. *T* 1958.47.4a14–16. Elsewhere he states, "Here, this *Visualization Sutra* has the *samādhi* of Buddha-visualization as its main import." Ibid., 5a26.

58. Sato Tetsuei, *Tendai daishi no kenkyū,* pp. 567–568, 594–597. Sato suggests that followers of the T'ien-t'ai tradition compiled the commentary sometime

between the second half of the seventh and the first half of the eighth century. In Sato's view, the followers felt a need for a commentary on the *Kuan-ching,* due to its popularity and that the eminent exegetes of the other traditions, like Hui-yüan and Chi-tsang, had their commentaries.

The question of authenticity of authorship appears not to have been raised in China. In Japan during the Kamakura period, Ryōchū of the Jōdo school raised doubts regarding Chih-i's authorship since Genshin never once mentioned Chih-i's commentary in his *Ōjōyōshū (T* 2682.84). During the Tokugawa period, the Nichiren followers asserted the apocryphal nature of this commentary. For a detailed discussion of the borrowed *Commentary* passages in the compilation of this 'apocryphal' text, see Sato, *Tendai daishi,* pp. 270–594.

59. Ocho, *Chūgoku bukkyō,* vol. 3, p. 159.

60. Mochizuki, *Chūgoku jōdokyōri-shi,* p. 90. There are reasons to believe that Hui-yüan did, in fact, take a personal interest in Maitreya devotion. There is also an account in the *Further Biographies* on the biography of Ling-kan, which relates a story of his rebirth in the Tuṣita Heaven and meeting Hui-yüan there. See *T* 2060.50.518b21.

61. *T* 1851.44.834a23–b28. Hui-yüan classifies the pure lands into three categories: (1) phenomenal pure lands, (2) form pure land, and (3) true pure lands. Although the heavens are regarded as somewhat inferior to Amitābha's Sukhāvatī and since the means for rebirth are "defiled pure acts" for the former as compared to "pure acts" for the latter, both are similarly included among phenomenal pure land.

62. See Mochizuki, *Chūgoku jōdokyōri-shi,* p. 135. For more examples of such inscriptions with a syncretistic outlook, see Matsumoto Bunzaburo, *Shina bukkyō ibutsu* (Tokyo: Kōbundō, 1942), pp. 286–299.

63. They are respectively *T* 453.14; 454.14; 456.14; 452.14.

64. Nogami, *Chūgoku jōdokyo-shi,* pp. 69–79. Yuki sees orthodox Pure Land Buddhism as that based on the concept of *mo-fa,* "Shina bukkyō ni okeru mappō shisō no koki," *Tōhō gappō: Tokyo* 6 (1936):214. Morimitsu, more recently, expresses the same view, "Chūgoku shisō-shi ni okeru zendō no chi'i," p. 14.

65. *T* 2060.50.490c26–29.

66. Mochizuki has alluded to this point, but not in any detail in connection with Hui-yüan. See Mochizuki, *Chūgoku jōdokyōri-shi,* pp. 63–69. A separate research is needed to thoroughly treat such topics as the role of devotion among scholarly monks to a particular Buddha or Bodhisattva.

67. *T* 1958.47.14b9–16.

68. Mochizuki Shinko, Matsumoto Bunzaburo, Fujino Ritsuzen, Nogami Shunjo and others have questioned the traditional view of regarding this text to

be the *Kuan-ching.* Fujino and Nogami further argue that the text under question was the *Rebirth Treatise.* For a detailed discussion, see Ching-fen Hsiao, *The Life and Teaching of T'an-luan* (Ph.D. dissertation, Princeton Theological Seminary, 1967), pp. 51–56. Hsiao concurs with Fujino and Nogami.

69. See Mochizuki, *Chūgoku jōdokyōri-shi,* pp. 63–65, 71–72; Nogami, *Chūgoku jōdokyō-shi,* pp. 48–49.

70. *T* 2060.50.608a8–10 (Hui-kuang); *T* 2060.50.484c12–13 (Tao-p'ing); *T* 2060.50.497b17–18 (Ling-yü). Cf. *Mochizuki,* pp. 67, 130.

71. *T* 1524.26.

72. One of the earliest surviving texts to use this short title was Tao-cho's *An-le chi,* written around the mid-seventh century. See *T* 1958.47.7c7.

73. The only discussion of this—and only an allusion at that—is found in Hirakawa Akira, "Jōdokyō no yōgo ni tsuite," p. 6. He suggests Tao-ch'o's *An-le chi* as the earliest to employ "*Ching-t'u*" but remains silent regarding the usage of "*Wang-sheng lun*" (*Rebirth Treatise).*

74. His *Lüeh-lun an-le ching-t'u i* refers to *Rebirth Treatise* as *Wu-liang-shou lun. T* 1957.47.1a15. See Leo Pruden, trans., "A Short Essay on the Pure Land," pp. 74–95.

75. *T* 1949.37.183a19, 184b11, 15, 22ff.

76. Mikogami Eryu, *Ōjōronchū kaisetsu,* pp. 13.

77. *T* 2146.55.141a26, *T* 2153.55.407c28–29, *T* 2154.55.541a22, *T* 2157.55.941a14, *T* 2149.55.269b3.

78. In *An-le chi, T* 1958.47.7c7, 25ff. In *Pure Land Treatise, T* 1963.97c12ff. In *Ching-t'u shih-i lun, T* 1961.47.78c5–6, 81a11.

79. There is, however, no firm evidence to conclude that the *Commentary* was the earliest text to employ this title, because of the small number of surviving works from north China during the period between the translation of the *Rebirth Treatise* by Bodhiruci (ca. 530) and Hui-yüan's compilation of the *Commentary.*

80. *T* 2060.50.497c18. This, of course, assumes that this recorded title in the *Further Biographies* was the original title that Ling-yü himself used and not subsequently ascribed to it by Tao-hsüan.

81. *T* 2124.50.141a26.

82. *T* 1745.37.107c10–11. For original passages, see *T* 1524.26.231a14, 232a3–4. The same passage appears once in the verse section and once in the prose section, respectively. The exclusion clause regarding women, and so forth preoccupied later Pure Land apologists against the criticism of rival schools.

83. *T* 1524.26.231b5.

**Notes Chapter 4**

1. The relevant texts are the *Wu-liang-shou ching, Rebirth Treatise* and the *Kuan-ching.* As a good example, the *Ching-t'u shih-i lun,* a late seventh century text falsely attributed to Chih-i, cites these three together as scriptural authority. *T* 1961.47.78c5–6. Hōnen, the founder of the Jōdo School regarded the same three and the *A-mi-t'o-fo ching* as the scriptures that espoused the Pure Land teaching. See *T* 2608.83.2a4–5.

2. See above, notes 19 and 20 of chapter 3.

3. *Ch'u san-tsang chi chi, T* 2145.55.22a8.

4. They are found in his commentaries on the *Wu-liang-shou ching* (*T* 1745.37.91a3-c1), *Nirvāṇa-sūtra* (*T* 1764.37.613a3–b17), *Vimalakīrti-sūtra* (*T* 1776.38.421a16–c22), *Wen-shih ching* (*T* 1793.39.512c10–19), *Śrīmālādevī-sūtra* (*ZZ* 1.30.4.276a3–c9), *Daśabhūmika-śāstra* (*ZZ* 1.71.2.134a15–c13). While they are in large measure the same, there are slight variations among them. The commentary on the *Nirvāṇa-sūtra,* for example, has only the first two essentials, while the *Wen-shih ching* and the *Śrīmālādevī-sūtra* commentaries set up a sixth category, which distinguishes the Three Piṭakas, the sutra, the *vinaya* and the *abhidharma.*

5. The category of the two Piṭakas appears in the *Ti-ch'ih ching* (*T* 1581.30.958c2–3) and that of the five kinds of speakers in the *Ta chih tu lun* (*T* 1509.25.66b5–6).

6. *T* 1745.37.91b5–7, and *T* 1764.37.613b3–6. The sutra passage in the *Ti-ch'ih ching* (*T* 1581.30.958b29–c2) differs from Hui-yüan's citation, in that it includes the Pratyekabuddhas along with the Śrāvakas.

7. *T* 1746.37.613b6–8.

8. It, however, should be noted that the relevant section is missing from his commentary on the *Daśabhūmika-śāstra* (*ZZ* 1.61.3.202).

9. *T* 1749.37.173a7–10.

10. Liu-ch'iu's classification is reported by Hui-yüan in *Mahayana Encyclopedia, T* 1851.44.465a8–23. Hui-kuan's classification is reported by Chi-tsang in *San-lun hsüan-i, T* 1852.45.5b4–14. Cf. Yoshizu Yoshihide, "Jōyōji-eon no kyōhanron," pp. 210–211.

11. *T* 1931.46.774c9ff.

12. *T* 1851.44.465b2–5.

13. *T* 1776.38.421b–12. Similar passages are found in *T* 1745.37.91a16–20, *T* 1764.37.613a16–20, *ZZ* 1.30.4.276b8–11, and *ZZ* 1.71.2.134b10–13.

14. *T* 1851.44.809b23–26. I have rendered the passage explaining the reason for his leaving Hinayana as: "Even after having obtained the Hinayana fruit, he realized that there was still more [to be accomplished]."

15. *T* 1745.37.91a20–23, *T* 1776.38.421b12–17, *T* 1764.37.613a20–28, *ZZ* 1.30.4.276b11–15, *ZZ* 71.2.134b13–17.

16. The *T'an-luan Commentary, T* 1819.40.826a25.

17. *T* 1745.37.91a25–26, *T* 1764.637.13a25.

18. *T* 1745.37.91b9; *ZZ* 1.30.4.276c8–9; *T* 1776.38.421b28; *ZZ* 1.71.2.134c11. The position on the *Daśabhūmika-sūtra* is expressed in Hui-yüan's commentary on Vasubandhu's commentary on the sutra.

19. *T* 1793.39.512c10; *T* 1764.37.613b12.

20. *T* 1745.37.91b9–12.

21. *T* 1749.37.173a10–15.

22. Ibid., p. 174a15–b1.

23. Ibid., p. 173b1–4.

24. *T* 1753.37.247a16–22.10; *T* 1509.25.66b5–6 (*Ta chih tu lun*). See note 17 of chapter 6 below.

25. *T* 1752.37.232c20–23.

26. For the *Chih-i Commentary,* see the following note. The commentary by Chi-tsang includes the fifth and third essentials. (*T* 1752.37.232c21–22, 234c3–15) Tao-ch'o's *An-le chi* employs the third, fourth, and fifth essentials. (*T* 1958.47.4a11, 5a23–c10; 4a12–16; 4a16–19) *Shan-tao Commentary* shows the first, second, third, and fifth essentials. (*T* 1753.247a16–27)

27. *T* 1750.37.188c18–21.

28. Ocho Enichi, *Chūgoku būkkyo,* vol. 3, pp. 165–173.

29. Fujieda Akira, "Shōmangyō gisho," pp. 486–487.

30. Ocho, *Chūgoku bukkyō* , vol. 3, p. 169. For the *Taishō* editions of the three commentaries, see *T* 1694.33; *T* 1693.33; *T* 1775.38.

31. Ocho, *Chūgoku bukkyō,* vol. 3, p. 169.

32. Ibid., p. 173.

33. Ibid., pp. 169–178.

34. *T* 1715.33.574c13–575b17. Cf. Ocho, *Chūgoku bukkyō,* vol. 3, 178–180.

35. Fujieda, "Shōmangyō gisho," p. 486.

36. *T* 1819.40.826a24–b10.

37. Ibid., p. 826b28–29.

38. Ibid., p. 826b29–c1.

39. Ocho cites this passage that is said to appear in *Fa-hua wen-chu* (*T* 1718.34). See his *Chūgoku bukkyō,* vol. 3, p. 182, line 3.

40. *T* 1749.37.174a5, 11–12, 177b14–17, 186a21–22.

41. Fujieda, pp. 478–479.

42. Ocho, *Chūgoku bukkyō,* vol. 3, pp. 193–196.

43. Ibid., p. 194.

44. Ibid., pp. 193–196.

45. See Hōnen, *Senchaku-shū, T* 2608.83.2a4–6.

46. Kogatsuin Jinrei, *Jōdoronchū kōgi,* pp. 91–92; Roger Corless, "T'an-luan's Commentary on the Pure Land Discourse: An Annotated Translation and Soteriological Analysis of the *Wang-sheng-lun chu* (*T* 1819)," Ph.D. diss., University of Wisconsin, 1973, pp. 13–15.

47. Taya Hiroshi, "Donran no senjutsuchū," *Ōtani Gakuhō* 23–6 (1942): 521–533. Moreover, the emphasis on the Pure Land sutras does not automatically demonstrate that T'an-luan treated them as a set.

48. *T* 1819.40.834a14–20.

49. Translation by Corless, "T'an-luan's Commentary on the Pure Land Discourse," pp. 13–14. For the *T'an-luan* passage, see *T* 1819.40.826b12–14.

50. Kogatsuin, *Jōdoronchū kōgi,* p. 92; Corless, "T'an-luan's Commentary on the Pure Land Discourse," pp. 13–14.

51. The treatise either is cited or its passages quoted as scriptural source, for example, in Tao-ch'o's *An-le chi* (*T* 1958.47.7c7), Chia-tsai's *Pure Land Treatise* (*T* 1963.47.84c23, 89a16, c5, 91b4) *Ching-t'u shih-i lun* (*T* 1961.47.78c5, 80b7, 81a11), and *Nien-fo ching* (*T* 1966.47.126c18, etc.). The treatise attracted the attention of these exegetes particularly for its exposition of the Five Contemplative Gates and of the controversial question of rebirth in the Pure Land for women and the disabled, whose rebirth the treatise repudiated. *T* 1525.26.231b10–14, 232a3–4.

The *Ching-t'u shih-i lun* ascribed to Chih-i is now believed to have been compiled much later, sometime between 694–774. See Leo Pruden, trans., "The Ching-t'u Shih-i-lun," pp. 127–130.

52. The *Rebirth Treatise* passage states, "The verse says, 'In the realm of the Mahayana virtuous faculties, all are equal and without despised names. Women,

those with incomplete faculties and the classes of two vehicles are not reborn [there]'". (*T* 1525.26.232a3–4) The *Kuan-ching,* on the other hand, permits rebirth of the Hinayanists because the three middle grades of those who are reborn in the Pure Land (the object of the fifteenth visualization) are Hinayanists. (345b8–c9)

53. *T* 1749.37.184b11–16.

54. *T* 365.12.346b1–4.

55. *T* 1749.47.184b21–26.

56. Ibid., p. 184b26–c9.

57. Ibid., pp. 183b8–184a15. Similar reconciliations among the Pure Land scriptures are also found in his *Wu-liang-shou ching i-shu. T* 1745.37.107b3ff.

58. *T* 2646.83.590a14ff.

59. E. B. Cowell, F. Max Müller and J. Takakusu trans., *Buddhist Mahayana Texts.* Sacred Books of the East, vol. 49. (1985, reprint. Delhi: Motilal Benarsidass, 1965), p. 1.

60. *T* 1749.37.179a6ff.

61. *T* 1959.47.6b27ff, *T* 1963.47.86b28, and *T* 1753.37.246b10ff, respectively. The term is also found in Chi-tsang's commentary, but it does not appear to be a reference to the *Wu-liang-shou ching,* since the latter is referred to as "*Shuang-chuan ching.*" *T* 1752.37.234b19ff.

62. *Chih-i Commentary, T* 1750.37.193b11ff.

63. Hui-kan's *Shih ching-t'u ch'ün-i ching, T* 1950.47.43c15ff.

64. Chi-tsang's commentary, *T* 1752.37.234c5ff.

65. Other such abbreviations include *Nirvāṇa-sūtra* as *Nieh-p'an,* Vasubandhu's commentary on the *Daśabhūmika-sūtra* as *Ti-lun* and the *P'u-sa ti-ch'ih ching* (*T* 1581) as *Ti-ch'ih.*

*Kuan-ching* is the short title by which the *Kuan wu-liang-shou ching* has commonly been known. Its earliest usage is found in the *Biographies of Eminent Monks.* (*T* 2059.50.402a24) The Japanese Pure Land Buddhists also adopted this short name as its common title. The rationale behind this abridgement poses no problem. Unlike the case with *Ta-ching* it apparently was derived simply as an abbreviation of the original title of this sutra.

66. *T* 1749.37.183b9–10.

67. *T* 1948.47.4c15–16, 5a3.

68. *T* 2145.55. (a) 11c12, 12a24, and (b) 13a3, 14a22.

69. *T* 2146.55. (a) 119b24, 25, 26, and (b) 117c19, 23.

70. *T* 2147.55.158c4.

71. *T* 2034.49. (a) 50b7, 91b14, and (b) 89c16.

72. *T* 2148.55.191b20.

73. *T* 1958.47.4c15–16.

74. *T* 1961.47.78c12. Modern scholarship is in general agreement that this was not an actual work by Chih-i as the text states. For a summary of the findings of Japanese scholarship on this subject, see Leo Pruden trans., "The Ching-t'u Shih-i lun," pp. 126–129.

75. *T* 2184.55.1171c19.

76. *Nakamura,* p. 915a–b.

77. *T* 2147.55.157a3. This entry is found next to that of Kumārajīva's translation of the same sutra, *Wu-liang-shou fo ching.*

78. The *Ch'u san-tsang chi chi* lists *A-mi-t'o ching* as an alternate title for this sutra. However, all of the subsequent catalogues referred to the sutra by the other title, and it was in the *K'ai-yüan lu* that Chih-sheng listed "*A-mi-t'o ching*" as the primary title and "*Wu-liang-shou ching*" as the alternate (*T* 2154.55.512c9–10).

79. *T* 1958.47.19a14.

80. Ibid., 19a12–19. Other sutras include the *Sui-yüan shih-fang wang-sheng ching, Wu-liang ch'ing-ching chüeh ching* and *Wang-sheng ching.* Tao-ch'o also mentions *śāstras* in this 'Pure Land' category, such as those written by Nāgārjuna and Vasubandhu.

81. Ch'i's (632–682) *A-mi-t'o ching shu* (*T* 1757.37.313a17,18) refers to it as *Hsiao a-mi-t'o,* but in contrast to the *Ta a-mi-t'o ching* (*T* 362.12). Similar titles are found in Chia-ts'ai's *Pure Land Treatise* (*T* 1963.47.92c20, 94b20).

**Notes Chapter 5**

1. Fujiwara Ryosetsu, *Nembutsu shisō,* p. 153; Yuki Reimon, "Kangyōsho ni okeru zendō shakugi," pp. 908–909; Nogami Shunjo, *Chūgoku jōdokyō-shi,* pp. 224–227.

2. *T* 1749.37.182c23–183a26.

3. Ibid., p. 183a26–b9.

4. Yuki Reimon, "Kangyōsho ni okeru zendō shakugi," p. 920.

5. Ohara Shojitsu, *Zendō kyōgaku,* p. 87. The same fourth cause is omitted in, Masaki Haruhiko, "Kangyōsho ni okeru kubon no mondai," p. 263. Fujiwara Ryosetsu, however, acknowledges this point in his *Nembutsu shisō,* p. 157.

6. *T* 2682.84.78c2–6.

7. *T* 1749.37.183c16–17.

8. Yuki, "Kangyōsho ni okeru zendō shakugi," pp. 908–909. For a more detailed discussion of Yuki's view, see chapter 6. Nogami, *Chūgoku jōdokyō-shi,* pp. 224–227.

9. *T* 1819.40.839b4–6.

10. *T* 1819.40.835c2–8.

11. *T* 1819.40.833c27–834a12.

12. For the original *Kuan-ching* passage, see *T* 366.12.346a12–26.

13. *T* 1957.47.3c26–28. The authenticity of T'an-luan's authorship of this work was questioned quite early by Japanese Tendai scholar-monk, Shōshin (ca. mid-twelfth century to early thirteenth. For textual background and an English translation of this treatise, see Leo Pruden, "A Short Essay on the Pure Land," pp. 74–95.

14. *T* 1524.26.231b11–13. The five are worship, praise, vow, visualization and transference of merit. Hui-yüan was aware of the Five Contemplative Gates because he cites them immediately prior to the enumeration of his Four Causes.

15. T 1753.37.272a28–b10.

16. Ohara, *Zendo kyōgaku,* pp. 186–187; Honpa Hongwanji Mission of Hawaii ed., *Shinshū Seiten* (Honolulu: The Honpa Hongwanji Mission of Hawaii, 1955), p. 167; Morimitsu Jusaburo, "Chūgokushisōshi-jo ni okeru zendō no ichi," p. 18.

17. *T* 1753.37.272b1–9.

18. Shan-tao's "chanting" corresponds to Hui-yüan's "reciting of Mahayana sutras" under "cultivation of pure acts" (second cause, p. 183a28, 176b28–c4); "visualization" to "visualization" (first cause, p. 183a27); "worship" to "worship" under "devotion" (fourth cause, p. 183b8); "oral recitation" to "recitation" under the same "devotion" (p. 183b8); "praise and offering" to "praise" under "devotion" (p. 183b8). Only "offering" has no counterpart in Hui-yüan's list.

19. *T* 1749.37.173a15, 174c28.

20. This modern Japanese sectarian understanding was already clearly expressed by Tokugawa scholars such as Rei'ō. Rei'ō delineated twenty-two points of differences between Shan-tao's position and that of the 'heretical' masters, of whom Hui-yüan is the primary target. As the seventh of the twenty-two points, Rei'ō criticizes Hui-yüan for 'incorrectly' regarding Buddha-visualization *samādhi* as the same as Buddha-contemplation *samādhi.* For Rei'ō, the two are different, as the latter meant '*samādhi* of oral recitation.' *Shinshū Zensho,* vol. 5, p. 16. See the introduction above for the enumeration of the twenty-two points. For an ex-

ample of modern orthodox scholars who have perpetuated this view, see Ohara, *Zendō kyōgaku,* pp. 141 and 184, and Fujiwara, *Nembutsu shisō,* pp. 215–221.

21. Allan Andrews, "Nembutsu in the Chinese Pure Land tradition," *The Eastern Buddhist,* 3:2 (1970). This article addresses a broader question of the "*nien-fo*" practice in a much larger context; Minoru Kiyota, "Buddhist Devotional Meditation: A Study of the *Sukhāvatīvyūhopadeśa,*" in *Mahayana Buddhist Meditation: Theory and Practice,* edited by Minoru Kiyota (Honolulu: University of Hawaii, 1978), 249–296. This is a study primarily on the treatise attributed to Vasubandhu the *Sukhāvatīvyūhopadeśa*; Fukushima Koya, "Jyōyōji eon no shikan shisō," *Tōhōgaku* 36 (1968):15–28. While this article alludes to the subject of visualization, its main concern is to elucidate the subject of *chih-kuan* in the context of its development within Chinese Buddhism.

22. *T* 1749.37.173a12–14.

23 Ibid., p. 173b19–21.

24. *T* 1749.37.173b21–c11. For the original passage in the *Vimalakīrti- sūtra,* see *T* 475.14.554c29–555a2.

25. See note 36 below.

26. *T* 1749.37.173c2–14.

27. Ibid., p. 173c4–8.

28. See *Bussho,* vol. 2, p. 180b. According to this entry, this sutra was in one fascicle and translated by Kumārajīva; the sutra is listed in the *K'ai-yüan lu* fascicle 14 and in the *Tei-yüan lu* fascicle 24.

29. *T* 643.15.645–697. Translated by Buddhabhadra (359–429), it has been argued by modern scholars that it served as one of the models for the compilation in China of the *Kuan-ching.* See Fujita Kotatsu, *Genshijōdo shisō,* pp. 126–130. The *Bussho* (Vol. 2, p. 180b), however, does not list *Kuan fo san-mei ching* as a variant title of this sutra.

30. *T* 1581.30.941b26–29. The "Stage [of Rejoicing]" is the first Bhūmi.

31. For the commentary on this sutra, see *ZZ* 1.71.2 and 3. Further studies are required to determine the reasons for Hui-yüan's failure in not citing scriptural sources in this case.

32. *T* 1581.30.941b29–c1.

33. Hui-yüan uses "vision" and "visualization" interchangeably. See *T* 1749.-37.173c6, 11.

34. Ibid., 173c10–11. Hui-yüan's position is evinced in the statement, "What is being expanded on here in this *Sutra* is the visualization derived from unrefined pure-faith as a form of Response-body visualization."

35. *T* 1579.30.555c27–556a6.

36. Wogihara, Unrai, ed. *Bodhisattvabhūmi: A Statement of Whole Course of the Bodhisattva* (Tokyo: Sankibō Buddhist Book Store, 1971), pp. 330:14–331:2.

37. *T* 1911: 46.21b15–c6.

38. *T* 1749.37.173c2–3.

39. *T* 1911.46.21b16–17, 19–20.

40. Ibid., 21c6–7.

41. Ibid., 21c10.

42. *T* 1749.37.184c5.

43. *T* 1851.44.716a14–15.

44. *T* 1749.37.182c6–7, 12.

45. *T* 1851.44.811c25–26.

46. *T* 1851.44.811b13–15.

47. *T* 1749.37.181c14–15.

48. In its Chinese translation, see *T* 1579.30.552c28ff; *T* 1581.30.929c19.

49. Ohara, *Zendō kyōgaku,* p. 141.

50. *T* 1851.44.677a5–6; c17–18; 788c2–3.

51. Rei'ō, *Bussetsu kanmuryōjukyō kōki,* p. 22.

52. Ohara, *Zendō kyōgaku,* p. 232.

53. Ibid., p. 232; Masaki, "Kangyōsho ni okeru kubon no mondai," pp. 266–267; Hirose, *Kangyōsho ni manabu - Gengi-bun* 2, p. 389.

54. *T* 1851.44.677c17–18.

55. *T* 1753.37.247c22–28.

56. This was, then, an insertion by Shan-tao that attempted, in my view, to accentuate Hui-yüan's higher ranking of the nine grades in contrast to his own lower assignment of ranks.

57. This is deduced from his statements that: (1) both *fan-fu* and *sheng-jen* are reborn in the Pure Land (*T* 1963.47.88b15); and (2) the highest of the high grades is ranked the initial mind of the Ten-Transferences (Inner Pṛthagjanas) and the middle of the high grades ranked the initial mind of the Ten-Faiths (Outer Pṛthagjanas) (87b23, 87b27–28). Since these two grades are the highest of the nine grades,

and if *sheng-jen* (Āryapudgalas) are reborn, then Chia-ts'ai must have considered beings of these grades as Āryapudgalas.

58. For example, Hui-kan (fl. second half of seventh century) does not share this position. In his *Shih ching-t'u ch'ün-i lun,* he expresses a position that agrees with Hui-yüan rather than with his teacher, Shan-tao. Also, according to Kogatsuin Jinrei, the Fa-hsiang Schools that developed on the basis of two of the translations of the *Mahāyāna-saṃgraha* differed on this issue. The followers of the earlier Paramārtha version regarded beings of the Ten-Understandings and above to be Āryapudgalas, but expounders of the Hsüan-tsang translations treated all stages below the Bhūmis as Pṛthagjanas. Kogatsuin Jinrei, *Jōdoronchū kōgi,* p. 97.

59. *T* 1749.37.179a17–18.

60. Ibid., p. 179a13–15. Hui-yüan cites from the *Jen-wang ching* five kinds of Insight of Non-arising, which are attained in the five different stages: (1) Lineage and Practice of Resolution, (2) second and third Bhūmis, (3) fourth, fifth, and sixth Bhūmis, (4) seventh, eighth, and ninth Bhūmis, and (5) tenth Bhūmi and above. Ibid., p. 179a8–15.

61. The *Kuan-ching* states, "Then the Buddha said to Vaidehī, 'You and all sentient beings ought to single-mindedly restrain your thoughts in one place and perceive the Western Quarter.'" *T* 365.12.341c28–29.

62. Ibid., 341c23–24.

63. The nine grades constitute the object of the fourteenth, fifteenth, and sixteenth visualizations, with three grades associated with each of the visualizations. *T* 365.12.344c9–346a26.

64. See Chia-ts'ai's *Pure Land Treatise, T* 1965.47.87a18–88b23; Wŏnhyo's *Yusim allakto, T* 1965.47.115c4–118a18; Huai-kan's *Shih ching-t'u ch'ün-i lun, T* 1960.47.67b15–17.

65. See Ohara, *Zendō kyōgaku,* pp. 231–242; Fujiwara, *Nembutsu shisō,* pp. 190; Hirose Takashi, *Kangyōsho ni manabu: gengibun ni,* pp. 352–391. For a discussion of Hui-yüan's higher ranking relative to that of Chia-ts'ai, see Nabata Ojun, *Kazai jōdoron no kenkyū* (Kyoto: Hozokan, 1928), pp. 73–82. For Shantao's position, see *T* 1753.37.247c22–249b8.

66. *T* 1749.37.182a12–c22.

67. The distinctions among the three lower grades are on the transgressions committed.

68. *T* 1753.37.248b7–250a8.

69. *T* 1753.37.248a8–15, 25, b2. This difference has long been recognized among orthodox writers. See, for example, Kashiwabara Yugi, *Kangyō gengibun kōyō* (Kyoto: Ango jimusho, 1955), p. 222.

70. *T* 1749.37.184a15–27.

71. Ibid., p. 184a27–b10.

72. Ibid., p. 182a7–9.

73. *T* 1963.47.87b7–9.

74. See Ohara, *Zendō kyōgaku,* p. 235. Ohara states:

> In contrast to these views [of Hui-yüan, Chia-ts'ai and others], Shan-tao stated in the "Hsüan-i fen" (first chapter in the *Shan-tao Commentary*), "clearly [taught the sutra] for the Pṛthagjanas but not for Āryapudgalas" and "[The sixteen visualizations] were taught solely for sentient beings who are continually wallowing [in *saṃsāra*], and not for the Āryapudgalas of Mahayana and Hinayana." Thus, Shan-tao determined the nine grades to be all Pṛthagjanas, and pointed out and criticized the incorrectness of the views of the masters.

See Hirose, *Kangyōsho ni manabu: gengibun,* p. 393. Hirose also quotes Shan-tao's statement cited above (the second of the two quotations cited by Ohara) to show the manner and the basis on which Shan-tao refuted the position of the masters.

75. *T* 1749.37.173a9–10.

76. Ibid., p. 182c5–8. See note 44 above for full citation of the passage.

77. T 1753.37.249c8–9.

78. T 1753.37.248a14–15.

79. See Rei'ō, *Bussetsu kanmuryōjukyō kōgi,* p. 16; Yuki, "Kangyōsho ni okeru zendō shakugi," p. 916.

80. *T* 1749.37.179a8–15. *Jen-wang ching* translated by Kumārajīva, the version that Hui-yüan more than likely consulted, describes the Five Insights, but the description (at least based on its *Taishō* edition) does not reveal the rankings for each of the insights as explicitly and as clear cut as in Hui-yüan's enumeration. See *T* 245.8.826b21–827a7. The later version translated by Amoghavajra, on the other hand, does include rankings for the Five Insights that correspond more closely to Hui-yüan's description. See *T* 246.8.836b14–837a4.

81. However, this is not quite in keeping with his above description in the *Jen-wang ching* that states that the Insight of Non-arising is realized in the seventh, eighth, and ninth Bhūmis. According to the *Jen-wang ching,* it is the Insight of Accordance that is attained in the fourth, fifth, and sixth Bhūmis. But this discrepancy is not as serious as it appears, for this Insight of Accordance is technically not very different from the Insight of Non-arising. In describing the former insight based on the *Jen-wang ching,* Hui-yüan states, "[it] is the realm of suchness and is in accordance with the [Insight] of Non-arising [of dharmas]." (179a12) This

could very well have been the reason that Hui-yüan included the Insight of Accordance (= fourth, fifth and sixth Bhūmis) with the Insight of Non-arising.

82. Hui-yüan does not list the first Bhūmi of the *Jen-wang ching* description, but this is probably a simple omission by Hui-yüan since he includes the first Bhūmi as one of the stages of Insight of Faith in the *Mahayana Encyclopedia.* See *T* 1851.44.701c27–28.

83. *T* 1749.37.182a19–21.

84. Ibid., p. 182b20–c16.

85. Ohara, *Zendō kyōgaku,* p. 232; Nobuo Haneda, "The Development of the Concept of *Pṛthagjana,* Culminating in Shan-tao's Pure Land Thought: The Pure Land Theory of Salvation of the Inferior" (Ph.D. diss., University of Wisconsin, Madison, 1979), pp. 110, 114.

86. *T* 1749.37.182a15–16.

87. Ibid., p. 182c20–22.

88. Ibid., p. 185c9–10.

89. For a representative view, see Ohara, *Zendō kyōgaku,* p. 232.

90. Nogami Shunjo, *Chūgoku jōdokyō-shi,* pp. 178–183. He suggests the category of the nine grades may have had as its model the practice of dividing people into nine classes as discussed in "*Ku-chin-jen-piao*" of the *Han-shu,* or the practice of laws regarding the nine grades of officials that was established in the Ts'ao-wei period (220–265) for the purpose of appointing and promoting officials.

91. *T* 1545.28.21b5–8. The Hinayana stages prior to the Insight into the Path (*darśana-mārga*) are divided into nine grades: *uśma-gata* into lowest of the low, middle of the low and highest of the low; *murdhān* into lowest of the middle, middle of the middle and highest of the middle; *kṣamana* into lowest of the high and middle of the high; *laukikāh agra-dharmāḥ* as highest of the high.

92. *T* 1851.44.676b5–8. Here, Hui-yüan specifically mentions that they are "divided into nine kinds," a comment that is not found in the original passage above.

93. The commentaries on the *Avatamsaka-sutra* by Hui-kuang (*T* 2756.85) and by Ling-yü (*ZZ* 1–88–1) have survived in their fragments. All three of them are credited with commentaries on the *Daśabhūmika-śāstra,* and that of Fa-shang has come down to us (*T* 2799.85). As for the *Ti-ch'ih ching,* Hui-kuang and Ling-yü wrote commentaries on it. See *T* 2060.50.497c15; 607c23. Ocho Enichi points out the importance of these texts for members of the 'Hui-kuang' lineage. See his *Chūgoku bukkyō,* vol. 3, pp. 158–159.

94. Other common categories include "name," "essence and nature," "characteristics" and "person."

95. *T* 1851.44.700a8-9; 701a2-11.

96. Ibid., 685c27-686a2; 709c20-710a1.

97. See discussion in chapter 2 of this study.

98. *T* 1753.37.244c13-245a15.

99. *T* 2760.85.249c10, 250a17-18, b22, c9, 251a19, b4, b25, 252a6-7, b9-10.

100. *T* 1963.47.87b12-88a10-11.

101. *T* 1750.37.193b28-c1.

102. *T* 1753.37.247c22-249b8. See note 68 above.

103. *T* 1963.47.87b1-88a21.

104. Etani, *Jōdokyō no shin kenkyū,* pp. 355-391.

105. Etani Ryusho, "Koshitsusho ryūkō no kanmuryōjukyō no kenkyū," p. 86. Etani lists the quoted texts and the number of citations of the texts.

106. Etani, *Jōdokyō no shin kenkyū,* p. 381. Lung-hsing then goes on to state, "after this (the position expressed by Hui-yüan and Dharma Master Li), many of the masters [began] to speak [of ranking the nine grades] prior to the Bhūmis [departing from Hui-yüan's comparatively high ranking]." This statement points to a general tendency towards a lower ranking, as seen in Lung-hsing's citation of the ranking attributed to Dharma Master Ch'i, who was a disciple of the famous Hsüan-tsang (596-664).

107. *T* 1960.47.67b15-17.

108. See note 64 above.

109. Nogami, *Chūgoku jōdokyō-shi,* pp. 74-77. Yuki sees orthodox Pure Land Buddhism as based on the belief in the Last Period of Dharma. See his "Shina bukkyō ni okeru mappō shisō no kōki," *Tōhō gappō: Tokyo* 6 (1936): 214. Morimitsu, more recently, expresses the same view in "Chugokushisō-shi ni okeru zendō no ch'i," in *Zendō kyōgaku no kenkyū,* p. 14.

**Notes Chapter 6**

1. Yuki Reimon, "Kangyōsho ni okeru zendō shakugi," *Tsukamoto Festschrift,* pp. 908-909.

2. Agawa Kantatsu, "Jōdo resso yori mitaru jōyō," pp. 849-855; Fukagai Jiko, "Zendō to jōyōji eon," in pp. 1265-1280; Etani, "Zui-tō jidai no kangyō kenkyū shikan," *Tsukamoto Festschrift,* p. 125.

3. The four issues are: (1) the placement of the *Kuan-ching* within the overall Buddhist literature, (2) the meditative and non-meditative good acts, (3) the rank of the nine grades, and (4) the classification of pure lands.

4. *T* 1753.37.246a11–16. The seven gates are: (1) stating the preface, (2) explaining the title, (3) elucidating the import, (4) revealing the difference in the speaker of the sutra, (5) examining the two gates of the meditative and non-meditative good, (6) reconciling the sutras and sastras, and (7) examining the benefits for Vaidehī.

5. *T* 1753.37.247a16–22.

6. The three essentials are enumerated in the *Commentary,* p. 173a3–15.

7. *T* 1753.37.247a23–25.

8. *T* 1749.37.173a15–b1.

9. *T* 1958.47.4a11–12, 5a23–26.

10. Rei'ō, *Kanmuryōjukyō kōki,* pp. 26b–27a; Yuki, "Kangyōsho ni okeru zendō shakugi," p. 920; Hirose, *Kangyōsho ni manabu: gengibun,* pp. 287–295.

11. Julian Pas, "Shan-tao's Commentary on the *ABAS.*" Ph.D diss., McMaster University, 1973, pp. 503–518. That the term "Buddha-contemplation" as used in sixth and seventh century China signified more than one form of Buddhist practice has been pointed out by previous writers. Cf. Allan Andrews, "Nembutsu in the Chinese Pure Land tradition," p. 34.

12. Rei'ō, *Kanmuryōjukyō kōki,* 26b; Yuki, "Kangyōsho ni okeru zendō shakugi," p. 920; Ohara, *Zendō kyōgaku,* p. 187.

13. Ohara, *Zendō kyōgaku,* p. 187; Rei'ō, *Kanmuryōjukyō kōki,* p. 17. Rei'ō equates Buddha-visualization with the "essential gate of Śākyamuni's teaching" and of Buddha-contemplation with the "universal vow of Amitābha's teaching." He goes on to argue that the former teaching is simply a means leading to the latter, which constitutes, in essence, the main import of the *Kuan-ching.* In support of his view, he argues that the Buddha-contemplation is mentioned in the transmission section of the sutra but not the Buddha-visualization. Yuki also expresses the same point in his "Kangyōsho ni okeru zendō shakugi," pp. 916–917.

14. *T* 1753.37.247a23–25. For Hui-yüan's list, see *T* 1749.37.173b2–4.

15. *T* 1958.47.4a17–18.

16. *T* 1509.25.66b5–6. This could be a scriptural source from which Hui-yüan based his list.

17. For Chi-tsang's list, see *T* 1752.37.232c21–22. The Chinese terms are:

| *Ta chih tu lun:* | *Hui-yüan:* | *Tao-ch'o:* | *Shan-tao* |
|---|---|---|---|
| *fo-tzu* | *fo-tzu* | *fo-tzu* | *fo* |

| | | | |
|---|---|---|---|
| *fo ti-tzu* | *sheng ti-tzu* | *sheng ti-tzu* | *sheng ti-tzu* |
| *hsien-jen* | *shen-hsien* | *chu-t'ien* | *t'ien-hsien* |
| *chu-t'ien* | *t'ien kuei-shen* | *shen-hsien* | *kuei-shen* |
| *hua-jen* | *pien-hua* | *pien-hua* | *pien-hua* |

18. Kashiwabara, *Kangyō gengibun kōyō,* p. 147.

19. *T* 1749.37.178a19–21, b9–11, c4.

20. *T* 1750.37.193b25–26; 1753.37.247b4ff.

21. *T* 1753.37.247b22–25.

22. *T* 1753.37.247c8–10. It should, however, be pointed out that Shan-tao did disagree with Hui-yüan's understanding of the terms "speculation" (*szu-wei*) and "meditation" (*cheng-shou*)—terms which appear in the *Kuan-ching*—which Hui-yüan equated with "non-meditative good acts" and "meditative good acts," respectively. Shan-tao argued on the basis of the *Avataṃsaka-sūtra* that these two sutra terms were merely synonyms for "*samādhi,*" and thereby should not be regarded as terms with differing meanings.

23. For example, Ohara, *Zendō kyōgaku,* pp. 148–158.

24. *T* 1753.37.247b2–4; 277c4–6.

25. Ibid., p. 270b10–12.

26. Ibid., p. 272a29–b9.

27. Ibid., p. 272b6–9.

28. Yuki, "Kangyōsho ni okeru zendō shakugi," p. 918.

29. This, of course, assumes that the surviving manuscripts basing the *Taishō* edition are not corrupt.

30. *T* 1753.37.248a1. Hui-yüan, to the contrary, states, "The Inner and Outer Prthagjana [groups] who are prior to the stage of Path of Insight (*darśana-mārga*) . . . are said to be of the middle of the middle grades." (182c13–14)

31. *T* 1753.37.247c26–27.

32. *T* 1749.37.182b4–5.

33. *T* 1753.37.247c28.

34. *T* 1749.37.182a13–b20.

35. For Hui-yüan, only those of the Bhūmi stages are Āryapudgalas.

36. *T* 1753.37.248a8–b1.

37. Ibid., 248b2.

38. Ibid., 248b4–5.

39. *T* 1753.37.248b9–12.

40. *T* 365.12.344c14–16. There is the possibility that Shan-tao was working with a different rescension of the *Kuan-ching* from those used in the compilation of the extant *Taishō* edition. There is, however, no compelling reason to believe this to be the case, and it is more likely that this was an interpolation by Shan-tao. Cf. Nobuo Haneda, "The Development of the Concept of *Pṛthagjana,* p. 160.

41. See note 36 above.

42. *T* 1753.37.250b12–14.

43. Yuki, "Kangyōsho ni okeru zendō shakugi," p. 918.

44. *T* 1851.44.834a23–836a21 (characteristics) and 836a21–c7 (cause).

45. Ibid., 834a24ff (from the point of view of characteristics) and 836a21ff (point of view of cause).

46. T'an-luan's classification is explained in the following passage:

> "Nature" is the original meaning. This word means that this Pure Land accords with the true reality (*dharmatā*).

Compared to the sophisticated scheme of Hui-yüan's, this simply regards the Pure Land as separate from true reality but in accord with it. *T* 40.828b27.

47. Mochizuki, pp. 97–98.

48. *T* 44.834a28–b6.

49. Ibid., p. 834b4–28.

50. Ibid., p. 834b28–c9.

51. Ibid., p. 834c11–19.

52. Ibid., p. 835a3–12.

53. Ibid., p. 835b23–26.

54. Ibid., p. 835b4–5, 16–17.

55. Ibid., p. 835b10–13, 28–29.

56. *T* 1753.37.250b14–20.

57. Ibid., p. 213a8–9.

58. See Mochizuki, *Chūgoku jōdokyōri-shi,* p. 141 (Tao-ch'o), pp. 150–155 (She-lun proponents), pp. 165–168 (Chia-ts'ai), pp. 203–204 (K'uei-chi). "She-lun

proponents," according to Mochizuki, refers to such students of *Mahāyāna-saṃgraha* as Tao-ch'i (d. 637), Fa-ch'ang (d. 645), and Chih-yen (602–668).

59. Fujita Kotatsu, *Zendō,* Jinrui no chiteki-isan 18, (Tokyo: Kodansha, 1985), pp. 22–23.

60. In commenting on the opening lines of the *Kuan-ching,* Shan-tao divides up the lines in the same manner as Hui-yüan did and, though more elaborate, the meaning is virtually the same. For example, Shan-tao explains "*fo*" (Buddha) as "*hua-chu*" (master who converts), which was the same term used by Hui-yüan, and like Hui-yüan Shan-tao explains "*tsai wang-she-ch'eng*" ("residing in Rājagṛha") as "the place of sermon." *T* 1851.37.252b21–23.

61. The eight are: (1) purity, (2) non-malodorousness, (3) lightness, (4) chill, (5) malleableness, (6) beauty, (7) appropriateness when drunk, and (8) no illness after having drunk. *T* 1753.37.265a9–12 (*Shan-tao Commentary*), p. 179c1–3 (*Commentary*).

62. *T* 1753.37.261b11, 262b16, 267a19.

## Notes Translation, Part One

1. In Hui-yüan's view, "Pṛthagjana" refers to those below the first Bhūmi, differing from Shan-tao and other orthodox Pure Land proponents who regarded them to be below the Ten-Faiths stages. See chapter 5 of this study.

2. This work is not extant; see *Bussho* 4–50a–b.

3. *T* 806.

4. *T* 465.

5. *T* 353.

6. *T* 143.

7. *T* 128.

8. *T* 1509.25.66b5–6.

9. As the quotation below further indicates, the first category of *dharmas* leads to positive or pleasant results, while the second leads to negative or unpleasant results; the third category is undeterminable.

10. *T* 1581.

11. *T* 475.14.554c29–555a2.

12. These auspicious marks of great persons originated outside Buddhism and were later adopted as features of the Buddha. Interest in the marks increased in the first century A.D. with the widespread practice of visualization focused on

the use of Buddha images with these auspicious marks. These marks include white hair between the eyebrows, light from between the eyebrows, Buddha's circle of light, the mound of flesh on the head, and a moustache and web between fingers. Several versions of the thirty-two marks are found in Buddhist texts, and those attributes that were not included among the thirty-two were eventually together grouped to make up the eighty secondary marks. The auspicious marks are listed in, for example, the *Lakkhana suttanta* (*Dīgha-nikāya* III, No. 30), the *Mahāvastu* and the *Ta chi tu lun* (*T* 1509.24). Cf. *Ryūkoku,* pp. 127–128.

13. Cf. *T* 371.12.357a5–9.

14. I have gone with the alternate reading; Hui-yüan's *Wu-liang-shou ching i-shu* has virtually the same passage and it reads "pi" ("must") and not "nu" ("woman"). *T* 1745.37.92a18.

15. The Five Desires are generally the five desires arising from the objects of the five senses: sight, sound, smell, taste, and touch.

16. As punishment, the transgressing monks are given the 'silent treatment' by the other monks. See *Wu-fen lu, T* 1421.22.192a8–19.

17. "*śīta-vana*" literally meaning "cold grove"; a place for exposing corpses.

18. I have taken the alternate reading provided in the edited text: "ming" *(life)* instead of "*ming*" (rendering; name).

19. Unlike the first meaning, whose essence was expressed by first character "fearful" (in "fearful of Māra"), these next two meanings are expressed in both characters, "mendicant priest" and "pure life."

20. The phrase, "beings of the enlightenment" with regard to the Bodhisattvas derives, as we shall see below, from the *Ti-ch'ih lun.* See p. 175c23 in the *Commentary.*

21. Wisdom obtained as a result of having eliminated all defilement of blind afflictions (*kleśa*).

22. Wisdom about the non-substantiality or emptiness of *dharmas.*

23. While the exact meaning is unclear, a possible meaning of "common path" (*kung-tao*) and "uncommon path" (*pu-kung-tao*) may, respectively, be "common teaching" and "uncommon teaching." The former encompasses Buddha's meritorious attributes that are found in common with all beings on the Path, while the latter includes attributes common to other Buddhas or Bodhisattvas.

24. Of the four continents located in each of the four directions of Mt. Sumeru, Jambūdvīpa is the southern continent and came to be regarded as India.

25. "Broken finger" is an epithet of Ājataśatru, who, according to a well-known Buddhist parable, received his broken finger when as a newborn baby, his father Bimbisāra dropped him from a high tower. For a full story of this parable, see the synopsis of the *Sutra* at the beginning of this translation.

26. They are the ability to (1) go freely wherever one wants to go, (2) see everything in the world or in the future, (3) distinguish every sound in the world, (4) intuit how others think, and (5) know the previous lives of others as well as one's own.

27. I have taken the variant reading.

28. This phrase and those similar to it are found throughout the text. They are intended to denote phrases which Hui-yüan sees as bridging the prior and the following sections.

29. The eight are enumerated in the next paragraph of the text. They include the Five Precepts plus the additional three and are designed for the lay followers to lead a life similar to the monastics for six days of a lunar month, the eighth, fourteenth, fifteenth, twenty-third, twenty-ninth, and thirtieth.

30. *T.*1646 and *T.*1509, respectively.

31. Hui-yüan refers readers on several occasions to this encyclopedic text attributed to him. See chapter 2 for discussion of this work.

32. I have chosen to read it "chi" rather than "i."

33. "Sahā World-realm" is the realm where we dwell. See next note for "evil Destinies."

34. The three evil Destinies are those of the hungry ghosts, beasts, and hell beings. Hui-yüan discusses them in detail starting the next paragraph in the text.

35. *T.*1552. *Abhidharmasārapratikīrnaka-[śāstra]*.

36. Hui-yüan differentiates, here and elsewhere, between characteristic and meaning.

37. Of the compound, the former is foreign and the latter Chinese.

38. The white curled hair (*ūrṇa-keśa*) is one of the thirty-two marks of a great man.

39. One of the 'seven kinds of jewels' found in Buddhist texts. Cf. *Ryūkoku,* pp. 28, 122–123.

40. The characters *szu-wei* (to think) and *cheng-shou* (to concentrate) literally mean "thinking" and "right acceptance" respectively. "To think" is one of the eightfold noble path, while "right acceptance" came to mean "meditation." See *Ryūkoku,* p. 21 No. 2.

41. This classification of the Āryapudgala stages is divided into Stream-winner, Once-returner, Non-returner, and Perfected One. See appendix 1.

42. This statement does not make sense. The *Sutra* states that the Pure Land is "not far," yet Hui-yüan explains that the Land is ten-thousand times a hundred-million lands away.

43. Dependent and main rewards are based on past karmic actions. The "main rewards" refer to living beings, while the "dependent rewards" refer to the physical environment on which the living beings 'depend,' such as the land, pond, trees, and so forth. See *Bukkyōgaku jiten,* p. 42a. As discussed in chapter 6, these two categories were adopted by many of the subsequent commentators of the *Sutra.*

44. I have read this as referring to the three *highest* grades, for the people of these grades perform the three pure acts. Besides, it cannot be referring to all grades, since the *Sutra* expounds a total of nine grades.

45. This in contrast with the practice of insight (*vipaśyanā*). *Nakamura,* p. 506d.

46. The ten calls for refraining from: (1) killing, (2) stealing, (3) committing adultery, (4) telling a lie, (5) being duplicitous, (6) slandering, (7) equivocating, (8) being covetous, (9) being angry, and (10) holding perverted views. See *Ryūkoku,* p. 124. The "three heresies" refer to the first three of the above ten transgressions, the "four transgressions" to the next four and the "three evils" to the last three. However, no separate chapter or entry devoted to the ten virtuous acts can be found in the *Mahayana Encyclopedia.*

47. The ten precepts for the novices are refraining from (1) killing living beings, (2) taking what has not been given, (3) misconduct in sexual matters, (4) telling lies, (5) drinking liquor, (6) wearing adornments and perfume, (7) enjoying singing and dancing, (8) sleeping in large, raised beds, (9) eating after noon, and (10) possessing gold, silver, and other precious metals.

48. These three refuges are the Buddha, Dharma, and Sangha. See *T* 1851.44.654ff.

49. The four are (1) sexual intercourse with a woman, (2) stealing, (3) killing a human being, and (4) falsely asserting that one is a saint or possess supernatural faculties. These are grounds for expulsion from the sangha. It seems that the light transgressions refer to the remaining precepts such as the partaking of alcoholic drinks, as Hui-yüan mentions below.

50. The "sanctioned instructions" refer to the general instruction that the Buddha gives before discoursing on the visualizations.

51. Based on *Wu-liang-shou ching,* the Five Evils refer to transgression of the five lay precepts, the Five Pains to the pain of the punishment by a king for the transgression and the Five Burnings to the suffering from succumbing to the three evil Destinies that are akin to being physically burned. These are discussed below in the *Commentary,* p. 179b5–10. Also, see *Nakamura,* pp. 353d, 372d, 368c.

52. This suggests an 'eternal' Buddha Śākyamuni with universalized qualities.

53. *T* 245.8.826b21–827a7 (Kumārajīva translation) and *T* 246.8.836b14–837a4 (Amoghavajra translation).

54. Lineage and Practice of Resolutions follow immediately below the Bhūmi stages on the Path system. See appendix 1.

55. See note 51 above. For the original sutra passage, see *T.*360.12.275c23ff.

56. *Mahayana Encyclopedia, T.*1851.44.834a1–837c7.

57. Hui-yüan uses *kuan-ch'a* in the same sense as *kuan.*

**Notes Translation, part two**

1. "Accomplished feature" refers to the state in which the object of visualization is clearly formed in the practitioner's mind so that, as the *Sutra* states, "you see things clearly and distinctly just as you might see the palm of your hand" (343a28).

2. *T* 1851.44.837c10–844c15.

3. See Hui-yüan's definition above, p. 174b20ff.

4. This third phrase differs from the first in that it includes the character "this" and also "concludes" the first phrase.

5. The *Sutra* states, "Buddha, Tathāgata, Samyaksambuddha" (343a23) instead of "Buddha Amitābha," which appears to be Hui-yüan's substitution.

6. This refers to subsegment one of segment one of the eighth visualization. See p. 180a3–5 above.

7. It seems more appropriate for this to be read as "features" (*hsiang*) rather than as "proper conduct" (*i*), since this section has the same aim as subsegment one which discusses "features."

8. According to *Abhidharmakośa-śāstra,* "*koṭi*" is a high number equal to 10 to the seventh power, and a "*nayuta*" refers to a higher number, generally 10 to the 11th power. See *Ryūkoku,* p. 129. A "*yojana*" is about nine miles.

9. A measure of length equal to 360 paces.

10. It should be three-hundred and twenty thousand.

11. This section with the numbers is somewhat unclear and requires further examination of its calculations and assumptions.

12. The five Destinies are heavenly beings, human, hungry ghosts, beasts, and hell.

13. For rankings of the Path, see appendix 1.

14. On several occasions, Hui-yüan resorts to this interesting method ("in the context of those of superior capabilities") for reconciling the discrepancies he sees between this *Sutra* and other scriptures in the time involved in attaining a certain rank. In this case the difference concerns the Insight of Non-arising, where

this *Sutra* espouses "immediate" obtainment upon rebirth, while Hui-yüan realizes that normally "it actually takes great amount of time."

15. The largest unit of time. A Kalpa is so long that only parables are able to approximate its length. In the *Ta chih tu lun* (fascicle 38), a Kalpa is said to be the time required for a person to wear down a stone mountain of forty *li* (approx. 75,600 English feet) high by rubbing it with a light garment once every one hundred years. See *Nakamura,* p. 392b.

16. The Uncountable Kalpa refers to largest unit of number in the Indian system, described as 10 to the 51st power.

17. Its original meaning is unclear. The notion that such wisdom is acquired at the rank of the Ten-Dwellings appears in the *P'u-sa ying-lo pen-ying ching* (*T* 24.1011c). This set of stages corresponds to the Lineage stage discussed here by Hui-yüan. But the idea that this wisdom is acquired at the first Bhūmi (Stage of Rejoicing is found in the *Avataṃsaka-sūtra* (*T* 9.547b). See *Ryūkoku,* p. 92 No 1.

18. See 182a29–b3 above. The argument is that the 'starting point' in the *Sutra* is at a higher level than that in the *Ti-ch'ih ching.*

19. See 182b5–6 above for the earlier statement. Further, it seems that "final stage" would make more sense than "initial stage" (*shih-ch'u*) as the text states, since the thrust of Hui-yüan's argument concerns, as above, the higher starting point in reaching the first Bhūmi.

20. See 182b4–5 above for the earlier statement. Hui-yüan argues that the *Sutra* espouses a goal that is at the low end.

21. From the ongoing logic of the argument, it only makes sense to read this sentence with "not" inserted so that it reads, "it was *not* stated. . . ."

22. A variant reading can be ". . . are roughly the same."

23. For the three Āryapudgala fruits, see appendix 1.

24. As one of two kinds of transmigration, "*fen-tuan* [*sheng-szu*]" refers to unenlightened beings who, on account of blind passions, receive limited life spans and physical bodies of specific dimensions. They are caught in the cycle of transmigration with this limitation. In contrast, "*pien-i* [*sheng-szu*]" refers to enlightened beings who are no longer subject to the above limitations and are able to take on any physical form at will in the transmigratory realm to carry out the task of saving others. See *Bukkyōgaku jiten,* p. 263b.

25. See above note.

26. I have taken the variant reading, *ching* (sutra) instead of *chu* (dwelling).

27. A translation of the Sanskrit term *kalyāṇa-mitra,* a "virtuous friend," refers to a teacher who guides the seekers on the Buddhist Path.

28. The *Kuan-ching* speaks of a person of the middle of the lowest grade hearing the names of the Buddha, Dharma, and Sangha. See p. 345b25–26.

29. The six objects of these mindfulness practices are: Buddha, Dharma, Sangha, precepts, merits of renunciation and merits of deity. See *Ryūkoku,* p. 78 No. 2.

30. The term "*chieh-liao*" here does not mean "understanding" as one might normally expect. The *Sutra* means rather steadfast faith as when it says, Upon hearing the highest truth, their minds are not perplexed or shaken" (345a6). Cf. *Ryūkoku,* p. 85.

31. *T* 360.12.272c6–8.

32. (see above 178a18–23) The five are: (1) to kill one's mother, (2) to kill one's father, (3) to kill an Arhat, (4) to injure or spill blood of the Buddha, and (5) to destroy the harmony of the Sangha. See *Ryūkoku,* p. 93 No. 5.

33. I am taking the variant reading, for, by so doing, the two correspond to Dharma-body and Rewarded-body.

34. I have taken the variant reading, "flower."

35. Good Destinies generally refer to the heavenly and human (and, at times, titan (*aśura*) Destinies.

36. "*Erh-yin*" (the second [section deals with] the causes) should be included for better reading as suggested by the *Taishō* editor.

37. The character "*ch'eng*" (accomplish) is not found in the *Taishō* edition of the *Kuan-ching* (p. 345a5).

38. See *Ryūkoku,* pp. 92, note No. 1.

39. There are ambiguities in this paragraph, particularly the last sentence that makes more sense with the insertion.

40. The passage makes more sense if "*hsien*" (revelation) is read "*kuan*" (visualization).

41. I have taken the variant reading.

42. See *Ryūkoku,* p. 112.

# Glossary

**English and Sanskrit (selected)**

| | |
|---|---|
| Amitābha: | Buddha of Immeasurable Light |
| Amitāyus: | Buddha of Immeasurable Life—this and "Amitābha" refer to the same Buddha. |
| Arhat: | "One worthy of reverence"—perfected sage in the highest stage, who has attained nirvana. |
| Āryapudgala: | Sage in the Bhūmi stages above the Pṛthagjana stages |
| Bhikṣu: | Buddhist monk |
| Bhūmi: | Path stages of the Āryapudgalas |
| Bodhisattva: | Mahayana follower of high ranking, generally above Ten-Faiths stages |
| Destinies: | *gati*—realms of existence of the heavenly beings, human, titans, hungry ghosts, beasts, and hell beings |
| *dharmas*: | Fundamental elements of existence |
| Dharma: | Teaching, doctrine—ultimate reality |
| Hinayana: | "The small vehicle"—a pejorative term coined by the Mahayanists to refer to the teachings of the earlier schools. |
| Insight of Non-arising of *dharmas:* | *dharmānutpattika-kṣānti*—insight into the non-substantial nature of all phenomenal existence |
| Jambūdvīpa: | The continent to the south of Mt. Meru, where India is believed to be located. |
| Kalpa: | Aeon—an extremely long span of time |

| | |
|---|---|
| Path: | *mārga*; stages of cultivation leading to enlightenment |
| Piṭaka: | Collection of writings |
| Pratyekabuddha: | A Buddha "for himself alone," who does not share his enlightenment with others. |
| Pṛthagjana: | Ordinary seeker below the Āryapudgala stages such as Ten-Faiths, Lineage, and Practice of Resolution. |
| Pure Land: | Amitābha's world-realm (*loka-dhātu*), Sukhāvatī |
| pure lands: | The world-realms of other 'transcendent' Buddhas |
| Sahā: | This world-realm where Buddha Śākyamuni appeared and where Jambūdvīpa is located. |
| *śāstra* | Commentary, treatise |
| *stūpa*: | Relic monument of the Buddha |
| Śrāvaka: | "hearer"—follower of Hinayana teaching |
| Śramaṇa: | "striver"—Buddhist monk |
| Stream-winner: | *srotāpanna*; lowest of the four stages of sage, below those of the Once-returner, Non-returner and Arhat—one who has entered the stream leading to nirvana. |
| Sukhāvatī | "Realm of Utmost Bliss"—the Pure Land of Amitābha located in the western direction. |

**Chinese, Korean, and Japanese: Proper Names, Technical Terms, and Titles of Works (selected)**

| | |
|---|---|
| A-lo-ho | 阿羅訶 |
| A-lo-han | 阿羅漢 |
| A-lu-ho | 阿盧訶 |
| A-mi-t'o | 阿彌陀 |
| *A-mi-t'o ching* | 阿彌陀經 |
| A-mi-t'o fo | 阿彌陀佛 |

| | |
|---|---|
| *A-mi-t'o san-yeh-san-fo-sa-lou-fo-t'an kuo-tu-jen-tao ching* | 阿彌陀三耶三佛薩 樓佛檀過度人道經 |
| *An-le chi* | 安樂集 |
| An-le ching-t'u | 安樂淨土 |
| An-le kuo | 安樂國 |
| An-yang shih-chieh | 安養世界 |
| *Anyōshō* | 安養抄 |
| *bonpu* (also, *bonbu*) | 凡夫 |
| *Bussetsu kanmuryō-jukyō-kōki* | 佛說觀無量壽經講記 |
| Chajang | 慈藏 |
| Ch'an | 禪 |
| *ch'an-hui* | 懺悔 |
| *ch'an-mo* | 懺摩 |
| Ch'ang-an | 長安 |
| *chao-mu hsü* | 昭穆序 |
| *chen* | 眞 |
| *chen ching-t'u* | 眞淨土 |
| *chen-fo wu-hsiang* | 眞佛無像 |
| *ch'en* | 晨 |
| Ch'en-hui | 陳慧 |
| *chen-shen* | 眞身 |
| *chen-shen kuan* | 眞身觀 |
| *chen-shih chien* | 眞實見 |
| *chen-ti* | 眞諦 |
| *cheng* | 正 |

| | |
|---|---|
| *ch'eng* | 稱 |
| *ch'eng-ch'i-ming* | 稱其名 |
| *cheng-hsin hsü* | 証信序 |
| *ch'eng-hsiang* | 成相 |
| *ch'eng-hsin* | 誠心 |
| Ch'eng-kuan | 澄觀 |
| *ch'eng-ming* | 稱名 |
| *cheng-pao* | 正報 |
| *cheng-ting-yeh* | 正定業 |
| *Ch-eng-shih lun* | 成實論 |
| *cheng-shou* | 正受 |
| *cheng-tsung* | 正宗 |
| Ch'eng-tu | 成都 |
| Ch'i | 齊 |
| Ch'i-ch'ao shang-t'ung | 齊朝上統 |
| Chi-chün | 汲郡 |
| Chi-lo | 極樂 |
| *ch'i-men* | 七門 |
| *chi-mieh jen* | 寂滅忍 |
| Chi-tsang | 吉藏 |
| Chia-ts'ai | 迦才 |
| *Chia-yeh-shan-ting ching* | 伽耶山頂經 |
| Chiang-liang-yeh-she | 畺良耶舍 |
| Chiang-ling | 江陵 |
| *chiao* | 教 |
| Chiao-chih | 交趾 |

| | |
|---|---|
| *chiao-chih-ta-hsiao* | 教之大小 |
| *chiao-chih-tsung-ch'ü* | 教之宗趣 |
| *chieh-hsing* | 解行 |
| *chieh-liao* | 解了 |
| *chien* (gradual) | 漸 |
| *chien* (vision) | 見 |
| Chien-k'ang | 建康 |
| Chien-yeh | 建業 |
| *chih* | 至 |
| *ch'ih* | 尺 |
| Chih-ch'ien | 支謙 |
| Chih-hu Szu | 陟岵寺 |
| Chih-i | 智顗 |
| *chih-kuan* | 止觀 |
| Chih-li | 智禮 |
| Chih Lou-chia-ch'en | 支婁迦讖 |
| Chih-tun | 支遁 |
| Chih-yen | 智儼 |
| Chikō | 智光 |
| Ch'in-chin | 秦晋 |
| *Chin-kang ming ching* | 金剛明經 |
| *Chin-kang po-jo lun shu* | 金剛般若論疏 |
| *Chin kuang-ming ching shu* | 金剛明經疏 |
| *chin-yüan fen-pieh* | 近遠分別 |

| | |
|---|---|
| *Ching-fan-wang pan-nieh-p'an ching* | 淨飯王般涅槃經 |
| Ch'ing-hua Szu | 清化寺 |
| *ching* | 經 |
| *ching i-shu* | 經義疏 |
| *ching-kuo* | 淨國 |
| *ching-ming pu-t'ung* | 經名不同 |
| Ching-t'ai | 靜泰 |
| Ching-ti | 靜帝 |
| *ching-t'u* | 淨土 |
| *ching-t'u chiao* | 淨土教 |
| *ching-t'u fa-men* | 淨土法門 |
| *ching-t'u i-men* | 淨土一門 |
| *Ching-tu san-mei ching* | 淨度三昧經 |
| *ching-t'u tsung* | 淨土宗 |
| *Ching-t'u lun* | 淨土論 |
| *Ching-t'u shih-i lun* | 淨土十疑論 |
| Ching-yeh | 淨業 |
| Ching-ying Hui-yüan | 淨影慧遠 |
| Ching-ying Szu | 淨影寺 |
| *chiu-p'in wang-sheng* | 九品往生 |
| Chou | 周 |
| *chu* (commentary) | 注，註 |
| *chü* (limited) | 局 |

| | |
|---|---|
| *ch'u* | 處 |
| Chü-ch'ü Ching-sheng | 沮渠京聲 |
| *Chu fa-hua ching* | 注法華經 |
| *chu-fa shih-hsiang* | 諸法實相 |
| *Ch'u san-tsang chi chi* | 出三藏記集 |
| *ch'u-sheng* | 畜生 |
| *Chu ta-p'in ching* | 注大品經 |
| *chu-t'ien-kuei* | 諸天鬼 |
| *Chu wei-mo ching* | 注維摩經 |
| *chu-yeh* | 助業 |
| *chüan* | 卷 |
| *Chuang-tzu* | 莊子 |
| *chüeh* | 覺 |
| *chüeh-ch'a* | 覺察 |
| *chüeh-wu* | 覺悟 |
| Ch'üeh Kung-tse | 闕公則 |
| *chung* | 終 |
| *Chung-ching mu-lu* | 衆經目錄 |
| *chung-hsiang chieh* | 衆香界 |
| *chung-hsing* | 種性 |
| Chung-nan Shan | 終南山 |
| *chung-sheng yüan* | 衆生緣 |
| *Dai-kyō* | 大經 |
| Eichō | 永超 |
| *erh-ti* | 二諦 |
| *fa* | 法 |

| | |
|---|---|
| Fa-ch'eng | 法誠 |
| *fa-ch'i hsü* | 發起序 |
| *fa-chieh yüan-ch'i fa-men* | 法界緣起法門 |
| Fa-ching | 法經 |
| *Fa-ching lu* | 法經錄 |
| Fa-chao | 法照 |
| *fa-hsing t'u* | 法性土 |
| *Fa-hua* | 法華 |
| *Fa-hua ching shu* | 法華經疏 |
| *Fa-hua lun* | 法華論 |
| *Fa-ku ching* | 法鼓經 |
| *fa-mieh* | 法滅 |
| Fa-lang | 法朗 |
| Fa-lin | 法林 |
| Fa-pao | 法寶 |
| Fa-shang | 法上 |
| *fa-shen* | 法身 |
| *fa-tao ch'ang* | 法道場 |
| Fa-tsang | 法藏 |
| Fa-ts'ung | 法聰 |
| Fa-tu | 法度 |
| *fa-yü* | 法喻 |
| *fa-yüan* | 法緣 |
| Fa-yun | 法雲 |
| *fan-fu* | 凡夫 |
| Fang-ch'i | 方啓 |
| *Fang-teng ta-chi ching* | 方等大集經 |

| | |
|---|---|
| Fei Ch'ang-fang | 費長房 |
| *fei-pang cheng-fa* | 誹謗正法 |
| Fen-chou | 汾州 |
| *fen-pieh* | 分別 |
| *fen-tuan [sheng-szu]* | 分段生死 |
| *fo* | 佛 |
| *fo-hsing* | 佛性 |
| *fo-kuo* | 佛國 |
| *fo-li chien* | 佛力見 |
| *Fo-shuo kuan wu-liang-shou ching shu* | 佛說觀無量壽經疏 |
| *Fo-tsu li-tai t'ung-tsai* | 佛祖歷代通載 |
| *Fo-tsu t'ung-chi* | 佛祖統紀 |
| *fo-ti-tzu* | 佛弟子 |
| *fo-tzu* | 佛自 |
| *fo-yüan* | 佛緣 |
| *fo-yüan li* | 佛願力 |
| *fu-jen* | 伏忍 |
| Genryūkoku | 源隆國 |
| Genshin | 源信 |
| *hao* | 好 |
| *heng-ho sha* | 恒河沙 |
| *hōmetsu* | 法滅 |
| Ho-nan Pao-shan | 河南寶山 |
| Hōnen | 法然 |
| *hou* Shan-tao | 後善導 |

| | |
|---|---|
| *Hsi-fang yao-chüeh shih-i t'ung-kuei* | 西方要決釋疑通規 |
| Hsi-shan | 西山 |
| *hsiang* | 相 |
| *hsiang ching-t'u* | 相淨土 |
| *Hsiao-chüan wu-liang-shou ching* | 小卷無量壽經 |
| *Hsiao wu-liang-shou ching* | 小無量壽經 |
| *hsien-jen* | 仙人 |
| *hsin-jen* | 信忍 |
| Hsin-hsing | 信行 |
| *hsin shih fo* | 心是佛 |
| *hsin tso fo* | 心作佛 |
| *Hsin wu-liang-shou ching* | 新無量壽經 |
| *hsing* | 行 |
| *hsing-te* | 行德 |
| *hsiu* | 修 |
| *hsiu-hsin* | 修心 |
| *hsiu-kuan* | 修觀 |
| *hsiu-to-lo* | 修多羅 |
| *hsiu-yeh* | 修業 |
| *hsü* | 序 |
| *Hsü kao-seng chuan* | 續高僧傳 |
| *Hsü-mo-t'i nü ching* | 須摩提女經 |
| Hsüan-chung Szu | 玄中寺 |

| | |
|---|---|
| *hsüan-hsueh* | 玄學 |
| *hsüan-t'an* | 玄談 |
| Hsüan-ti | 宣帝 |
| Hsüan-tsang | 玄奘 |
| *hua-chu* | 化主 |
| *hu-fa p'u-sa* | 護法菩薩 |
| *hua-fo* | 化佛 |
| *hua-jen* | 化人 |
| *hua-shen* | 化身 |
| *hua-t'u* | 化土 |
| Hua-yen | 華嚴 |
| *Hua-yen [ching] shu* | 華嚴經疏 |
| Huai-chou | 懷州 |
| Hui-chiao | 慧皎 |
| Hui-ch'ih | 慧持 |
| Hui-ch'ung | 迴向 |
| *hui-hsiang* | 迴向發願心 |
| *hui-hsiang fa-yuan hsin* | 慧休 |
| Hui-hsiu | 慧日 |
| Hui-jih | 慧可 |
| Hui-k'o | 慧觀 |
| Hui-kuan | 慧光 |
| Hui-kuang | 慧寵 |
| Hui-shun | 慧順 |
| Hui-szu | 慧思 |
| Hui-wen | 慧文 |
| Hui-ying | 慧影 |

| | |
|---|---|
| Hui-yüan | 慧(惠)遠 |
| Hwangnyong-sa | 黃龍寺 |
| Hyonil | 玄一 |
| *i* (meaning) | 義 |
| *i* (recollection) | 憶 |
| *i-chi* | 義記 |
| *i-hsin chuan-chu* | 一心專注 |
| *i-hsing* | 易行 |
| *i-hsing tao* | 易行道 |
| *i-pao* | 依報 |
| *i-shih* | 一時 |
| *i-shu* | 義疏 |
| *i-yüeh* | 一越 |
| *jen* | 人 |
| *jen-fa* | 人法 |
| *Jen-pen-yü-sheng ching-chu* | 人本欲生經注 |
| *Jen-wang ching* | 仁王經 |
| *Jōdo ron* | 淨土論 |
| Jōdo-Shinshū | 淨土眞宗 |
| Jōdoshū | 淨土宗 |
| *ju-fa* | 如法 |
| *ju-lai-tsang* | 如來藏 |
| *ju-lai-tsang hsing* | 如來藏性 |
| *ju-lai-tsang yüan-ch'i* | 如來藏緣起 |
| *ju-shih* | 如是 |
| *k'ai-fa hsü* | 開發序 |
| K'ang Seng-k'ai | 康僧鎧 |

| | |
|---|---|
| Kao-tu | 高都 |
| *Ken jōdo shinjitsu kyōgyōshō mon'rui* | 顯淨土眞實教行證文類 |
| *k'o-tuan* | 科段 |
| Ku-hsien-ku Szu | 古賢谷寺 |
| *K'u-shu ching* | 枯樹經 |
| *kuan* | 觀 |
| *kuan-ch'a* | 觀察 |
| *Kuan-ching* | 觀經 |
| "Kuan-ching hsüan-i fen" | 觀經玄義分 |
| *kuan-fo* | 觀佛 |
| *kuan-fo san-mei* | 觀佛三昧 |
| *Kuan fo san-mei ching* | 觀佛三昧經 |
| *Kuan fo san-mei hai ching* | 觀佛三昧海經 |
| *Kuan hsü-k'ung-tsang p'u-sa ching* | 觀虛空藏菩薩經 |
| *Kuan mi-le p'u-sa shang-sheng tou-shuai-t'ien ching* | 觀彌勒菩薩上生兜率天經 |
| *Kuan p'u-hsien p'u-sa hsing-fa ching* | 觀普賢菩薩行法經 |
| *Kuan wu-liang-shou-fo ching chi* | 觀無量壽佛經記 |
| *Kuan wu-liang-shou-fo ching shu miao-tsung ch'ao* | 觀無量壽佛經疏 妙宗鈔 |
| *Kuan wu-liang-shou ching i-shu* | 觀無量壽經義疏 |

| | |
|---|---|
| *Kuan wu-liang-shou ching shu* | 觀無量壽經疏 |
| *Kuan-yin ching* | 觀音經 |
| *Kuang hung-ming-chi* | 廣弘明集 |
| *kuang kuan* | 廣觀 |
| [K'uei-]chi | 窺基 |
| *kuei-hsiang* | 歸向 |
| *kuei-hsiang chih li* | 歸向之力 |
| *kuei-shen* | 鬼神 |
| *kung-tao* | 共道 |
| *kuo* (effect) | 果 |
| *kuo* (transgression) | 過 |
| *Lao-tzu* | 老子 |
| *li* (distance) | 里 |
| *li* (noumenal) | 理 |
| *li* (worship) | 禮 |
| Li | 李 |
| Li-chan | 梨湛 |
| Li fa-shih | 李法師 |
| *li-i* | 利益 |
| *li-shih wu-ai* | 理事無礙 |
| *li-t'a* | 利他 |
| *Li-tai fa-pao chi* | 歷代法寶記 |
| Li Te-lin | 李德林 |
| Liang Wu-ti | 梁武帝 |
| *lien-she* | 蓮社 |
| Ling-kan | 靈幹 |
| Ling-yü | 靈裕 |

| | |
|---|---|
| Liu-ch'iu | 劉虬 |
| *liu ta-te* | 六大德 |
| *liu-t'ung* | 流通 |
| Lu | 魯 |
| Lu-shan Hui-yüan | 廬山慧遠 |
| *Lu-shan lien-tsung pao chien* | 廬山蓮宗寶鑑 |
| *lüeh-kuan* | 略觀 |
| *Lüeh-lun an-le ching-t'u i* | 略論安樂淨土義 |
| *Lun-yü* | 論語 |
| Lung-hsing | 龍興 |
| Lung-men | 龍門 |
| *miao ching-t'u* | 妙淨土 |
| *Mi-le hsia-sheng ching* | 彌勒下生經 |
| *Mi-le-hsia-sheng ch'eng-fo ching* | 彌勒下生成佛經 |
| *Mi-le ta-ch'eng-fo ching* | 彌勒大成佛經 |
| *Mi-le wen ching* | 彌勒問經 |
| *Miao-fa lien-hua ching shu* | 妙法蓮華經疏 |
| *ming* | 名 |
| *mo-fa* | 末法 |
| *nan* | 難 |
| *nei-fan* | 內凡 |
| *Nei-tien lu* | 內典錄 |
| *nei-yu kuan* | 內有觀 |
| *nembutsu* | 念佛 |

| | |
|---|---|
| *Nieh-p'an ching* | 涅槃經 |
| *nien* | 念 |
| *nien-fo* | 念佛 |
| *Nien-fo ching* | 念佛鏡 |
| *nien-fo san-mei* | 念佛三昧 |
| *Nien-fo san-mei pao-wang lun* | 念佛三昧寶王論 |
| *Ōjō ron* | 往生論 |
| *Ōjō yōshū* | 往生要集 |
| *pa chieh-t'uo* | 八解脫 |
| *pa-pei* | 八背 |
| *pai-fa ming* | 百法明 |
| *pai-lien she* | 白蓮社 |
| *Pan-jo ching* | 般若經 |
| Pao-liang | 寶亮 |
| *Pao p'u-tzu* | 抱朴子 |
| *pao-shen* | 報身 |
| *pao-t'u* | 報土 |
| Pao-yün | 寶雲 |
| *p'an-chiao* | 判教 |
| Pei-shan | 北山 |
| *piao-fa* | 表法 |
| *pieh* | 別 |
| *pieh-ch'ing* | 別請 |
| *pieh-hsien* | 別顯 |
| *pieh-hsü* | 別序 |
| *pieh-shih i* | 別時意 |
| *pien-hua* | 變化 |

pien-i [sheng-szu] 變易生死

Pŏbwi 法位

*pu-kung-tao* 不共道

*p'u-sa seng* 菩薩僧

*P'u-sa ti-ch'ih ching* 菩薩地持經

*p'u-sa tsang* 菩薩藏

*pu-szu-i chieh-t'uo* 不思議解脫

Pu-t'i sa-to 菩提薩埵

*pu t'ui-chuan* 不退轉

Rei'ō 靈暀

Ryōchū 艮忠

*Sa-ho-t'an t'ai-tzu ching* 薩和檀太子經

*san-ching yeh* 三淨業

*san-hsin* 三心

*san-i* 三義

*san-men* 三門

San-miao san-fo-t'o 三藐三佛陀

*san-ming* 三明

*Sanron-shū shō sho* 三論宗章疏

*san-shan* 散善

*se-shen* 色身

*senchaku hongan nembutsu-shū* 選擇本願念佛集

Seng-chao 僧肇

Seng-hsien 僧顯

Seng-szu 僧思

| | |
|---|---|
| *Sha-men pu-ching wang-che lun* | 沙門不敬王者論 |
| Shao-k'ang | 少康 |
| Shao-lin Szu | 少林寺 |
| *shan* | 善 |
| *shan-ch'ü* | 善趣 |
| Shan-tao | 善導 |
| *shan-tsai* | 善哉 |
| *Shan-wang huang ti ching* | 善王皇帝經 |
| *shang-t'ung* | 上統 |
| She-lun | 攝論 |
| *She ta-ch'eng lun* | 攝大乘論 |
| *shen-hsien* | 神仙 |
| *shen-hsin* | 深心 |
| *sheng-jen* | 聖人 |
| *Sheng-man ching* | 勝鬘經 |
| *Sheng-man ching i-chi* | 勝鬘經義記 |
| *Sheng-man pao-k'u* | 勝鬘寶窟 |
| *sheng-wen* | 聲聞 |
| *sheng-wen tsang* | 聲聞藏 |
| *sheng-tao men* | 聖道門 |
| *sheng ti-tzu* | 聖弟子 |
| *shih* (beginning) | 如 |
| *shih* (objects) | 事 |
| *shih* (time) | 時 |
| *Shih-ching* | 時經 |

| | |
|---|---|
| *shih ching-t'u* | 事淨土 |
| *Shih ching-t'u ch'ün-i lun* | 釋淨土群疑論 |
| *shih-chu* | 十住 |
| *shih-ch'u* | 始處 |
| *shih-fa* | 事法 |
| *shih-hsiang* | 實相 |
| *shih-hsin* | 十信 |
| *shih-hsing* | 十行 |
| *shih-hui ching-lun* | 釋會經論 |
| *shih hui-hsiang* | 十迴向 |
| *shih-i tsa-ching lu* | 失譯雜經錄 |
| *shih-nien* | 十念 |
| *shih-pao t'u* | 實報土 |
| *shih shan-yeh* | 十善業 |
| *shih-shih* | 事事 |
| *shih-shih wu-ai* | 事事無礙 |
| *shih-ti* | 世諦 |
| *Shih-ti ching-lun i-chi* | 十地經論義記 |
| *Shih-ti [ching-lun i-]shu* | 十地經論義疏 |
| *Shih wang-sheng ching* | 十往生經 |
| *shinjin* | 信心 |
| *Sinp'pyŏn chejong kyojang ch'ongnok* | 新編諸宗教藏總錄 |
| Shinran | 親鸞 |
| *shōdōmon* | 聖道門 |
| *shoshi* | 諸師 |

| | |
|---|---|
| *Shou-ching* | 壽經 |
| *shu* | 疏 |
| *Shuang-chüan ching* | 雙卷經 |
| *shūgaku* | 宗學 |
| *shun-jen* | 順忍 |
| *shuo-jen* | 說人 |
| *shuo-jen ch'a-pieh* | 說人差別 |
| *so-piao* | 所表 |
| *so-shuo* | 所說 |
| *Sui-yüan shih-fang wang-sheng ching* | 隨願十方往生經 |
| *Sung kao-seng chuan* | 宋高僧傳 |
| Szu-ch'uan | 四川 |
| *Szu-fen lü* | 四分律 |
| *szu-hsiang kuan-ch'a i-nien* | 思想觀察憶念 |
| *szu-men* | 四門 |
| *szu-wei* | 思惟 |
| *Ta a-mi-t'o ching* | 大阿彌陀經 |
| *Ta-ch'eng ch'i-hsin lun i-shu* | 大乘起信論義疏 |
| *Ta-ch'eng i-chang* | 大乘義章 |
| *Ta-chi ching* | 大集經 |
| *Ta chih tu lun* | 大智度論 |
| *Ta-ching* | 大經 |
| *Ta-fa-shih hsing-chi* | 大法師行記 |
| Ta-hai | 大海 |

| | |
|---|---|
| Ta-hsing-shan Szu | 大興善寺 |
| *t'a-li* | 他力 |
| *Ta-nieh-p'an-ching chi-chieh* | 大涅槃經集解 |
| *Ta-pan nieh-p'an ching i-chi* | 大般涅槃經義記 |
| *[Ta-pan] nieh-p'an [ching i-]shu* | 大般涅槃經義疏 |
| *ta pi-ch'iu* | 大比丘 |
| *Ta-p'in ching* | 大品經 |
| *ta p'u-sa* | 大菩薩 |
| *ta-pu-yu-hsiao* | 大不由小 |
| *t'a sheng chih kuan* | 他生之觀 |
| *ta-ts'ung-hsiao-ju* | 大從小入 |
| *Ta wu-liang-shou ching* | 大無量壽經 |
| Ta-yin | 大隱 |
| *t'an* | 歎 |
| T'an-hung | 曇弘 |
| Tan-ku | 丹谷 |
| T'an-luan | 曇鸞 |
| *tan-neng* | 但能 |
| T'an-yen | 曇衍 |
| *tao* | 道 |
| Tao-ch'ang | 道場 |
| Tao-ch'o | 道寵 |
| Tao-ch'ung | 道綽 |
| *tao chung-sheng* | 道衆生 |
| Tao-p'ing | 道憑 |

| | |
|---|---|
| Tao-sheng | 道生 |
| Tao-yin | 道誾 |
| *tariki* | 他力 |
| *te fen-pieh* | 德分別 |
| *t'i* | 體 |
| *tieh-ch'ien ch'i-hou* | 牒前起後 |
| *t'ien* | 天 |
| *t'ien kuei-shen* | 天鬼神 |
| *t'ien-hsien* | 天仙 |
| T'ien-t'ai | 天台 |
| *Ti-ch'ih ching* | 地持經 |
| *Ti-ch'ih ching-lun* | 地持經論 |
| *Ti-ch'ih ching lun i-chi* | 地持經論義記 |
| *Ti-ch'ih [lun i-]shu* | 地持論義疏 |
| Ti-lun | 地論 |
| Ti-lun shih | 地論師 |
| Ti-yü | 地獄 |
| Ting-chou | 定州 |
| *ting-san* | 定散 |
| *Tō'iki dentō mokuroku* | 東域傳燈目錄 |
| To-t'o-a-chia-tu | 多陀阿伽度 |
| *tsa* | 雜 |
| *Tsa-hsin [lun]* | 雜心論 |
| *Tsan a-mi-t'o fo chieh* | 讚阿彌陀佛偈 |
| *tsan-t'an kung-yang* | 讚歎供養 |

| | |
|---|---|
| Tse-chou | 澤州 |
| *Tseng-shu fa-men* | 增數法門 |
| *ts'u-chien* | 粗見 |
| *ts'u ching-hsin chien* | 麁(麤)淨信見 |
| *tsui* | 罪 |
| *ts'un* | 寸 |
| *tsung* | 宗 |
| *tsung-ch'ü* | 宗趣 |
| *tsung-kuan* | 總觀 |
| Tu-shun | 杜順 |
| *tu-sung* | 讀誦 |
| *t'u wu fang-hsien* | 上無方限 |
| *tun* | 頓 |
| *tun-chiao* | 頓教 |
| Tun-huang | 敦煌 |
| *t'ung* | 通 |
| *t'ung-ch'ing* | 通請 |
| *t'ung-hsien* | 通現 |
| *t'ung-hsü* | 通序 |
| Tung-shan | 東山 |
| *tzu-li* | 自利 |
| Tz'u-min | 慈愍 |
| *tzu wang-sheng kuan* | 自往生觀 |
| Ŭich'ŏn | 義天 |
| Ŭijok | 義寂 |
| Ŭisang | 義湘 |
| *wai-fan* | 外凡 |

| | |
|---|---|
| *wai-kuan se* | 外觀色 |
| *wang-sheng* | 往生 |
| *wang-sheng chieh* | 往生偈 |
| *wang-sheng ching-t'u fa-men* | 往生淨土法門 |
| *Wang-sheng lun* | 往生論 |
| *Wang-sheng lun-chu* | 往生論註 |
| *wei* | 位 |
| *wei-ching* | 僞經 |
| *wei-li* | 威力 |
| *Wei-mo ching* | 維摩經 |
| *Wei-mo i-chi* | 維摩義記 |
| *Wei-mo ching i-chi* | 維摩經義記 |
| Wei Shih-tu | 衛士度 |
| *Wei wu san-mei ching* | 惟務三昧經 |
| *wei-yüan* | 唯願 |
| *wen* (hearing) | 聞 |
| *wen* (passages) | 文 |
| *wen-ch'ü* | 文曲 |
| *Wen-shih ching* | 溫室經 |
| *Wen-shih [ching i-shu]* | 溫室經義疏 |
| Wen-ti | 文帝 |
| *wo-wen* | 我聞 |
| Wŏn'gwang | 圓光 |
| Wŏnhyo | 元曉 |
| Wu | 武 |

| | |
|---|---|
| Wu-chen Szu | 悟眞寺 |
| *wu-cheng-hsing* | 五正行 |
| *wu-chung hsüan-i* | 五重玄義 |
| *wu-k'u* | 五苦 |
| *Wu-liang ch'ing-ching p'ing-teng-chüeh ching* | 無量淸靜平等覺經 |
| *Wu-liang-i* | 無量義 |
| Wu-liang-kuang | 無量光 |
| Wu-liang-shou | 無量壽 |
| *Wu-liang-shou ching* | 無量壽經 |
| *Wu-liang-shou ching i-shu* | 無量壽經義疏 |
| *Wu-liang-shou ching lun* | 無量壽經論 |
| *Wu-liang-shou kuan [ching i-shu]* | 無量壽觀經義疏 |
| *Wu-liang-shou kuan ching tsan-shu* | 無量壽觀經讃述 |
| *Wu-liang-shou ta-ching* | 無量壽大經 |
| *Wu-liang-shou ching yu-po-t'i-she yüan-sheng chieh* | 無量壽經優波提舍願生偈 |
| *Wu-liang-shou yu-po-t'i-she ching lun* | 無量壽優波提舍經論 |
| *wu-nien men* | 五念門 |
| *wu-o* | 五惡 |

| | |
|---|---|
| *wu-shao* | 五燒 |
| *wu-sheng jen* | 無生忍 |
| *wu-shih pa-chiao* | 五時八教 |
| *Wu-ti* | 武帝 |
| *wu-t'ung* | 五痛 |
| *wu-yao* | 五要 |
| *wu-yüan tz'u* | 無緣慈 |
| *Yao-wang yao-shang kuan ching* | 藥王藥上觀經 |
| Yeh | 鄴 |
| Yen-ts'ung | 彥悰 |
| *yin* | 因 |
| *Yin-ch'ih-ju ching-chu* | 蔭持入經注 |
| *yin-yüan* | 因緣 |
| *Ying-lo ching* | 瓔珞經 |
| *ying-shen* | 應身 |
| *ying-shen kuan* | 應身觀 |
| *yü* | 喻 |
| *Yü-chia-shih ti-lun* | 瑜伽師地論 |
| *Yü-lan-p'en ching* | 盂蘭盆經 |
| *Yü-yeh ching* | 玉耶經 |
| *yüan* | 願 |
| *Yüan-chao* | 元照 |
| *Yüan-chia* | 元嘉 |
| *yüan-chüeh* | 緣覺 |
| *Yuan fa-shih* | 遠法師 |
| *Yüan fa-shih chieh* | 遠法師解 |
| *Yüan-sheng* | 願生 |

| | |
|---|---|
| *yüan-ying t'u* | 圓應土 |
| Yün-kang | 雲崗 |
| *yung* | 用 |
| *Yusim allakto* | 遊心安樂道 |

# Selected Bibliography

## Dictionaries and Collections

*A Dictionary of Chinese Buddhist Terms*. 1937. Reprint. Delhi: Motilal Banarsidass, 1977.
*Buddhist Hybrid Sanskrit Dictionary*. 1953. Reprint. Delhi: Motilal Banarsidass, 1970.
*Bukkyō daijiten*. Oda Tokunō. Tokyo: Daizō shuppan kabushiki gaisha, 1954.
*Bukkyōgo daijiten (shukusatsuban)*. Nakamura Hajime. Tokyo: Toppan insatsu kabushikgaisha, 1981.
*Bukkyōgaku jiten*. Ed. Taya Raishun, et al. Kyoto: Hōzōkan, 1955.
*Bussho kaisetsu daijiten*. Ed. Ono Genmyō. 12 vols.; Tokyo: Tōkyō shoseki, 1975.
*Butten kaidai jiten*. Ed. Mizuno Kōgen, et al. Tokyo: Shunjūsha, 1966.
*Dai nihon zokuzōkyō*. Ed. Nakano Tatsue. 750 vols. Kyoto: Zōkyō shoin, 1905–12.
*Jōdoshū zensho*. Kyoto: Jōdoshūten kankōkai, 1929 and 1930.
*Mathews' Chinese-English Dictionary*. Cambridge: Harvard Univ., 1963.
*Mochizuki bukkyō dai jiten*. Mochizuki Shinkō. 10 vols. Tokyo: Sekai seiten kankō kyōkai, 1929–1937.
*Taishō shinshū daizōkyō*. Ed. Takakusu Junjirō and Watanabe Kaigyoku. 100 vols. Tokyo: Taishō issaikyō kankōkai, 1924–1932.
*Shinshū shōgyō zensho*. Ed. Shinshū shōgyō zensho hensanjo. Kyoto: Daiyagi kōbundō, 1941.
*Shinshū zensho*. Ed. Tsumaki Naoyoshi. Kyoto: Zōkyōshoin, 1914.
*The Korean Buddhist Canon: A Descriptive Catalogue*. Berkely: Univ. of Calif. Press, 1979.

## Primary Works: (By Title)

*A-mi-t'o ching*. *T* 366.
*A-mi-t'o san-yeh-san-fo-sa-lou-fo-t'an kuo-tu-jen-tao ching*. *T* 362.
*An-le chi*. Tao-ch'o. *T* 1958.
*Any*ōshō. Genryūkoku. *T* 2686.
*Bussetsu kanmuryōjukyō kōki*. Rei'ō. *Shinshū Zensho* Vol. 5, pp. 1–298.
*Ching-t'u lun*. Chi a-ts'ai. *T* 1963.
*Ching-tu san-mei ching*. *ZZ* 1.87.4.
*Ching-t'u shih-i lun*. Chih-i. *T* 1961.

*Ch'u san-tsang chi chi.* Sen-yu. *T* 2145.
*Chung-ching mu-lu.* Ch'ing-t'ai. *T* 2148.
*Chung-ching mu-lu.* Fa-ching. *T* 2146.
*Chung-ching mu-lu.* Yen-tsung. *T* 2147.
*Fo-tsu t'ung-chi.* Chih-p'an. *T* 2035.
*Fo-tsu li-tai t'ung-tsai.* Nien-ch'ang. *T* 2036.
*Hsi-fang yao-chüeh shih-i t'ung-kuei.* [K'uei-]chi *T* 1964.
*Hsü kao-seng chuan.* Tao-hsüan. *T* 2060.
*Jen-wang ching.* *T* 245.
*K'ai-yüan lu.* Chih-sheng. *T* 2154.
*Kao-seng chuan.* Hui-chiao. *T* 2059.
*Ken jōdo shinjitsu kyōgyōshō monrui.* Shinran. *T* 2646.
*Kuan fo san-mei hai ching.* *T* 642.
*Kuan wu-liang-shou ching i-shu.* Chi-tsang. *T* 1752.
*Kuan wu-liang-shou ching i-shu.* Hui-yüan *T* 1745.
*Kuan wu-liang-shou fo ching i-shu.* Yüan-chao. *T* 1754.
*Kuan wu-liang-shou fo ching shu.* Shan-tao. *T* 1753.
*Kuang hung-ming chi.* Tao-hsüan. *T* 2103.
*Lüeh-lun an-le ching-t'ui i.* T'an-luan. *T* 1957.
*Nei-tien lu.* Tao-hsüan. *T* 2149.
*Nien-fo ching.* Tao-ching and Shan-tao. *T* 1966.
*Nien-fo san-mei pao-wang lun.* Fei-hsi. *T* 1967.
*Ōjōyōshū.* Genshin. *T* 2682.
*Sanron-shū shō sho.* *T* 2686.
*Senchaku hongan nembutsu-shū.* Hōnen. *T* 2608.
*She ta-ch'eng lun-shih.* Vasubandhu. *T* 1595.
*Shih ching-t'u ch'ün-i lun.* Huai-kan. *T* 1960.
*Shih-chu p'i-p'o-sha lun.* Nāgārjuna. *T* 1521.
*Shih wang-sheng ching.* *ZZ* 1.87.4.
*Sui-yüan shih-fang wang-sheng ching.* *T* 1331.
*Sung kao-seng chuan.* San-ning. *T* 2061.
*Ta-ch'eng i-chang.* Hui-yüan. *T* 1851.
*Ta chih tu lun.* Nāgārjuna. *T* 1521.
*Wu-liang ch'ing-ching p'ing-teng-chüeh ching.* *T* 361.
*Wu-liang-shou ching.* *T* 360.
*Wu-liang-shou ching i-shu.* Hui-yüan. *T* 1749.
*Wu-liang-shou ching yu-po-t'i-she yüan-sheng chieh* Vasubandhu. *T* 1524.
*Wu-liang-shou ching yu-po-t'i-she yüan-sheng chieh-chu* (*Wang-sheng lun-chu*). T'an-luan. *T* 1819.
*Yusim allakto.* Wŏnhyo. *T* 1965.

**Modern Sources: (By Author)**

*Books: Japanese Language Sources*

*Bukkyō-gaku kankei: Zasshi ronbun bun'rui mokuroku,* Kyoto: Nagata bunshodō, 1975.

Etani Ryūkai. *Jōdokyō no shin kenkyū.* Tokyo: Sankibō busshorin, 1976.

Fujita Kōtatsu. *Genshi jōdo-shisō no kenkyū.* Tokyo: Iwanami shoten, 1970.

———. *Zendō.* Jinrui no chiteki-isan 18. Tokyo: Kōdansha, 1985.

Fujiwara Ryōsetsu. *Nembutsu no kenkyū.* Kyoto: Nagata bunshodō, 1957.

Hirai Shunei. *Chūgoku hanya shisō-shi.* Tokyo: Shunjū-sha, 1976.

Hirose Takashi. *Kangyōsho ni manabu: gengibun.* Kyoto: Hōzōkan, 1979–1980.

———. *Kangyōsho ni manabu: jobungi ichi.* Kyoto: Hōzōkan, 1982.

———. *Kangyōsho ni manabu: jobungi ni.* Kyoto: Hōzōkan, 1982.

Inouye Mitsusada. *Nihon jōdokyō seiritsushi no kenkyū.* Tokyo: Yamakawa shuppansha, 1956.

Kamata Shigeo. *Chūgoku bukkyō shisō-shi kenkyū.* Tokyo: Shunjūsha, 1968.

Kajiyama Yūichi. *Satori to ekō.* Tokyo: Kōdansha, 1983.

Kashiwabara Yūgi. *Kangyō gengibun koyo.* Kyoto: Ango jimusho, 1955.

Kishi Kakuyū. *Zoku zendō kyōgaku no kenkyū.* Yamaguchi: Kishi Kakusho, 1966.

Kōgatsuin Jinrei. *Jōdoronchū kōgi.* Kyoto: Hōzōkan, 1974.

Makita Tairyō. *Gikyō kenkyū.* Kyoto: Kyōto daigaku jinbun kagaku kenkyūjo, 1976.

———. *Chūgoku bukkyōshi kenkyū.* Vol. 1. Tokyo: Daitō shuppansha, 1981.

Matsumoto Bunzaburō. *Shina bukkyō ibutsu.* Tokyo: Kōbundō, 1942.

Mayeda, Sengaku. *Genshibukkyō-seiten no seiritsushi kenkyū.* Tokyo: Sankibo-busshorin Publishing Co., Ltd., 1964.

Mikogami Eryū. *Ōjōronchū kaisetsu.* Kyoto: Nagata bunsho-dō, 1969.

Mochizuki Shinkō. Daijōkishinron no kenkyū. Tokyo: Kanao bun'eidō, 1921.

———. *Chūgoku jōdokyōri-shi.* Kyoto: Hōzōkan, 1932.

———. *Jōdokyō no kigen oyobi hatten.* 1930. Reprint. Tokyo: Sankibō, 1977.

———. *Jōdokyō no kenkyū.* 1930. Tokyo: Nihon tosho sentā, 1977.

Nogami Shunjō. *Chūgoku jōdokyō-shi.* Kyoto: Hōzōkan, 1981.

Nabata Ōjun. *Kazai jōdoron no kenkyū.* Kyoto: Hōzōkan, 1928.

Ochō Enichi. *Chūgoku bukkyō no kenkyū.* Vol. 1. Kyoto: Hōzōkan, 1958.

———. ed. *Hokugi bukkyō no kenkyū.* Kyoto: Heirakuji shoten, 1970.

———. *Chūgoku bukkyō no kenkyū.* Vol. 2. Kyoto: Hōzōkan, 1971.

———. *Chūgoku bukkyō no kenkyū.* Vol. 3. Kyoto: Hōzōkan, 1979.

Ogasawara Senshū. *Chūgoku-jōdokyōke no kenkyū.* Kyoto: Heirakuji shoten, 1951.

Ōhara Shōjitsu. *Zendō kyōgaku no kenkyū.* Kyoto: Nagata bunshodō, 1974.

Ono Genmyō. *Dai jō bukkyō geijutsu-shi no kenkyū.* Tokyo: Kanao-bun'endō, 1927.

———. *Bukkyō no bijutsu to rekishi.* Tokyo: Kanao-bun'endō, 1937.

Satō Tetsuei. *Tendai daishi no kenkyū.* Kyoto: Hyakkaen, 1961.

Sugiyama Jirō, *Gokurakujōdo no kigen.* Tokyo: Chikuma shobō, 1984.

Tōdō Kyōshun. *Muryōjukyōronchū no kenkyū.* Kyoto: Bukkyō bunka kenkyūjo, 1958.

*Tsukamoto hakushi shōjukinen: bukkyō shigaku ronshū*. Kyoto: Tsukamoto hakushi shōjukinen kankōkai, 1961. (*Tsukamoto Festschrift*)
Tsukamoto Zenryū. *Gisho shakurōshi no kenkyū*. Kyoto: Bukkyō-bunka kenkyū-jo shuppan, 1961.
———. *Tōchūki no jōdokyō*. 1933. Reprint. Kyoto: Hōzōkan, 1975.
Yabuki Keiki, *Amidabutsu no kenkyū*. Tokyo: Heigo shuppansha, 1911.
Yamaguchi Kōen. *Tendai jōdokyō-shi*. Kyoto: Hōzōkan, 1957.
Yamaguchi Susumu. *Seshin no jōdoron*. Kyoto. Hōzōkan, 1966.
Yamamoto Bukkotsu. *Dōshaku kyōgaku no kenkyū*. Kyoto. Nagata bunshodō, 1959.

*Monographs: English Language Sources*

Chappell, David. ed. *Buddhist and Taoist Practice in Medieval Chinese Society*. Honolulu: University of Hawaii Press, 1987.
Ch'en, Kenneth. *Buddhism in China*. Princeton: Princeton University Press, 1964.
———. *Chinese Transformation of Buddhism*. Princeton University Press, 1973.
Cowell, E. B., F. Max Müller and J. Takakusu, trans. *Buddhist Mahayana Texts*. Sacred Books of the East Vol. XLIX. 1895. Reprint. Delhi: Motilal Benarsidass, 1965.
Davids, Rhys T. W. *The Questions of King Milinda* Part I. 1890. Reprint. New York: Dover Publications, Inc., 1963.
Fujiwara, Ryōsetsu. *The Way to Nirvana*. Tokyo: The Kyoiku Shincho Sha Co., Ltd., 1974.
Kawamura, Leslie, ed. *The Bodhisattva Doctrine in Buddhism*. Ontario, Canada: Wilfrid Laurier University Press, 1981.
Kloetzli, Randy. *Buddhist Cosmology*. Delhi: Motilal Banarsidass. 1983.
Lancaster, Lewis. *The Korean Buddhist Canon: A Descriptive Catalogue*. Berkeley: University California Press, 1979.
Robinson, Richard and Willard Johnson. *The Buddhist Religion: A Historical Introduction*. Belmont, California: Wadsworth Publishing Company, 1970.
Ryūkoku Univ. Translation Center, ed. and annotated. *Sutra of Contemplation on the Buddha of Immeasurable Life as Expounded by Śākyamuni Buddha*. Kyoto: Ryukoku Univ., 1984.
Sponberg, Alan and Helen Hardacare, eds. *Maitreya, the Future Buddha*. Cambridge: Cambridge Univ. Press, 1988.
Takasaki, Jikidō. *A Study on the Ratnagotravibhāga (Uttaratantra)*. Series Orientale Roma XXXII. Roma: Istituto Italiano Per Il Medio Ed Estremo Oriente, 1966.
———. *An Introduction to Buddhism*. Translated by Rolf W. Giebel. Tokyo: Toho Gakkai, 1987.
Wogihara, Unrai, ed. *Bodhisattvabhūmi: A Statement of Whole Course of the Bodhisattva*. Tokyo: Sankibo Buddhist Book Store, 1971.
Zürcher, Erik. *The Buddhist Conquest of China*. Leiden: E.J. Brill, 1959.

*Articles: Japanese Language Sources*


Agawa Kantatsu. "Jōdo resso yori mitaru jōyō". In *Imaoka kyōju kanreki kinen ronbunshū.* Edited by Taishō daigaku jōdogaku kenkyūkai. Tokyo: Taishō daigaku jōdogaku kenkyū, 1933, pp. 830–891.

Andō Toshio. "Hokugi nehangaku no dentō to shoki no shironshi." In *Hokugi bukkyō no kenkyū.* Edited by Ōchō Enichi. Kyoto: Heirakuji shoten, 1970.

Etani Ryūkai. "Koshitsusho ryūkō no kanmuryōjuki no kenkyū." *Indogaku bukkyōgaku kenkyū* 8-1 (1960):84–92.

———. "Zui-tō jidai no kangyō kenkyū shikan." *Tsukamoto Festschrift,* pp. 125–135.

Fujieda Akira. "Hokuchō ni okeru *Shōmangyō* no denshō." *Tōhō gappō: Kyoto* 40 (1969):325–349.

———. "Shōmangyō gisho." In *Shōtoku taishi-shū.* Edited by Ienaga Saburō et al. Nihon taikei. Tokyo: Iwanami shoten, 1975.

Fujii Kyōkō "Pelliot Ch. 2091 *Shōman-giki* kange zankan shahon ni tsuite". *Shōtoku taishi kenkyū* 13 (1979):27–37.

Fukagai Jikō. "Zendō to Jōyōji-eon." In *Tōyōgaku ronshū,* edited by Morimitsu jūsaburō hakushi kōju kinen jigyōkai. Kyoto: Hōyū shoten, 1979. pp. 1265–1280.

Fukihara Shōshin. "Jōyōji eon no busshō-setsu." In *Hokugi bukkyō no kenkyū.* Edited Ōchō Enichi. Kyoto: Heirakuji shoten, 1970. pp. 203–260.

Fukushima Kōya. "Jōyōji eon no shikan shisō." *Tōhōgaku* 36:15–28.

Haneda Nobuo. "Dōshaku zendō nisshi no kangyō gebon-kan hikaku," *Shinran kyōgaku* 37 (1980): 76–81.

Hirakawa Akira. "Jōdokyō no yōgo ni tsuite." In *Bukkyō ni okeru jōdo shisō.* Edited by Nihon bukkyō gakkai. Kyoto: Heirakuji, 1977.

Kagawa Kōyu. "Shōmyo shisō no keisei." *Indogaku bukkyōgaku kenkyū* 11-1 (1963):45–46.

Komaru Shinji. "Kanmuryōjukō to shōmyōshisō." In *Bukkyō shisō no shomondai.* Hirakawa Akira hakushi koju kinenronshū. Tokyo: Shunjūsha, 1985.

Masaki, Haruhiko. "Kangyōsho ni okeru kubon no mondai." In *Bukkyō kyōri no kenkyū.* Tamura Yoshirō hakushi kanreki kinenronshū. Tokyo: Shunjūsha, 1982.

Morimitsu Jūsaburō. "Chūgokushisō-shi ni okeru zendō no chi'i." In *Zendō kyōgaku no kenkyū,* edited by Bukkyō daigaku zendō kyōgaku kenkyūkai. Kyoto: Tōyō bunka shuppan, 1980.

Nakamura Hajime. "Jōdo sanbukyō no kaisetsu." *Jōdo sanbukyō.* Vol. 2. Tokyo: Iwanami shoten, 1964.

Ogasawara Senshū. "Kōshōkoku no bukkyō kyōgaku." In *Tsukamoto Festschrift,* pp. 136–147.

Takahashi Kōji. "Eon to zendō no busshin-ron." In *Zendō kyōgaku no kenkyū.* Edited by Bukkyō daigaku zendō kyōgaku kenkyūkai. Tokyo: Tōyō bunka shuppan, 1980, pp. 79–96.

Taya Hiroshi. "Donran no senjitsuchū ni inyō saretaru shomoku no chōsa." *Ōtani Gakuhō* 23-6 (1942):521–533.

Tōdō Kyōshun. "Zendō kyōgaku ni okeru gikyōten: tokuni *Jūōjō kyō* o megutte". *Ōryō shigaku* 3 and 4 (1977):319–337.

Tsujimori Yōshū. "Daijōgishō kaidai." *Kokuyaku issaikyō: shoshūbu 13,* pp. 362–366.

Tsukamoto Zenryū. "Hokushū no haibutsu ni tsuite." *Tōhō gakuhō, Kyōto* 16 (1948): 29–101; 18 (1950): 78–111.

———. "Shina jōdokyō no tenkai." *Shina bukkyō shigaku* 3-3 and 4 (Dec. 1939):13.

———. "Hokushū no shūkyō haiki-seisaku no hōkai." *Bukkyō shigaku* 1 (1949): 3–31.

———. "Kangyōsho ni okeru zendō shakugi no shisōshi teki igi." *Tsukamoto Festschrift,* pp. 907–924.

Yamada Meiji. "Kangyō kō: muryōju-butsu to amida-butsu." *Ryūkoku daigaku ronshū* 408 (1976):76–95.

Yamaguchi Kōen. *Tendai jōdokyō-shi.* Kyoto: Hōzōkan, 1967.

Yoshizu Yoshihide. "Kyōritsuron inyō yori mita daijōgi shō no seikaku." *Komazawa daigaku bukkyō-gakuba ronshū* 2 (1971):123–137.

———. "Eon no *Kishinron-sho* o meguru shomondai (jo)." *Komazawa daigaku bukkyō-gakubu ronshū* 3 (1972): 82–97.

———. "Daijōgishō hasshikigi kenkyū." *Komazawa daigakubu bukkyō-gakubu kenkyū kiyō* 30 (1972):141–161.

———. "Jironshi to iu kōshō ni tsuite." *Komazawa daigaku bukkyō-gakubu kenkyū kiyō* 31 (1973):307–323.

———. "Eon *Daijōkishinron-gisho* no kenkyū." *Komazawa daigaku bukkyō-gakabu kenkyū kiyō* 34 (1976): 151–173.

———. "Jōyōji-eon no kyōhanron." *Komazawa daigaku bukkyō-gakubu kenkyū-kiyō* 35 (1977):205–226.

———. "Daijōgishō no seiritsu to jōyōji eon no shisō (1)." *Sanzō* 165 (1978):1–8.

———. "Daijōgishō no seiritsu to jōyōji-eon no shisō (2)." *Sanzō* 166 (1978):1–8.

Yūki Reimon. "Shina bukkyō ni okeru mappō shisō no kōki." *Tōhō gappō: Tokyo* 6 (1936):205–215.

———. "Zui-tō no chūgoku-teki shin bukkyō soshiki no ichirei to shite no *Kegon hokkai kanmon* ni tsuite." *Indogaku bukkyōgaku kenkyū* 6 (1958): 276–281.

———. "Kangyōsho ni okeru zendō shakugi no shisōshiteki igi." *Tsukamoto Festschrift,* pp. 907–924.

———. "Chūgoku bukkyō no keisei." Edited by Miyamoto Shōson, et al. *Kōza Bukkyō IV: Chūgoku bukkyō.* Tokyo: Daizō shuppan, 1967, pp. 79–104.

*Articles: English Language Sources*

Andrews, Allan. "Nembutsu in the Chinese Pure Land tradition." *The Eastern Buddhist* 3-2 (Oct., 1970): 20–45.[4–12]

Corless, Roger. "T'an-luan: Taoist Sage and Buddhist Bodhisattva." In *Buddhist and Taoist Practice in Medieval Chinese Society.* Ed. David W. Chappell. Honolulu. University of Hawaii Press, 1987.

Donner, Neal. "The Mahayanization of the Chinese Dhyana Tradition." *The Eastern Buddhist* (1977): 49–64.

Harrison, Paul. "Buddhānusmrti in the *Pratyutpanna-buddha-saṃmukhāvasthita-samādhi-sūtra.*" *Journal of Indian Philosophy* 6 (1978):35–57.

Ishida, Mitsuyuki. "Fragmented Copied Manuscripts of the *Wu liang shou ching kuan tsan-shu,*" *Monumenta Serindica* I.

Kiyota, Minoru. "Buddhist Devotional Meditation: A Study of the *Sukhāvatīvyū-hopadeśa.*" In *Mahāyāna Buddhist Meditation: Theory and Practice.* Ed. Minoru Kiyota. Honolulu: University of Hawaii, 1978.

Mukherjee, B. N. "A Mathura Inscription of the Year 26 and of the Period of Huvishka." *Journal of Ancient Indian History* Vol. XI (University of Calcutta, 1979):82–84.

Pas, Julian. "Shan-tao's Interpretation of the Meditative Vision of Buddha Amitayus." *History of Religion* 14–2 (Nov., 1974): 96–116.

———. "The *Kuan-wu-liang-shou Fo-ching*: Its Origin and Literary Criticism." In *Buddhist Thought and Asian Civilization.* Eds. Leslie Kawamura and Keith Scott. Emeryville, California: Dharma Publishing, 1977.

———. "The Meaning of Nien-fo in the three Pure Land Sutras." 7–4 *Studies in Religion* (1978):403–413.

Pruden, Leo. trans. "The *Ching-t'u Shih-i lun.*" *The Eastern Buddhist* 6–1 (May, 1973):126–157.

———. trans. "A Short Essay on the Pure Land," *The Eastern Buddhist* 8–1 (May, 1975):74–95.

Rowell, Teresina. "The Background and Early Use of the Buddha-kṣetra Concept." *The Eastern Buddhist* 3–4 (July, 1934):199–246; 4–2 and 3 (March, 1935):379–431; 7–2 (June, 1937):131–176.

Schopen, Gregory. "Sukhāvatī as a Generalized Religious Goal in Sanskrit Mahāyāna Sūtra Literature," *Indo-Iranian Journal* 19 (1977):177-210.

———. "The Inscription on the Kuṣān Image of Amitābha and the Character of Early Mahāyāna in India." *Journal of the International Association of Buddhist Studies* 10–2 (1987): 119.

*E) Unpublished Works*

Chappell, David W. "Tao-ch'o (562–645): A Pioneer of Chinese Pure Land Buddhism." Ph.D. dissertation. Yale University, 1976.

Corless, Roger. "T'an-luan's Commentary on the Pure Land Discourse: An Annotated Translation and Soteriological Analysis of the *Wang-sheng-lun chu* (T 1819)," Ph.D. Dissertation, University of Wisconsin, 1973.

Haneda, Nobuo. "The Development of the Concept of *Pṛthagjana,* Culminating in Shan-tao's Pure Land Thought: The Pure Land Theory of Salvation of the Inferior." Ph.D. Dissertation, Univ. of Wisconsin, Madison, 1979.

Hsiao, Ching-fen. "The Life and Teachings of T'an-luan." Th.D. Dissertation, Princeton Theological Seminary, 1967.

Pas, Julian. "Shan-tao's Commentary on the *ABAS.*" Ph.D. Dissertation, McMaster University, Canada, 1973.

Seah, Ingram Samuel. "Shan-tao, His Life and Teachings." Ph.D. Dissertation, Princeton Theological Seminary, 1975.

# Index